de Ruvigny's
ROLL OF
HONOUR
1914–18

de Ruvigny's
ROLL OF
HONOUR
1914–18

A BIOGRAPHICAL RECORD OF MEMBERS
OF HIS MAJESTY'S NAVAL AND MILITARY
FORCES WHO FELL IN THE GREAT WAR 1914-1918

"And he Passed over…
and all the Trumpets sounded
for him on the other side."

INDEX

Name	Photo	Part No.	Page No.
ABBAY, Marmaduke John Norman	P	1	1
ABBEY, John Gibson		5	1
ABBISTON, William		2	1
ABBOT, John		1	1
ABBOTT, Albert		1	1
ABBOTT, Arthur Leonard Victor		2	1
ABBOTT, Charles Thomas	P	1	1
ABBOTT, Duncan William Sydney Elphinstone		2	1
ABBOTT, Ernest William		1	1
ABBOTT, Frederick Charles	P	1	1
ABBOTT, Geoffrey Dyett		2	1
ABBOTT, James		4	1
ABBOTT, Reginald Frederick William		2	1
ABBOTT, Robert		1	1
ABBOTT, Sidney Adolphus	P	2	1
ABBOTT, The Rev. William David		5	1
ABBOTTS, Harry	P	1	1
ABBS, Tom William Robert		1	1
ABEL, Claud Cecil		1	1
ABEL, Sam	P	3	1
ABELL, William Henry		2	1
ABELSON, Edward Gordon		3	1
ABERCROMBIE, John Balfour Symington	P	2	1
ABERCROMBIE, John Fergus	P	5	1
ABERCROMBIE, Robert Henry Chester	P	1	1
ABERDEEN, James	P	1	1
ABERNETHY, David Ross		3	1
ABRAHAM, Geoffrey William Popperrell		3	1
ABRAHAMS, Reginald Arthur		3	1
ABRAM, Ernest William		1	1
ABRAMS, Frederick		1	1
ABRAMS, Harold James		1	1
ABRATTHAT, William		1	1
ACHURCH, Henry Graham		4	1
ACKERS, William James		2	1
ACKLAND, Edwin George		5	1
ACKLAND-ALLEN, Hugh Thomas		2	5
ACKROYD, John Cavill		4	1
ACKROYD, Willie		3	1
ACTON, Arthur Cawley		4	1
ACTON, Charles Annesley		3	1
ACTON, Samuel		2	1
ACTON, William Albert	P	1	1
ADAIR, William Finlay		2	1
ADAM, Alan Gordon Acheson	P	2	1
ADAM, Alexander Rollo		3	1
ADAM, Alexander Thomson		3	1
ADAM, Allan	P	5	1
ADAM, Frank Dalziel	P	5	1
ADAM, James Christopher		5	1
ADAM, Robert	P	5	1
ADAM, Ronald William	P	3	1
ADAM, Thomas		1	1
ADAMES, Alfred Henry		2	1
ADAMS, A H		3	1
ADAMS, Albert	P	3	1
ADAMS, Alexander Jackson		3	1
ADAMS, Alfred Edwin		3	1
ADAMS, Auriol Charles Andrew	P	3	2
ADAMS, C		2	1
ADAMS, Charles John Norman		5	1
ADAMS, Clare Robert		1	1
ADAMS, David Scott	P	2	1
ADAMS, Ernest Alexander Hector		1	1
ADAMS, F H		2	1

Name	Photo	Part No.	Page No.
ADAMS, Francis Henry		1	1
ADAMS, Frederic James		2	1
ADAMS, Frederick		1	1
ADAMS, Geoffrey Lloyd	P	1	1
ADAMS, George		1	2
ADAMS, George	P	5	1
ADAMS, George Austin	P	5	1
ADAMS, George James		3	2
ADAMS, George Stopford	P	1	2
ADAMS, George Thomas		1	2
ADAMS, Henry Eustace	P	2	2
ADAMS, John Goold	P	1	2
ADAMS, Laurence Kingston	P	1	2
ADAMS, Ord	P	3	2
ADAMS, Richard Allen Alexander		4	1
ADAMS, Robert Job		1	2
ADAMS, Roland		1	2
ADAMS, Thomas Edward Albert		5	2
ADAMS, Thomas Henry	P	1	2
ADAMS, Thomas Henry		4	1
ADAMS, W		2	2
ADAMS, Walter		1	2
ADAMS, Walter Frederick		1	2
ADAMS, William	P	1	2
ADAMS, William		3	2
ADAMS, William		5	2
ADAMS, William Frederick		1	2
ADAMSON, Alexander		4	1
ADAMSON, David		1	2
ADAMSON, Francis Douglas		2	2
ADAMSON, George		5	2
ADAMSON, Gilbert Edgar		5	2
ADAMSON, Harold William		3	2
ADAMSON, James	P	3	2
ADAMSON, John Edward		1	2
ADAMSON, Robert		5	2
ADAMSON, Thomas		1	2
ADAMSON, Walter Benjamin		1	2
ADAMSON, William		2	2
ADAMSON, William	P	5	2
ADCOCK, Joseph Robert		2	2
ADDAMS-WILLIAMS, Donald Arthur	P	1	380
ADDIE, Thomas	P	5	2
ADDISON, Alexander		2	2
ADDISON, Philip Francis		3	2
ADDISON, Robert Henry		4	1
ADDLEY, Edward		1	2
ADDY, Edward	P	1	2
ADDYMAN, William John		1	2
ADEANE, Henry Robert Augustus	P	1	2
ADEY, Frederick James		2	2
ADIE, David		2	2
ADKINS, James Francis Basil	P	3	2
ADKINS, Leonard		2	2
ADLAM, Arthur Wills	P	1	3
ADLER, Harry George Vergottini	P	5	2
ADLINGTON, Leslie Douglas		5	2
ADMANS, Walter George	P	1	3
ADSETTS, William Henry		2	2
ADSHEAD, Albert Guest		3	2
ADSHEAD, William		1	3
AFFLECK, Lewis Alexander		1	3
AFFLECK, William	P	4	1
AFFLECK, William Francis		4	1
AGATE, Norman Stanford	P	4	1

Name	Photo	Part No.	Page No.	Name	Photo	Part No.	Page No.
AGATES, Arthur James		3	2	**ALDERSLEY,** Eustace		3	3
AGER, James Alfred		1	3	**ALDERSON,** Henry	P	1	4
AGGER, Frank Edward	P	2	2	**ALDERSON,** Joseph	P	1	4
AGLIONBY, Arthur Hugh		5	2	**ALDERTON,** Arthur		1	4
AGNEW, J		2	2	**ALDERTON,** Charles		1	4
AGNEW, J		3	2	**ALDINGTON,** J		2	3
AGNEW, Nathaniel		1	3	**ALDISS,** Harry		1	4
AGNEW, W J		3	2	**ALDOUS,** Cecil		1	4
AGNEW, William S		2	2	**ALDOUS,** Walter Robert	P	2	3
AIKENHEAD, Frank Quarrier		3	2	**ALDOUS,** William		1	4
AIKENHEAD, Robert	P	1	3	**ALDRED,** John William		1	4
AINAND, Charles		1	3	**ALDRIDGE,** David		1	4
AINDOW, Frank Norman		1	3	**ALDRIDGE,** Ernest Sidney		1	4
AINGE, George Alfred		1	3	**ALDRIDGE,** George		2	3
AINGER, Harold		1	3	**ALDRIDGE,** Henry	P	5	3
AINGER, John		1	3	**ALDRIDGE,** Reginald John Petty Devenish	P	1	4
AINLEY, Charles Ernest	P	1	3	**ALDRIDGE,** Stanley	P	5	3
AINLEY, Hefford William Ernest	P	3	2	**ALDRIDGE,** Thomas		1	4
AINSLEY, George Henry		1	3	**ALDRIDGE,** Thomas		5	3
AINSLEY, Leonard Crombie	P	2	2	**ALDRIDGE,** William		1	4
AINSLIE, Denys Alfred Lafoue	P	1	3	**ALDWINCKLE,** Ernest Henry		3	3
AINSLIE, Edward		1	3	**ALDWINCKLE,** Ralph		3	3
AINSLIE, John Elliot		2	2	**ALEXANDER,** A F		3	3
AINSLIE, John Gordon		3	2	**ALEXANDER,** Arthur		4	2
AINSLIE, Walter Gordon		5	2	**ALEXANDER,** Arthur		5	3
AINSWORTH, John Stirling		2	3	**ALEXANDER,** C		2	3
AINSWORTH, Philip		1	3	**ALEXANDER,** Charles		1	4
AINSWORTH, William		1	3	**ALEXANDER,** Charles Henry		4	2
AIRLIE, John		2	3	**ALEXANDER,** Ernest		1	4
AITCHISON, Ronald A C	P	1	3	**ALEXANDER,** George Luard	P	3	3
AITCHISON, Thomas Frank	P	5	2	**ALEXANDER,** Harry	P	2	3
AITCHISON, Walter		4	1	**ALEXANDER,** Harry		2	4
AITKEN, Andrew		5	2	**ALEXANDER,** Herold Percy	P	3	3
AITKEN, Emil Leonard Dow		4	1	**ALEXANDER,** James	P	1	4
AITKEN, James Charles Lamont		4	1	**ALEXANDER,** James		2	4
AITKEN, James Home	P	1	3	**ALEXANDER,** James		3	3
AITKEN, James Russell	P	4	1	**ALEXANDER,** R		2	4
AITKEN, James Tod		2	3	**ALEXANDER,** Reginald		2	4
AITKEN, John	P	4	1	**ALEXANDER,** Thomas		1	4
AITKEN, John Christie		2	3	**ALEXANDER,** William		3	3
AITKEN, John Walter		5	2	**ALEXANDER,** William John		3	4
AITKEN, Peter	P	4	2	**ALEXANDRE,** John William	P	3	4
AITKEN, Sidney Charles		1	3	**ALFORD,** Adolphe John		5	3
AITKEN, William		4	2	**ALFORD,** Frank		2	4
AITKENS, Albert Reginald Knight	P	2	3	**ALFORD,** Thomas William Barker		2	4
AITKENS, Cyril Arthur Charles	P	2	3	**ALFORD,** W J		3	4
AITON, Andrew Alfred		1	3	**ALGAR,** Arthur Archibald	P	2	4
AKED, George	P	1	4	**ALGEO,** Norman	P	3	4
AKEHURST, Alexander James	P	1	4	**ALGIE,** Robert		1	4
AKEHURST, William		3	3	**ALINGTON,** Geoffrey Hugh		3	4
AKERMAN, Charles Savidge Annand		2	3	**ALINGTON,** Gervase Winford Stoven	P	5	3
AKERMAN, Joseph		2	3	**ALISON,** George Newdegate	P	2	4
AKERMAN, Thomas William		2	3	**ALLAN,** Adam		5	3
ALBERY, Charles Ernest	P	3	3	**ALLAN,** Alexander	P	3	4
ALBONE, Arthur Henry	P	4	2	**ALLAN,** Archibald		4	2
ALBUTT, George		2	3	**ALLAN,** Charles	P	1	4
ALCOCK, Alfred David		5	3	**ALLAN,** David		2	4
ALCOCK, Henry		1	4	**ALLAN,** Frank		2	4
ALDANA, Juan Manuel	P	3	3	**ALLAN,** Frank Cecil		3	4
ALDER, Cyril Charles		2	3	**ALLAN,** George Cowie		3	4
ALDER, David		1	4	**ALLAN,** George Waldo		2	4
ALDER, William Stanley	P	1	4	**ALLAN,** James		2	4
ALDERMAN, Ernest William	P	4	2	**ALLAN,** James		2	4
ALDERMAN, Frederick George		4	2	**ALLAN,** James		4	2
ALDERMAN, William Percy		2	3	**ALLAN,** James		5	3

Name	Photo	Part No.	Page No.
ALLAN, James Edward		3	4
ALLAN, James Grant	P	2	4
ALLAN, James Mcdonald		4	2
ALLAN, John Cruickshank		3	4
ALLAN, John Mein		1	4
ALLAN, John Turnbull		5	3
ALLAN, Joseph		3	4
ALLAN, Peter		1	4
ALLAN, Peter Rodger		5	3
ALLAN, Thomas Martin		1	4
ALLAN, William H		2	4
ALLAN, William Harry	P	3	4
ALLAN, William Lewis Campbell		2	4
ALLAN HAY, Edward James	P	5	81
ALLAN-BLACK, Hugh Mcalister	P	5	16
ALLARD, D		2	4
ALLARD, Donald		1	5
ALLARD, William		2	4
ALLARD, William	P	5	3
ALLARD, William Henry	P	5	3
ALLASON, Lionel Theophilus		2	4
ALLCHIN, Albert George		1	5
ALLCOCK, Alfred		2	4
ALLCOCK, Herbert Ernest	P	1	5
ALLCORN, Herbert		1	5
ALLDEN, Stanley Trowse		2	4
ALLEBONE, Horace		3	4
ALLEN, Albert		4	2
ALLEN, Alexander		2	4
ALLEN, Alfred		2	4
ALLEN, Alfred Thomas		2	4
ALLEN, Alphaeus		4	2
ALLEN, Andrew Edward	P	4	2
ALLEN, Archibald Stafford	P	2	4
ALLEN, Arthur		2	4
ALLEN, Arthur James		1	5
ALLEN, Charles		2	4
ALLEN, Daniel		1	5
ALLEN, Francis Leslie		2	5
ALLEN, Frank Reginald	P	2	5
ALLEN, Frederick James	P	3	4
ALLEN, George		2	5
ALLEN, George		2	5
ALLEN, Harry		5	3
ALLEN, Harvey Percy	P	2	5
ALLEN, Henry		1	5
ALLEN, Henry		1	5
ALLEN, Henry Seymour	P	4	2
ALLEN, J		4	3
ALLEN, Jeffreys Somerset	P	3	4
ALLEN, John	P	4	3
ALLEN, John Cecil		1	5
ALLEN, John Edric Russell	P	4	3
ALLEN, John Francis		1	5
ALLEN, John Francis		2	5
ALLEN, John Hugh	P	1	5
ALLEN, John Robert		2	5
ALLEN, Lewis Ralph		2	5
ALLEN, Marshall Claude		1	5
ALLEN, Richard		2	5
ALLEN, Richard E		2	5
ALLEN, Stephen		3	5
ALLEN, Thompson	P	1	5
ALLEN, Wellington Lyster		3	5
ALLEN, Wilfred James		2	5
ALLEN, William		2	5
ALLEN, William Benjamin	P	1	5
ALLEN, William Francis		2	5
ALLEN, William Lynn		1	5
ALLENBY, Augustus Heathcote	P	1	5
ALLERTON, Henry S		2	5
ALLEYN, Joseph		1	5
ALLFORD, W		2	5
ALLFREY, Frederick De Vere Bruce		2	5
ALLGOOD, Bertram		2	5
ALLGOOD, Henry George		2	5
ALLIES, Sidney		2	5
ALLIN, Harold Wyse	P	3	5
ALLINGHAM, Frederick G		2	5
ALLINGTON, Joseph		5	3
ALLINSON, Joseph		1	5
ALLISON, Dan Walter		1	5
ALLISON, G		2	5
ALLISON, Garrett		2	5
ALLISON, George		2	5
ALLISON, George		4	3
ALLISON, George		5	3
ALLISON, Hazlett Samuel	P	3	5
ALLISON, J		2	5
ALLISON, James		2	5
ALLISON, James Steele Reid		3	5
ALLISON, John		2	5
ALLISON, John Malcolm		1	5
ALLISON, Robert		1	5
ALLISON, Sidney		3	5
ALLISON, William		2	5
ALLISON, William George	P	1	5
ALLMAN, G		3	5
ALLOT, J		2	5
ALLOT, J		3	5
ALLOWAY, William Henry		1	5
ALLPORT, Alan Hiatt		3	5
ALLSOP, Alfred	P	2	5
ALLSOP, Bertram	P	2	5
ALLSOP, Ernest Henry	P	2	6
ALLUM, George		1	5
ALLVEY, William		2	6
ALLWRIGHT, Alfred Walter		1	5
ALMOND, James William Harry	P	3	5
ALMOND, Joseph Sydney		4	3
ALSBURY, James		1	5
ALSTON, Claude Mccaul		2	6
ALSTON, George E		2	6
ALSTON, Rowland Evelyn		3	5
ALTOFT, George Herbert		3	5
ALTOFT, Harold		3	5
AMASS, A		2	6
AMBER, Frederick		2	6
AMBLER, Frederick	P	2	6
AMBLER, George	P	3	5
AMBROSE, William Charles John		1	5
AMES, Frederick		2	6
AMES, John		1	5
AMES, William Kerr		2	6
AMIES, Arthur George		3	5
AMIES, Nathaniel George Read		2	6
AMIES, Stephen John		1	5
AMOR, Ernest John	P	3	6
AMOS, A H		2	6
AMOS, Albert Edward		1	5

Name	Photo	Part No.	Page No.
AMOS, Arthur George		4	3
AMOS, Charles Byron	P	1	6
AMOS, Gilbert Stratton		2	6
AMOS, John Vince		4	3
AMOS, Joseph Herbert		2	6
AMPHLETT, Edward Baylie	P	1	6
AMPLEFORD, Frederick		1	6
AMPT, Norman Crosland	P	2	6
AMY, Raulin Anthoine John	P	1	6
ANCILL, Harry Pearce		1	6
ANDERSON, Abdy Fellowes	P	1	6
ANDERSON, Alan James Ramsay		2	6
ANDERSON, Alexander Clairmonte		1	6
ANDERSON, Alexander Webster		2	6
ANDERSON, Archibald Joseph	P	3	6
ANDERSON, Arthur Ashley		3	6
ANDERSON, Charles Alexander Kenneth	P	1	6
ANDERSON, Charles Ogilvy	P	2	6
ANDERSON, Charles Walter	P	2	7
ANDERSON, Colin Knox		2	7
ANDERSON, David		2	7
ANDERSON, David	P	3	6
ANDERSON, David		3	6
ANDERSON, David George Marcus		3	6
ANDERSON, David Horace	P	2	7
ANDERSON, David Lyall		3	6
ANDERSON, Eddie		3	6
ANDERSON, Edward		2	7
ANDERSON, Edward Emil		5	3
ANDERSON, Ernest Lionel Lane		2	7
ANDERSON, Fred		4	3
ANDERSON, Frederick Kinloch		1	6
ANDERSON, George John	P	2	7
ANDERSON, Gerard Rupert Laurie		2	7
ANDERSON, Henry Kemp	P	1	6
ANDERSON, Henry Lawrence		2	7
ANDERSON, Henry Small		1	6
ANDERSON, J		2	7
ANDERSON, James		2	7
ANDERSON, James		4	3
ANDERSON, James Alexander		3	6
ANDERSON, James Skelton	P	3	6
ANDERSON, John		1	6
ANDERSON, John		3	6
ANDERSON, John Grant	P	1	6
ANDERSON, John Kemp		3	6
ANDERSON, John Reginald	P	4	3
ANDERSON, John Robert		1	7
ANDERSON, John William		4	3
ANDERSON, Kenneth Angus	P	1	7
ANDERSON, Mervyn Kebble	P	1	7
ANDERSON, Percival Robert	P	2	7
ANDERSON, R		4	3
ANDERSON, Reginald William Christie	P	1	7
ANDERSON, Robert		2	7
ANDERSON, Robert Ballantine		3	6
ANDERSON, Robert Graham Wilson		2	7
ANDERSON, Robert Samuel		1	7
ANDERSON, Robertson Topping		5	3
ANDERSON, Samuel		1	7
ANDERSON, T		4	3
ANDERSON, Thomas		2	7
ANDERSON, Thomas		2	7
ANDERSON, Thomas		2	7
ANDERSON, Thomas	P	3	7
ANDERSON, Thomas		5	4
ANDERSON, Thomas Harold		4	3
ANDERSON, Thomas K		2	7
ANDERSON, W		2	7
ANDERSON, William	P	2	7
ANDERSON, William		2	7
ANDERSON, William	P	5	4
ANDERSON, William Arthur		1	7
ANDERSON, William James	P	2	8
ANDERSON, William John		1	7
ANDERSON, William John	P	2	8
ANDERSON, William Trevor	P	3	7
ANDERSON BEY, George Whitefield	P	1	7
ANDERTON, James		1	7
ANDERTON, John Wainwright		1	7
ANDERTON, William Lyon	P	1	7
ANDREW, Frederick Russell	P	1	8
ANDREW, George Hubert		4	3
ANDREW, Harry		1	8
ANDREW, Harry Townsend	P	3	7
ANDREWS, Charles Cyril		2	8
ANDREWS, Charles George William		2	8
ANDREWS, Charles Neville		4	3
ANDREWS, Charles Raymond		5	4
ANDREWS, Christopher Boyd	P	1	8
ANDREWS, Edward Norman	P	5	4
ANDREWS, Edward Richard Lawrence	P	2	8
ANDREWS, Edward Silvester	P	1	8
ANDREWS, Ernest Charles		5	4
ANDREWS, Ernest Thomas		4	3
ANDREWS, Frank	P	4	3
ANDREWS, Frederick Charles	P	1	8
ANDREWS, Frederick Charles		2	8
ANDREWS, Frederick George		1	8
ANDREWS, Frederick John		1	8
ANDREWS, Henry George		5	4
ANDREWS, Herbert Henry		2	8
ANDREWS, J		3	7
ANDREWS, James		1	8
ANDREWS, James Josiah		1	8
ANDREWS, Maynard Percy	P	2	8
ANDREWS, Peter		2	8
ANDREWS, R		2	8
ANDREWS, Robert Freeman		3	7
ANDREWS, Sydney		2	8
ANDREWS, William		2	8
ANGAS, Lionel George		5	4
ANGEL, Horace Albert Edward	P	5	4
ANGELL, Charles		2	8
ANGELL, J G H		2	8
ANGELL, T		2	8
ANGELL, W F		2	8
ANGUS, Archibald	P	2	8
ANGUS, Bruce Robertson		3	7
ANGUS, George Quinton		3	7
ANGUS, James Filshie Macfarlane	P	3	7
ANGUS, Norman John		3	7
ANGUS, Robert Edward	P	4	3
ANGUS, Stewart	P	2	8
ANKETELL-JONES, Henry Moutray	P	3	161
ANNABELL, Frederick Felix		1	8
ANNALLS, Charles George		2	9
ANNAND, Allan Young	P	3	7
ANNAND, Frank		3	7
ANNAND, Wallace Moir	P	1	8

Name	Photo	Part No.	Page No.
ANNANDALE, Charles James	P	3	7
ANNE, Crathorne Edward Isham Charlton	P	3	7
ANNESLEY, Francis		1	8
ANNESLEY, Hon. Arthur		1	8
ANNESLEY, James Ferguson St. John		3	8
ANNING, H P		2	9
ANNING, Hubert Percy	P	1	8
ANNING, James W		2	9
ANNIS, Robert		1	8
ANNIS, Walter		2	9
ANSCOMBE, Edgar S		2	9
ANSELL, Albert		1	8
ANSELL, Charles Hart		1	8
ANSELL, Charles Percy		3	8
ANSELL, Charles William		1	8
ANSELL, George Frederick		3	8
ANSELL, George Kirkpatrick		2	9
ANSELL, George Thomas	P	2	9
ANSELL, Sidney H		2	9
ANSELL, Walter		1	8
ANSELL, William		1	8
ANSELL, William Christopher		1	8
ANSON, F		2	9
ANSON, Robert		2	9
ANSON, Thomas		4	3
ANSON, Wilfrid Gordon		3	8
ANSTEY, Albert Edward		2	9
ANSTEY, Alfred Richard John		3	8
ANSTEY, George Alexander	P	1	9
ANSTEY, Thomas John Edmund	P	2	9
ANSTICE, John Spencer Ruscombe	P	1	9
ANSTISS, Henry Cecil		1	8
ANSTRUTHER, Thomas		2	9
ANTHONY, H		2	9
ANTHONY, Tom		5	4
ANTILL, Alfred Mansfield	P	1	9
ANTONY, E W		2	9
ANTRAM, Herbert Wilkins		5	4
ANTROBUS, Cecil Hugh	P	2	9
ANTROBUS, Charles Alexander	P	2	9
ANTROBUS, Edmund	P	1	9
APLIN, Elphinstone D'oyley	P	1	9
APLIN, K S		2	9
APPELGVIST, Frans Ludwig		2	9
APPLEBY, Harold C S		2	9
APPLES, Peter John		4	3
APPLETON, Charlie		2	10
APPLETON, Edgar	P	2	10
APPLEYARD, Walter D'ancie	P	1	9
APPS, Owen William		2	10
APPS, Thomas		2	10
ARBER, Archibald Guy	P	2	10
ARBON, Alfred John		5	4
ARBUTHNOT, Ashley Herbert		2	10
ARBUTHNOT, Kenneth Windham	P	1	9
ARBUTHNOTT, John	P	3	8
ARCHDALE, Charles William	P	3	8
ARCHDALE, George Mervyn	P	3	8
ARCHER, Fred		1	9
ARCHER, George		1	9
ARCHER, Harry		3	8
ARCHER, John William	P	3	8
ARCHER, John William Butts	P	1	9
ARCHIBALD, James		5	4
ARCHIBALD, William	P	1	10

Name	Photo	Part No.	Page No.
ARDEN, Humphrey Warwick		3	8
ARDIN, William T		2	10
ARGENT, Charles J		2	10
ARGENT, James		2	10
ARGENT, William Robert		1	10
ARGO, Alexander Whyte		3	8
ARGUE, P		2	10
ARKCOLL, Frederick Thomas		4	4
ARKWRIGHT, Frederic George Alleyne	P	2	10
ARLAIN, Edwin		1	10
ARMES, Herbert Alfred		4	4
ARMES, John Henry		1	10
ARMITAGE, Francis Arthur William	P	4	4
ARMITAGE, John Basil	P	3	9
ARMITAGE, Joseph		3	9
ARMITAGE, Thomas William		1	10
ARMITAGE, Wilfred		4	4
ARMOUR, James		2	10
ARMOUR, John		5	4
ARMSTRONG, Arthur Keith		2	10
ARMSTRONG, Charles Arthur	P	2	10
ARMSTRONG, Charles Martin		4	4
ARMSTRONG, Elleray Francis		1	10
ARMSTRONG, George		2	11
ARMSTRONG, George	P	4	4
ARMSTRONG, George	P	5	4
ARMSTRONG, George Leighton	P	1	10
ARMSTRONG, Henry Louis Winthrop		2	11
ARMSTRONG, J		2	11
ARMSTRONG, Jack		5	4
ARMSTRONG, James		1	10
ARMSTRONG, John		1	10
ARMSTRONG, John Graham		3	9
ARMSTRONG, Joseph		4	4
ARMSTRONG, Louis		3	9
ARMSTRONG, Robert		1	10
ARMSTRONG, Sydney John		2	11
ARMSTRONG, Wilfred		3	9
ARMSTRONG, William James		5	5
ARMSTRONG, William Maurice	P	3	9
ARMSTRONG, William Percival		2	11
ARMSTRONG, William Wilberforce	P	4	4
ARMSTRONG-LUSHINGTON-TULLOCH, **Graham** De Montmorency		4	216
ARNELL, Albert Colin		3	9
ARNELL, Alfred	P	3	9
ARNELL, Clement		2	11
ARNELL, James Alexander	P	1	10
ARNETT, Arthur Edward		3	9
ARNETT, Henry J		2	11
ARNOLD, B		3	9
ARNOLD, Cecil		5	5
ARNOLD, Charles Edgar		1	10
ARNOLD, E		3	9
ARNOLD, Ferdinand Franck William	P	1	10
ARNOLD, George Horace		2	11
ARNOLD, Harry Richard	P	1	10
ARNOLD, Henry		1	10
ARNOLD, Hugo Cholmondeley		3	9
ARNOLD, John		2	11
ARNOLD, John James		5	5
ARNOLD, John Samuel		5	5
ARNOLD, Robert		1	10
ARNOT, Cyril William	P	4	4
ARNOT, James Allan		2	11

Name	Photo	Part No.	Page No.
ARNOTT, Harold	P	2	11
ARNOTT, Hugh		5	5
ARNOTT, Robert		2	11
ARNOTT, Robert Louis Irving		5	5
ARROL, Colin A	P	3	10
ARRONDEAN, George		2	11
ARROWSMITH, Alfred Edgar		5	5
ARROWSMITH, Thomas James		4	4
ARTHUR, Alexander		5	5
ARTHUR, Charles	P	1	10
ARTHUR, David	P	3	10
ARTHUR, E		2	11
ARTHUR, George Mcleod		3	10
ARTHUR, Herbert George	P	1	10
ARTHUR, James Andrew	P	3	10
ARTHUR, John Clark	P	3	10
ARTHUR, Richard Victor	P	1	11
ARTHURS, J		2	11
ARTHURS, J		3	10
ARUNDELL, Albert		2	11
ASBREY, Harold Wilfred		5	5
ASBURY, Arthur Gerard		1	11
ASCOTT, Vincent John Dawson	P	1	11
ASCROFT, Robert Geoffrey Lees	P	1	11
ASH, Basil Claudius		2	11
ASH, Basil Drummond	P	1	11
ASH, Henry T		2	11
ASH, John	P	2	11
ASH, John Clement		4	4
ASH, Joseph		2	11
ASH, Wilfrid John	P	1	11
ASH, William Joseph		3	10
ASHBROOK, William Chrimes		4	4
ASHBY, A H		2	11
ASHBY, Edwin		4	5
ASHBY, George		1	11
ASHBY, George William	P	2	11
ASHBY, Leslie	P	5	5
ASHCROFT, J		2	11
ASHDOWN, John	P	5	5
ASHENDEN, Harry		2	11
ASHER, Alexander	P	4	5
ASHFORD, Isaac Dobson		3	10
ASHFORD, Sidney Herbert		3	10
ASHFORD, W		3	10
ASHLEY, Albert Richard		2	11
ASHMAN, Lionel Alfred		3	10
ASHTON, Edward Stanley John Charles		1	11
ASHTON, Edwin	P	1	11
ASHTON, Eli	P	2	11
ASHTON, Ernest		2	11
ASHTON, Frank	P	3	10
ASHTON, Frank		4	5
ASHTON, Frederick William	P	2	12
ASHTON, Frederick William		5	5
ASHTON, Henry		4	5
ASHTON, Henry Frederick		4	5
ASHTON, J T		3	10
ASHTON, John	P	2	12
ASHTON, John T		2	12
ASHTON, Joseph George Ripley		3	10
ASHTON, Norman	P	5	5
ASHTON, Walter Charles	P	3	10
ASHURST, James		1	11
ASHWORTH, Edmund		1	11

Name	Photo	Part No.	Page No.
ASKEW, Henry Adam	P	1	11
ASKEW, John Henry		1	12
ASKEW, Joseph		2	12
ASKEW, William		3	10
ASLETT, Francis George		2	12
ASLIN, George		1	12
ASLIN, Robert	P	2	12
ASPINALL, Reginald Clarence		4	5
ASPINALL, Samuel		2	12
ASPREY, Bernard Noel		2	12
ASSITER, Alfred		1	12
ASTILL, William Frederick	P	3	11
ASTLEY, Christopher Basil		4	5
ASTON, Ernest Edward		4	5
ASTON, H		3	11
ATCHESON, John	P	1	12
ATHERTON, F		3	11
ATKIN, Albert Frank Fowler		3	11
ATKIN, Jesse Marson		2	12
ATKIN, John Claude		1	12
ATKINS, Arthur Clare	P	2	12
ATKINS, Charles G		2	12
ATKINS, Charles John		2	12
ATKINS, Edmund Joseph		1	12
ATKINS, Frank Stanley	P	1	12
ATKINS, Henry Albert		2	12
ATKINS, Herbert De Carteret	P	2	12
ATKINS, James		1	12
ATKINS, John		1	12
ATKINS, Lewis William Henry		2	12
ATKINS, Robert		2	12
ATKINS, Sidney James		5	5
ATKINS, Walter Ernest		2	12
ATKINSON, Alfred		4	5
ATKINSON, Alfred George		1	12
ATKINSON, Andrew George	P	1	12
ATKINSON, Arnold Francis Crossley		5	5
ATKINSON, Charles	P	2	12
ATKINSON, F		3	11
ATKINSON, George Arthur		4	5
ATKINSON, Guy Cheselden Reuell	P	2	13
ATKINSON, Henry	P	4	5
ATKINSON, James Percy		2	13
ATKINSON, John Broadwood		2	13
ATKINSON, John Cyril		2	13
ATKINSON, John Thomas		2	13
ATKINSON, Miles Linzee		3	11
ATKINSON, Noel Mitford Henson	P	2	13
ATKINSON, Norman		3	11
ATKINSON, Samuel Arnold		4	5
ATKINSON, Walter William		5	5
ATKINSON, William Fewlass	P	2	13
ATKINSON, William Joseph	P	1	12
ATKINSON, William Noel	P	1	12
ATLAY, Hugh Wordsworth	P	2	13
ATTENBORROW, Ernest		2	13
ATTERBURY, William James		1	12
ATTEWELL, Frederick David		3	11
ATTHILL, L		3	11
ATTLEE, James Mervyn	P	1	12
ATTREALL, Albert		1	12
ATTREE, Benjamin		1	12
ATTREL, Ernest Charles		1	12
ATTWATER, Ernest		4	5
ATTWATER, Richard		1	12

Name	Photo	Part No.	Page No.
ATTWELL, William Henry		5	6
ATTWOOD, Algernon Foulkes	P	1	12
ATTWOOD, Arthur		1	12
ATTWOOD, Arthur Charles		1	12
ATTWOOD, Charles	P	1	13
ATTWOOD, George F		2	13
ATTWOOD, William		4	5
ATWELL, Alfred	P	4	5
ATWELL, Robert Erskine		5	6
AUBIN, Alfred Charles	P	1	13
AUBREY, William George	P	3	11
AUCHINLECK, Daniel George Harold		2	13
AUDEN, Geoffrey William		5	6
AUDSLEY, Joseph Cameron		3	11
AUDSLEY, William Thomas		5	6
AULD, Frederick Arnot		4	5
AULD, George Lockhart	P	2	13
AULD, Robert Yeudall		5	6
AUSTEN, Hubert		2	13
AUSTEN, Samuel Ernest		2	13
AUSTEN, William Frank		1	13
AUSTIN, A		3	11
AUSTIN, Albert		2	13
AUSTIN, Alfred		2	13
AUSTIN, Aubrey John		2	14
AUSTIN, Cyril Frederic	P	1	13
AUSTIN, D T		3	11
AUSTIN, Eric Mannington		3	11
AUSTIN, Ernest James	P	4	6
AUSTIN, Frank Ernest		3	11
AUSTIN, Frederick William		1	13
AUSTIN, George		1	13
AUSTIN, Harold Lunn Ferrier		3	11
AUSTIN, Harry		4	6
AUSTIN, W		3	11
AUSTIN, William	P	4	6
AUTON, Charles James		2	14
AVELING, Lancelot Neville	P	1	13
AVERAILL, R		3	11
AVERILL, A		3	11
AVERILL, Albert		1	13
AVERIS, Frank George		2	14
AVERY, Alfred		2	14
AVERY, Percy	P	5	6
AVILA, L F		3	11
AVIS, Frederick George	P	4	6
AVIS, Harry		1	13
AVIS, Ralph Cutts		1	13
AVIS, William		1	13
AWDRY, Carol Edward Vere	P	1	13
AXFORD, F H		3	11
AXON, Walter Henry		1	14
AXON, William Charles		2	14
AXUP, Victor Emmanuel		1	14
AYERS, Percy Daniel		3	11
AYLES, John Henry		4	6
AYLESBURY, Alexander		4	6
AYLETT, William		2	14
AYLING, Ebenezer		2	14
AYLING, Harry		2	14
AYLING, William		1	14
AYRE, Rodney		3	11
AYRES, Clement		5	6
AYRES, James George		3	12
AYRES, James Henry		2	14

Name	Photo	Part No.	Page No.
AYRTON, Harry	P	3	12
AYTON, William Henry		2	14
AYTOUN, Robert Merlin Graham		2	14
BABBINGTON, George Stephen	P	3	12
BABER, Thomas Edward		1	14
BACHE, Albert Henry		3	12
BACHELOR, Frank		1	14
BACHMANN, Friedrich Marcus August		4	6
BACK, John Richard		1	14
BACKHOUSE, Frederick John		3	12
BACKHOUSE, Henry		2	14
BACKHOUSE, Hubert Edmund	P	2	14
BACKHOUSE, John William		3	12
BACKWAY, Thomas Albert Henry		4	6
BACON, Alan Harvey		2	14
BACON, Basil Kenrick Wing	P	1	14
BACON, Dudley Francis Cecil		2	14
BACON, Sidney Roger Claude		4	6
BADCOCK, Arthur Ernest		4	6
BADCOCK, Arthur Lawrence	P	2	14
BADDELEY, Edward Lawrence	P	1	14
BADDELEY, Lionel Richard Logan	P	1	14
BADDER, Sidney Joseph		1	14
BADDON, Donald		2	14
BADENOCH, James		1	14
BADETSCHER, John Henry		2	14
BADGER, Charles Sidney	P	2	14
BAGGIN, R		3	12
BAGGS, G		3	12
BAGGS, Harold Frank		3	12
BAGGULEY, James Lionel		5	6
BAGLEY, Arthur Davies	P	1	14
BAGLEY, Frank Adams	P	2	14
BAGLEY, Thomas William Aston	P	2	14
BAGNALL, John Charles		5	6
BAGSHAWE, Leonard Vale	P	1	14
BAIGENT, S S		3	12
BAILEY, A J		2	15
BAILEY, Albert Henry	P	2	15
BAILEY, Albert Henry	P	3	12
BAILEY, Archibald Ernest		1	14
BAILEY, Arthur Charles	P	5	6
BAILEY, Arthur Edward	P	1	14
BAILEY, Arthur William		5	6
BAILEY, Dermot Harvey	P	3	12
BAILEY, E		3	12
BAILEY, Edward		2	15
BAILEY, F W		3	12
BAILEY, Francis John		3	12
BAILEY, Frederick Joseph		1	14
BAILEY, Frederick Maurice		3	12
BAILEY, G H		2	15
BAILEY, George Henry		1	14
BAILEY, Henry	P	3	12
BAILEY, Horace Horatio		3	12
BAILEY, J		3	13
BAILEY, James		2	15
BAILEY, John James	P	1	14
BAILEY, Leonard		5	6
BAILEY, Thomas Dismore	P	1	15
BAILEY, W H		3	13
BAILEY, W H V		3	13
BAILEY, Wallace James		1	15
BAILEY, Walter H		2	15
BAILEY, William		1	15

Name	Photo	Part No.	Page No.
BAILEY, William		1	15
BAILEY, William		2	15
BAILEY, William Ernest		4	6
BAILEY, William Henry		1	15
BAILEY, William Henry		3	13
BAILEY, William James		2	15
BAILLIE, Charles		3	13
BAILLIE, Douglas Anderson		1	15
BAILLIE, Duncan		2	15
BAILLIE, Evan Henry	P	2	15
BAILLIE, George		2	15
BAILLIE, Ian Henry	P	1	15
BAILLIE, John	P	4	6
BAILLIE, Sir Gawaine George Stuart		1	15
BAILWARD, Theodore	P	1	15
BAILY, Albert		3	13
BAILY, George		2	15
BAILY, Stuart Underwood	P	5	6
BAIN, Charles	P	2	15
BAIN, Herbert		5	7
BAIN, J		3	13
BAIN, John		4	6
BAIN, Robert Ronald Cochrane		2	15
BAIN, Walter Duncan		2	15
BAINBRIDGE, Carlyle	P	5	7
BAINBRIDGE, John Stuart	P	5	7
BAINBRIDGE, Thomas Lindsay	P	1	15
BAINES, D		3	13
BAINES, Jack Gordon Barrymore		4	6
BAINTON, Thomas Walter Peveril		2	15
BAIRD, A		3	13
BAIRD, Alexander		3	13
BAIRD, Alexander Charles Henry		2	15
BAIRD, Colin	P	1	15
BAIRD, J		2	15
BAIRD, Robert Smellie		4	7
BAIRD, Stanley Charles		1	15
BAIRD, W		2	15
BAIRD, William	P	4	7
BAIRD, William Archibald	P	3	13
BAIRD, William Frank Gardiner		1	15
BAKER, A		3	13
BAKER, Albert Charles		2	16
BAKER, Alfred		2	16
BAKER, Arthur		2	16
BAKER, Aubrey Halliwell	P	2	16
BAKER, Basil Howard		4	7
BAKER, Cecil Douglas		3	13
BAKER, Charles Gilbert	P	4	7
BAKER, Charles William Edwin	P	2	16
BAKER, Cyril Victor		5	7
BAKER, Edward		2	16
BAKER, Edward		2	16
BAKER, Edward Benjamin		2	16
BAKER, Edward James		1	15
BAKER, Edwin Joseph		1	15
BAKER, Ernest John	P	4	7
BAKER, F		3	13
BAKER, F		3	13
BAKER, F C		3	13
BAKER, Fernley Edward	P	4	7
BAKER, Francis Charles		4	7
BAKER, Fred Badcock		2	16
BAKER, Frederick		2	16
BAKER, Frederick Charles		3	13

Name	Photo	Part No.	Page No.
BAKER, Frederick William	P	1	15
BAKER, G		2	16
BAKER, George		2	16
BAKER, George		5	7
BAKER, George Brandon		1	15
BAKER, George Robert		2	16
BAKER, H		3	13
BAKER, Henry Tillet		1	16
BAKER, James		2	16
BAKER, James Henry	P	1	16
BAKER, John		1	16
BAKER, John		2	16
BAKER, John		3	13
BAKER, John		4	7
BAKER, John E		2	16
BAKER, John William	P	1	16
BAKER, Marshall		1	16
BAKER, Osbert Clinton	P	1	16
BAKER, Roger Dyke	P	2	16
BAKER, W		3	13
BAKER, W J		3	13
BAKER, W T		3	13
BAKER, William	P	2	16
BAKER, William Arthur		5	7
BAKER, William Henry		1	16
BAKER, William Henry		2	16
BAKER, William J		2	16
BAKER, William John		1	16
BAKEWELL, J E		3	13
BALBIRNIE, John Victor Elphinstone	P	5	7
BALCOMBE, Frederick		1	16
BALCOMBE, Henry Charles George		3	13
BALCOMBE, W		3	13
BALDERSON, Henry Leslie Paxton	P	2	16
BALDIE, G		5	7
BALDIE, John Halley		3	13
BALDING, Robert		1	16
BALDING, William David		2	17
BALDOCK, Claude Henry	P	4	7
BALDOCK, James		2	17
BALDOCK, Stanley Clifford		4	7
BALDOCK, Stephen Thomas		5	7
BALDOCK, William Robert		1	16
BALDRICK, J		3	13
BALDWIN, A		2	17
BALDWIN, Allen Aquila	P	5	7
BALDWIN, Anthony Hugh	P	1	16
BALDWIN, Cuthbert Godfrey	P	3	13
BALDWIN, David Aitken	P	2	17
BALDWIN, E		3	13
BALDWIN, Edwin Harold Arthur		4	7
BALDWIN, Ernest		5	7
BALDWIN, H		2	17
BALDWIN, Hugh Laurents Chenevix		2	17
BALDWIN, John Oswald		3	13
BALDWIN, Josiah		1	16
BALDWIN, Terence Kennet James		4	7
BALDWIN, William Frederick	P	5	7
BALE, Herbert	P	4	7
BALFE, S		3	13
BALFOUR, Robert Frederick		2	17
BALFOUR MELVILLE, James Elliot	P	2	224
BALHARRIE, David		4	7
BALKWILL, William Horniman	P	3	13
BALL, Albert Ransome	P	1	16

Name	Photo	Part No.	Page No.
BARKER, Herbert		1	19
BARKER, Noah	P	1	19
BARKER, Richard Vincent		2	18
BARKER, Sam	P	3	15
BARKER, Samuel		2	18
BARKER, Thomas William		3	15
BARKER, William		1	19
BARKER, William	P	2	18
BARKER, William		2	18
BARKER, William		2	18
BARKLAMB, Edward Charles		2	18
BARKS, Herbert		1	19
BARKS, Isaac		1	19
BARLEY, H		3	15
BARLEY, John	P	1	19
BARLEY, Leslie William	P	2	19
BARLIN, George	P	4	8
BARLING, Henry William		1	19
BARLING, Percy		2	19
BARLING, William Bingham	P	1	20
BARLOW, Charles Ernest		1	20
BARLOW, Geoffrey Petrie	P	3	15
BARLOW, James William		1	20
BARLOW, John Robert		4	8
BARLOW, Thomas Arthur		1	20
BARLOW, Thomas Richards		3	15
BARMES, W		3	15
BARMFED, J		3	15
BARNARD, Charles Henry		3	15
BARNARD, Humfrey Denzil	P	5	9
BARNARD, Philip		1	20
BARNARD, Reuben George		1	20
BARNARD, William Henry		1	20
BARNARDIER, James		1	20
BARNARD-SMITH, William Woodthorpe Barnard		3	252
BARNBROOK, John		2	19
BARNDEN, Frederick Thomas		1	20
BARNES, A H		3	15
BARNES, A W		3	15
BARNES, Abraham	P	2	19
BARNES, Arthur		1	20
BARNES, Arthur Frederick		1	20
BARNES, Arthur James		4	8
BARNES, Charles		1	20
BARNES, Charles Edward		1	20
BARNES, Charles Roger Gorell		5	9
BARNES, Clements David James	P	3	15
BARNES, David Samuel		2	19
BARNES, Douglas Meston	P	1	20
BARNES, Edward Ernest		1	20
BARNES, Eric		2	19
BARNES, Frederick		1	20
BARNES, Frederick Francis	P	1	20
BARNES, Frederick George		2	19
BARNES, George Ernest	P	2	19
BARNES, George William		1	20
BARNES, H		3	15
BARNES, Herbert Plume		1	20
BARNES, Hugh Cyril		4	8
BARNES, Hugh Cyril		5	9
BARNES, John		1	20
BARNES, John	P	4	8
BARNES, John William		1	20
BARNES, Owen		3	15
BARNES, Philip Charles		1	20
BARNES, S		3	15
BARNES, Stephen		2	19
BARNES, Sydney George	P	2	19
BARNES, Sydney James		1	20
BARNES, Thomas		1	20
BARNES, W		3	15
BARNES, William		1	21
BARNES, William Alfred	P	5	9
BARNES, William George		5	9
BARNES, William Joseph		1	21
BARNETT, Denis Oliver		3	15
BARNETT, Francis Gerald		4	8
BARNETT, H		3	16
BARNETT, James	P	1	21
BARNETT, Knight	P	1	21
BARNETT, Robert Allan		5	9
BARNETT, S		3	16
BARNETT, S W		3	16
BARNETT, W		2	19
BARNETT, W		3	16
BARNETT, William		1	21
BARNETT, William		2	19
BARNETT, William		5	9
BARNETT, William Stuart	P	1	21
BARNHARDT, Frederick John	P	1	21
BARNICOTT, Cyril		2	19
BARNSBY, Joseph Albert		4	9
BARNSLEY, Alan		2	19
BARNSLEY, Cyril Jevon		3	16
BARNSLEY, Harry		5	9
BARON, Thomas		1	21
BARONIAN, Haron	P	3	16
BARR, Charles		2	19
BARR, Donald Robertson		5	9
BARR, J		2	19
BARR, James H		5	9
BARR, Samuel Tudor	P	1	21
BARR, Thomas Henry		1	21
BARRACK, James Ferguson		4	9
BARRACLOUGH, G		3	16
BARRACLOUGH, Gilbert		2	19
BARRAND, Sydney		5	9
BARRASS, Alfred Leonard		1	21
BARRAT, William Topley	P	3	16
BARRATT, Albert Ernest	P	5	9
BARRATT, Charles Wylly		1	21
BARRATT, James		1	21
BARRATT, Percival John		1	21
BARRELL, Alfred James		5	10
BARRELL, Henry		5	10
BARRELL, William Herbert		5	10
BARRETT, Alec		3	16
BARRETT, Alfred		5	10
BARRETT, Alfred Victor		5	10
BARRETT, Archie James		3	16
BARRETT, Bernard Thomas	P	4	9
BARRETT, Charles John Chard	P	1	21
BARRETT, F		2	19
BARRETT, George	P	2	19
BARRETT, Horace Reginald George		2	19
BARRETT, Hugh Henry Guy	P	1	22
BARRETT, John Edwin		4	9
BARRETT, Joseph		1	22
BARRETT, Lindsay Alfred	P	3	16

Name	Photo	Part No.	Page No.
BARRETT, Philip Godfrey		2	19
BARRETT, Robert Simon		1	22
BARRETT, T R		4	9
BARRETT, Walter		3	16
BARRETT, William		1	22
BARRETT, William George John		1	22
BARRIE, John		2	20
BARRIE, John		5	10
BARRINGER, George		2	20
BARRINGTON, Aubrey Leonard Bertram		4	9
BARRINGTON, Noel Scot	P	1	22
BARRON, Edward		2	20
BARRON, James	P	4	9
BARROW, Edmund Sproston Knapp	P	3	16
BARROW, Richard		2	20
BARROW, Richard Henry		2	20
BARROW, Wilfrid Gordon	P	2	20
BARROWMAN, Robert Wishart	P	3	17
BARRS, Alfred		4	9
BARRS, Thomas Edward	P	5	10
BARRY, J C		2	20
BARRY, James		1	22
BARRY, John Francis		1	22
BARRY, Wiiliam Thomas Henry		3	17
BARSBY, George		1	22
BARSON, Percy		1	22
BARSTOW, John Baillie		1	22
BARTER, Harry Stanley		1	22
BARTER, William Charles		1	22
BARTHEY, Edward		2	20
BARTHOLOMEW, Jim		5	10
BARTHOLOMEW, William John Hargreaves		3	17
BARTHROPP, Sidney Alfred Nathaniel Shafto	P	1	22
BARTLE, Frederic		4	9
BARTLE, Thomas William		3	17
BARTLEET, Henry Booth		5	10
BARTLETT, Austin George Henry	P	2	20
BARTLETT, Charles Frederick		1	22
BARTLETT, Charles H		2	20
BARTLETT, Cyril	P	4	9
BARTLETT, F		3	17
BARTLETT, Frederick		4	9
BARTLETT, Frederick Dudley		5	10
BARTLETT, Geoffrey Edward Rose	P	1	22
BARTLETT, George		5	10
BARTLETT, George		5	10
BARTLETT, Harry Steven	P	3	17
BARTLETT, Henry Arthur		1	22
BARTLETT, Herbert W P		2	20
BARTLETT, Joe		1	22
BARTLETT, Lionel Arthur		2	20
BARTLETT, R		3	17
BARTLETT, V P		3	17
BARTLETT, W		3	17
BARTLEY, Arthur	P	4	9
BARTLEY, Arthur		5	10
BARTLEY, John Arthur		2	20
BARTLEY, Michael	P	2	20
BARTLEY, William James		3	17
BARTON, Albert		2	20
BARTON, Alfred		2	20
BARTON, Alfred Richard	P	2	20
BARTON, Edwin William	P	3	17
BARTON, Ernest	P	1	22
BARTON, Francis Hewson		2	20
BARTON, Frederick St.John		3	17
BARTON, Gilbert Johnson		1	22
BARTON, Harold Remington		5	10
BARTON, Harold William Ferguson	P	1	22
BARTON, Harry Frederick		3	17
BARTON, Henry		1	22
BARTON, Hugh Fabian		2	20
BARTON, J		4	9
BARTON, James Thomas		1	22
BARTON, John Thomas		1	22
BARTON, Reginald Ernest	P	5	10
BARTON, Thomas Eyre		3	17
BARTON, Thomas Lawrence		2	20
BARTON, Vivian Alfred		3	17
BARTON, W		3	17
BARTON, William Dunn		3	17
BARTRAM, Alan		3	17
BARTROP, W B		3	18
BARTTELOT, Nigel Kenneth Walter	P	1	23
BARUGH, T W		3	18
BARWELL, Edward Egerton		2	20
BARWELL, Humphrey Eames		4	9
BASFORD, Bromley Alfred		3	18
BASHFORD, Alfred		1	23
BASHFORD, Henry Fletcher		2	21
BASKERVILLE, Gilbert Thomas	P	1	23
BASKERVILLE, Hedley		1	23
BASNETT, J		3	18
BASNETT, John	P	1	23
BASS, A J		3	18
BASS, Henry		1	23
BASS, John		5	10
BASS, Philip Burnet	P	2	21
BASSETT, Percy Nicholas		3	18
BASSETT, Victor Charles		1	23
BASTABLE, Sampson Edward		5	10
BASTARD, Reginald George		1	23
BASTARD, William	P	1	23
BASTERFIELD, William Joseph		2	21
BATCHELOR, Albert	P	5	10
BATCHELOR, Benjamin Edwin		1	23
BATCHELOR, Cyril Edward		4	9
BATCHELOR, George		1	23
BATCHELOR, Harold James		1	23
BATCHELOR, William George		4	9
BATCHELOR, William John		5	10
BATE, John Richard		3	18
BATE, T		3	18
BATE, Thomas	P	3	18
BATE, Thomas Henry		1	23
BATE, Walter	P	3	18
BATEMAN, Bernard Montague Basil		2	21
BATEMAN, Charles	P	3	18
BATEMAN, Claude John		1	23
BATEMAN, Frank		1	23
BATEMAN, J		2	21
BATEMAN, Joseph		2	21
BATEMAN, Wilfrid Reginald		4	9
BATEMAN, William Thomas		1	23
BATES, A		3	18
BATES, F		2	21
BATES, Frank		1	23
BATES, George		1	23
BATES, George Richard		2	21
BATES, James Christopher		1	23

Name	Photo	Part No.	Page No.
BATES, Percy G		2	21
BATES, Stanes Geoffrey	P	1	23
BATES, Stanley Knight	P	1	23
BATES, William Daniel		5	10
BATES, William George Henry	P	1	23
BATEY, Edward Henry		1	24
BATEY, Robert	P	1	24
BATH, Allen Henry		2	21
BATH, John Euel Witherden	P	2	21
BATHGATE, W		3	18
BATHIE, George		2	21
BATHO, John	P	2	21
BATHURST, Nelson Standish		4	10
BATSON, Alfred William	P	1	24
BATSON, Robert Evelyn		3	18
BATSON, William Stewart		3	18
BATT, John Albert Alias Frank		1	24
BATT, Norman Harold		1	24
BATTAMS, H		2	22
BATTARBEE, Herbert		1	24
BATTARBEE, P A		2	22
BATTEN, A		2	22
BATTEN, Arthur		1	24
BATTEN, J		2	22
BATTEN, John Henry Strode		1	24
BATTEN, Joseph		1	24
BATTEN, William Henry		1	24
BATTENBERG, His Highness Prince Maurice Victor Donald	P	1	24
BATTERHAM, James		1	24
BATTERSBY, Augustus Wolfe	P	1	24
BATTERSBY, Caryl Lionel Morse	P	3	18
BATTERSBY, Charles Fremoult Preston	P	1	25
BATTERSBY, Eric May		2	22
BATTERSBY, James Henry		2	22
BATTERSBY, James Wilfred		4	10
BATTESON, J F		2	22
BATTLE, Edward Charles Vulliamy		2	22
BATTY, Charles Frederick		3	18
BATTY, Christopher		1	25
BATTY, William	P	3	18
BATTY, William Henry	P	1	25
BATY, Robert	P	1	25
BATY, Thomas		1	25
BAUCHOP, Arthur	P	1	25
BAUCHOP, Spence		5	10
BAUMBACH, John		3	18
BAVERSTOCK, Alfred George		1	25
BAVIN, Anthony James		3	19
BAVIN, Nigel Benjamin	P	1	25
BAVISTER, William E		2	22
BAX, George Thomas	P	3	19
BAXENDALE, Philip		4	10
BAXENDINE, Andrew Richard	P	5	11
BAXENDINE, John Young	P	5	11
BAXTER, Alexander Walls		5	11
BAXTER, Alfred Joyce		1	25
BAXTER, Arthur		2	22
BAXTER, Bernard Eyre	P	1	25
BAXTER, Charles		2	22
BAXTER, David	P	5	11
BAXTER, Frederick Henry		2	22
BAXTER, James Patrick		1	25
BAXTER, John Henry		1	25
BAXTER, Leslie William	P	4	10
BAXTER, Philip John Wood		2	22
BAXTER, Ralph Frederick		2	22
BAXTER, W		2	22
BAXTER, William Charles		2	22
BAYES, Christopher Henry		2	22
BAYFIELD, Alfred		1	25
BAYLEY, Albert Edward		1	25
BAYLEY, George Baird	P	1	25
BAYLEY, Joseph William		2	22
BAYLIS, Henry		2	22
BAYLISS, John Edwin		3	19
BAYLISS, Reginald Blencowe	P	3	19
BAYLISS, William	P	3	19
BAYLY, Charles George Gordon	P	1	25
BAYLY, Lancelot Myles	P	5	11
BAYNES, Alfred		2	22
BAYNES, James	P	1	26
BAZELEY, Rolland A	P	2	22
BEACH, Edgar		2	22
BEACH, Ernest		1	26
BEACH, George Frederick		4	10
BEACH, Lionel Hadwen Fletcher	P	5	11
BEACHAM, Henry	P	4	10
BEACHER, L G C		3	19
BEADELL, Percy Charles		2	22
BEADLE, A T		2	22
BEADLE, Jesse Augustus	P	1	26
BEADON, Basil Herbert Edwards	P	1	26
BEAGLEHOLE, Arthur	P	4	10
BEAK, Douglas Eliot	P	5	11
BEAL, Edgar		2	22
BEAL, James Henry	P	2	22
BEALE, Clifford William		3	19
BEALE, Edgar		3	19
BEALE, Harry	P	4	10
BEALE, James		1	26
BEALE, Simion		2	22
BEALING, S T		3	19
BEAMES, Alfred Edward		1	26
BEAMS, William Thomas		2	22
BEAN, Charles Reginald		2	22
BEAN, Frederick James		1	26
BEAN, George		1	26
BEAN, Harold Knowles		3	19
BEAN, John Thomas		2	22
BEAN, Maurice Gordon		2	22
BEAN, Samuel John		1	26
BEANEY, Albert Edward		1	26
BEANEY, Alfred		2	23
BEANEY, James		1	26
BEANLAND, Harry		1	26
BEANLAND, Joseph Wilfrid		2	23
BEANLANDS, Frederick Alexander	P	5	11
BEARD, Fred		1	26
BEARD, Walter Edmund		2	23
BEARDER, A		3	19
BEARMAN, Walter John		1	26
BEARMAN, Willie George		1	26
BEARNE, Arthur Henry		1	26
BEASANT, E		2	23
BEASLEY, David Southon		2	23
BEASLEY, Herbert Frederick	P	3	19
BEASLEY, James Joyce	P	2	23
BEATON, A		2	23
BEATON, George Tait	P	2	23

Name	Photo	Part No.	Page No.
BEATON, Harry	P	3	19
BEATON, Kenneth Corbett		3	19
BEATSON, Frederick	P	1	26
BEATTIE, Frederick George	P	3	19
BEATTIE, G		3	19
BEATTIE, Isaac	P	1	26
BEATTIE, J		2	23
BEATTIE, J		2	23
BEATTIE, J		2	23
BEATTIE, Robert-Grant		2	23
BEATTIE, T		3	19
BEATTIE, William		2	23
BEATTIE, William		3	19
BEATTIE, William Marshall	P	5	11
BEATTIE-BROWN, William		3	38
BEATTY, Eric Edge	P	3	20
BEAUCHAMP, Edward Archibald		2	23
BEAUFORT, Francis Hugh	P	1	26
BEAUFORT, Ostcliffe Harold	P	1	27
BEAUMONT, Cyril J		2	23
BEAUMONT, Eric Paton	P	4	10
BEAUMONT, Harold		5	12
BEAUMONT, Joseph Arthur		4	10
BEAUMONT, R		3	20
BEAUMONT, Sidney Arthur		4	11
BEAUMONT, W		3	20
BEAUMONT-NESBITT, Wilfrid Henry		4	143
BEAVER, Arthur Louis		2	23
BEAVER, Percival Granville	P	5	12
BEAVER, Wilfred Norman		3	20
BEAVES, Frederick		2	23
BEAVIS, Leonard E		2	23
BEAVIS, Thomas		2	23
BEAVON, Thomas		2	23
BEBBINGTON, Joseph		3	20
BECHER, Henry Owen Dabridgcourt		1	27
BECHER, Henry Sullivan		2	23
BECHER, John Pickard	P	2	23
BECHER, Maurice Andrew Noel	P	1	27
BECHER, William Stewart	P	2	24
BECK, Arthur		1	27
BECK, Charles Broughton Harrop	P	2	24
BECK, Frank Reginald	P	2	24
BECK, George		3	20
BECK, Harry Harold		3	20
BECK, Herbert Harvey		2	24
BECK, John Stanley		3	20
BECK, Joseph		1	27
BECK, Robert Leonard		1	27
BECK, T		3	20
BECKER, Albert Raphael		2	24
BECKERWICK, Moses		2	24
BECKETT, David William		2	24
BECKETT, Richard		1	27
BECKETT, William Henry		3	20
BECKHURTS, J W		3	20
BECKLEY, William		2	24
BEDBOROUGH, W		3	20
BEDBROOK, Ernest Arthur St. George	P	5	12
BEDDA, H		3	20
BEDDOW, John Frederick Heber		5	12
BEDDOW, M		3	20
BEDDOW, Richard Charles		1	27
BEDFORD, Charles	P	3	20
BEDFORD, Conrad Thomas	P	1	27

Name	Photo	Part No.	Page No.
BEDFORD, H		3	20
BEDFORD, Harold		1	27
BEDFORD, Herbert		1	27
BEDFORD, William Arthur	P	2	24
BEDNALL, Benjamin Charles		3	20
BEE, Charles Lovering		3	20
BEE, Harry		1	27
BEEBEE, T H		3	20
BEECH, Albert		1	27
BEECH, Ernest	P	2	24
BEECH, Frederick W		2	24
BEECH, John		4	11
BEECH, John Robert	P	2	24
BEECH, Norman William		3	20
BEECHAM, Arthur Robert		1	27
BEECHAM, Thomas		2	24
BEECHER, J		2	24
BEECHING, John		1	27
BEECHING, Luke		1	27
BEECROFT, George	P	1	27
BEEMAN, Arthur C		2	24
BEER, A		3	20
BEER, Albert Henry		2	24
BEER, Edward George		4	11
BEER, Frederick James	P	1	27
BEER, George Henry		1	28
BEER, Harry		1	28
BEER, Henry Oliver		2	25
BEER, John Henry		2	25
BEER, William Edward		1	28
BEERLING, Thomas William		1	28
BEESLEY, Anthony Blyton		5	12
BEESLEY, Dick		1	28
BEETON, W R P		3	20
BEGBIE, Alfred Vincent	P	3	20
BEGG, Alexander		1	28
BEGG, Kenneth Humphreys		3	20
BEGG, Peter Gall	P	3	21
BEGLEY, Denis Francis		1	28
BEGLEY, William B		2	25
BEHENNA, William Henry		1	28
BEHENNAH, Alfred Dunn		3	21
BEHRENS, Robert Philip	P	1	28
BEIRN, C		3	21
BEIRNE, William	P	4	11
BELAND, George		2	25
BELCHER, A		3	21
BELCHER, Albert		1	28
BELCHER, J		4	11
BELCHER, W		3	21
BELCHER, Wilfrid Frank	P	3	21
BELCHIER, Frank Elliot	P	1	28
BELDHAM, Arthur		1	28
BELDOM, George Noah		1	28
BELDON, S		3	21
BELL, (Alfred) Ray Lancaster	P	1	28
BELL, A		3	21
BELL, Alan Robert	P	1	28
BELL, Albert Henderson		1	28
BELL, Albert Victor		5	12
BELL, Albert William		1	28
BELL, Alexander		1	28
BELL, Alexander Murray-Macgregor	P	1	28
BELL, Alfred Herbert	P	2	25
BELL, Archibald Mccutcheon		5	12

Name	Photo	Part No.	Page No.
BELL, Arthur Walton		4	11
BELL, C		3	21
BELL, Cedric Molesworth	P	1	28
BELL, Charles Henry		4	11
BELL, Charles Ockley	P	1	28
BELL, Christopher		2	25
BELL, David		1	28
BELL, Edgar Allan		3	21
BELL, Eric Victor		2	25
BELL, F		3	21
BELL, Fred	P	1	29
BELL, George		2	25
BELL, George		2	25
BELL, George Henry		2	25
BELL, George Sinclair		1	29
BELL, H		3	21
BELL, H		4	11
BELL, James Jim		2	25
BELL, John		4	11
BELL, John Alfred Rudolph	P	4	11
BELL, John Murray	P	2	25
BELL, John Murray	P	3	21
BELL, John William		1	29
BELL, Joseph	P	3	21
BELL, Joshua		1	29
BELL, Lauriston Percival Edward	P	1	29
BELL, Leslie James	P	2	25
BELL, Malcolm Arthur Russell		2	25
BELL, Norman		4	11
BELL, O L		3	21
BELL, Percy	P	3	21
BELL, Percy Watts	P	5	12
BELL, R		3	21
BELL, Reginald George		4	11
BELL, Richard Harold		3	21
BELL, Robert De Hougham Mark	P	2	25
BELL, Robert William Harry	P	5	12
BELL, Samuel		3	21
BELL, Sydney James	P	2	26
BELL, Thomas		2	26
BELL, Thomas		4	11
BELL, Thomas Frederick	P	3	21
BELL, Thomas Hector		3	21
BELL, Tom	P	3	21
BELL, Wilson		3	22
BELLAIRS, Edward Dunstan	P	1	29
BELLAIRS, William	P	1	29
BELLAMY, G		3	22
BELLAMY, Victor Samuel		1	29
BELLAS, William		1	29
BELLERBY, Tom		1	29
BELLFIELD, William		2	26
BELLINGER, R		3	22
BELLINGER, William Frederick		1	29
BELLINGHAM, Percival Edmund		3	22
BELLINGHAM, Roger Charles Noel	P	1	29
BELLINGHAM, Thomas Henry		1	29
BELL-WEDGE, William George		2	309
BELSTEN, Walter Sidney	P	1	29
BELSTEN, William Henry	P	1	29
BEMROSE, Harold		4	11
BENBOW, Edwin Louis	P	4	11
BENCH, C		3	22
BENDALL, Arthur Victor		3	22
BENDING, George Jesse		1	29

Name	Photo	Part No.	Page No.
BENDYSHE, Richard Nelson	P	1	29
BENHAM, D K		2	26
BENHAM, John Percy	P	1	30
BENHAM, John Russell	P	1	30
BENISON, Robert Burton		2	26
BENITZ, Frank Allyn	P	5	12
BENJAMIN, John Duxfield	P	5	12
BENN, Frank Edward		2	26
BENNET, A		3	22
BENNET, Charles Hosken	P	5	13
BENNET, Helena Stewart	P	5	13
BENNET, Trevor Moutray		3	22
BENNETT, A		3	22
BENNETT, A E		3	22
BENNETT, Adam Addison		2	26
BENNETT, Albert Edward		1	30
BENNETT, Alfred Henry		5	13
BENNETT, Charles	P	4	12
BENNETT, Clarence	P	3	22
BENNETT, Edward James	P	3	22
BENNETT, Ernest Henry		1	30
BENNETT, Frank Henry		1	30
BENNETT, Frank Thomas		2	26
BENNETT, Frederick Benjamin	P	1	30
BENNETT, G		3	22
BENNETT, George		1	30
BENNETT, George Robert	P	2	26
BENNETT, Hugh Donald	P	1	30
BENNETT, James		1	30
BENNETT, James Stewart Hutchison		4	12
BENNETT, John Thomas		5	13
BENNETT, John William	P	2	26
BENNETT, L		3	22
BENNETT, Noel	P	2	26
BENNETT, Philip Dennis		5	13
BENNETT, Thomas Edmund		3	22
BENNETT, Thomas Henry		1	30
BENNETT, Victor Ernest Edward		1	30
BENNETT, W		3	22
BENNETT, W		3	22
BENNETT, W S		3	22
BENNETT, William		2	26
BENNETT, William Henry Hesp		1	30
BENNEY, Edward Harvey		3	22
BENNEYWORTH, Frank		2	26
BENNING, Murray Stuart		2	26
BENNINGTON, Alexander John		3	22
BENNION, Bert		3	22
BENNION, Reginald Walley		1	30
BENNION, William		2	26
BENNITT, Brooke Hector Pershouse		5	13
BENSON, B W		4	12
BENSON, Hugh Cecil		1	30
BENSON, John Penrice	P	1	30
BENSON, M		4	12
BENSON, Richard Erle	P	1	30
BENSON, T S		4	12
BENSON, Thomas Brooke	P	1	31
BENSON, W Benjamin		2	27
BENSON, William John		4	12
BENSTEAD, Charles		1	31
BENSTEAD, Edward		1	31
BENT, John		1	31
BENTALL, Ernest Hammond		2	27
BENTHAM, J		4	12

Name	Photo	Part No.	Page No.	Name	Photo	Part No.	Page No.
BENTLEY, Archibald Arthur Douglas		3	23	BERRY, William Thomas	P	5	13
BENTLEY, Arthur	P	2	27	BERRYMAN, James		1	32
BENTLEY, Arthur Francis John	P	5	13	BERRYMAN, Stanley	P	5	14
BENTLEY, C A		4	12	BERRYMAN, Sydney		1	32
BENTLEY, Charles Arthur Campbell		2	27	BERTIE, Ninian Mark Kerr	P	1	32
BENTLEY, Clarence Leslie	P	1	31	BERTRAM, George Stanley		2	27
BENTLEY, Claude Louis		3	23	BERTRAM, Phillip		1	32
BENTLEY, Freeland Martell	P	1	31	BESANT, W J		3	23
BENTLEY, Geoffrey Malcolm		1	31	BESLY, Barton Hope		2	27
BENTLEY, Gerald Wilson		1	31	BESS, Ernest F		2	27
BENTLEY, H		4	12	BEST, Alfred James		5	14
BENTLEY, Hellewell		3	23	BEST, Herbert		1	32
BENTLEY, Henry		3	23	BEST, Jack	P	4	12
BENTLEY, Kenneth Haddon		1	31	BEST, James		2	27
BENTLEY, William John		5	13	BEST, Thomas	P	2	27
BENTLY, J		3	23	BEST, Walter Henry		5	14
BENTON, E		2	27	BESTLEY, H		3	23
BENTON, Samuel Westwood		3	23	BESTONSO, John Richard	P	3	23
BENTZON, Sydney Malcolm		1	31	BETHELL, Charles Francis Ithell		3	23
BENVIL, Robert		2	27	BETHELL, Herbert Edward	P	5	14
BENYON, Godfrey Berkeley John	P	1	31	BETHUNE, Alexander Douglas	P	2	27
BENYON, Joseph	P	3	23	BETHUNE, Alexander Douglas	P	5	14
BERARD, Charles Delphis	P	1	31	BETHUNE, Alick	P	5	14
BERESFORD, William		1	31	BETHUNE, F		2	27
BERESFORD, William		1	31	BETHUNE, Norman Mcleod		5	14
BERISFORD, Leonard	P	3	23	BETT, Kenneth Graeme	P	4	12
BERKELEY, Maurice Kenneth Fitzhardinge	P	1	31	BETT, Roderick St. George		5	14
BERKLEY, M F K		2	27	BETTELEY, Fred		5	14
BERLEIN, Charles Maurice		1	32	BETTELEY, Harry		5	14
BERLEIN, Leslie Herman		1	32	BETTERIDGE, J		3	23
BERNARD, Bernard Frederick Paul		2	27	BETTIS, Albert		1	32
BERNARD, Hilton		5	13	BETTLES, B		3	23
BERNARD, Laurence Arthur		2	27	BETTNEY, F W		3	23
BERNARD, Robert	P	1	32	BETTNEY, Robert		2	27
BERNERS, Hamilton Hugh		2	27	BETTS, A		3	23
BERNEY, D		3	23	BETTS, Conrad Coryton	P	4	12
BERNHARDT, Martin		1	32	BETTS, Frank William John		3	24
BERRIDGE, Harry		1	32	BETTS, Gordon W G	P	1	32
BERRIDGE, John Frederick Harry		1	32	BETTS, John William		1	32
BERRY, Albert J		2	27	BETTS, Robert Sidney	P	3	24
BERRY, Albert Victor		5	13	BETTS, Thomas Henry	P	1	32
BERRY, Alfred		1	32	BETTY, Joseph		2	27
BERRY, Alfred Edward		1	32	BEVAN, Ernest Victor		1	32
BERRY, Alfred Robert	P	1	32	BEVAN, Gordon Frederick		1	32
BERRY, Douglas W		2	27	BEVAN, Henry		2	27
BERRY, Edward Alfred		1	32	BEVAN, J		3	24
BERRY, Ernest Frank		3	23	BEVAN, Percy		1	32
BERRY, F		3	23	BEVAN, Reginald James		1	32
BERRY, Francis	P	3	23	BEVAN, Richard Vincent	P	1	33
BERRY, Frederick Ernest		5	13	BEVERIDGE, Arthur Douglas	P	3	24
BERRY, G		3	23	BEVERIDGE, David		1	33
BERRY, H S O		2	27	BEVERIDGE, David Alexander	P	1	33
BERRY, Harry Albert		4	12	BEVERIDGE, John		1	33
BERRY, Henry		4	12	BEVERIDGE, Robert Mcauslan	P	1	33
BERRY, Herbert L		2	27	BEVERLEY, Arthur		1	33
BERRY, Ira Sidney		1	32	BEVERLEY, Michael		4	12
BERRY, J		3	23	BEVERLY, George		4	12
BERRY, Robert		5	13	BEVINGTON, Fred		5	14
BERRY, S		3	23	BEVIR, Cyril Edward Felix	P	2	27
BERRY, Sidney Field	P	5	13	BEVIS, Edward Albert Frank		1	33
BERRY, Thomas	P	1	32	BEVIS, Horace		4	12
BERRY, Thomas		5	13	BEVIS, William		1	33
BERRY, Thomas Sidney		1	32	BEVON (ALIAS BEVAN), Harold Samuel		2	27
BERRY, W E		3	23	BEW, Reginald Norman	P	2	28
BERRY, W H		3	23	BEWICKE-COPLEY, Redvers Lionel Calverley		3	62

Name	Photo	Part No.	Page No.
BEWLEY, Joseph Charles Layborn	P	2	28
BEWS, William		3	24
BEYFUS, Harold Emanuel	P	1	33
BEYNON, William Charles		3	24
BEZER, Reuben		1	33
BIAGGI, Ernest Frederick		2	28
BIANCHI, J		3	24
BIBB, George Frederick		1	33
BIBBY, John Patrick		1	33
BICKERDIKE, Robert	P	4	12
BICKERSTETH, Stanley Morris		3	24
BICKERTON, Frederick Richard	P	1	33
BICKERTON, William		5	14
BICKHAM, Arthur Rushton		5	14
BICKLEY, George Howard	P	4	12
BICKNELL, Arthur Victor		4	13
BICKNELL, Frank		2	28
BICKNELL, H		3	24
BICKNELL, Henry William	P	4	13
BICKNELL, John Joseph		2	28
BICKNELL, Montague		2	28
BIDDLE, James Pearson	P	5	15
BIDDLE, W F		2	28
BIDDLECOMBE, Edward George		1	33
BIDDLECOMBE, W H		2	28
BIDDLE-COPE, Anthony Cyprian Prosper	P	1	93
BIDGOOD, W F P		3	24
BIGG, H J		3	24
BIGGAR, Alexander		2	28
BIGGAR, Kenneth	P	2	28
BIGGE, Hon. John Neville	P	1	33
BIGGERSTAFF, J		2	28
BIGGIN, Haydn Vincent		4	13
BIGGINS, Richard		2	28
BIGGINS, Robert		5	15
BIGGS, Edward	P	2	28
BIGGS, George Edward		1	33
BIGGS, Henry Nelson		3	24
BIGGS, Walter J		2	28
BIGGS, William Joseph		2	28
BIGNELL, Arthur Thomas		2	28
BIGNELL, V		3	24
BIGNELL, William Henry	P	3	24
BILES, Albert Ernest		4	13
BILL, Rodney Edward		5	15
BILLING, Charles George	P	1	33
BILLING, Horace		4	13
BILLING, Samuel Alfred		1	33
BILLING, Samuel Alfred		4	13
BILLINGHAM, G		3	24
BILLINGS, T J		3	24
BILLINGTON, John William	P	5	15
BILLINGTON, Leslie Charles	P	1	34
BILNEY, Edwin Arthur		1	34
BILTON, Edward Barnard	P	3	24
BILTON, Joseph	P	1	34
BIMROSE, Charles		5	15
BINDLEY, Horace		1	34
BINFIELD, T		3	24
BINGEN, Charles		3	24
BINGHAM, Charles Henry		1	34
BINGHAM, Charles Jeffrey Slade	P	1	34
BINGHAM, David Cecil		2	28
BINGHAM, Frank Miller	P	1	34
BINGHAM, J		3	24

Name	Photo	Part No.	Page No.
BINGHAM-BRYDEN, Edward Carruthers	P	1	58
BINGLEY, John William		1	34
BINKS, Arthur		3	24
BINNIE, Alexander	P	4	13
BINNIE, Arthur Drybrough		5	15
BINNIE, David Willis	P	3	25
BINNIE, James		5	15
BINNIE, William Meek		4	13
BINNS, G W		3	25
BINNS, George Edward		4	13
BINNS, Percy Vere		4	13
BINNY, Steuart Scott	P	3	25
BINSTED, Henry Joseph John		4	13
BINSTEED, Gerald Charles	P	1	34
BIRCH, A		3	25
BIRCH, Arthur		1	34
BIRCH, Arthur Edward		1	34
BIRCH, Edward		2	28
BIRCH, Eric Wykeham	P	3	25
BIRCH, Harold Lee		3	25
BIRCH, Percy		2	28
BIRCH, Percy G		2	28
BIRCH, Sydney James	P	2	28
BIRCH, William Claud Kennedy	P	4	13
BIRCH, William Elric Hawthorne	P	1	34
BIRCH, William Joseph		1	34
BIRCHALL, Arthur Percival Dearman	P	1	34
BIRCHAM, Edward Henry		4	13
BIRD, Alan Ernest	P	5	15
BIRD, Arthur	P	2	28
BIRD, Bertie		5	15
BIRD, Clement Eustace		5	15
BIRD, Cuthbert		1	35
BIRD, E		3	25
BIRD, Edward		1	35
BIRD, Edward		1	35
BIRD, Eric James		3	25
BIRD, Francis Clifford		1	35
BIRD, Frank	P	3	25
BIRD, Frank Edward	P	1	35
BIRD, Harry		2	28
BIRD, Harry Godwin		4	13
BIRD, Horatio Parkyns	P	5	15
BIRD, John Greville Hobart		2	28
BIRD, John Woodall		4	13
BIRD, Richard De Burgho		4	14
BIRD, Samuel		2	29
BIRD, Stephen Carmen	P	1	35
BIRD, T S		2	29
BIRD, W		3	25
BIRD, Walter Charles		4	14
BIRD, Wiiliam James		3	25
BIRD, Wilfred Stanley	P	1	35
BIRD, William		3	25
BIRDSEYE, Douglas Martin		4	14
BIRDWOOD, Gordon Alic Brodrick		2	29
BIRDWOOD, Herbert Frederick		3	25
BIRDWOOD, Richard Lockington		2	29
BIRKBECK, Edward	P	2	29
BIRKBECK, Morris	P	2	29
BIRKBY, Henry Alexander	P	3	25
BIRKETT, Harold Wreford		3	26
BIRKETT, William		2	29
BIRNEY, John Gordon	P	3	26
BIRNIE, Gerald		5	15

Name	Photo	Part No.	Page No.
BODEN, Frederick		5	17
BODIMEADE, Henry Charles		1	40
BODKIN, Geoffrey		1	40
BODKIN, Thomas		3	28
BODY, William Henry	P	1	40
BOEATER, Alfred		1	40
BOENING, Charles		4	16
BOGGUST, A H		3	28
BOGLE, Frank		5	17
BOGLE, George Lockie		3	28
BOGNE, Douglas		4	16
BOGUE, Robert Alexander		3	28
BOILEAU, Edward Bulmer Whicher	P	5	17
BOILEAU, Frank Ridley Farrer		2	32
BOIS, Dudley Gillespy	P	2	32
BOISSIER, William Arthur Marshall		4	16
BOLAND, David		2	32
BOLAND, H C		3	28
BOLAND, Patrick Joe		2	32
BOLD, Harold Edward		1	40
BOLDY, George		4	16
BOLES, Hastings Fortescue	P	1	40
BOLITHO, Fleetwood John		1	40
BOLITHO, William Torquill Macleod	P	1	40
BOLLAND, Horace Albert	P	3	28
BOLLAND, Theodore Julian		1	40
BOLLARD, T		3	28
BOLST, Nuel Jocelyn	P	2	32
BOLSTER, E		4	16
BOLSTER, George Emil	P	1	41
BOLSTRIDGE, Alex		3	28
BOLTER, Charles Albert		4	16
BOLTON, A		3	29
BOLTON, Charles	P	1	41
BOLTON, Ernest James		1	41
BOLTON, George		1	41
BOLTON, Gilbert Benson	P	3	29
BOLTON, Harry Hargreaves	P	1	41
BOLTON, Herbert Frederick	P	3	29
BOLTON, James Frederick		1	41
BOLTON, John	P	1	41
BOLTON, John		1	41
BOLTON, Joseph Crook	P	1	41
BOLTON, Maurice Baldwin	P	5	17
BOLTON, Walter	P	4	16
BOLTON, Wilfred		1	41
BOLTON, Wilfred		1	41
BOLTON, William		1	41
BOLTON, William Henry		2	33
BON, Robert		1	41
BOND, Frederick Noel	P	2	33
BOND, G		3	29
BOND, H		2	33
BOND, H		3	29
BOND, Herbert Francis Crispin		3	29
BOND, John		2	33
BOND, Joseph	P	1	41
BOND, Joseph Cameron	P	2	33
BOND, Oliver Hugh Devereux	P	1	41
BOND, Robert Harold		2	33
BOND, Samuel		1	41
BOND, Thomas Morgan	P	1	42
BOND, Walter		1	42
BOND, William James		2	33
BONE, Albert Edward		5	17
BONE, Charles	P	2	33
BONE, David		2	33
BONE, Harry		1	42
BONE, Henry George		3	29
BONE, Percy John		5	17
BONE, William George Alfred	P	1	42
BONELL, Herbert	P	2	33
BONFIELD, Edward W		2	33
BONFIELD, James George		1	42
BONHAM, Harry B		3	29
BONHAM-CARTER, Guy	P	1	73
BONIFACE, Albert		2	33
BONIFACE, Arthur Frederick	P	2	33
BONIFACE, Charles William		2	33
BONIFACE, Victor Gordon John		1	42
BONNAR, William Mcgregor	P	1	42
BONNELL, Ralph		2	33
BONNELLA, Douglas Cutler		3	29
BONNER, Augustine	P	3	29
BONSER, C		3	29
BONSER, Ernest William		2	33
BONTOFT, J		3	29
BONVALOT, Edward St. Laurent		2	33
BOOKER, Charles William Henry		3	29
BOOKER, Frederick		2	33
BOOKER, John		2	33
BOON, Charles		2	34
BOON, H		3	29
BOON, James		3	29
BOON, T J		3	29
BOONE, Charles Frederick De Bohun	P	1	42
BOONE, Henry Griffith		3	29
BOONE, W T		2	34
BOORER, Walter James	P	1	42
BOORMAN, Cyril Adlington	P	1	42
BOOSEY, Frederick Cecil	P	2	34
BOOSEY, Rupert George	P	2	34
BOOT, Arthur	P	1	42
BOOTE, John Arthur	P	5	17
BOOTH, F		3	29
BOOTH, Frederick James		4	16
BOOTH, Geroge Thomas		1	42
BOOTH, H		3	29
BOOTH, H		3	29
BOOTH, John		1	42
BOOTH, John		5	17
BOOTH, Joseph Frank		3	29
BOOTH, Patrick Dick	P	4	16
BOOTH, Robert Hutchinson		3	29
BOOTH, Roland Hartley		1	42
BOOTH, Thomas		1	42
BOOTH, Tom		1	42
BOOTH, W		3	29
BOOTHAWAY, Arthur	P	1	42
BOOTHBY, James Robert	P	1	42
BOOTHER, James		2	34
BOR, Thomas Humphrey	P	3	30
BOREHAM, Charles William		1	43
BOREHAM, John William		2	34
BORLAND, William Anderson		3	30
BORLAND, William Barr		2	34
BOROUGH, Alaric Charles Henry		3	30
BORRETT, Alfred Frank Cyril		4	16
BORSBERRY, Thomas Frederick		4	16
BORST, Charles Louis	P	5	17

Name	Photo	Part No.	Page No.
BORTHWICK, Joseph Little		2	34
BORTON, Cyprian Edward		3	30
BOSANQUET, Armytage Percy		3	30
BOSANQUET, Lionel Arthur	P	1	43
BOSANQUET, Sidney Courthope	P	1	43
BOSCAWEN, The Hon. Vere Douglas		2	34
BOSELEY, H		3	30
BOSEMAN, John		1	43
BOSHER, Charles Walter		1	43
BOSHER, Ronald Frederick		1	43
BOSTOCK, Archibald Thomas		2	34
BOSTOCK, Edward Lyon		3	30
BOSTOCK, Neville Stanley		3	30
BOSTON, Joseph Henry	P	4	16
BOSWELL, Benjamin	P	1	43
BOSWELL, Joseph Norman		1	43
BOSWORTH, Arthur Wright		2	34
BOSWORTH, J		3	30
BOSWORTH, Philip Charles Worthington		2	34
BOSWORTH, W		3	30
BOSWORTH, W		3	30
BOTHAM, Charles Henry		3	30
BOTHWELL, Alexander		4	17
BOTHWELL, Duncan William		5	18
BOTHWELL, Frank		5	18
BOTHWELL, William		1	43
BOTLEY, Albert Wickstead		1	43
BOTT, Charles Stuart		3	30
BOTT, George		5	18
BOTTERILL, Stuart	P	5	18
BOTTGER, Abbin Ernest Henry		1	43
BOTTING, Edward Charles		1	43
BOTTING, George		1	43
BOTTING, William Rolph		3	30
BOTTOMLEY, Albert		1	43
BOTTOMLEY, John Wood		2	34
BOTTOMLEY, Thomas Reginald	P	1	44
BOUCHER, Alan Estcourt		3	30
BOUCHER, Alfred Henry	P	5	18
BOUCHER, Harold Ernest	P	1	44
BOUCHIER, L J		3	30
BOUGHEY, Anchitel Edward Fletcher		5	18
BOUGHTON, Ernest George	P	1	44
BOUGHTON, Frederick William		5	18
BOULD, Maurice Alfred	P	4	17
BOULDEN, Reuben William Henry		1	44
BOULOGNE, Jordan		1	44
BOULT, Thomas		1	44
BOULTER, Richard Henry	P	2	34
BOULTON, Frederick Wilson		3	30
BOULTON, Henry Edward		2	35
BOULTON, Herbert Sydney		4	17
BOULTON, James Forster	P	1	44
BOULTON, Thomas		4	17
BOUNDS, H		3	30
BOUNDY, C		3	30
BOURGES, John (Jean)	P	1	44
BOURKE, Bertram Walter		1	44
BOURKE, Eustace George Walter	P	1	44
BOURKE, James Patrick		1	45
BOURKE, Thomas Leslie		5	18
BOURNE, Austin Spencer		3	30
BOURNE, Ernest		1	45
BOURNE, John Pulsford	P	5	18
BOURNE, P A		3	30
BOURNE, Robert Stanley		5	18
BOURNE, S		3	30
BOURNE, Sydney Ryder		2	35
BOURNE, Thomas C		2	35
BOURNS, Charles	P	1	45
BOURROUGHS, C		3	30
BOUSFIELD, Eustace	P	2	35
BOUSFIELD, Mary Cawston		5	18
BOUSFIELD, Sidney Robert	P	2	35
BOUSTEAD, Harry Atheling Russell	P	3	31
BOUTLE, Sydney		1	45
BOVET, William	P	5	18
BOVIS, Daniel		2	35
BOWDEN, Albert John		1	45
BOWDEN, C H		3	31
BOWDEN, Edward Ratcliffe	P	1	45
BOWDEN, Horace George Cecil	P	3	31
BOWDEN, James		4	17
BOWDEN, Sidney George		5	18
BOWDEN-SMITH, Walter Adrian Carnegie	P	2	279
BOWELL, Frederick James		1	45
BOWEN, Cuthbert Edward Latimer	P	1	45
BOWEN, Edward		1	45
BOWEN, Geroge Frederick		1	45
BOWEN, Henry	P	1	45
BOWEN, Herbert		4	17
BOWEN, Rees		4	17
BOWEN-COLTHURST, Robert Macgregor	P	1	90
BOWER, Frederic William		4	17
BOWER, Henry Raymond Syndercombe		2	35
BOWERS, Arthur Hugh Maunsell		2	35
BOWERS, Henry Walter		4	17
BOWERS, J T		3	31
BOWERS, Percival Conway	P	1	45
BOWES, Edwin		3	31
BOWES, Robert Edward		1	45
BOWES, William Edward		1	45
BOWES LYON, Charles Lindsay Claude	P	1	232
BOWES-WILSON, George Hutton		1	382
BOWGETT, C V		3	31
BOWHAY, Eustace Gilbert		3	31
BOWIE, Albert Campbell		3	31
BOWIE, John		3	31
BOWIE, William Robert	P	4	17
BOWKER, Francis Jearrad	P	2	35
BOWKER, William		4	17
BOWL, Albert Henry Thomas	P	2	35
BOWLBY, A		3	31
BOWLBY, Geoffrey Vaux Salvin	P	1	45
BOWLBY, George Elliott Lowes		3	31
BOWLER, F		3	31
BOWLER, Herbert L		2	35
BOWLES, Bertie		3	31
BOWLES, Bertram Frank	P	3	31
BOWLES, James Arthur		2	35
BOWLEY, Albert		2	35
BOWLEY, Harry Edwin		1	45
BOWLEY, Thomas Henry		2	35
BOWMAN, Frederick		1	45
BOWMAN, Geoffrey Glendinning		4	17
BOWMAN, George		2	35
BOWMAN, J		2	35
BOWMAN, James		1	45
BOWMAN, Leslie Spencer		3	31
BOWMAN, Matthew	P	2	35

Name	Photo	Part No.	Page No.
BOWMAN, William Powell	P	3	31
BOWN, Cyril Walter	P	4	17
BOWTLE, Frederick Clement		5	18
BOWYER, Charles Alexander		1	45
BOWYER, Richard Grenville		4	17
BOWYER, William Henry		1	45
BOX, Frederick Archibald		3	31
BOX, Frederick James		1	45
BOX, Joseph William		1	45
BOX, L		3	31
BOX, Reginald George		4	17
BOXALL, Caryl Lermitte	P	1	46
BOXALL, Charles Bert		1	46
BOXALL, Frederick George		4	17
BOXER, Hugh Edward Richard	P	2	36
BOXER, William Tremain		3	31
BOXWELL, Francis Jeffares Tilson		1	46
BOYACK, Alexander Ian		4	18
BOYCE, Charles		2	36
BOYCE, Gilbert Revill		2	36
BOYCE, John Henry	P	1	46
BOYD, Alexander		2	36
BOYD, Alexander		2	36
BOYD, David		1	46
BOYD, E		2	36
BOYD, Edward Fenwick		2	36
BOYD, George Finlayson		3	32
BOYD, Harold Alexander		1	46
BOYD, John		3	32
BOYD, Nigel John Lawson	P	1	46
BOYD, Percy Gernon	P	1	46
BOYD, William Allan West		2	36
BOYD, William Ballantine	P	4	18
BOYD, William Noel Lawson	P	5	19
BOYD-MOSS, Ernest William		1	262
BOYES, Reginald John		3	32
BOYINGTON, F		3	32
BOYLE, Charles		4	18
BOYLE, David Erskine		2	36
BOYLE, H		3	32
BOYLE, Herbert Charles		2	36
BOYLE, Hon. James	P	1	46
BOYLE, J		2	36
BOYLE, T		2	36
BOYLE, Thomas		1	46
BOYLE, Thomas William	P	1	46
BOYLE, Timothy		2	36
BOYLE, William		1	46
BOYLE, William		2	36
BOYLE, William Duguid		2	36
BOYS, Charles Henry		1	46
BOYSON, Harry Billingham	P	5	19
BOYTON, Victor Henry Thompson	P	3	32
BRABAZON, Hon. Ernest William Maitland Molyneux	P	1	47
BRABROOK, Arthur Henry	P	1	47
BRABROOKE, William Robert		4	18
BRACE, George Edgar		3	32
BRACEY, Humphrey Alfred	P	1	47
BRACEY, Victor Charles Edelsten		3	32
BRACHER, George		1	47
BRACKEN, John		1	47
BRACKEN, Samuel		2	36
BRACKLEY, Albert J		2	36
BRACKLEY, B		3	32

Name	Photo	Part No.	Page No.
BRACKSTONE, Henry		1	47
BRADBEER, Francis Henry		4	18
BRADBERRY, Cyril Christopher David		5	19
BRADBROOK, William Herbert Claude		3	32
BRADBURN, J		4	18
BRADBURY, Edward		2	36
BRADBURY, Edward Chapness		1	47
BRADBURY, Edward Kinder	P	1	47
BRADBURY, George	P	5	19
BRADBURY, William	P	5	19
BRADBURY, William Arthur	P	2	36
BRADDEN, Albert		5	19
BRADDOCK, Arthur Leslie		1	47
BRADDOCK, Harry		1	47
BRADDON, Hubert Frederick	P	5	19
BRADFORD, A		4	18
BRADFORD, Arthur Jesse George	P	1	47
BRADFORD, Frederick Daniel	P	5	19
BRADFORD, George Richard	P	1	48
BRADFORD, Samuel George		2	36
BRADFORD, Sir Evelyn Ridley	P	1	47
BRADFORD, Thomas		2	36
BRADFORD, W R		4	18
BRADING, A		3	32
BRADLEY, A		2	36
BRADLEY, Cyril Montague		3	32
BRADLEY, Eric Jatinga		1	48
BRADLEY, Frederick Hoysted		5	19
BRADLEY, G		3	32
BRADLEY, Geoffrey Montague		2	36
BRADLEY, Harry		2	36
BRADLEY, Harry		4	18
BRADLEY, James		5	19
BRADLEY, John Thomas	P	2	36
BRADLEY, L		3	32
BRADLEY, N		2	36
BRADLEY, Reginald John		1	48
BRADLEY, Spencer Maxwell	P	3	32
BRADLEY, Thomas		1	48
BRADLEY, Thomas H		4	18
BRADLEY, Walter Frederick		5	19
BRADLEY, Walter Robinson		5	19
BRADLEY, William		2	36
BRADLEY, William Ferguson		4	18
BRADLEY, William H		2	36
BRADOCK, John Milward		5	19
BRADSHAW, Alfred Alexander		2	36
BRADSHAW, Arthur		5	20
BRADSHAW, Arthur Edwin		2	37
BRADSHAW, E		3	32
BRADSHAW, Ernest Edwin	P	3	32
BRADSHAW, Frank Seymour	P	1	48
BRADSHAW, George Ramson		1	48
BRADSHAW, James Henry		2	37
BRADSHAW, Joseph	P	2	37
BRADSHAW, Matthew		1	48
BRADSHAW, Richard		2	37
BRADSHAW, W		3	33
BRADSTREET, Gerald Edmund	P	2	37
BRADY, Edmund		1	48
BRADY, Edmund		2	37
BRADY, Francis Thomas		5	20
BRADY, J		2	37
BRADY, Joseph		5	20
BRADY, W C		2	37

Name	Photo	Part No.	Page No.	Name	Photo	Part No.	Page No.
BRAIK, John	P	1	48	**BREEDS,** George		2	38
BRAILSFORD, H		3	33	**BREEN,** Thomas Francis Pennefather		5	20
BRAILSFORD, H		3	33	**BREEZE,** John		1	49
BRAINE, Carl Svend		5	20	**BREMER,** Francis Agustus		1	49
BRAITHWAITE, A		2	37	**BREMMER,** Frederick		2	38
BRAITHWAITE, Francis Joseph		2	37	**BREMNER,** Harry Joyce	P	3	33
BRAITHWAITE, Joseph		1	48	**BREMNER,** Henry Sadler	P	1	49
BRAKSPEAR, Ronald William		2	37	**BREMNER,** Huntly William Bruce		5	20
BRAMALL, Horace		1	48	**BREMNER,** James		1	49
BRAMBLE, T		3	33	**BRENAN,** Byron Edward	P	1	49
BRAMBLE, Thomas Henry	P	2	37	**BRENCHLEY,** Arthur		1	49
BRAMHAM, William		3	33	**BRENCHLEY,** George Charles		1	49
BRAMIDGE, W		3	33	**BRENCHLEY,** James George		2	38
BRAMLEY, Arthur		3	33	**BRENCHLEY,** Robert Henry	P	1	49
BRAMLEY, Cyril Richard		3	33	**BREND,** William		2	38
BRAMLEY, Harold		1	48	**BRENNAN,** James	P	2	38
BRAMPTON, Cyril Herbert James		4	18	**BRENNAN,** John Henry		2	38
BRAMWELL, William		2	37	**BRENNAN,** John J		2	38
BRANCH, John St. Patrick		2	37	**BRENNAN,** Thomas John	P	2	38
BRAND, Ernest Stanley		1	48	**BRENNOCK,** Patrick		4	18
BRAND, James William	P	4	18	**BRENNOCK,** Thomas Bolger		4	18
BRAND, John	P	2	37	**BRENNOCK,** William		4	18
BRANDER, John		3	33	**BRENT,** Douglas Leslie		4	18
BRANDON, John Cooper		1	48	**BRERETON-BARRY,** William Roche		3	17
BRANDON, Percy		2	37	**BRESLIN,** Andrew	P	1	50
BRANFILL, Capel Lisle Aylett	P	2	37	**BRESLIN,** Peter		1	50
BRANNAN, C		3	33	**BRETT,** Charles		1	50
BRANNIGAN, P		2	37	**BRETT,** Charles		1	50
BRANSBURY, Vernon Dudley Bramsdon		2	37	**BRETT,** Charles Arthur Hugh	P	1	50
BRANT, John Samuel		5	20	**BRETT,** Frederick W		2	38
BRANT, Robert		2	37	**BRETT,** James Patrick		2	38
BRANTINGHAM, George		1	48	**BRETT,** William Henry	P	4	18
BRANTOM, Frank	P	5	20	**BRETTELL,** Samuel Thomas		1	50
BRASH, Edmund		5	20	**BREWER,** C		3	33
BRASH, Prentise Stephen		1	48	**BREWER,** Charles		2	38
BRASH, Robert		5	20	**BREWER,** Frank		1	50
BRASHAW, Joseph Arthur	P	1	48	**BREWER,** John Harold	P	1	50
BRASHIER, William		1	48	**BREWER,** Joseph Henry		2	38
BRASIER, Leonard George		1	48	**BREWER,** Richard Leslie	P	3	33
BRASS, William	P	1	48	**BREWER,** William Arthur	P	1	50
BRASSEY, Albert		5	20	**BREWIN,** William Henry Frank		1	50
BRASTED, Frederick Elliott		3	33	**BREWIS,** Alfred Percy	P	3	34
BRATTLE, Ernest William		2	37	**BREWIS,** Robert Henry Watkin		2	38
BRATTLE, William		1	48	**BREWOOD,** Henry		2	38
BRAY, Cecil Herbert	P	1	48	**BREWSTER,** Herbert John		1	50
BRAY, Derrick Reginald Pamphilon	P	1	49	**BRIAN,** Herbert Cecil	P	1	50
BRAY, George		1	48	**BRIARD,** Ernest Felix Victor	P	2	38
BRAY, Horace		1	49	**BRICE,** Albert		3	34
BRAY, S		3	33	**BRICE,** Henry Copeland	P	1	50
BRAYSHAW, Edwin Austin		2	37	**BRICE-SMITH,** John Kenneth	P	1	332
BRAZIE, Horace Charles		4	18	**BRICKELL,** Cecil Douglas	P	5	20
BRAZIER, A H		4	18	**BRICKETT,** Ralph		1	50
BRAZIER, Alfred		1	49	**BRICKNELL,** Thomas		3	34
BRAZIER, Benjamin William	P	1	49	**BRICKWOOD,** Arthur Cyril	P	1	51
BRAZIER, Frederick Owen		1	49	**BRICKWOOD,** George W		2	38
BRAZIER, Hammond G W		2	37	**BRIDGE,** Herbert Walter	P	2	38
BRAZIER, James		1	49	**BRIDGELAND,** Hubert Edward	P	1	51
BRAZIER, Walter Ernest		1	49	**BRIDGER,** Arthur Wilfred (Artie)	P	3	34
BREACH, John	P	1	49	**BRIDGER,** Frank	P	5	20
BREAM, Charles		1	49	**BRIDGER,** Percy William		3	34
BRECHIN, G		2	37	**BRIDGER,** W C		3	34
BRECHIN, John		3	33	**BRIDGER,** Walter		5	20
BRECKELL, Ralph Leicester	P	1	49	**BRIDGES,** Arthur		4	18
BREE, Edward Russell Stapylton		5	20	**BRIDGES,** James Taylor		2	38
BREED, George Alfred	P	1	49	**BRIDGES,** Richard James		5	20

Name	Photo	Part No.	Page No.
BRIDGES, William		2	38
BRIDGES, William Robert		3	34
BRIDGFORD, Stanley Lyon		4	18
BRIDGLAND, Charles	P	2	38
BRIDGLAND, Neville Linton		2	38
BRIDLE, Percy William		5	20
BRIEN, James		2	38
BRIERLEY, Charles Leonard		2	39
BRIERLEY, Horace James		2	39
BRIERLEY, James	P	4	19
BRIERLEY, W		3	34
BRIERLY, Alwin Huard	P	1	51
BRIERS, A		3	34
BRIERS, Cyril Ernest		2	39
BRIGDEN, Cecil Herbert		2	39
BRIGDEN, Herbert		4	19
BRIGDEN, Reginald Wilfrid	P	4	19
BRIGGS, Cecil Reginald		2	39
BRIGGS, Charley	P	1	51
BRIGGS, Claude	P	3	34
BRIGGS, George Clark	P	1	51
BRIGGS, Harry		5	21
BRIGGS, Horace Henry	P	3	34
BRIGGS, John		2	39
BRIGGS, Robert W		2	39
BRIGGS, Thomas	P	5	21
BRIGHT, Frank Arnold		2	39
BRIGHT, Harry John		4	19
BRIGHT, Richard J		2	39
BRIGHT, T		2	39
BRIGHT, William		2	39
BRIGHT, William C	P	2	39
BRIGHTMORE, E J H		3	34
BRIGHTWELL, George		2	39
BRIGHTY, Charles Edward		2	39
BRILL, William		2	39
BRIMBLE, Cyril George Michael	P	1	51
BRIMBLECOMBE, Thomas		1	51
BRIMLEY, John		2	39
BRIND, Ralph Montacute	P	2	39
BRINDLE, James	P	1	51
BRINDLE, William		5	21
BRINDLEY, Roland		3	34
BRINDLEY, Thomas Leslie St.John		1	51
BRINDLEY, Victor George	P	5	21
BRINE, George William	P	5	21
BRINGLOE, Thomas		1	51
BRINKLEY, John W		2	39
BRINKWORTH, Harold Rupert		3	34
BRISELDEN, Thomas Harold		3	34
BRISTER, Sydney James		3	34
BRISTON, William		2	39
BRISTOW, Arthur Thomas		1	51
BRISTOW, Frederick Charles		2	39
BRISTOW, John		2	39
BRISTOW, Leonard		2	39
BRISTOW, Thomas		2	39
BRISTOWE, Robert Owen	P	1	51
BRISTOWE, Stanley	P	1	52
BRISTOWE, Vivian Ernest John		3	34
BRISTOWE CARE, Graham		3	47
BRITT, Albert Henry		1	52
BRITTAIN, Reginald George Cousins		3	34
BRITTAIN, Richard Arthur Henry	P	4	19
BRITTEN, Edward William		2	39
BRITTEN, Henry Champness		2	40
BRITTEN, J A Mcl. S		2	40
BRITTEN, Thomas		2	40
BROAD, Alfred Evans	P	2	40
BROAD, Arthur Percy		2	40
BROAD, Edward		1	52
BROAD, Ernest		3	35
BROAD, Francis Boase		5	21
BROAD, George Alfred		1	52
BROAD, John Eric		5	21
BROAD, Walter	P	1	52
BROADBENT, Cecil Hoyle		3	35
BROADBRIDGE, Alfred		2	40
BROADHURST, Gerald Henry	P	2	40
BROADHURST, Joseph Henry		1	52
BROADHURST, T		3	35
BROADLEY, Charles J		2	40
BROADLEY, Harry	P	3	35
BROADLEY, Walter Stanley		4	19
BROADLEY, William		2	40
BROADLEY-SMITH, Alan Francis		1	332
BROADRICK, George Fletcher	P	2	40
BROADRICK, James George		1	52
BROADWAY, Charles Victor		5	21
BROADWAY, Hugh Alexander	P	1	52
BROADWELL, Thomas		1	52
BROADWOOD, Maximilian Francis	P	1	52
BROCK, Eric George		3	35
BROCK, John		1	52
BROCK, John Ramsay	P	1	52
BROCK, Percy Douglas		5	21
BROCKBANK, Robert		5	21
BROCKBANK, Stegfried Harrison	P	1	52
BROCKBANKS, William Nicholson		2	40
BROCKELBANK, Laurence Seymour	P	1	53
BROCKIE, David	P	1	53
BROCKIE, John		4	19
BROCKLEBANK, Ralph Royds	P	3	35
BROCKLEBANK, William		3	35
BROCKLEHURST, Edward Henry		1	53
BROCKLEHURST, J W Clarke		2	40
BROCKLESBY, Dennis		1	53
BROCKMAN, Arthur Thomas		2	40
BROCKWAY, Robert William		5	21
BROCKWAY, T H G		3	35
BROCKWELL, Albert Edward		2	40
BROCKWELL, Claud Butler		4	19
BROCKWELL, George Thomas		2	40
BROCKWELL, William James		1	53
BRODIE, Ewen James	P	1	53
BRODIE, Mark Moyle		3	35
BRODIE, P		2	40
BRODIE, Patrick		2	40
BRODIE, Stanley Gordon		3	35
BRODIE, Walter Lorrain	P	5	21
BRODIE, William		4	19
BRODRICK, Eric William		3	35
BRODRICK-ENGLISH, James Falconar	P	4	53
BROLLY, Hugh		2	40
BROMAGE, Edgar Reginald		2	40
BROMAGE, H		3	35
BROMHEAD, Thomas E		2	40
BROMLEY, Cuthbert	P	1	53
BROMLEY, Herbert Assheton	P	1	53
BROMLEY, John		2	40

Name	Photo	Part No.	Page No.	Name	Photo	Part No.	Page No.
BROMLEY, John Ledger		5	22	BROUGH, Alexander		2	41
BROMWICH, Harry Freeman		3	35	BROUGH, Hugh		1	55
BRONSDON, Arthur Edwin		5	22	BROUGHTON, Ernest Chamier	P	1	55
BROOK, Arthur	P	3	35	BROUGHTON, William		2	41
BROOK, Edwin	P	2	40	BROUN, Ernest Scott		2	41
BROOK, John Harold	P	3	35	BROWN, A		3	37
BROOK, Lowie Ellis	P	3	36	BROWN, Aitken	P	4	19
BROOKBANK, William Alfred		4	19	BROWN, Albert		2	41
BROOKE, George		2	40	BROWN, Albert Victor		1	55
BROOKE, Henry Brian		5	22	BROWN, Albert Edward		1	55
BROOKE, James Anson Otho	P	1	54	BROWN, Albert Moore		1	55
BROOKE, Patrick Harry		5	22	BROWN, Albert William	P	1	55
BROOKE, Victor Reginald	P	1	54	BROWN, Alexander Balfour		1	55
BROOKE, Vivian Cyril	P	1	54	BROWN, Alfred		2	41
BROOKE, Walter	P	1	54	BROWN, Alfred Hughes		4	20
BROOKE, Willie	P	4	19	BROWN, Andrew Drinnan		2	41
BROOKER, George		2	41	BROWN, Anthony William Scudamore	P	3	37
BROOKER, Horance Brian	P	1	54	BROWN, Archibald Campbell		5	22
BROOKER, William James		1	54	BROWN, Arthur		2	41
BROOKES, C G		3	36	BROWN, Arthur Anthony	P	4	19
BROOKES, Henry Richard		2	41	BROWN, Arthur Edward		1	55
BROOKES, Herbert Ernest Victor	P	3	36	BROWN, Arthur Gwilliam		3	37
BROOKFIELD, Harold John	P	3	36	BROWN, Arthur Kennish	P	1	55
BROOKING, Arthur Richard		3	36	BROWN, Arthur Richard		2	41
BROOKING, Charles William		1	54	BROWN, Bertram		1	55
BROOKMAN, Sydney George		2	41	BROWN, C		3	37
BROOKS, Alfred Harold		1	54	BROWN, Cecil Arthur	P	3	37
BROOKS, Arthur James		5	22	BROWN, Charles		1	55
BROOKS, Augustus	P	1	54	BROWN, Charles Alfred		1	55
BROOKS, Cecil Edmund		3	36	BROWN, Charles Ernest	P	4	20
BROOKS, Charles		2	41	BROWN, Charles Ernest Edward	P	5	22
BROOKS, Charles Edward		3	36	BROWN, Charles Shutwell		3	37
BROOKS, Fred		4	19	BROWN, Charles Tolme		3	37
BROOKS, G		3	36	BROWN, Clive Andrews		5	22
BROOKS, G L		3	36	BROWN, D		2	41
BROOKS, George		1	54	BROWN, D		2	41
BROOKS, George		3	36	BROWN, David		2	41
BROOKS, George F		2	41	BROWN, David		2	42
BROOKS, Harold Walton	P	5	22	BROWN, David Alison		5	22
BROOKS, Henry		5	22	BROWN, David Hepburn		2	42
BROOKS, James Vincent		1	54	BROWN, David Sangster		3	37
BROOKS, M		3	36	BROWN, Donald	P	4	20
BROOKS, Rowland Causer	P	1	54	BROWN, Donald	P	5	22
BROOKS, W D		3	36	BROWN, Donald Livingstone	P	4	20
BROOKSBANK, Hugh Godfrey	P	1	55	BROWN, E		3	37
BROOKSBANK, Stamp		5	22	BROWN, Edward	P	1	56
BROOM, Cecil Roy Hamilton		3	36	BROWN, Edward		2	42
BROOM, Reginald John		4	19	BROWN, Edward		2	42
BROOMAN, Arthur Frank		3	36	BROWN, Eric Francis		3	37
BROOMAN, Gordon Leonard		2	41	BROWN, Ernest George		2	42
BROOMAN, Horace		3	36	BROWN, Ernest William		5	23
BROOME, Geoffrey George	P	2	41	BROWN, Frank	P	2	42
BROOME, William	P	3	36	BROWN, Frank		2	42
BROOMHAM, William		1	55	BROWN, Frank		5	23
BROPHY, G		3	36	BROWN, Frank Edmund		5	23
BROSTER, Jessep		1	55	BROWN, Frank William Radford		3	37
BROSTER, W		2	41	BROWN, Frederic Hubert		3	37
BROSTON, Thomas		2	41	BROWN, Frederick Arthur		3	37
BROTCHIE, Robert Traill	P	1	55	BROWN, Frederick Charles		3	37
BROTHERIDGE, George Hawkins		5	22	BROWN, Frederick G		2	42
BROTHERS, C		3	36	BROWN, Frederick George		1	56
BROTHERS, William Ernest		2	41	BROWN, Frederick George		2	42
BROTHERSTON, Robert Thomas	P	1	55	BROWN, Frederick George		2	42
BROTHERTON, A		2	41	BROWN, Frederick Harold		3	37
BROTHERTON, Richard	P	1	55	BROWN, Frederick James		1	56

Name	Photo	Part No.	Page No.	Name	Photo	Part No.	Page No.
BROWN, Frederick William		1	56	**BROWN,** Maberley Lens	P	5	23
BROWN, G		2	42	**BROWN,** Norman	P	1	56
BROWN, George		1	56	**BROWN,** Norman Mcleod	P	1	56
BROWN, George		1	56	**BROWN,** Osbert Harold	P	2	43
BROWN, George		2	42	**BROWN,** Oscar		1	57
BROWN, George		2	42	**BROWN,** Philip Anthony	P	2	43
BROWN, George		2	42	**BROWN,** Philip George Mortimer	P	1	57
BROWN, George Edward		2	42	**BROWN,** R		2	43
BROWN, George Frederick		1	56	**BROWN,** R W		3	38
BROWN, George Joseph		3	37	**BROWN,** Ralph		5	23
BROWN, George Paul		2	42	**BROWN,** Richard Gavin	P	2	43
BROWN, George Percy		2	42	**BROWN,** Richard Stanley	P	3	38
BROWN, George Robert		2	42	**BROWN,** Robert		2	43
BROWN, George Shipton		1	56	**BROWN,** Roland C		2	43
BROWN, George William	P	1	56	**BROWN,** Sidney Edgar		3	38
BROWN, Gerald Knapton	P	3	37	**BROWN,** Sydney Bunten		2	43
BROWN, H J		3	38	**BROWN,** Sydney James		3	38
BROWN, Harold Masters	P	2	42	**BROWN,** Sylvester Samuel	P	5	23
BROWN, Harris Victor		4	20	**BROWN,** T		4	20
BROWN, Harry		2	42	**BROWN,** Thomas		2	43
BROWN, Harry		2	42	**BROWN,** Thomas Walter	P	5	23
BROWN, Harry	P	3	38	**BROWN,** Tom	P	4	20
BROWN, Harry James		1	56	**BROWN,** W C		3	38
BROWN, Hedley		1	56	**BROWN,** Walter		2	43
BROWN, Henry Augustus		1	56	**BROWN,** Walter Gilbert		1	57
BROWN, Henry Cecil		5	23	**BROWN,** William		2	43
BROWN, Henry George		4	20	**BROWN,** William		4	20
BROWN, Herbert Henry		1	56	**BROWN,** William Archibald Ross		4	20
BROWN, Herbert James	P	3	38	**BROWN,** William George		2	43
BROWN, Horace Raymond		3	38	**BROWN,** William H		4	20
BROWN, Hubert William		2	42	**BROWN,** William John	P	2	44
BROWN, J		2	42	**BROWN,** William John		3	38
BROWN, J		2	42	**BROWN,** William Leonard	P	3	38
BROWN, J		2	42	**BROWN,** William Robert		4	20
BROWN, Jack Robert Alexander	P	2	42	**BROWN,** William Robertson		5	23
BROWN, James		1	56	**BROWN (ALIAS BROWNING),** William		1	57
BROWN, James		1	56	**BROWNE,** Arthur George	P	1	57
BROWN, James		2	42	**BROWNE,** F		3	39
BROWN, James		3	38	**BROWNE,** Frederick Macdonell	P	2	44
BROWN, James Alexander Charles		4	20	**BROWNE,** Geoffrey Dennis		3	39
BROWN, James Cartmell Dennison		1	56	**BROWNE,** George	P	2	44
BROWN, James Edwin		2	42	**BROWNE,** George Brownlie	P	3	39
BROWN, James Graham	P	2	43	**BROWNE,** Gordon Stewart		1	57
BROWN, James Turner	P	3	38	**BROWNE,** Harold Vernon	P	1	57
BROWN, James Waddel		2	43	**BROWNE,** Hew Edwards	P	3	39
BROWN, James Westhall	P	5	23	**BROWNE,** Hon. Maurice Henry Dermot	P	2	44
BROWN, James William		2	43	**BROWNE,** J		2	44
BROWN, John	P	2	43	**BROWNE,** J		3	39
BROWN, John		2	43	**BROWNE,** John		4	21
BROWN, John	P	3	38	**BROWNE,** Lionel Charles		3	39
BROWN, John	P	3	38	**BROWNFIELD,** Reginald John		2	44
BROWN, John	P	4	20	**BROWNING,** Charles Hunter		2	44
BROWN, John		5	23	**BROWNING,** F		3	39
BROWN, John Alexander	P	1	56	**BROWNING,** Frank Herbert		1	57
BROWN, John Edward		2	43	**BROWNING,** Herbert John		4	21
BROWN, John Edward Guy	P	1	56	**BROWNING,** J E		3	39
BROWN, John Richard	P	3	38	**BROWNING,** James Alexander	P	1	57
BROWN, John Samuel		1	56	**BROWNING,** Robert		2	44
BROWN, John Samuel		1	56	**BROWNLEE,** Gilbert		3	39
BROWN, John Sydney		2	43	**BROWNLEE,** James Alexander		1	57
BROWN, John William	P	2	43	**BROWNLEY,** G		3	39
BROWN, Joseph F		2	43	**BROWNLIE,** J		3	39
BROWN, Keith Andrews		5	23	**BROWNLOW,** Mark		1	57
BROWN, Leonard Marshall		3	38	**BROYD,** Ernest John		1	58
BROWN, Lionel		2	43	**BRUCE,** Albert Edward Percy		3	39

Name	Photo	Part No.	Page No.
BRUCE, Alfred		1	58
BRUCE, C		3	39
BRUCE, Charles James	P	3	39
BRUCE, Charles Thomas	P	2	44
BRUCE, David		2	44
BRUCE, George Macdonald	P	5	24
BRUCE, Gervase Ronald		1	58
BRUCE, Harry Kendal Walpole	P	2	44
BRUCE, James		3	39
BRUCE, James Smith	P	4	21
BRUCE, John Elliott Lidderdale	P	1	58
BRUCE, Jonathan Maxwell	P	1	58
BRUCE, The Hon. Henry Lyndhurst		2	44
BRUCE, The Hon. Robert		2	45
BRUCE, Thomas Greenfield		2	45
BRUCE, Thomas Robert		3	39
BRUCE, William		2	45
BRUCE, William Arthur Mccrae		1	58
BRUCE, William Smith		3	39
BRUCE, William Thomas		2	45
BRUCE, Wyndle James		2	45
BRUM, Samuel John		2	45
BRUMAN, Albert Victor	P	4	21
BRUMBLEY, Walter James Joshua		4	21
BRUMBY, Herbert		2	45
BRUMBY, Thomas John		2	45
BRUMPTON, Ernest William		1	58
BRUNGER, Robert		5	24
BRUNS, Thomas John		1	58
BRUNSDON, W T		3	39
BRUNTLETT, John Edwin		4	21
BRUNTON, Edward Henry Pollock		2	45
BRUNTON, Robert		3	39
BRUNWIN-HALES, Greville Oxley		4	73
BRUSH, George W		2	45
BRUTTON, Eric West	P	4	21
BRYAN, Alfred Lionel	P	4	21
BRYAN, Arthur Edwin		3	39
BRYAN, Edgar William		4	21
BRYAN, Edward		2	45
BRYAN, James		3	40
BRYAN, Thomas		2	45
BRYAN, W		4	21
BRYAN-BROWN, Guy Spencer		4	21
BRYANT, A		4	21
BRYANT, Albert		2	45
BRYANT, Alfred		2	45
BRYANT, Alfred Miles	P	5	24
BRYANT, Charles Frederick		5	24
BRYANT, Charles Marrable	P	2	45
BRYANT, Charles William		1	58
BRYANT, Ernest Gladstone		3	40
BRYANT, Frederick James Mansel		3	40
BRYANT, George		2	45
BRYANT, George		5	24
BRYANT, George		5	24
BRYANT, H J		3	40
BRYANT, Harvey		5	24
BRYANT, Henry Edward		1	58
BRYANT, John William		1	58
BRYANT, Reginald		2	45
BRYANT, Reginald Charles Arnold	P	2	45
BRYANT, Reginald Eyre	P	3	40
BRYANT, Richard		1	58
BRYANT, Sidney		2	45

Name	Photo	Part No.	Page No.
BRYANT, Sydney Doggett	P	3	40
BRYANT, Thomas		2	45
BRYANT, Thomas Henry		1	58
BRYANT, W		3	40
BRYCE, David Greig	P	2	45
BRYCE, Thomas Burt	P	3	40
BRYDSON, R		3	40
BRYER, A T		3	40
BRYETT, Frederick A		2	45
BRYNE, Harry Benjamin Cyril		2	45
BRYSON, James Harvey		5	25
BRYSON, John		5	25
BUBB, G		3	40
BUCHAN, D		2	45
BUCHAN, Ernest Norman	P	2	46
BUCHAN, J		3	40
BUCHANAN, Alexander		5	25
BUCHANAN, Archibald Ure		2	46
BUCHANAN, David Niel Griffiths	P	3	40
BUCHANAN, Duncan Allan	P	1	58
BUCHANAN, G		3	40
BUCHANAN, J		2	46
BUCHANAN, James Herbert	P	1	58
BUCHANAN, James Robert	P	4	22
BUCHANAN, John Campbell		5	25
BUCHANAN, John Daniel	P	2	46
BUCHANAN, Robert Gills	P	2	46
BUCHANAN, T		3	40
BUCHANAN, William		1	59
BUCHANAN, William Alfred		2	46
BUCHANAN, William Arthur Irvine		3	40
BUCHANAN-BAILLIE-HAMILTON, Arthur	P	1	170
BUCHANAN-DUNLOP, Colin Napier	P	2	107
BUCK, A		3	40
BUCK, Arthur Percy		4	22
BUCK, Donald William	P	3	40
BUCK, Frederick		1	59
BUCK, Joseph G		2	46
BUCK, Thomas Cyril	P	1	59
BUCK, W		3	40
BUCKERFIELD, J		3	40
BUCKETT, Henry		1	59
BUCKINGHAM, Albert		1	59
BUCKINGHAM, Alfred Thomas		1	59
BUCKINGHAM, Aubrey Webster	P	1	59
BUCKINGHAM, James		1	59
BUCKINGHAM, William Edward		1	59
BUCKINGHAM, William James	P	5	25
BUCKLAND, A H		2	46
BUCKLAND, Edgar		2	46
BUCKLAND, Ernest Blas Frank		3	40
BUCKLAND, John Arnold	P	3	41
BUCKLAND, William Ernest		4	22
BUCKLE, Albert		2	46
BUCKLE, Henry		2	46
BUCKLE, Henry White		1	59
BUCKLE, Mathew Perceval		2	46
BUCKLEY, Clarence James	P	1	59
BUCKLEY, Eric James Kershaw	P	5	25
BUCKLEY, Ernest	P	2	46
BUCKLEY, F		3	41
BUCKLEY, George		5	25
BUCKLEY, Humphrey Paul Stennett		4	22
BUCKLEY, James Willie		3	41
BUCKLEY, Joseph Arnold		5	25

Name	Photo	Part No.	Page No.
BUCKLEY, Moses Miller Shaw		1	59
BUCKMAN, Sidney		4	22
BUCKNELL, Harry Hill		4	22
BUCKNILL, John Charles	P	1	59
BUCKNILL, Llewellyn Morris	P	1	60
BUCKNOLE, Walter Samuel		1	60
BUCKTROUT, Horace		1	60
BUCKWORTH-HERNE-SOAME, Richard Everard		4	192
BUDD, George William		5	25
BUDD, Thomas William		3	41
BUDD, Wrinch Joseph Charles	P	1	60
BUDDEN, Ronald Anderson	P	3	41
BUDDON, Charles Clark		4	22
BUDENBERG, Donald Harlow		5	25
BUDGE, Alexander Simpson	P	2	46
BUDGETT, Edwin George		3	41
BUGBY, George Joseph		2	46
BUGLER, William George		5	25
BUHAGIAR, Carmelo		1	60
BUICK, David	P	5	25
BUIE, Hugh	P	5	25
BULKELEY, Llewelyn Ah		4	22
BULKELEY, Thomas Henry Rivers		2	46
BULL, Alfred George		1	60
BULL, Arthur Edward	P	1	60
BULL, Arthur Joseph		2	47
BULL, Benjamin Allen		3	41
BULL, Bernard William		1	60
BULL, Charles		2	47
BULL, Frederick Charles		2	47
BULL, Godfrey John Oswald	P	1	60
BULL, Herbert		1	60
BULL, Leo Francis		2	47
BULL, Philip		1	60
BULL, Robert Edward Bristow		2	47
BULL, Thomas Richard		2	47
BULL, William		2	47
BULL, William Alfred		1	60
BULLASS, Harry	P	3	41
BULLER, Frederick Derick Edwin	P	1	60
BULLER, Lesley Montagu		5	25
BULLEY, Edward		2	47
BULLIN, Thomas J		2	47
BULLINARIA, Henry William		1	60
BULLOCK, Arthur Ernest	P	2	47
BULLOCK, Arthur Ernest	P	2	47
BULLOCK, E		3	41
BULLOCK, George William		1	60
BULLOCK, Gervas Frederic	P	3	41
BULLOCK, Thomas William		5	25
BULMAN, Thomas		1	60
BULPITT, William Arthur		1	60
BUMSTEAD, George William		3	41
BUNBURY, Godfrey Hugh St. Pierre	P	3	41
BUNBURY, Wilfred Joseph		4	22
BUNCE, Charles Henry		1	60
BUNCE, Charles Ralph Thomas		1	60
BUNCE, Edward		1	60
BUNCE, John Henry	P	1	60
BUNDY, Samuel Thomas		3	42
BUNKER, Charles John	P	5	26
BUNKER, John Thomas		2	47
BUNN, Alfred		5	26
BUNN, Ernest Arthur		5	26
BUNN, Ernest Walton		5	26
BUNN, George		1	60
BUNN, George William		5	26
BUNYAN, Benjamin James		1	60
BUNYAN, G		2	47
BURBERRY, Sydney John		2	47
BURBRIDGE, Benjamin		2	47
BURBRIDGE, Walter		1	60
BURCH, Arthur Thomas		1	61
BURCH, William John		1	61
BURCHALL, George		2	47
BURCHELL, Fred		1	61
BURCHELL, Frederick Hugh		1	61
BURCHELL, John Jasper		2	47
BURCHETT, Arthur		1	61
BURCHILL, Thomas		1	61
BURDEKIN, Geoffrey Eric	P	1	61
BURDEN, Clive Britten	P	4	22
BURDESS, Thomas	P	2	47
BURDETT, F		3	42
BURDETT, Halford Gay		3	42
BURDETT, Thomas George Deane	P	3	42
BURDISS, William		1	61
BURDOCH, W		2	47
BURDON, Edward	P	1	61
BURDON, John	P	2	47
BURDON, Rowland	P	3	42
BURGES, Eric Laurence Arthur Hart		2	47
BURGES, William Armstrong	P	1	61
BURGESS, Albert Henry		2	48
BURGESS, Alfred		2	48
BURGESS, Andrew	P	2	48
BURGESS, Arthur Henry		2	48
BURGESS, C		3	42
BURGESS, Cyril Douglas William	P	3	42
BURGESS, Frank		2	48
BURGESS, Harold	P	3	42
BURGESS, Herbert William	P	1	61
BURGESS, John	P	4	22
BURGESS, John Donald		1	61
BURGESS, Nathaniel Gordon		4	22
BURGESS, P		3	42
BURGESS, Richard		1	61
BURGESS, William		1	61
BURGESS, William		2	48
BURGESS, William Henry		2	48
BURGESS, William Henry George		1	61
BURGOYNE, Frederick		2	48
BURGOYNE-WALLACE, Douglas Burgoyne	P	1	364
BURINI, Charles Lewis	P	1	61
BURK, Roderick		2	48
BURKE, Charles James	P	5	26
BURKE, Cornelius		1	61
BURKE, Edmund	P	5	26
BURKE, F		2	48
BURKE, George		4	23
BURKE, James		2	48
BURKE, James		2	48
BURKE, John		2	48
BURKE, John Errol	P	2	48
BURKE, Joseph		3	42
BURKE, Thomas		1	61
BURKE, Thomas Campbell	P	1	61
BURKE, William		2	48
BURKETT, Walter	P	1	62
BURKIN, William Thomas		2	48

Name	Photo	Part No.	Page No.
BURKINSHAW, Charles Ernest		2	48
BURLEIGH, Joseph Gordon Foster		3	42
BURLEY, Henry	P	2	48
BURLING, William George		5	26
BURMESTER, Eric		2	48
BURN, Arthur George Mccausland		2	48
BURN, Arthur Herbert Rosdew		2	48
BURN, Cuthbert		5	26
BURN, John	P	1	62
BURN, William		1	62
BURNAND, Cyril Francis	P	1	62
BURNARD, Eric Mountjoy		2	48
BURNARD, Leonard		1	62
BURNE, Maurice		2	48
BURNELL, George Cuthbertson	P	1	62
BURNELL, John Sidney		1	62
BURNESS, James	P	4	23
BURNET, Robert	P	1	62
BURNET, William		3	42
BURNETT, Arthur		5	26
BURNETT, Charles		1	62
BURNETT, Francis		1	62
BURNETT, G		2	48
BURNETT, George		1	62
BURNETT, J		4	23
BURNETT, Noel Fletcher	P	1	62
BURNETT, Thomas Newcomen Corry		4	23
BURNETT, Wilfred		2	48
BURNETT, William Josiah		4	23
BURNEY, Gilbert Edward Burney	P	2	48
BURNHAM, Charles Richard		1	62
BURNIE, Donald		2	49
BURNLEY-CAMPBELL, Colin William	P	2	56
BURNS, Albert Horace	P	1	63
BURNS, Alfred		2	49
BURNS, Bertie Daniel		2	49
BURNS, David		1	63
BURNS, G J		2	49
BURNS, Harry Walter	P	1	63
BURNS, Islay Ferrier		3	42
BURNS, J		2	49
BURNS, J		2	49
BURNS, James		2	49
BURNS, James		4	23
BURNS, James Drummond	P	2	49
BURNS, James Rattray	P	4	23
BURNS, John		1	63
BURNS, Lawrence		2	49
BURNS, Michael		1	63
BURNS, Thomas		1	63
BURNS, Thomas		5	26
BURNS, W		2	49
BURNS, William		1	63
BURNS, William Gordon	P	1	63
BURNSIDE, Walter		5	26
BURR, Alfred Percy		4	23
BURR, Andrew Fowler		5	26
BURR, George		4	23
BURR, Harold		1	63
BURR, William Simpson	P	2	49
BURRARD, Norman Sidney		1	63
BURRELL, Alexander	P	1	63
BURRELL, Frederick		1	63
BURRELL, George Owen	P	3	42
BURRELL, John William	P	1	63
BURRELL, Richard George	P	1	63
BURRELL, T		2	49
BURRELL, William Matthew	P	1	63
BURRIDGE, Arthur Charles	P	1	63
BURRIDGE, Frederick William		1	63
BURRIDGE, Henry Gardiner (Lal)	P	1	63
BURRINGTON, Gilbert	P	3	42
BURRINGTON, Harley		1	64
BURROW, Thomas	P	1	64
BURROW, William John		2	49
BURROWES, Guy Walter		2	49
BURROWS, A		3	42
BURROWS, A E		3	43
BURROWS, Alexander		2	49
BURROWS, Arthur Andrew		2	49
BURROWS, Bertie		3	43
BURROWS, E		2	49
BURROWS, Harry	P	2	49
BURROWS, J		3	43
BURROWS, John		2	49
BURROWS, Leonard Righton	P	2	49
BURROWS, Leopold Charles		1	64
BURROWS, Samuel Joseph		1	64
BURROWS, T S		3	43
BURROWS, Thomas		2	49
BURROWS, William Frederick		3	43
BURSNALL, Francis George		1	64
BURSTOW, Albert E		2	49
BURT, Andrew		2	49
BURT, Andrew	P	2	50
BURT, Bernard		4	23
BURT, Henry George		2	50
BURT, James		4	23
BURT, Robert William		1	64
BURT, Thomas		2	50
BURT, William Charles	P	5	26
BURT, William James	P	2	50
BURTENSHAW, A E		3	43
BURTENSHAW, Harry		2	50
BURT-MARSHALL, William Marshall	P	1	245
BURTON, Alfred	P	2	50
BURTON, Alfred	P	4	23
BURTON, Alfred William		1	64
BURTON, C		3	43
BURTON, Charles Samuel		3	43
BURTON, Edward Thomas		2	50
BURTON, Ernest Henry	P	5	26
BURTON, G N J		3	43
BURTON, Gerard William	P	2	50
BURTON, Gilbert		5	27
BURTON, H		3	43
BURTON, Henry		2	50
BURTON, Herbert		4	23
BURTON, James Albert		1	64
BURTON, John		1	64
BURTON, R		3	43
BURTON, R		3	43
BURTON, Rees Thomas		1	64
BURTON, Richard	P	2	50
BURTON, Thomas		2	50
BURTON, Thomas		2	50
BURTON, Thomas		2	50
BURTON, W J		3	43
BURTON, Walter		4	23
BURTON, Walter		5	27

Name	Photo	Part No.	Page No.
BURTON, William Harry	P	1	64
BURTON-FANNING, Newel Edward Eden	P	5	57
BURTONSHAW, William A		2	50
BUSBY, John Leonard		3	43
BUSBY, Maurice Frederick		2	50
BUSH, Albert	P	3	43
BUSH, Alfred John		3	43
BUSH, Archibald R		2	50
BUSH, Arthur Douglas		1	64
BUSH, Charles Frederick		1	64
BUSH, Charles Gerald	P	5	27
BUSH, E		2	50
BUSH, H G De Lisle		4	23
BUSH, James Cromwell		3	43
BUSH, Vivian		2	50
BUSH, W		2	50
BUSHBY, Frederick		2	50
BUSHELL, A		3	43
BUSHELL, A		3	43
BUSHELL, J		2	50
BUSHELL, John William		2	50
BUSHELL, William Stanley	P	2	50
BUSHELL, William Theodore	P	1	64
BUSHNELL, A		3	43
BUSHNELL, Arthur		2	50
BUSHNELL, G H		3	43
BUSHNELL, Henry Owen		4	23
BUSK, Edward Teshmaker	P	1	64
BUSKIN, Alexander Frank	P	2	50
BUSKIN, George Arthur Keith		4	23
BUSS, Hilary Thomas		3	43
BUSWELL, Edward Tom		3	43
BUSWELL, Frederic Henry		2	51
BUTCHARD, Robert Archibald	P	2	51
BUTCHER, Charles		2	51
BUTCHER, Charles		2	51
BUTCHER, Charles Geoffrey	P	1	64
BUTCHER, E E		2	51
BUTCHER, Edward Francis		2	51
BUTCHER, F		3	43
BUTCHER, Frederick		3	43
BUTCHER, Frederick William	P	3	43
BUTCHER, Harold Thomas	P	2	51
BUTCHER, Harry Stanley		1	65
BUTCHER, Henry Townsend	P	2	51
BUTCHER, Thomas Edward		2	51
BUTCHER, William		1	65
BUTCHER, William		2	51
BUTCHER, William		4	23
BUTCHER, William Guy Deame		3	43
BUTFOY, Thomas		2	51
BUTLAND, William Henry	P	3	44
BUTLER, Albert G		2	51
BUTLER, Albert Thomas		3	44
BUTLER, Archibald Harry		2	51
BUTLER, Bernard Arnold Barrington	P	5	27
BUTLER, C		3	44
BUTLER, C H		3	44
BUTLER, Charles		1	65
BUTLER, Charles Dixon	P	4	24
BUTLER, Clifford Hicks	P	3	44
BUTLER, Desmond George		4	24
BUTLER, Edward George		2	51
BUTLER, Francis Mourilyan		5	27
BUTLER, Frederick		1	65

Name	Photo	Part No.	Page No.
BUTLER, Frederick		2	51
BUTLER, Frederick		2	51
BUTLER, Frederick Harold	P	2	51
BUTLER, Frederick William		2	52
BUTLER, G		3	44
BUTLER, George William		2	52
BUTLER, Harry William		1	65
BUTLER, Herbert		2	52
BUTLER, John		1	65
BUTLER, John	P	1	65
BUTLER, John		1	65
BUTLER, John Fitzhardinge Paul		3	44
BUTLER, John Ormonde		5	27
BUTLER, Joseph		2	52
BUTLER, P		3	44
BUTLER, Robert Alexander		3	44
BUTLER, Walter		1	65
BUTLER, William		2	52
BUTLER, William Henry	P	3	44
BUTLER, William Lewis		1	65
BUTLER, William Percy		3	44
BUTLER-WRIGHT, Neville Ormonde	P	2	323
BUTLER-WRIGHT, Vivian Arthur	P	2	323
BUTT, Jesse A		2	52
BUTT, O		4	24
BUTT, Richard Acton		3	44
BUTT, Thomas	P	3	44
BUTTERFIELD, Reginald Herbert	P	3	44
BUTTERISS, R		3	44
BUTTERLY, Thomas Joseph		4	24
BUTTERWICK, Alexander Middleton	P	1	65
BUTTERWORTH, A		3	44
BUTTERWORTH, A		3	44
BUTTERWORTH, George Robert		2	52
BUTTERWORTH, Hugh Montagu		2	52
BUTTERWORTH, J		3	44
BUTTLE, Albert Edward	P	5	27
BUTTON, Frank		2	52
BUTTON, John Samuel		1	65
BUTTON, Stanley		3	44
BUXTON, Arthur Robert		2	52
BYATT, Harry Vivian Byatt	P	1	65
BYCROFT, Walter Herbert		2	52
BYE, Frank Edwin		1	65
BYE, Henry		2	52
BYE, James		2	52
BYERS, James		4	24
BYFIELD, Edgar		4	24
BYFIELD, Harold		2	52
BYFORD, Harry Alfred		2	52
BYGOTT, Frank		3	45
BYGRAVE, Bernard		2	52
BYHAM, Edward Arthur George		1	65
BYNG, Arthur Maitland		2	52
BYRES, William Smith Diack		4	24
BYRNE, Edward	P	3	45
BYRNE, Erl Stanley Frederic		5	27
BYRNE, Herbert Henry		1	65
BYRNE, Hugh Vyvyan Edward		4	24
BYRNE, James		1	65
BYRNE, Leo Francis		3	45
BYRNE, M		4	24
BYRNE, P		4	24
BYRNE, Patrick		3	45
BYRNE, Thomas		1	65

Name	Photo	Part No.	Page No.
BYRNE, W		4	24
BYRON, Arthur		2	52
BYRON, William		4	24
BYWATERS, E		3	45
CABLE, J		3	45
CABLE, Walter	P	2	52
CABLE, William Walter	P	2	52
CADDEN, H		3	45
CADE, William Albert	P	5	27
CADELL, Assheton Biddulph		3	45
CADGER, William Law		1	65
CADMAN, Charles Joseph	P	4	24
CADMAN, Henry		4	24
CADMAN, Isaiah		1	65
CADMAN, Samuel		3	45
CADMAN, William	P	3	45
CADOGAN, Henry Osbert Samuel		2	52
CADOGAN, The Hon. William George Sydney		2	52
CADOGAN, William		2	52
CADZOW, Robert	P	4	24
CAESAR, Augustus Benjamin		1	65
CAFFYN, Harold Hunt		1	65
CAHILL, Henry T		2	52
CAHILL, Henry Thomas		1	65
CAHILL, J J		4	24
CAHILL, Maurice		2	52
CAHILL, Thomas		2	52
CAILE, John Allison		2	52
CAIN, Henry T		2	52
CAINAN, David Walter		1	65
CAIRD, Ernest Thomson		4	24
CAIRD, James Robert	P	1	65
CAIRD, John Hay		2	52
CAIRNIE, Gilbert James Bryan	P	1	65
CAIRNS, A		2	53
CAIRNS, George Morton	P	2	53
CAIRNS, J		2	53
CAIRNS, James		2	53
CAIRNS, John	P	1	66
CAIRNS, John Anderson Gibson	P	2	53
CAIRNS, Joseph		2	53
CAIRNS, Robert Albert		2	53
CAIRNS, Samuel		2	53
CAIRNS, T		3	45
CAIRNS, Thomas Charles		4	25
CAIRNS, Thomas George		4	25
CAIRNS, Walter		2	53
CAIRNS, William		2	53
CAISEY, Henry	P	2	53
CAKE, W C		3	45
CALDECOTT, John Leslie		2	53
CALDER, Colin Stewart	P	3	45
CALDER, Edwin		3	45
CALDER, Kenneth William		2	53
CALDER, W		3	45
CALDERBANK, J		3	45
CALDERWOOD, William Sewell		4	25
CALDICOTT, George		3	45
CALDWELL, Quintin		2	53
CALDWELL, Robert Seddon	P	5	27
CALDWELL, S		3	45
CALE, Albert		1	66
CALEB, Clement Daryl Nicoll		3	45
CALKIN, Brian Penry Bernard		4	25
CALKIN, John Ernest	P	3	45
CALLAER, Harry Osmond		4	25
CALLAGHAN, James		3	46
CALLAGHAN, John Corneleous		2	53
CALLAGHAN, T		2	53
CALLANDER, Arthur William	P	1	66
CALLER, Edward		2	53
CALLEY, Oliver John	P	1	66
CALLINGHAM, Frederick		2	53
CALLOW, William C		2	53
CALMAN, J		2	53
CALOW, F L		3	46
CALROW, Denis		2	53
CALROW, William Robert Launcelot	P	1	66
CALVER, J		2	53
CALVERLEY, James		1	66
CALVERLEY, Lawrence Basil		1	66
CALVERT, G		3	46
CALVERT, Herbert Edwin		1	66
CALVERT, Herbert Tom	P	2	54
CALVERT, John Dutton	P	1	66
CALVERT, Robert		2	54
CALVERT, William James		2	54
CAMBIE, Edward Maurice Baldwin	P	2	54
CAMBRIDGE, George William	P	1	66
CAMERON, A		2	54
CAMERON, A		2	54
CAMERON, A		2	54
CAMERON, A F		2	54
CAMERON, Alexander		4	25
CAMERON, Alexander		5	27
CAMERON, Alexander Crawford		2	54
CAMERON, Allan George	P	1	66
CAMERON, Archie		1	66
CAMERON, Arthur Ian Douglas	P	1	66
CAMERON, Colin		5	27
CAMERON, D		2	54
CAMERON, David Morton		5	27
CAMERON, Donald	P	2	54
CAMERON, Donald		5	28
CAMERON, Donald Alexander		3	46
CAMERON, Donald Ewan	P	1	67
CAMERON, Donald Ronald Colin	P	2	54
CAMERON, Duncan Alexander	P	4	25
CAMERON, Evan Stuart	P	1	67
CAMERON, Francis Blake		3	46
CAMERON, Hector William Lovett	P	2	54
CAMERON, Hugh		5	28
CAMERON, Ian Gilmour		3	46
CAMERON, J		2	54
CAMERON, J		3	46
CAMERON, James	P	2	54
CAMERON, James Finlayson	P	2	54
CAMERON, James Hope		2	54
CAMERON, John		5	28
CAMERON, John		5	28
CAMERON, John Gordon	P	4	25
CAMERON, John Kennedy		2	55
CAMERON, John Munn		3	46
CAMERON, John Thomas		5	28
CAMERON, Joseph		1	67
CAMERON, Morton Augustus	P	1	67
CAMERON, Napier Charles Gordon		2	55
CAMERON, Nathaniel		4	25
CAMERON, Neil Kennedy	P	2	55
CAMERON, Pedro		1	67

Name	Photo	Part No.	Page No.
CAMERON, Peter	P	2	55
CAMERON, Robert Brown		3	46
CAMERON, Roy Douglas		2	55
CAMERON, Thomas Albert		1	67
CAMERON, William	P	2	55
CAMERON, William		2	55
CAMERON, William		2	55
CAMERON, William Henry Veitch		2	55
CAMERON, William Matheson	P	1	67
CAMERON, William Mcarthur		3	46
CAMFFERMAN, Alexander	P	1	67
CAMFIELD, A		3	46
CAMFIELD, William		1	67
CAMM, Philip O		2	55
CAMNOCK, Alexander Mclean		2	55
CAMP, Albert		2	55
CAMP, Harold C		2	55
CAMPANY, William		2	55
CAMPBELL, A		2	55
CAMPBELL, A		2	55
CAMPBELL, Alexander		1	67
CAMPBELL, Alexander Boswell	P	3	46
CAMPBELL, Allan William George		2	55
CAMPBELL, Andrew		5	28
CAMPBELL, Angus		2	55
CAMPBELL, Benjamin	P	3	46
CAMPBELL, Brabazon		2	55
CAMPBELL, C		2	55
CAMPBELL, Charles		5	28
CAMPBELL, Charles Arthur		2	55
CAMPBELL, Charles Sidney		5	28
CAMPBELL, Charles Smith		3	46
CAMPBELL, Charles Wilson		5	28
CAMPBELL, Colin Frederick Fitzroy	P	1	67
CAMPBELL, Colin Richmond	P	4	25
CAMPBELL, D		3	46
CAMPBELL, Donald	P	1	67
CAMPBELL, Donald Henry Bruce	P	1	68
CAMPBELL, Donald William Auchinbreck		2	55
CAMPBELL, Duncan	P	1	68
CAMPBELL, Edward Gill		4	25
CAMPBELL, Evan Mcdonald		3	46
CAMPBELL, Frederick James		1	68
CAMPBELL, Geoffrey Arthur	P	2	56
CAMPBELL, George		4	25
CAMPBELL, George Edward Forman	P	1	68
CAMPBELL, George Jackson		1	68
CAMPBELL, H		2	56
CAMPBELL, Harold Edgar		1	68
CAMPBELL, Henry		4	26
CAMPBELL, Hugh		2	56
CAMPBELL, Ivar		3	46
CAMPBELL, J		2	56
CAMPBELL, J		2	56
CAMPBELL, J		2	56
CAMPBELL, J		3	46
CAMPBELL, James		1	68
CAMPBELL, James		2	56
CAMPBELL, James		2	56
CAMPBELL, James		2	56
CAMPBELL, James		4	26
CAMPBELL, James Henderson		3	46
CAMPBELL, John		1	68
CAMPBELL, John	P	2	56
CAMPBELL, John Davies		1	68

Name	Photo	Part No.	Page No.
CAMPBELL, John Gordon	P	1	68
CAMPBELL, John Guy	P	3	46
CAMPBELL, Keith Morehead Gunning	P	1	68
CAMPBELL, Kenneth Gordon	P	2	56
CAMPBELL, Kenneth James	P	1	68
CAMPBELL, Kenneth Mckenzie	P	1	68
CAMPBELL, Malcolm Dring		1	68
CAMPBELL, Malcolm James	P	1	69
CAMPBELL, Matthew James		4	26
CAMPBELL, Montagu Irving Mitchell	P	3	47
CAMPBELL, Murdoch Cameron Prentice		5	28
CAMPBELL, Neil	P	5	28
CAMPBELL, Neil Leslie	P	2	56
CAMPBELL, Norman		2	56
CAMPBELL, Norman Adam		4	26
CAMPBELL, Peter Mclellan		4	26
CAMPBELL, R		2	56
CAMPBELL, Richard Graham		4	26
CAMPBELL, Robert	P	1	69
CAMPBELL, Robert Charles Cowburn	P	1	69
CAMPBELL, Robert Henry Clark		5	28
CAMPBELL, Robert John		2	56
CAMPBELL, S		2	56
CAMPBELL, Stanley		4	26
CAMPBELL, Stewart Prince Falls		5	28
CAMPBELL, T		2	56
CAMPBELL, T		2	56
CAMPBELL, T		3	47
CAMPBELL, Thomas Grier		2	56
CAMPBELL, W		2	56
CAMPBELL, W		3	47
CAMPBELL, Walter Mellish		3	47
CAMPBELL, William		3	47
CAMPBELL, William Percy		2	56
CAMPION, Edward		2	57
CAMPION, Frederick T		2	57
CAMPION, Robert Percy		2	57
CAMPION, Walter Ernest		2	57
CAMPION, William Charles		2	57
CAMPKIN, Edward		2	57
CANDLISH, Joseph Hilton		4	26
CANDY, Philip Sadler	P	1	69
CANE, Leonard Dobbie		3	47
CANE, Lionel Alfred Francis		2	57
CANE, Thomas		2	57
CANE, William Henry		5	28
CANE, William Robert		2	57
CANFIELD, William		2	57
CANHAM, Herbert		1	69
CANHAM, Robert		2	57
CANIM, John		2	57
CANN, Charles		1	69
CANN, John Henry		2	57
CANN, Robert Henry		1	69
CANNELL, J		3	47
CANNELL, S		3	47
CANNON, Charles Edwin		1	69
CANNON, Hugh Stanley	P	1	69
CANNON, Maxwell		2	57
CANNONS, Frank John		1	69
CANTELL, G R		3	47
CANTILLON, John	P	2	57
CANTON, Charles John	P	1	69
CANTON, G		3	47
CANTON, Herbert Westrup		1	69

Name	Photo	Part No.	Page No.
CASH, George Richard		1	73
CASH, William Henry		3	49
CASHEN, William		2	61
CASHMAN, John		2	61
CASHMORE, James		4	28
CASLEY, Hugh De Chastelai	P	1	73
CASLON, Thomas White	P	2	61
CASS, Charles Bouchier		5	30
CASS, James Oliver		5	30
CASSELLS, Samuel		3	49
CASSIDY, Cyril Martin		1	73
CASSIDY, John	P	2	62
CASSIDY, William		4	28
CASTELL, Charles		5	30
CASTLE, Albert Edward		2	62
CASTLE, Fred		2	62
CASTLE, George Phil	P	1	73
CASTLE, George Richard		2	62
CASTLE, John		1	73
CASTLE, John George		1	73
CASTLE, Joseph		2	62
CASTLE, William Edward	P	2	62
CASTLEDINE, Montagu Cyril	P	1	73
CASTLES, W		3	49
CASTLETON, Claud Charles	P	3	49
CATCHPOLE, A		3	50
CATCHPOLE, Ernest		3	50
CATER, James Percival	P	4	28
CATES, Arthur Kenneth		4	28
CATES, George Edward		3	50
CATHCART, Augustus Ernest		2	62
CATHCART, James		3	50
CATHING, Albert Henry		2	62
CATO, Edward		2	62
CATOR, R		3	50
CATT, Bert		1	73
CATT, Bert		2	62
CATT, Edward		1	73
CATT, Percy Henry		1	73
CATTANACH, John		2	62
CATTERMOLE, Henry L		2	62
CATTO, Alexander		3	50
CATTO, Alexander		5	30
CATTON, Isaac		4	28
CAUDERY, George Henry		2	62
CAUDWELL, W		3	50
CAUGHTREY, Joseph Edward Mackintosh		5	30
CAULDER, Albert		2	62
CAULFEILD, James Crosbie	P	1	73
CAULFIELD, Joseph		2	62
CAULFIELD, William		3	50
CAUNTER, E J		3	50
CAUSER, John		2	62
CAUSON, Francis		2	62
CAUSON, Sidney Albert	P	2	62
CAUSTON, J W		2	62
CAUTLEY, William Oxenham	P	1	74
CAVALIER, George Alfred	P	2	62
CAVANAGH, A		2	62
CAVANAGH, F		2	62
CAVE, B		2	63
CAVE, C		3	50
CAVE, Eric Arthur	P	2	63
CAVE, Sidney Edwin		4	28
CAVELL, Frank Corneluis		1	74

Name	Photo	Part No.	Page No.
CAVELL, Stanley Herbert		4	28
CAVENDISH, George F		2	63
CAVENDISH, Godfrey Lionel John	P	1	74
CAVENDISH, Lord John Spencer		1	74
CAVEY, Albert E		2	63
CAVEY, Sidney	P	1	74
CAW, Harry		3	50
CAWARD, C		2	63
CAWKILL, Stanley		3	50
CAWKWELL, A E		3	50
CAWKWELL, Albert Holloway		5	30
CAWLEY, Harold Thomas	P	1	74
CAWLEY, James		2	63
CAWLEY, John Stephen		1	74
CAWOOD, William Benjamin Crane		2	63
CAWS, Stanley Winther	P	2	63
CAWSE, Samuel George		1	75
CAWSON, George		2	63
CAWSON, John		2	63
CAWTE, Henry Arthur		2	63
CAWTHERAY, H		3	50
CAWTHORNE, John Raymond		2	63
CAWTHORNE, Vernon Whitfield	P	2	63
CAWTHRA, Harold		1	75
CAYFORD, George Everett		3	50
CAYME, Bernard Glyde	P	1	75
CECIL, George Edward		1	75
CECIL, The Hon. William Amherst		2	63
CECIL, Thomas J		4	28
CECIL, William Henry		4	28
CESARI, Sydney Fraser Mcalpine	P	2	63
CHADBAND, John Stanley	P	2	63
CHADD, Benjamin		1	75
CHADDOCK, J		3	50
CHADDOCK, Jonathan		2	63
CHADWICK, F		3	50
CHADWICK, Frederick James	P	1	75
CHADWICK, Harry	P	3	50
CHADWICK, John William	P	3	50
CHADWICK, Richard Markham	P	1	75
CHAFER, Herbert John		1	75
CHAFF, Ernest		2	63
CHAFFER, Ernest Albert		2	63
CHAFFEY, George H		2	63
CHALCROFT, Walter Charles		2	63
CHALK, A		3	50
CHALK, Henry Benjamin		5	30
CHALLEN, William Augustus	P	2	64
CHALLIS, Arthur Bracebridge		5	30
CHALLIS, Frank Walter		1	75
CHALLIS, Frederick Charles		1	75
CHALLIS, Walter		1	75
CHALLIS, Walter James		2	64
CHALLONER, Alan Crawhall	P	1	75
CHALMERS, Alexander	P	2	64
CHALMERS, Alexander		3	50
CHALMERS, Alexander		3	50
CHALMERS, Archibald Douglas	P	5	30
CHALMERS, David		3	50
CHALMERS, Duncan		2	64
CHALMERS, John Binny		2	64
CHALMERS, John Hunter	P	4	28
CHALMERS, John Stuart		4	28
CHALMERS, William Mcmillan		2	64
CHALMERS, William Robert		1	76

Name	Photo	Part No.	Page No.
CHAMBERLAIN, Arthur Ernest		2	64
CHAMBERLAIN, E		3	51
CHAMBERLAIN, Henry Osman		2	64
CHAMBERLAIN, John		2	64
CHAMBERLAIN, Percy Edward	P	5	31
CHAMBERLAIN, Thomas William		2	64
CHAMBERLAIN, W		3	51
CHAMBERLAIN, William Masters		3	51
CHAMBERS, Albert Alfred		2	64
CHAMBERS, Albert Edward		2	64
CHAMBERS, Albert Norris	P	2	64
CHAMBERS, Alexander		3	51
CHAMBERS, Alfred George	P	4	29
CHAMBERS, Antony Gerald		3	51
CHAMBERS, Charles Thomas		3	51
CHAMBERS, David Macdonald		3	51
CHAMBERS, Edward		1	76
CHAMBERS, Edward Chandos Elliot	P	2	64
CHAMBERS, Francis		3	51
CHAMBERS, Francis H		2	65
CHAMBERS, Francis James		5	31
CHAMBERS, Hedley		5	31
CHAMBERS, John		2	65
CHAMBERS, Percy		1	76
CHAMBERS, Thomas Henry		2	65
CHAMBERS, Victor Leethem		3	51
CHAMBERS, Wilfrid John		3	51
CHAMBERS, William		1	76
CHAMBERS, William Henry		2	65
CHAMP, Francis Logan		1	76
CHAMP, Wilfred George		2	65
CHAMPION, A G		2	65
CHAMPION, Charles Edward		4	29
CHAMPION, Edward Thomas		1	76
CHAMPION, Frederick Harry		3	51
CHAMPION, Henry William		4	29
CHAMPION, Reginald James		3	51
CHAMPION, Victor Alfred Richard	P	1	76
CHAMPION DE CRESPIGNY, Claude Norman	P	1	109
CHAMPLIN, William Albert		4	29
CHAMPS, Sidney		1	76
CHANCE, Andrew Ferguson	P	2	65
CHANCE, Edward		2	65
CHANCE, Guy Ogden De Peyster		2	65
CHANCE, Joseph		1	76
CHANCELLOR, Geoffrey Ellis	P	3	51
CHANCELLOR, Samuel		1	76
CHANDLER, Arthur C		2	65
CHANDLER, Charles William		1	76
CHANDLER, Clive Hereward		2	65
CHANDLER, G		2	65
CHANDLER, Henry Norman	P	1	76
CHANDLER, J R		3	51
CHANDLER, James Thomas		2	65
CHANDLER, John Kellman		1	76
CHANDLER, Joseph		2	65
CHANDLER, Norman		1	76
CHANDLER, W T J		3	51
CHANNING, Edward John	P	3	51
CHAPLIN, Arthur		1	76
CHAPLIN, Charles Sidney		2	65
CHAPLIN, Charles Slingsby	P	1	76
CHAPLIN, David Henry		5	31
CHAPLIN, Edward Robert		1	76

Name	Photo	Part No.	Page No.
CHAPLIN, Frederick Hardress	P	3	51
CHAPLIN, Humphrey Marmaduke	P	1	76
CHAPMAN, A		3	52
CHAPMAN, Alexander W		4	29
CHAPMAN, Alfred		1	76
CHAPMAN, Arthur		4	29
CHAPMAN, Arthur Thomas	P	1	76
CHAPMAN, Charles Herbert		3	52
CHAPMAN, Charles Stirling	P	2	65
CHAPMAN, Clement		1	77
CHAPMAN, D		2	65
CHAPMAN, Edgar		2	65
CHAPMAN, Edgar Arthur		4	29
CHAPMAN, Edward George		4	29
CHAPMAN, Edward Henry	P	1	77
CHAPMAN, Edward Wynne		2	65
CHAPMAN, Eli		2	65
CHAPMAN, Eric		2	65
CHAPMAN, Ernest Robert Braybrook	P	3	52
CHAPMAN, Ewart Frederick		2	65
CHAPMAN, F		3	52
CHAPMAN, F C		3	52
CHAPMAN, Frank James Albert		1	77
CHAPMAN, Frank James Albert		2	65
CHAPMAN, Fred Charles		1	77
CHAPMAN, Frederick		1	77
CHAPMAN, Frederick Major		5	31
CHAPMAN, G H		3	52
CHAPMAN, George		2	65
CHAPMAN, George		2	65
CHAPMAN, George Ernest	P	1	77
CHAPMAN, George John		2	65
CHAPMAN, George Martin	P	1	77
CHAPMAN, Gordon Humphrey	P	2	65
CHAPMAN, Harry Reynolds	P	1	77
CHAPMAN, Herbert Alfred	P	1	77
CHAPMAN, Horace	P	3	52
CHAPMAN, James		2	65
CHAPMAN, Joe		1	77
CHAPMAN, Joe	P	2	65
CHAPMAN, John		2	65
CHAPMAN, John		4	29
CHAPMAN, John Richard		2	66
CHAPMAN, Leonard George		2	66
CHAPMAN, Perceval Christian	P	1	77
CHAPMAN, Peter Thomas		2	66
CHAPMAN, Philip George	P	1	78
CHAPMAN, Richard Keppel George Sutton	P	1	78
CHAPMAN, Robert		2	66
CHAPMAN, Robert		2	66
CHAPMAN, Robert		2	66
CHAPMAN, Samuel		4	29
CHAPMAN, Theodore Victor		3	52
CHAPMAN, Victor Fuller		4	29
CHAPMAN, Wilfrid Hubert	P	1	78
CHAPMAN, William		4	29
CHAPMAN, William Alfred	P	1	78
CHAPPEL, William Eldon	P	3	52
CHAPPELL, Albert		5	31
CHAPPELL, Charles John		4	29
CHAPPELL, H		3	52
CHAPPELL, Harold		3	52
CHAPPELL, Moses	P	2	66
CHAPPELL, Sydney		2	66
CHAPPELL, W J		3	52

Name	Photo	Part No.	Page No.	Name	Photo	Part No.	Page No.
CHILTON, Frank		1	80	CHRISTOPHER, Leonard De Lona	P	1	81
CHILTON, Frank		2	68	CHRISTY, Stephen Henry		2	69
CHILTON, Free		1	80	CHRISTY, Thomas Hills	P	4	30
CHILTON, James		5	31	CHRYSTAL, James		2	69
CHILVERS, Alexander Victor		2	68	CHRYSTALL, William	P	4	31
CHILVERS, John		2	68	CHRYSTIE, John	P	1	81
CHILVERS, Matthew Limbert	P	2	68	CHUBB, Alan Travers		3	54
CHILVERS, Percy Ernest		1	80	CHUDLEIGH, F M		3	54
CHILVERS, William George		2	68	CHUDLEY, C		3	54
CHIMES, Douglas Percy		4	30	CHUDLEY, John Frederick	P	1	81
CHING, Hugh (Alias Hugh William Power)	P	1	80	CHUICH, Stanley Twy Miras		4	31
CHIPCHASE, Charles Wilson		1	80	CHUMLEY, Horace		2	69
CHIPIBASE, Charles		2	68	CHURCH, Denis Frederic		3	54
CHISHOLM, Alexander		1	80	CHURCH, E W		3	55
CHISHOLM, Charles		2	68	CHURCH, George		3	55
CHISHOLM, Donald Alexander Gordon		2	68	CHURCH, R		3	55
CHISHOLM, J		3	53	CHURCH, R J		3	55
CHISHOLM, Robert Darling	P	2	68	CHURCH, Reginald		2	69
CHISHOLM, Roderick		2	68	CHURCHER, Bryan Thomas	P	5	31
CHISHOLM, Stephenson		3	53	CHURCHER, Ernest Frederic Claude		2	69
CHISHOLM, William Malcolm		2	68	CHURCHER, Frederick William Thomas	P	4	31
CHISHOLM, William Turner		3	54	CHURCHILL, Albert Edward		2	69
CHISIM, John		1	80	CHURCHILL, Arthur Norton Hickling	P	2	70
CHISLETT, Angus Robert Joseph	P	3	54	CHURCHILL, Charles Edward		5	31
CHISMON, Arthur William		2	68	CHURCHILL, David Edwin Stanley		1	81
CHISNALL, George Henry	P	1	80	CHURCHILL, James Henry		3	55
CHITTENDEN, Arthur George	P	3	54	CHURCHILL, John Wilfred		1	81
CHITTENDEN, Arthur Grant Bourne		2	68	CHURCHILL, R T		3	55
CHITTENDEN, Frank		1	80	CHURCHWARD, Thomas Joseph	P	4	31
CHITTENDEN, Thomas		2	68	CHUTE, Challoner Francis Trevor	P	1	81
CHITTICK, T		3	54	CIVILIAN-SILLS, Stephen		1	326
CHITTY, Arthur		2	69	CLAIR, William		1	82
CHITTY, Arthur William		2	69	CLAIRMONTE, George Egerton	P	2	70
CHITTY, Herbert Henry		2	69	CLAMP, Laurence Pearson		5	31
CHITTY, Thomas William	P	2	69	CLANCEY, Trevor John		2	70
CHIVAS, Edwin John	P	1	80	CLANCY, J		3	55
CHIVERS, Harold	P	3	54	CLANCY, Joseph		2	70
CHOATE, Richard William		2	69	CLANNACHAN, Edward		2	70
CHOLMELEY, Humphrey Jasper	P	3	54	CLAPHAM, Barnard Aubrey	P	3	55
CHOLMELEY, Sir Montagu Aubrey Rowley		2	69	CLAPP, Albert George		1	82
CHOLMLEY, George Francis	P	1	81	CLAPP, William Gilbert Elphinstone		3	55
CHOLMONDELEY, Charles Almeric John	P	1	81	CLAPPEN, Wilfrid Joseph		3	55
CHONEY, William		2	69	CLARE, Jabez Benjamin		4	31
CHORLEY, Dudley Cecil	P	1	81	CLARE, Samuel John		1	82
CHOULES, J H		3	54	CLARE, William James	P	3	55
CHOWN, Herbert		1	81	CLARIDGE, Alfred James Robert	P	2	70
CHRISTIAN, Harold		5	31	CLARK, Albert		3	55
CHRISTIAN, Henry Clyne	P	3	54	CLARK, Albert E		2	70
CHRISTIAN, Robert Burns	P	3	54	CLARK, Alexander Macleod		4	31
CHRISTIE, Albert William Ernest	P	2	69	CLARK, Alexander Smith		3	55
CHRISTIE, Andrew	P	2	69	CLARK, Andrew		5	31
CHRISTIE, Denis Halsted		5	31	CLARK, C S		3	55
CHRISTIE, Dennis Peter	P	4	30	CLARK, Charles		3	55
CHRISTIE, Dugald Roderick (Derick)		3	54	CLARK, D		2	70
CHRISTIE, Frederick	P	4	30	CLARK, D		2	70
CHRISTIE, John		2	69	CLARK, D		3	55
CHRISTIE, John		4	30	CLARK, Donald		4	31
CHRISTIE, Robert Erskine		4	30	CLARK, Edward		1	82
CHRISTIE, William Charles		2	69	CLARK, Eric Alan	P	4	31
CHRISTIE-MURRAY, Maurice	P	4	141	CLARK, Ernest Edward		2	70
CHRISTISON, Robert Colin		3	54	CLARK, F W		3	55
CHRISTMAS, Henry Victor		4	30	CLARK, Frank		4	31
CHRISTMAS, Leslie Frederick		4	30	CLARK, Frank		5	31
CHRISTMAS, Walter	P	5	31	CLARK, Frank Watson	P	5	32
CHRISTOPHER, J W		3	54	CLARK, Frederick James		1	82

Name	Photo	Part No.	Page No.
COLE, Reginald Price		4	34
COLE, Richard		2	74
COLE, Sidney Lionel Flinn	P	1	88
COLE, W R		3	58
COLE, William Charles	P	1	88
COLE, William George		3	58
COLEBROOK, Geoffrey Bathurst	P	2	74
COLEMAN, Charles James Bruce	P	5	34
COLEMAN, Edward Charles		3	58
COLEMAN, Eric Arthur Frank	P	3	58
COLEMAN, Fred Creighton		3	59
COLEMAN, Frederick		4	34
COLEMAN, G A		3	59
COLEMAN, George Henry		1	88
COLEMAN, George Mansfield		1	88
COLEMAN, George Thomas	P	4	34
COLEMAN, Herbert Edward Evatt		3	59
COLEMAN, J M		3	59
COLEMAN, John Morris		1	88
COLEMAN, John Roberts		5	34
COLEMAN, Reginald John	P	3	59
COLEMAN, Samuel George		1	88
COLEMAN, Sidney F		2	75
COLEMAN, Thomas Barnes		1	88
COLEMAN, William		1	88
COLEMAN, William Albert	P	1	88
COLEMAN, William Frederick		4	34
COLENUTT, Albert Edward		1	88
COLERIDGE, Colin Goss	P	4	34
COLES, Caleb James		4	34
COLES, Charles George	P	1	88
COLES, Donald M		2	75
COLES, E C		2	75
COLES, Edgar Ralph	P	1	88
COLES, Ewart John		1	88
COLES, F J		3	59
COLES, G		3	59
COLES, George		2	75
COLES, George		5	35
COLES, J W		3	59
COLES, James		2	75
COLES, Robert	P	1	88
COLES, Sidney Harcourt		2	75
COLES, Thomas Edward		2	75
COLES, William		2	75
COLES, William J T		2	75
COLES, William Thomas		2	75
COLL, Daniel		2	75
COLLAR, Ernest		2	75
COLLARD, B R		3	59
COLLARD, Phillip		2	75
COLLARD, William Edwin		3	59
COLLCUTT, Philip Martin Blake	P	5	35
COLLEN, Norman Owen	P	2	75
COLLER, E E		3	59
COLLES, Arthur Grove	P	1	88
COLLET, Charles Herbert	P	1	88
COLLETT, D		3	59
COLLETT, Frederick William		1	89
COLLETT, Reuben Kemp		2	75
COLLETT, Ronald Frederick		3	59
COLLIE, James Gordon		3	59
COLLIE, William	P	3	59
COLLIER, Albert		2	75
COLLIER, Alfred Ernest		1	89

Name	Photo	Part No.	Page No.
COLLIER, Frederick Henry		1	89
COLLIER, George		1	89
COLLIER, Reginald John		3	59
COLLIER, Thomas		1	89
COLLIER, Victor		2	75
COLLINDRIDGE, Jack	P	3	59
COLLINGE, William		1	89
COLLINGS, Sydney Clement		2	75
COLLINGS, T		3	59
COLLINGS, Thomas E		2	75
COLLINGS, Wallace		1	89
COLLINGWOOD, Thomas William		5	35
COLLINGWOOD, William		1	89
COLLINGWOOD-THOMPSON, Edward James Vibart		4	211
COLLINS, A		3	59
COLLINS, A E		3	59
COLLINS, Albert		2	75
COLLINS, Albert Shepherd		3	59
COLLINS, Albert Victor		3	59
COLLINS, Alfred Charles		2	75
COLLINS, Alfred John		2	75
COLLINS, Arthur Edward Jeune		2	75
COLLINS, Arthur Michael Austin	P	5	35
COLLINS, Charles		2	75
COLLINS, Charles Alfred		2	75
COLLINS, Charles James		1	89
COLLINS, Christopher	P	1	89
COLLINS, David		1	89
COLLINS, David		2	76
COLLINS, Edward		1	89
COLLINS, Edward William Elger		1	89
COLLINS, Ernest George Stephen		1	89
COLLINS, Finlay		5	35
COLLINS, Frederick		2	76
COLLINS, Frederick Leslie		2	76
COLLINS, H		2	76
COLLINS, H		3	60
COLLINS, H		3	60
COLLINS, H E		3	60
COLLINS, Harold George	P	4	34
COLLINS, Harry	P	1	89
COLLINS, Harry		1	89
COLLINS, Harry		2	76
COLLINS, Harry Ernest		2	76
COLLINS, Henry		2	76
COLLINS, Henry Silvester		1	89
COLLINS, Herbert Charles		1	89
COLLINS, J		3	60
COLLINS, J		3	60
COLLINS, J A		3	60
COLLINS, James		2	76
COLLINS, John		1	89
COLLINS, John		2	76
COLLINS, John		2	76
COLLINS, John A		5	35
COLLINS, John R		2	76
COLLINS, John W		2	76
COLLINS, John William		2	76
COLLINS, Joseph		2	76
COLLINS, Lionel Drummond Kyrle	P	3	60
COLLINS, Lionel F		5	35
COLLINS, Michael		2	76
COLLINS, Peter		2	76
COLLINS, Richard	P	1	89

Name	Photo	Part No.	Page No.
COLLINS, Richard		2	76
COLLINS, Samuel		1	89
COLLINS, Stanley Bertram		1	89
COLLINS, T		3	60
COLLINS, Thomas		1	89
COLLINS, W		2	76
COLLINS, W		3	60
COLLINS, W A		3	60
COLLINS, W C		3	60
COLLINS, Walter	P	5	35
COLLINS, William Edward		5	35
COLLINS, Willie George		1	89
COLLINSON, J		3	60
COLLINSON, John		2	76
COLLIS, Bertram Humphrey		2	76
COLLIS, J		3	60
COLLIS, William Samuel	P	2	76
COLLIS-BROWNE, Alfred Ulick		1	57
COLLISSON, Cedric Hazledine	P	1	89
COLLISSON, Evelyn Ernest Arnold		3	60
COLLMAN, Albert George		3	60
COLLOFF, Sydney	P	4	35
COLLOP, William (Alias Walter)		2	76
COLLYER, Frank Howard	P	2	76
COLLYER, James		2	76
COLMAN, George Ewart		4	35
COLQUHOUN, Archibald		4	35
COLQUHOUN, Frederick Gibson		3	60
COLQUHOUN, John		2	76
COLQUHOUN, Robert Crosthwaite	P	2	76
COLSON, William John	P	1	89
COLTART, David John		2	77
COLTART, R		3	60
COLTMAN, Charles Stanley		4	35
COLTON, Frederick William		4	35
COLUMBUS, Fred		1	90
COLVILL, George Chaigneau		3	60
COLVIN, Robert Alexander		1	90
COLYER, Reginald James		1	90
COMAN, Albert		2	77
COMBE, Boyce Anthony		2	77
COMBE, George Henry Richard		3	60
COMBE, S B		2	77
COMBER, William Ephraim	P	2	77
COMER, T		3	60
COMERFORD, Arthur		2	77
COMERY, W		3	60
COMLEY, Edwin		2	77
COMPER, G E		3	60
COMPTON, Charles Victor		3	60
COMPTON, Herbert J		2	77
COMPTON, John Hugh		2	77
COMPTON, Reginald		2	77
COMPTON-SMITH, Roger Noel	P	1	332
COMPTON-THORNHILL, Richard Anthony		4	212
COMRIE, F		2	77
COMYN, William Nugent		1	90
CONAGHAN, John		2	77
CONDER, John Albert		2	77
CONDER, W J		2	77
CONDI, Allan George		3	60
CONDON, T		2	77
CONDRON, Edward		1	90
CONDUITT, Robert Bruce	P	1	90
CONEY, Thomas		2	77

Name	Photo	Part No.	Page No.
CONFORD, Charles Edward	P	2	79
CONGDON, Richard Henry		1	90
CONGERTON, Thomas		2	77
CONGLETON, Henry Bligh Fortescue Parnell		2	77
CONLEY, A T		3	60
CONLIN, R		2	77
CONN, Edward Reginald		3	60
CONN, George Denholm	P	1	90
CONNEFF, John		3	60
CONNELL, C		3	60
CONNELL, Edward		2	77
CONNELL, George Sharp		2	77
CONNELL, Gilbert	P	1	90
CONNELL, J		3	60
CONNELL, Sydney Dennis		2	77
CONNELL, William		2	77
CONNELLAN, Peter Martin	P	1	90
CONNELLY, E		2	77
CONNELLY, William		2	77
CONNER, Richard		1	91
CONNETT, Henry		1	91
CONNOLLY, Albert		5	35
CONNOLLY, Edward	P	1	91
CONNOLLY, J		3	60
CONNOLLY, J W		3	60
CONNOLLY, James		2	77
CONNON, Ferguson		4	35
CONNOR, Albert William		5	35
CONNOR, Andrew Thomas		2	77
CONNOR, C		3	60
CONNOR, E		2	77
CONNOR, George		2	77
CONNOR, Harry Thomas		5	35
CONNOR, J		3	60
CONNOR, Luke		2	77
CONNOR, M		3	60
CONNOR, P		3	60
CONNOR, P		3	60
CONNOR, T		3	60
CONNOR, T		3	60
CONNOR, Thomas		2	77
CONNORS, W P		2	77
CONQUEST, Leonard Alexander		2	77
CONRADE, A E		2	77
CONROY, T		2	77
CONSTABLE, Douglas Oliphant		3	61
CONSTABLE, G N		2	77
CONSTABLE, H L		2	77
CONSTABLE, T		3	61
CONSTABLE, William	P	5	35
CONSTANTINE, Alfred		2	77
CONVERY, John (Alias Conwery)	P	2	77
CONWAY, C		3	61
CONWAY, Ernest H G		2	77
CONWAY, J		3	61
CONWAY, John	P	1	91
CONWAY, John Charles		1	91
CONWAY, Thomas		4	35
CONYNGHAM, Cecil Allen Taylour		2	77
COOCH, Charles Rollo		2	77
COOK, Albert Benjamin		3	61
COOK, Alfred John		1	91
COOK, Arthur		2	78
COOK, Bernard Henry		1	91
COOK, C		3	61

Name	Photo	Part No.	Page No.
COOPER, Joseph		2	79
COOPER, L		3	62
COOPER, Leonard Gosse	P	1	93
COOPER, Leonard Holme		4	36
COOPER, R		2	79
COOPER, Robert		4	37
COOPER, Samuel		2	79
COOPER, Sidney		2	79
COOPER, Sidney		2	79
COOPER, Sidney Douglas		2	79
COOPER, Stanley James		1	93
COOPER, T		3	62
COOPER, T G		3	62
COOPER, Thomas		1	93
COOPER, Thomas Wilfred	P	1	93
COOPER, W H		3	62
COOPER, Wilfrid Leonard		4	37
COOPER, Wilkinson Bond		2	79
COOPER, William		2	79
COOPER, William		2	79
COOPER, William Albert		2	79
COOPER, William Ferguson	P	5	36
COOTE, Alfred		4	37
COOTE, C		3	62
COOTE, Philip Stanley	P	2	79
COPE, Harry Fitzgerald	P	1	93
COPE, J		3	62
COPE, James		2	79
COPE, Michael William	P	1	93
COPE, William		2	79
COPELAND, Alfred	P	4	37
COPELAND, C F		2	79
COPELAND, F		3	62
COPELAND, Frank		2	79
COPELAND, Richard		5	36
COPELAND, Tom		1	93
COPELAND, William George		1	93
COPELAND, William John	P	1	93
COPLAND, Dudley Charles James		1	93
COPLAND, Leonard George		1	93
COPLAND, Maurice	P	1	93
COPLEY, John		2	79
COPPAGE, E		3	62
COPPEN, Edward G		2	79
COPPING, A		3	62
COPPING, James A		2	79
COPPINGER, Cyril Douglas	P	1	94
COPPINS, Hugh Joseph		1	94
COPPLESTONE, W E		3	62
COPSON, Ralph		4	37
CORBALLY, Louis William	P	1	94
CORBET, Sir Roland James	P	1	94
CORBETT, Dennis		2	79
CORBETT, Francis Alexander		3	62
CORBETT, G E		3	62
CORBETT, George		1	94
CORBETT, Gustave		4	37
CORBETT, Herbert Vincent		5	36
CORBETT, John Harold	P	5	37
CORBETT, Michael Patrick		1	94
CORBIN, Alonzo Joseph		1	94
CORBYN, Vernon Hector	P	1	94
CORCORAN, Patrick		2	79
CORCORAN, William		2	79
CORCORAN, William James	P	2	79

Name	Photo	Part No.	Page No.
CORCORAN, William Joseph		2	79
CORDELL, George		2	79
CORDELL, William		2	79
CORDEN, Arthur		2	79
CORDEN, Herbert Stennett		4	37
CORDER, Ernest		1	94
CORDER, Hugh Gerald Annerly	P	1	94
CORDERY, George		4	37
CORDIER, Albert		2	79
CORDIER, J		3	62
CORDINER, George Galloway		4	37
CORDINER, Harry Noble		4	37
CORDINER, Roy Grote	P	3	62
CORDNER, Alexander Allen	P	4	37
CORDOZO, G		2	79
CORDWELL, William Sam		1	94
COREN, Edward Walker	P	1	94
CORFIELD, Harry		1	94
CORFIELD, Hubert Vernon Anchitel		3	62
CORFIELD, James Edward	P	4	37
CORIN, Harold Edward	P	3	62
CORINGTON, Ernest	P	2	73
CORK, Edwin F		2	79
CORK, John Henry		1	94
CORK, John J		2	79
CORK, William Lovatt		5	37
CORKE, Arthur Noel	P	1	94
CORKE, Guy Harold		3	62
CORKE, Hubert William		3	63
CORKER, Edmund		2	79
CORKETT, William Frederick		2	79
CORKRAN, Reginald Seymour	P	1	94
CORLESS, John Stanley		5	37
CORLETT, William John	P	5	37
CORMACK, Alexander Sutherland		5	37
CORMACK, Hector		2	79
CORMACK, Hector Sutherland	P	4	37
CORMACK, J		3	63
CORMACK, John David		4	37
CORMACK, William		2	79
CORMAC-WALSHE, Edward Joseph	P	1	365
CORMICAN, Hugh Patrick		1	94
CORNBOROUGH, William		2	79
CORNELIUS, Cecil Victor Powell		2	79
CORNELIUS, P		3	63
CORNELIUS, Thomas Henry		2	79
CORNELL, Arthur John Henry		4	37
CORNELL, William		2	79
CORNER, Albert Just	P	1	94
CORNER, Otto Heinrich	P	1	95
CORNER, Stephen Henry	P	1	95
CORNFORD, Frederick Charles		5	37
CORNFORD, Walter Percy		4	37
CORNICK, Daniel		1	95
CORNISH, A		3	63
CORNISH, C A		3	63
CORNISH, Charles Lawson	P	1	95
CORNISH, Henry George William		1	95
CORNISH, John Edwin	P	2	80
CORNOCK, James		2	80
CORNWALL, Geoffrey		1	95
CORNWALL, Percy Henry		3	63
CORNWELL, Abijah		1	95
CORNWELL, James Hamlet		3	63
CORP, Nelson Bertram	P	4	37

Name	Photo	Part No.	Page No.	Name	Photo	Part No.	Page No.
COVER, Frank		1	97	COX, George		4	39
COVEY, Percy		2	81	COX, George E		2	82
COVILL, Cecil Ernest	P	5	38	COX, George Henry		2	82
COWAN, Alexander	P	5	38	COX, George Oswald		3	65
COWAN, Andrew		2	81	COX, George Pottinger	P	2	82
COWAN, Andrew Galbraith	P	1	97	COX, George William		2	82
COWAN, Douglas Henderson		2	81	COX, Harold Frank		4	39
COWAN, H		2	81	COX, Harry		1	97
COWAN, R		3	64	COX, Harry		5	38
COWAN, Robert Craig	P	1	97	COX, Horace Raymond		1	97
COWAN, Thomas		2	81	COX, Hubert Pomeroy	P	1	98
COWAN, William		2	81	COX, J		3	65
COWAN, William Hyslopp		2	81	COX, J H		3	65
COWARD, John Oswald (Joc)		5	38	COX, J J		3	65
COWARD, Leslie Graham	P	1	97	COX, James		2	82
COWDERY, William		5	38	COX, John		2	82
COWDRILL, Alfred Leonard		3	64	COX, Joseph Robert		2	82
COWELL, Claude		1	97	COX, Reginald John Ponsonby	P	2	82
COWELL, Norman Arthur	P	4	38	COX, Richard Arthur		1	98
COWELY, Sidney Francis		4	38	COX, S J		3	65
COWEN, Frederick A		2	81	COX, Swithin John		1	98
COWEN, Reginald Percival	P	2	81	COX, Sydney Douglas	P	1	98
COWIE, D		2	81	COX, Thomas		1	98
COWIE, John		3	64	COX, W		3	65
COWIE, W		3	64	COX, Walter		1	98
COWIE, William		5	38	COX, William		3	65
COWIE, William H		4	38	COX, William George		1	98
COWIESON, Robert Cruickshanks		5	38	COX, William George		2	82
COWLEY, F W		3	64	COX, William Henry		3	65
COWLEY, James		1	97	COXE, Arthur Nelson		2	82
COWLEY, James		2	81	COXHEAD, Guy Templeton		1	98
COWLEY, T		3	64	COXHEAD, Maurice Edward	P	3	65
COWLING, Paul		4	38	COXON, A G		3	65
COWLING, Walter Sidney	P	1	97	COXON, T		3	65
COWLISHAW, William Forster	P	5	38	COXWELL, William Stewart Gordon	P	5	39
COWNIE, D		3	64	COXWELL-ROGERS, Richard Hugh		1	311
COWNIE, John Burnett	P	1	97	COY, C T		3	65
COWNIE, Stanley George	P	3	64	COY, William John	P	4	39
COWPE, George Bleazard		3	64	COYLE, E		3	65
COWPER, Alexander		3	65	COYLE, J		3	65
COWPER, Alexander Ayre		5	38	COYLE, James		1	98
COWPER, Gordon		5	38	COYLE, P		3	65
COWPER, William Pearson		5	38	COYNE, J		3	65
COX, A J		2	82	COYNE, James		1	98
COX, A W		3	65	COYNE, Sidney Thomas		2	82
COX, Alan Edward George	P	1	97	COZENS, Leslie	P	2	82
COX, Albert		2	82	COZENS-BROOKE, John Gilbert Somerset		2	41
COX, Alwyne		2	82	CRABB, James		2	82
COX, Anthony		1	97	CRABTREE, William	P	1	98
COX, B		3	65	CRACKNELL, C		3	65
COX, C J		3	65	CRACKNELL, Frederick		1	98
COX, Charles		1	97	CRADOCK, George John		4	39
COX, Charles Albine		1	97	CRADOCK, Sir Christopher George Francis Maurice	P	1	98
COX, E		2	82				
COX, Edward		4	38	CRAGG, Geoffrey Ethelbert	P	1	99
COX, Edward James		2	82	CRAGG, Noel Henry	P	2	82
COX, Ernest Edward		4	38	CRAGGS, Thomas Walter		2	82
COX, Ernest Wilkin	P	1	97	CRAIG, Alexander		4	39
COX, F J		3	65	CRAIG, James		3	65
COX, Francis Thomas		1	97	CRAIG, John	P	3	65
COX, Francis William		1	97	CRAIG, T		3	65
COX, Frederick Henry		2	82	CRAIGIE, William George Smeaton	P	2	83
COX, Frederick John		2	82	CRAIK, James Gordon		4	39
COX, Frederick Ratcliffe		3	65	CRAIKE-PICKERING, Maurice Stanley Craike		4	157
COX, George		2	82	CRAM, C		3	65

Name	Photo	Part No.	Page No.
CRAMB, Robert		4	39
CRAME, Charles James	P	4	39
CRAMER ROBERTS, Walter Evelyn		5	143
CRAMP, E W		3	65
CRAMP, H W		3	65
CRAMPTON, Charles Theodore		1	99
CRAN, Alexander		5	39
CRAN, Ernest		3	65
CRAN, George Alfred Merson		5	39
CRAN, James Alexander		4	39
CRANE, A		3	65
CRANE, Charles Edward	P	1	99
CRANE, Frederick William	P	5	39
CRANE, George William David		3	65
CRANE, Sidney Arthur		4	39
CRANE, Thomas John		2	83
CRANE, William Henry	P	5	39
CRANEFIELD, Reginald Thomas	P	3	66
CRANK, John		5	39
CRANK, John Victor		5	39
CRANNEY, J		3	66
CRANSTON, Percival		2	83
CRANSTON, William Weir	P	4	39
CRAPPER, Thomas A		5	39
CRASCALL, Coulson Henry		1	99
CRASKE, Leslie Donald		4	39
CRASKE, W E		3	66
CRATHORNE, Frederick	P	5	39
CRAVEN, Edward		1	99
CRAVEN, G		3	66
CRAVEN, Thomas		1	99
CRAVEN, Thomas		1	99
CRAVEN, Thomas Berkley		4	39
CRAWFORD, Alexander Pratt		1	99
CRAWFORD, Charles Noel		3	66
CRAWFORD, D		2	83
CRAWFORD, Edward	P	1	99
CRAWFORD, George Bradford		2	83
CRAWFORD, H P		3	66
CRAWFORD, Hugh		1	99
CRAWFORD, J		3	66
CRAWFORD, Joseph		2	83
CRAWFORD, Richard Gilpin	P	1	99
CRAWFORD, Sydney George		5	39
CRAWFORD, Thomas		2	83
CRAWFORD, William John	P	1	99
CRAWHALL, Fritz Portmore		1	99
CRAWLEY, Arthur Edward		1	99
CRAWLEY, Eustace		2	83
CRAWLEY, Harold		1	100
CRAWLEY, Herbert Francis		3	66
CRAWLEY, James		1	100
CRAWLEY-BOEVEY, Edward Martin	P	1	40
CRAWSHAY, Mervyn		2	83
CRAYFORD, Victor		1	100
CRAYTON, J		3	66
CREAGH, Aubrey Osborne		1	100
CREAGH, Leo		2	83
CREAGH, O'moore Charles	P	4	39
CREAN, Theodore		1	100
CREASER, Walter		1	100
CREASEY, A S		3	66
CREASEY, Albert Edward		4	39
CREASEY, C		3	66
CREBER, Richard William		4	39

Name	Photo	Part No.	Page No.
CREE, William Cecil Holt		2	83
CREED, Frank		2	83
CREES, Ernest James		1	100
CREEVY, J		2	83
CREFIN, J		3	66
CREFT, George Tombeur	P	5	39
CREIGHTON, Robert		1	100
CRELLIN, William		2	83
CRELLIN, William Anderson Watson	P	5	39
CREMER, C		3	66
CRERAR, James		2	83
CRESSWELL, Arthur Edgcumbe		4	40
CRESSWELL, Edward Arthur	P	2	83
CRESSWELL, Ernest Alan	P	1	100
CRESSWELL, Francis Joseph		2	83
CRESSWELL, Frank		3	66
CRESSWELL, Herbert		4	40
CRESSWELL, John Leslie		1	100
CRESWELL, John Lancashire		3	66
CRESWELL, S		3	66
CREW, William Thomas		1	100
CREWS, William Henry		4	40
CRIBBES, John		5	40
CRICHTON, Gerald Edgecumbe		1	100
CRICHTON, Henry William Crichton	P	2	84
CRICHTON, Herbert Clowe		3	66
CRICHTON, Hubert Francis	P	1	100
CRICHTON, James	P	4	40
CRICHTON, John Stewart	P	2	84
CRICHTON, Joseph Michael Smith	P	1	100
CRICHTON-BROWNE, Cecil Harold Verdin	P	5	23
CRICHTON-STUART, Lord Ninian Edward	P	2	288
CRICK, George		2	84
CRICKITT, Cyril Granolt		4	40
CRIDDLE, Arthur Clarence		5	40
CRIDLAND, S		3	66
CRIGGIE, James		3	66
CRIGHTON, John	P	2	84
CRIGHTON, William Robertson		3	66
CRIPPIN, Harry William		3	66
CRIPPS, Ernest Arthur		4	40
CRIPPS, George		1	100
CRIPPS, Spencer Harry	P	1	100
CRISELL, W		3	66
CRISP, James Frederick		1	100
CRISP, Robert John		4	40
CRISP, Walter	P	2	84
CRISPIN, Hugh Trevor		2	84
CRISPIN, Thomas	P	2	85
CRISPIN, William	P	2	85
CRITCHER, Albert		1	100
CRITCHLEY, F B		3	66
CRITCHLEY, George Edgar	P	5	40
CRITCHLEY, Sidney Herbert		1	100
CRITCHLOW, S		3	66
CRITTENDEN, James Thomas		4	40
CRITTLE, Alfred Bertram	P	3	66
CROAD, George Charles		4	40
CROAD, Percy		4	40
CROCK, Thomas		1	100
CROCKER, A		3	66
CROCKER, Albert		2	85
CROCKER, Frederick Cyril	P	1	100
CROCKER, H		3	66
CROCKER, Henry T		2	85

Name	Photo	Part No.	Page No.
CROCKER, Otto		2	85
CROCKER, Samuel John		2	85
CROCKET, John		2	85
CROCKETT, M		3	66
CROCKETT, William David		2	85
CROCKFORD, Charles		1	100
CROCKFORD, L		3	66
CROFT, A		3	66
CROFT, Cyril Talbot Burney	P	2	85
CROFT, George Frederick		2	85
CROFT, John Frederick Manners		2	85
CROFT, Leslie Robert		2	85
CROFT, R		3	66
CROFT, Robert		2	85
CROFTON, Charles Woodward	P	1	100
CROFTON, Edward Vivian Morgan	P	3	67
CROFTON, Nora Norris		5	40
CROFTS, Edward Penn		4	40
CROLL, Charles		3	67
CROLL, David B		2	85
CROMAN, Arthur Birkett		5	40
CROMAN, William James		5	40
CROMB, David Rankin		3	67
CROMBIE, Alexander		2	85
CROMBIE, John Eugene		3	67
CROMBIE, William		3	67
CROMIE, Mourice Francis	P	1	101
CROMPTON, Harry Dent	P	4	40
CROMPTON, N		4	40
CROMPTON, Nigel George	P	2	85
CROMPTON, R		4	40
CRONK, Friend		1	101
CRONK, William Guy	P	1	101
CRONSHAW, J		3	67
CROOCKEWIT, Alexander Edward		4	40
CROOK, Albert Edward		3	67
CROOK, Albert George		1	101
CROOK, Albert William		5	40
CROOK, H		3	67
CROOK, Herbert		4	40
CROOK, Joseph		1	101
CROOK, Philip Joseph	P	4	40
CROOKE, Charles Croydon		5	40
CROOKE, Reginald Arthur	P	2	85
CROOKE, Walter		4	40
CROOME, Frederick George		2	86
CROOME, James		2	86
CROOM-JOHNSON, Brian	P	1	207
CROOTE, Walter Edwin	P	2	86
CROPPER, Alexander		3	67
CROSBIE, Charles		2	86
CROSBIE, Peter		2	86
CROSBIE, William James		2	86
CROSBY, John Clifford	P	1	101
CROSBY, John Metcalfe	P	3	67
CROSBY, Samuel		3	67
CROSHAW, Frank Herbert	P	3	67
CROSLAND, John Henry		1	101
CROSLAND, Trevor Allington	P	3	67
CROSLEY, Cecil	P	1	101
CROSS, Arthur Moulton		4	40
CROSS, Daniel		1	101
CROSS, David Ronald	P	1	101
CROSS, E F		3	68
CROSS, Edward Kenneth Leslie	P	3	68

Name	Photo	Part No.	Page No.
CROSS, Edwin		1	101
CROSS, George Ernest		5	40
CROSS, J		3	68
CROSS, J H		3	68
CROSS, Reginald Carlton	P	4	41
CROSS, T		3	68
CROSS, Thomas		2	86
CROSS, Thomas Edward Kynaston	P	3	68
CROSS, W		3	68
CROSS, William		4	41
CROSS, William Charles		1	101
CROSSFIELD, Wilfred		2	86
CROSSIN, Edward		1	101
CROSSLAND, Thomas		4	41
CROSSLEY, Arthur Sidney		4	41
CROSSLEY, Joseph William		3	68
CROSSMAN, Guy Danvers Mainwaring		3	68
CROSSMAN, R G		3	68
CROSSMAN, William Ronald Morley		2	86
CROSSON, W		3	68
CROUCH, A		3	68
CROUCH, Arthur Stanley	P	5	40
CROUCH, Arthur Walter		2	86
CROUCH, Charles		2	86
CROUCH, John Ady		4	41
CROUCH, John William		1	101
CROUCH, Lionel William		3	68
CROUCH, P		3	68
CROUCH, Percy J		2	86
CROUCHER, James F	P	3	68
CROUCHER, William		2	86
CROUSAZ, Cecil Francis	P	1	101
CROW, F		3	68
CROW, James		2	86
CROW, John Logan		2	86
CROWDER, Robert Ashley	P	4	41
CROWE, Albert Edward	P	2	86
CROWE, S		3	68
CROWE, William Maynard Carlisle		2	86
CROWHURST, J T		3	68
CROWHURST, S T		5	40
CROWLEY, Daniel		2	86
CROWLEY, P		3	68
CROWLEY, R		2	86
CROWLEY, Ralph Edwin		4	41
CROWTHER, George		5	40
CROWTHER, Lelsie Taylor	P	1	102
CROWTHER, Philip Townsend	P	3	68
CROWTHER, S N		3	69
CROWTHER, William Osborne		3	69
CROXSON, Henry Thomas	P	1	102
CROYSDALE, Marjorie		5	40
CROZIER, James Cyril Baptist	P	1	102
CROZIER, William		4	41
CROZIER, William Kerr		1	102
CRUDDAS, Sandwith George Peter		2	86
CRUICKSHANK, Andrew John Tuke		5	40
CRUICKSHANK, Donald Edward		5	40
CRUICKSHANK, E O		2	86
CRUICKSHANK, George		4	41
CRUICKSHANK, James		3	69
CRUICKSHANK, James	P	5	41
CRUICKSHANK, John Lawson	P	3	69
CRUICKSHANK, Kenneth George	P	3	69
CRUICKSHANK, Raymond Alfred	P	5	41

Name	Photo	Part No.	Page No.
CURTIS, Roy Barnett	P	1	103
CURTIS, S H		3	71
CURTIS, T		3	71
CURTIS, W		3	71
CURTIS, W H		3	71
CURTIS, Walter		1	103
CURTIS, Walter Arthur	P	1	103
CURTIS, William		2	89
CURTIS, William		2	89
CURTIS, William F		2	89
CURTIS-BEALS, Harry	P	4	10
CURTLER, Frederick Gwatkin		2	89
CURWEN, F G		2	89
CURWEN, Wilton		2	89
CUSACK, Eric Athanasius	P	1	103
CUSHION, Alfred Joseph		5	42
CUSSELL, Sidney William		1	103
CUSSEN, Robert		2	89
CUTFIELD, Harold		1	103
CUTHBERT, Charles Lamond		2	89
CUTHBERT, G		2	89
CUTHBERT, George Charles Prawl	P	3	71
CUTHBERT, James Harold		2	89
CUTHBERT, Robert Lancelot	P	2	90
CUTHBERTSON, Alexander		2	90
CUTHBERTSON, Allan Scott	P	4	42
CUTHBERTSON, G		2	90
CUTHBERTSON, Norman William		1	104
CUTHBERTSON, Samuel		2	90
CUTHBERTSON, Thomas	P	1	104
CUTHELL, Algernon Hubert	P	2	90
CUTLER, Charles Edwin	P	3	71
CUTLER, E H		2	90
CUTLER, Harold Arthur		5	42
CUTLER, T W		3	71
CUTLER, Walter		2	90
CUTLER, William Charles		1	104
CUTTER, G		3	71
CUTTER, Thomas		2	90
CUTTRIDGE, David William		1	166
CUTTRISS, J		3	71
CUTTS, Arthur H		2	90
CUTTS, James		2	90
CUTTS, Percival Charles	P	4	42
CUTTS, W		3	71
CUTTS, William Thomas		2	90
DABATE, D		2	90
DABNER, Robert		1	104
DABORN, Albert Benjamin		2	90
DABORN, Horace John		2	90
DACE, John		2	90
DACK, Charles E		2	90
DACK, Frank		2	90
DACRE, William R		2	90
DADD, Edmund Hilton	P	2	90
DADD, Reginald John		4	42
DADD, Stephen Gabriel	P	1	104
DADE, William		1	104
DADSON, Frederick		1	104
DADSON, J W		4	42
DADSWELL, Jonathan Charles		2	90
DADY, Henry		1	104
DAFT, H		3	71
DAGG, M		3	71
DAGLISH, Thomas Reuben		1	104
DAGMAR, Harry E		2	90
DAILY, Frank		2	90
DAINES, Horace William		1	104
DALBY, Herbert Charles	P	2	90
DALBY, M J		3	71
DALBY, Richard Alfred	P	2	90
DALE, C		3	71
DALE, D		3	71
DALE, F		2	90
DALE, Francis William		2	90
DALE, Frederick Edward		1	104
DALE, Harry		1	104
DALE, James William		1	104
DALE, John Cecil		1	104
DALE, Thomas M		2	90
DALE, Wellington Trevelyan	P	1	104
DALE, William Henry	P	2	90
DALE, William Percy		2	91
DALEY, Herbert		1	104
DALEY, Jeremiah		2	91
DALEY, Michael	P	1	104
DALEY, Michael	P	2	91
DALEY, William		1	104
DALEY, William		2	91
DALGARNO, Eric George		4	42
DALGETTY, Richard		2	91
DALGLIESH, Thomas Chalmers		2	91
DALGLISH, Alexander	P	2	91
DALGLISH, Charles Antoine De Guerry		1	104
DALL, John	P	5	42
DALLAS, Alexander		1	104
DALLAS, J		2	91
DALLAS, James Hunter		5	42
DALLY, William Henry		1	104
DALMAHOY, John Francis Cecil	P	1	104
DALOY, Michael		4	42
DALTON, Charles		2	91
DALTON, Charles		2	91
DALTON, Ernest		2	91
DALTON, Percy Nugent	P	3	71
DALTON, William Henry	P	1	105
D'ALTON, Charles Edward	P	2	91
D'ALTON, Henry St. Eloy	P	2	91
DALY, Alexander		4	42
DALY, Ernest Robert		2	91
DALY, Francis	P	1	105
DALY, J		3	71
DALY, John		2	91
DALY, Joshua	P	3	71
DALY, Robert Thompson	P	3	71
DALY, William Cecil Thomas	P	2	92
DALZIEL, Walter		3	71
DAMES, James William	P	1	105
DAMMS, A		2	92
DAMMS, William		5	42
DAMPIER, J		3	71
DANCE, H		3	71
DANCKWERTS, Richard William		2	92
DANCOCKS, W		3	71
DANCY, Ellis Albert		3	71
DANCY, Harold Valentine		4	42
DANCY, William Henry		2	92
DANDY, John		5	42
DANIEL, Alfred Austen	P	1	105
DANIEL, William		2	92

Name	Photo	Part No.	Page No.
DANIELL, Archibald Steuart Lindsey		2	92
DANIELL, Edward Henry Edwin		2	92
DANIELL, George Francis Blackburne	P	3	71
DANIELLS, Reginald		4	42
DANIELS, Arthur Edward		3	71
DANIELS, D		3	71
DANIELS, Ernest		1	105
DANIELS, George	P	4	42
DANIELS, George Reginald		4	43
DANIELS, Gilbert Joseph		5	42
DANIELS, Henry		2	92
DANIELS, James		1	105
DANIELS, John		1	105
DANIELS, John Albert		1	105
DANIELS, R		3	71
DANIELS, William		2	92
DANIELS, William Alfred		2	92
DANN, David George	P	1	105
DANN, Francis Joseph		1	105
DANN, H A		3	71
DANN, William James		2	92
DANSON, Francis Rudolf	P	2	92
DARBY, C		3	72
DARBY, Frederick		2	92
DARBY, Maurice Alfred Alexander	P	1	105
DARBY, Peter		3	72
DARBY, Reginald Montague		2	92
DARBY, Robert W		2	92
DARCHE, August Raoul	P	1	105
D'ARCY, J		2	92
D'ARCY-IRVINE, Charles William		2	179
DARGIE, James Paterson	P	2	92
DARGO, D		2	92
DARGUE, Edwin		5	42
DARLEY, Arthur Tudor	P	1	105
DARLEY, Arthur Tudor	P	5	42
DARLEY, Desmond John		3	72
DARLEY, John Evelyn Carmichael	P	5	42
DARLEY, W		3	72
DARLING, Albert Edward		5	43
DARLING, Claud Henry Wish		2	92
DARLING, Thomas		5	43
DARLING, William Joseph		5	43
DARLING, William Oliver Fortescue		2	92
DARLINGTON, George		2	92
DARNELL, Aubrey Hugh		5	43
DARNELL, R		3	72
DARNELL, William		1	105
DARNELL, William Henry		1	105
DARNILL, William Alfred	P	1	106
DARRINGTON, Harold Edgar		4	43
DARROCH, Alexander		1	106
DARROCH, James		2	92
DARROCH, James		3	72
DART, George William		1	106
DART, Goronwy Kinsey		3	72
DART, J		2	92
DART, Leslie West		2	92
DARTNALL, James C		2	92
DARTNELL, William Thomas		2	92
DARTON, Henry Theodore		1	106
DARTY, Edward		1	106
DARWELL, Claude Randall	P	2	93
DARWIN, Erasmus	P	1	106
DASH, Frederick John		1	106
DASHWOOD, Claude Burrard Lewes	P	2	93
DASHWOOD, Frank Leopold	P	1	106
DASKEL, A		2	93
DASTON, A		2	93
DAUBENY, Charles John Odinel		3	72
DAUBER, John Henry	P	2	93
DAUBERT, A		2	93
DAUGHTREY, John	P	2	93
DAUN, Edward Charles	P	1	106
DAVENPORT, Eli		3	72
DAVENPORT, Fred	P	3	72
DAVENPORT, P		3	72
DAVEY, Arthur		3	72
DAVEY, Arthur John		1	106
DAVEY, George W		2	93
DAVEY, H		3	72
DAVEY, Henry Thomas		2	93
DAVEY, John James		5	43
DAVEY, John Stanley		2	93
DAVEY, Sidney		5	43
DAVEY, T		3	72
DAVEY, W		3	72
DAVEY, William Alfred George	P	1	106
DAVID, Charlie		1	106
DAVID, George William Kent	P	2	93
DAVID, James Stanley		1	106
DAVID, Thomas William		5	43
DAVIDSON, Alexander	P	2	93
DAVIDSON, Alexander B		5	43
DAVIDSON, Alexander Bissett	P	1	106
DAVIDSON, Alexander Murray Stuart		1	106
DAVIDSON, Alfred James		3	72
DAVIDSON, Archibald		3	72
DAVIDSON, Arthur Robert		4	43
DAVIDSON, C		3	72
DAVIDSON, Christopher Edmund Grant	P	2	93
DAVIDSON, David		2	94
DAVIDSON, Donald		4	43
DAVIDSON, Douglas Byres		2	94
DAVIDSON, Duncan Hamlyn	P	1	107
DAVIDSON, George		3	72
DAVIDSON, George Maitland	P	4	43
DAVIDSON, Henry		3	72
DAVIDSON, J		2	94
DAVIDSON, J		2	94
DAVIDSON, J		3	72
DAVIDSON, James		1	107
DAVIDSON, James		2	94
DAVIDSON, James Reid		2	94
DAVIDSON, James Stevenson	P	3	72
DAVIDSON, John Glennie		4	43
DAVIDSON, John Henry		1	107
DAVIDSON, Malcolm		2	94
DAVIDSON, Peter Ferries		3	72
DAVIDSON, Ralph Ivan Meynell		2	94
DAVIDSON, Robert		3	72
DAVIDSON, Thomas Blackburn	P	2	94
DAVIDSON, Thomas Cumming		2	94
DAVIDSON, Thomas Hall		2	94
DAVIDSON, William		1	107
DAVIDSON, William		5	43
DAVIDSON, William Leslie	P	1	107
DAVIDSON, William Thomas Chorley		2	94
DAVIDSON-HOUSTON, Charles Elrington Duncan	P	2	173

Name	Photo	Part No.	Page No.
DAVIE, Frank		3	72
DAVIE, Thomas Mckeddie	P	4	43
DAVIES, Albert		1	107
DAVIES, Alfred		3	72
DAVIES, Amos	P	3	73
DAVIES, Arthur	P	1	107
DAVIES, Arthur Cyril Richards		2	94
DAVIES, Arthur Thomas		2	94
DAVIES, Charles		1	107
DAVIES, Charlie Richard		5	43
DAVIES, D		3	73
DAVIES, David	P	2	94
DAVIES, David Ethelston	P	3	73
DAVIES, David Henry		3	73
DAVIES, Edmund Percival Barrett		3	73
DAVIES, Edward		4	43
DAVIES, Emlyn Holt	P	4	43
DAVIES, Ernest Wilberforce		2	94
DAVIES, F W		3	73
DAVIES, Fairfax Llewellyn	P	3	73
DAVIES, Frederick Ernest		1	107
DAVIES, Frederick George		3	73
DAVIES, Frederick Owen		3	73
DAVIES, Garibaldi William		3	73
DAVIES, Garnet E		2	94
DAVIES, George		1	107
DAVIES, George Herbert		2	94
DAVIES, George Richard		5	43
DAVIES, George Roland		1	107
DAVIES, George William	P	1	107
DAVIES, H		3	73
DAVIES, Harold		1	107
DAVIES, Harold Casamajor		2	94
DAVIES, Harold Harper		3	73
DAVIES, Harry Llanover		2	94
DAVIES, Henry Robert Griffith		2	95
DAVIES, Hubert Charles		3	73
DAVIES, Hugh		3	73
DAVIES, Isaac		1	107
DAVIES, J		3	73
DAVIES, Jack Tyssil		3	73
DAVIES, James		1	107
DAVIES, John		3	74
DAVIES, John Eric	P	2	95
DAVIES, John Henry	P	2	95
DAVIES, John Henry		5	43
DAVIES, John Rhys	P	3	74
DAVIES, John Robert		1	107
DAVIES, Joseph Ithel Jehu	P	5	43
DAVIES, Kenneth George		3	74
DAVIES, Leonard	P	3	74
DAVIES, Levi		3	74
DAVIES, Llewellyn Crighton		4	43
DAVIES, Norman Burton		5	43
DAVIES, Percy Hier		5	43
DAVIES, R		3	74
DAVIES, Rhys Beynon		3	74
DAVIES, Richard	P	1	107
DAVIES, Sydney		5	43
DAVIES, T E		5	43
DAVIES, Thomas Reginald	P	3	74
DAVIES, Trevor		4	43
DAVIES, W C		2	95
DAVIES, Walter Llewelyn		3	74
DAVIES, William		2	95
DAVIES, William		3	74
DAVIES, William Arthur		5	43
DAVIES, William David		4	43
DAVIES, William Hopkin	P	3	74
DAVIES, William Joseph		5	44
DAVIES, William Lloyd		5	44
DAVILL, Percy Henry		1	106
DAVIN, William Maurice		4	43
DAVIS, Albert Henry		1	107
DAVIS, Albert Henry Ezra		3	74
DAVIS, Alfred		2	95
DAVIS, Alistair Ingram	P	5	44
DAVIS, Arthur Albion		1	107
DAVIS, Arthur Harris	P	5	44
DAVIS, Bernard Samuel	P	4	43
DAVIS, Cecil		2	95
DAVIS, Charles William		1	107
DAVIS, Edward John		5	44
DAVIS, Edward Samuel		1	107
DAVIS, Ernest George Frank		1	107
DAVIS, F		3	74
DAVIS, Frederick Joseph		3	74
DAVIS, George		2	95
DAVIS, George David		1	107
DAVIS, George Henry		4	44
DAVIS, George Makins		5	44
DAVIS, H		3	74
DAVIS, H		3	75
DAVIS, H R		2	95
DAVIS, Harold Charles	P	3	75
DAVIS, Harold Charles		4	44
DAVIS, Harold Eborall		4	44
DAVIS, Henry Ouseley		2	95
DAVIS, Henry William Warren	P	1	108
DAVIS, Howard	P	2	95
DAVIS, J		3	75
DAVIS, J A		2	95
DAVIS, J D		2	95
DAVIS, James		2	95
DAVIS, James		2	95
DAVIS, James		2	95
DAVIS, John		2	95
DAVIS, John		2	95
DAVIS, John Joseph		5	44
DAVIS, John North		5	44
DAVIS, Reginald William		1	108
DAVIS, Richard Arthur		5	44
DAVIS, Robert Emmanuel		3	75
DAVIS, Sidney James		1	108
DAVIS, Stanley		2	95
DAVIS, Stanley Wilberforce		4	44
DAVIS, Thomas		2	95
DAVIS, Vyvyan Oswald		5	44
DAVIS, W		3	75
DAVIS, William		2	95
DAVIS, William		2	95
DAVIS, William		5	44
DAVIS, William Rhys Lancelot	P	3	75
DAVISON, Charles Frederick		1	108
DAVISON, Charles George		1	108
DAVISON, Charles Henry George (Alias Charles Henry Pettman)		1	108
DAVISON, Edmund		3	75
DAVISON, F		3	75
DAVISON, George William		3	75

Name	Photo	Part No.	Page No.
DAVISON, George William		3	75
DAVISON, Harry		1	108
DAVISON, John Lilburne		3	75
DAVISON, Stuart		2	95
DAVISON, William		2	95
DAVISON, William Hope		3	75
DAVY, George Henry		1	108
DAW, Thomas		2	95
DAWBARN, William	P	5	44
DAWDRY, Thomas		1	108
DAWE, Frederick G		2	95
DAWES, Albert		1	108
DAWES, Frank		2	95
DAWES, Harold Henry	P	4	44
DAWES, Henry		2	95
DAWES, Oswald Stephen Bernard	P	3	75
DAWES, Robert		2	95
DAWES, Walter Richard Augustus Aston		2	95
DAWKIN, John		5	44
DAWKINS, Alfred		1	108
DAWKINS, Charles John Randle	P	1	108
DAWNAY, The Hon. Hugh		2	95
DAWSON, Albert George		1	108
DAWSON, Allan	P	3	75
DAWSON, Bernard G		2	95
DAWSON, Eric Lawrence		3	76
DAWSON, Harry		4	44
DAWSON, Henry Beal	P	1	108
DAWSON, Herbert Edward		2	95
DAWSON, Hubert	P	3	76
DAWSON, James		5	45
DAWSON, John		2	95
DAWSON, John		4	44
DAWSON, John Edwin		4	44
DAWSON, John Henry		5	45
DAWSON, John Thomas Gibson		1	108
DAWSON, Richard Long		2	95
DAWSON, Sydney Herbert		3	76
DAWSON, W		2	96
DAWSON, W		3	76
DAWSON, W		3	76
DAWSON, Wilfred Yelverton	P	1	108
DAWSON, William Ernest	P	5	45
DAWSON, William Robert Aufrere	P	5	45
DAWSON-SCOTT, John Kearsley	P	1	321
DAWTRY, W H		3	76
DAY, Albert Eustace	P	2	96
DAY, Arnold Ellis	P	1	108
DAY, Arthur George		5	45
DAY, Aubrey Oliver Fisher		1	108
DAY, Calvin Wellington	P	2	96
DAY, Charles		1	108
DAY, Charles Frederick		1	108
DAY, Charles Frederick		1	108
DAY, Charles George	P	1	108
DAY, Dennis Ivor	P	2	96
DAY, Ernest		2	96
DAY, Francis Innes		2	96
DAY, Frederick William		2	96
DAY, George		2	96
DAY, George		2	96
DAY, Harry		5	45
DAY, Henry		2	96
DAY, Henry John		1	108
DAY, Hubert Victor		3	76
DAY, J H Y		3	76
DAY, John		2	96
DAY, John		5	45
DAY, John Charles Sigismund	P	4	44
DAY, John Edward	P	3	76
DAY, John Henry		2	96
DAY, John Victor	P	1	108
DAY, John William		1	108
DAY, Joseph		2	96
DAY, Joseph		2	96
DAY, Maurice Charles	P	1	109
DAY, O G		3	76
DAY, Owen Heathcote Lacy	P	2	96
DAY, Percy		2	96
DAY, Reginald Charles William		1	109
DAY, Robert		2	96
DAY, Sydney A		2	96
DAY, Thomas		1	109
DAY, W		2	96
DAY, W		3	76
DAY, William		2	96
DAY, William		2	96
DAYMAN, William		5	45
DAYSH, Frederick Arthur George		1	109
DAYSH, William		5	45
DAYSON, Arthur Stanley		3	76
DE BURIATTE, John Philip	P	1	61
DE CALRY, Valerio Awly Magawly Cerati		5	46
DE CANN, Harold John		3	77
DE CASTRO, James Vivien Reynell	P	2	62
DE COURCY, Henry Joseph	P	3	64
DE COURCY-WILLIAMS, Almericus John Falkiner (Eric)	P	1	380
DE FONTAINE, Edward Harold		2	121
DE HOGHTON, Vere	P	2	98
DE JONGH, Frank	P	1	210
DE LATTRE, Reginald		4	45
DE PASS, Frank Alexander		2	98
DE PRET-ROOSE DE CALESBERG, Gaston	P	4	25
DE ROUGEMONT, Maurice Henry	P	1	314
DE STACPOOLE, Robert Andrew		2	282
DE STACPOOLE, Roderick Algernon Antony		2	282
DE STE.CROIX, Wilfred Hungerford	P	3	239
DE TRAFFORD, Henry Joseph	P	2	99
DE TUYLL, Baron Maurice Arthur	P	1	357
DE VAUX LAW, Cecil Robert	P	3	170
DE VERE BEAUCLERK, Nevill	P	1	26
DE VINE, Clayton Howard		3	78
DE VOY, James Wilson		1	112
DE WEND, Douglas Fenton		2	99
DE WINTON, Walter	P	1	112
DEACON, Charles		4	44
DEACON, Jack Mervyn	P	2	96
DEACON, John Henry		5	45
DEACON, Stanley Douglas		1	109
DEACON, T		3	76
DEACON, William George		2	96
DEACON, William James		1	109
DEADMAN, Charles		2	96
DEADMAN, Charles William	P	1	109
DEADMAN, E T		3	76
DEAKIN, Albert Ernest		4	44
DEAKIN, William Nicholas	P	5	45
DEAN, Albert Henry		1	109
DEAN, Alexander	P	4	44

Name	Photo	Part No.	Page No.
DEAN, Alfred		2	96
DEAN, Charles Alfred		1	109
DEAN, Charles Henry		3	76
DEAN, Cyril Edward Brietzcke	P	2	97
DEAN, Frank		2	97
DEAN, George		2	97
DEAN, Henry Edgar		3	76
DEAN, Horace Edgar		1	109
DEAN, J H		3	76
DEAN, Michael		2	97
DEAN, S		3	76
DEAN, William	P	5	45
DEAN, William Hugh		1	109
DEANE, Arthur Harold	P	3	76
DEANE, Bernard Reginald John		2	97
DEANE, Denis		2	97
DEANE, Ernest Cotton	P	2	97
DEANE, George Frederic Field	P	3	76
DEANE, Michael		2	97
DEANE, Thomas Henry James		3	76
DEANS, Albert Cecil	P	2	97
DEANS, John Ewart		5	45
DEANS, William		3	76
DEAR, Elias		2	97
DEAR, John		1	109
DEAR, Walter John		2	97
DEARDEN, Frederick		2	97
DEARDEN, Herbert		1	109
DEARIE, Richard		2	97
DEARING, H		3	76
DEARLOVE, A		3	76
DEARMAN, Thomas William		2	97
DEARMER, Christopher	P	2	97
DEARNALEY, Irvine	P	2	97
DEARNESS, Thomas Rarity		5	45
DEASE, Maurice James	P	1	109
DEATH, W A		3	77
DEBENHAM, Herbert	P	2	98
DEED, John Cyril	P	1	109
DEEGAN, John		2	98
DEELEY, George Thomas		3	77
DEELEY, H W		3	77
DEELEY, William John		4	44
DEEPLEY, James		2	98
DEEPROSE, William		2	98
DEERY, P		3	77
DEGNAN, J		3	77
DEIGHTON, Frederick Hamilton	P	1	109
DELAMAIN, Henry Creswell	P	1	110
DELAMERE, Harry Gilland		4	44
DELAN, E L		3	77
DELANEY, Ernest	P	1	110
DELANEY, J		3	77
DELANEY, Michael		2	98
DELANEY, P		3	77
DELANEY, William		4	44
DELAY, D		3	77
DELEPINE, Helenus George Sheridan	P	1	110
DELEVANTE, M		3	77
DELL, W T		3	77
DELLER, Harry George		1	110
DELMAR-WILLIAMSON, George Frederick		4	238
DELMEGE, Claude Philippe	P	1	110
DELMEGE, James O'grady	P	1	110
DELPLANQUE, C		3	77

Name	Photo	Part No.	Page No.
DELVES, Samuel Henry		3	77
DEMELLWEEK, Joseph James		3	77
DEMINAWAY, Archibald		5	46
DEMPSEY, David		2	98
DEMPSTER, Edwin Alleyn		5	46
DEMPSTER, Gilbert Green	P	3	77
DEMPSTER, James Dean		3	77
DEMPSTER, John		4	45
DEMPSTER, Robert Heaford		5	46
DEMPSTER, William Stratton		4	45
DENARD, Joseph		4	45
DENHAM, A		2	98
DENHAM, Fred		1	110
DENHAM, William	P	1	110
DENHOLM, Alexander		2	98
DENHOLM, Robert Miller	P	3	77
DENISON, Bertram Noel	P	1	110
DENISON, William Frank Evelyn		4	45
DENMAN, Clarence Benjamin		1	111
DENNAN, Frederick Mason		2	98
DENNER, Frederick		5	46
DENNETT, Stephen Hepworth		5	46
DENNETT, Walter		2	98
DENNIFF, Thomas		2	98
DENNING, John Edward Newdigate Poyntz		3	77
DENNIS, Charles		2	98
DENNIS, Clarence Francis Victor		1	111
DENNIS, Edward	P	4	45
DENNIS, Edward Henry		1	111
DENNIS, Ernest J		2	98
DENNIS, Ernest W		2	98
DENNIS, George Ernest		2	98
DENNIS, James Owen Cunningham		2	98
DENNIS, John		2	98
DENNIS, John Edmund William		3	77
DENNIS, L		3	77
DENNIS, Richard		2	98
DENNIS, Richard Henry	P	1	111
DENNIS, Russell		1	111
DENNIS, Thomas Albert		2	98
DENNIS, Thomas H		2	98
DENNIS, Thomas Ralph		2	98
DENNISON, J		2	98
DENNISON, W		3	77
DENNISS, H A		2	98
DENNISTOUN, John Hay		4	45
DENNY, Barry Maynard Rynd	P	1	111
DENNY, Claude Boggis		3	77
DENNY, James		4	45
DENNY, R E		2	98
DENNY, Robert		2	98
DENNY, Robert Edmund Barry	P	1	111
DENROCHE-SMITH, Archibald John	P	1	332
DENSHAM, Raphael D B		2	98
DENSON, Hubert Stanley	P	2	98
DENT, Arthur Evelyn	P	4	45
DENT, Austen Campbell		2	98
DENT, Frederick B		2	98
DENT, Herbert		2	98
DENT, Paxton Malaby		2	98
DENT, Reginald Teesdale	P	4	45
DENTON, Albert George		5	46
DENTON, Bernard	P	5	46
DENTON, Edgar	P	5	46
DENTON, F R		3	77

Name	Photo	Part No.	Page No.	Name	Photo	Part No.	Page No.
DENTON, Joseph Edward		5	46	DICK, David		3	78
DENTON, Mark		1	111	DICK, George	P	4	46
DENTON, W		3	77	DICK, H		2	99
DENYER, Charles Peter		1	111	DICK, James Kennedy		2	99
DEPLEDGE, Joseph Alfred		5	46	DICK, John		2	99
DERBYSHIRE, A W		3	77	DICK, John Mcniven	P	2	99
DERHAM, J		3	77	DICK, Richard Muir		2	99
DERING, Frederick Charles		1	111	DICK, Samuel Thomas		1	112
DERISLEY, Frank Martin	P	1	111	DICK, Thomas		2	99
DERISLEY, Herbert	P	1	111	DICK, Thomas Aitkin		5	47
DEROSA, Albert	P	5	46	DICK, William		2	99
DERRICK, John Leslie	P	3	77	DICKENS, C A		2	99
DERRICK, Tom	P	1	111	DICKENS, Cedric Charles	P	4	46
DERRILL, W		3	77	DICKENS, Leonard		4	46
DERWENT, Arthur Hubert	P	5	46	DICKENSON, Arthur		2	99
DERWENT, Thomas Edward	P	5	46	DICKENSON, Henry Martin		5	47
DES VOEUX, Frederick William	P	1	111	DICKENSON, Laurence Aubrey Fiennes Wingfield		1	112
DES VOEUX, Harold Charles		2	98	DICKENSON, Sidney Robert		5	47
DES VOEUX, Seymour	P	2	99	DICKER, Frank Ernest		2	99
DESBROW, George William	P	5	46	DICKER, Philip	P	3	78
DESMEULES, Joseph Edgar	P	1	111	DICKERSON, Thomas Alfred	P	3	78
DESMOND, James Jeremiah		2	98	DICKESON, E		3	78
DESPARD, Charles Beauclerk		4	45	DICKESON, Henry Edmund	P	1	112
DETMOLD, Phillip Walter		3	77	DICKEY, James		1	112
DETTNER, Walter Joseph		1	112	DICKIE, Henry Anderson	P	5	47
DEVALL, T		3	78	DICKIE, James		2	99
DEVANNEY, William George		1	112	DICKIE, Robert Bruce		4	46
DEVANNY, Peter		2	99	DICKINS, W A		3	78
DEVENISH, Donald Henry	P	4	45	DICKINSON, Albert Edward		4	46
DEVENPORT, Alfred	P	2	99	DICKINSON, Arthur Frowde	P	4	46
DEVER, Mandy		2	99	DICKINSON, Arthur Thomas Searle	P	2	100
DEVEREUX, Charles Emile		1	112	DICKINSON, Charles		2	100
DEVEREUX, Leonard Fred		3	78	DICKINSON, H		3	78
DEVEY, Mark		3	78	DICKINSON, John Edward	P	3	78
DEVINE, Bernard		2	99	DICKINSON, Lewis George	P	2	100
DEVINE, D F		3	78	DICKINSON, Ronald Francis Bickersteth	P	1	112
DEVINE, J		3	78	DICKINSON, Sydney Elden		2	100
DEVINE, James		2	99	DICKINSON, William Vicris	P	3	78
DEVINE, James		2	99	DICKSON, Alan James		2	100
DEVINE, M		2	99	DICKSON, Archibald William		3	78
DEVINE, P		3	78	DICKSON, C		3	78
DEVINE, R		2	99	DICKSON, Cyril Garlies		2	100
DEVINE, W		2	99	DICKSON, F J		3	78
DEVLIN, Francis Cc		3	78	DICKSON, G		2	100
DEVLIN, Henry Little	P	4	45	DICKSON, George		1	112
DEVONSHIRE, Alfred John		1	112	DICKSON, George		1	112
DEVONSHIRE, Horace		2	99	DICKSON, George Aitken	P	1	112
DEWAR, Alexander		2	99	DICKSON, Isaac		2	100
DEWAR, Alexander		2	99	DICKSON, James		1	112
DEWAR, Charles		3	78	DICKSON, James	P	3	79
DEWAR, D		3	78	DICKSON, James Struthers		1	112
DEWAR, James		4	46	DICKSON, John		1	112
DEWAR, Thomas Clark	P	1	112	DICKSON, Thomas	P	1	113
DEWARS, W		3	78	DICKSON, Thomas Rutherford		2	100
DEWBURY, John James	P	3	78	DICKSON, William		3	79
DEWDNEY, Clifford Mostyn French	P	4	46	DIEHL, Ralph		1	113
DEWEY, Noble	P	1	112	DIETRICH, Herman Edward		5	47
DEXTER, George Henry		1	112	DIGBY, John Kenelm	P	1	113
DEXTER, H		3	78	DIGBY, Reginald John		3	79
DEY, William	P	5	46	DIGGENS, Bert		5	47
DIAMOND, David Lawrie		3	78	DIGGINS, James Willis		2	100
DIAMOND, Richard		2	99	DIGGLE, John Harold		1	113
DIBBLE, A		3	78	DILBEROGLUE, Augustus	P	3	79
DIBSDALL, Ernest William		1	112	DILBEROGLUE, Richard Nicholas	P	3	79
DICK, Arthur James Seaber	P	4	46	DILKE, Hugh Stanley	P	1	113

Name	Photo	Part No.	Page No.
DOIG, David Breck		5	49
DOIG, James Crow		3	81
DOLAN, Bernard		1	114
DOLAN, Francis		4	47
DOLL, Philip Walter Rudolph		2	103
DOLLER, Colin		1	114
DOLLEY, Leonard Ernest		2	103
DOLLMAN, Walter M		2	103
DOLMAN, Percy		5	49
DOLPHIN, Eric John Western		1	114
DOLPHIN, Joseph Samuel		1	114
DOMINEY, George William		1	114
DOMING, Tom		2	103
DON, Frederick A	P	5	49
DON, James		2	103
DON, Louis Drummond	P	5	49
DON, William Shaw	P	5	49
DONACHEY, Wallace		1	114
DONACHY, John		2	103
DONALD, James		3	81
DONALD, Joseph		1	114
DONALD, Martie		1	114
DONALD, William		2	103
DONALDSON, Alexander		2	103
DONALDSON, Alexander		3	81
DONALDSON, David		4	47
DONALDSON, Gilbert Douglas		5	49
DONALDSON, John	P	1	114
DONALDSON, John		2	103
DONALDSON, Joseph Kenneth		2	103
DONALDSON, Robert		5	49
DONALDSON, Thomas Mcquarrie		5	49
DONALDSON, William Duncan		4	47
DONE, Thomas Montague		5	49
DONKERSLOOT, E		3	81
DONKIN, Reginald Lyons		1	114
DONN, David		4	47
DONNAN, Joseph George Alexander	P	1	114
DONNE, Ernest	P	5	49
DONNE, Leopold Douglas		4	47
DONNELLEY, William		1	114
DONNELLY, Arthur		2	103
DONNELLY, Hugh		1	114
DONNELLY, James		4	47
DONNELLY, John		2	103
DONNELLY, P		3	81
DONNELLY, Peter		2	103
DONNELLY, T		3	81
DONNELLY, W		3	81
DONNELLY, William	P	4	47
DONOGHUE, Jeremiah		2	103
DONOVAN, Alfred Norman	P	1	114
DONOVAN, Daniel		2	103
DONOVAN, Daniel		3	81
DONOVAN, Edgar Claude		4	48
DONOVAN, F G		3	81
DONOVAN, James		2	103
DONOVAN, T		3	81
DONOVAN, W		3	81
DOODY, Albert		2	103
DOOLEY, E		3	81
DOOLEY, W		3	81
DOONER, Alfred Edwin Claud Toke	P	1	114
DOOR, William James Stephen	P	5	49
DOPSON, William		1	114

Name	Photo	Part No.	Page No.
DORAN, A		3	81
DORAN, William		2	103
DORANS, William		2	103
DORBY, James		2	103
DOREY, William Henry		1	115
DORINGTON, Thomas Philip		2	103
DORLING, Ernest C		2	103
DORMAN, Leonard		2	103
DORMER, Cecil		5	50
DORMER, John		2	103
DORMER, William Charles	P	1	115
DORNAN, James		2	103
DORNAN, John		2	103
DORNAN, R		3	81
DORNING, Arthur		1	115
DORR, Harry		2	103
DORRAM, George		1	115
DORRITY, Adrian Kingsley		4	48
DORSEY, J		3	81
DORSEY, T		3	81
DOSSETT, Richard J		2	103
DOSWELL, C E		3	81
DOTHIE, Elvery Ashton	P	2	103
DOTHIE, John Howard	P	2	103
DOUBLEDAY, A C G		3	81
DOUDS, John		2	103
DOUGALL, Andrew	P	1	115
DOUGALL, Eric Stuart		4	48
DOUGALL, Walter		1	115
DOUGHTY, Fred	P	4	48
DOUGHTY, H		3	81
DOUGHTY, H		3	81
DOUGHTY, Richard		2	103
DOUGHTY, William		2	103
DOUGHTY-WYLIE, Charles Hotham Montagu	P	1	387
DOUGLAS, Alfred Sydney		1	115
DOUGLAS, Andrew		2	103
DOUGLAS, Andrew		5	50
DOUGLAS, Colin Langslow	P	2	104
DOUGLAS, Donald Gordon	P	3	81
DOUGLAS, E		3	81
DOUGLAS, G		3	81
DOUGLAS, George		2	104
DOUGLAS, George Archibald Percy	P	2	104
DOUGLAS, H		3	81
DOUGLAS, H		3	81
DOUGLAS, Ian Victor	P	4	48
DOUGLAS, J		2	104
DOUGLAS, James		2	104
DOUGLAS, James		2	104
DOUGLAS, John		2	104
DOUGLAS, John	P	3	81
DOUGLAS, Leslie Hall	P	1	115
DOUGLAS, Leslie Stuart	P	1	115
DOUGLAS, Richard		2	104
DOUGLAS, Robert Moir		2	104
DOUGLAS, Thomas	P	3	81
DOUGLAS, Thomas Herbert		4	48
DOUGLAS, Thomas William Stewart		3	81
DOUGLAS, W		2	104
DOUGLAS, William		3	81
DOUGLAS, William	P	5	50
DOUGLAS, William Sholto	P	1	115
DOUGLAS-CROMPTON, Sydney Harold Lionel	P	3	67

Name	Photo	Part No.	Page No.	Name	Photo	Part No.	Page No.
DOUGLAS-HAMILTON, Angus Falconar	P	2	154	**DOYLE,** J		3	82
DOUGLAS-PENNANT, Hon. Charles	P	1	286	**DOYLE,** J		3	82
DOUGLAS-PENNANT, The Hon. George Henry	P	1	286	**DOYLE,** John		3	82
DOVE, Charles William		1	115	**DOYLE,** John Joseph	P	1	116
DOVENER, Cyril Hawkesworth	P	3	81	**DOYLE,** M		3	82
DOVER, John Percy Newton		3	81	**DOYLE,** T		3	82
DOVEY, F		2	104	**DOYLE,** T		3	82
DOVEY, Frederick Arthur		5	50	**DOYLE,** Thomas		5	50
DOVEY, H		3	81	**DOYLE,** William Joseph Gabriel		3	82
DOVEY, Sidney Thomas		2	104	**DRACOTT,** F F		2	105
DOW, Andrew Thomas		1	115	**DRAGE,** Fred		2	105
DOWDALL, Frederick Charles	P	2	104	**DRAIN,** G		3	82
DOWDEN, J		3	81	**DRAKE,** Robert Edward		2	105
DOWDEN, Stephen William	P	1	115	**DRAKE,** Robert Flint		2	105
DOWDING, Arthur G		2	104	**DRAKE,** Samuel Bingham		4	48
DOWIE, David Carlyle		5	50	**DRAKE,** Sidney Joseph		2	105
DOWLEN, Mark		2	104	**DRAKE,** Thomas		1	116
DOWLING, A S		3	82	**DRAKE,** Thomas Harold	P	1	116
DOWLING, J R		3	82	**DRAKE,** Walter	P	3	82
DOWLING, James Thomas	P	1	115	**DRAKE,** William Arthur Victor		2	105
DOWLING, John James		1	115	**DRAKE,** William Samuel		3	82
DOWLING, P		2	104	**DRAPER,** Harry Thomas		1	116
DOWLING, William Edward		1	116	**DRAPER,** Hedley		3	82
DOWN, Frederick William		1	116	**DRAPER,** John Alfred William		5	50
DOWN, George Albert		5	50	**DRAPER,** John Eyre		2	105
DOWN, George Arthur		3	82	**DRAPER,** Joseph		2	105
DOWNEND, John Middleton	P	3	82	**DRAPER,** Reginald Thomas		4	48
DOWNER, Ronald Ernest		4	48	**DRAPER,** Sidney		2	105
DOWNES, Albert Ernest		1	116	**DRAPER,** William		2	105
DOWNES, Andrew	P	1	116	**DRAPER,** William		2	105
DOWNES, Archer Chernocke		1	116	**DRAY,** H		3	82
DOWNES, Ernest	P	5	50	**DRAY,** Thomas		1	116
DOWNES, H W		3	82	**DRAYNER,** William Bruce		1	116
DOWNES, J		3	82	**DREDGE,** Alexander Eagle		4	48
DOWNES, James		2	104	**DREDGE,** William George		1	116
DOWNES, Thomas		2	104	**DREVER,** George		1	116
DOWNES, Villiers Chernocke		1	116	**DREW,** Alan Appleby		1	116
DOWNEY, J M		3	82	**DREW,** Albert James		1	116
DOWNEY, John Michael		1	116	**DREW,** Edwin Joseph		1	116
DOWNEY, Sydney James Livingston		3	82	**DREW,** Henry James	P	5	50
DOWNHAM, G A		3	82	**DREW,** Leonard Victor	P	1	116
DOWNHAM, Harold	P	5	50	**DREW,** William Reginald Caple		1	116
DOWNIE, Colin		2	104	**DREWETT,** George Frederick		1	116
DOWNIE, Duncan		3	82	**DREWRY,** G		3	82
DOWNIE, James		1	116	**DREY,** Adolphe		4	48
DOWNIE, James Cruickshank		3	82	**DRING,** William	P	4	48
DOWNIE, John Stewart		3	82	**DRINKSWATER,** T		3	82
DOWNIE, Peter Houston	P	1	116	**DRINKWATER,** L		3	82
DOWNIE, William Barclay	P	3	82	**DRISCOLL,** Cornelius		1	116
DOWNING, G H		3	82	**DRISCOLL,** Joseph		2	105
DOWNS, George		2	104	**DRISCOLL,** T		3	82
DOWNS, J F		3	82	**DRIVER,** Arthur Maurice		1	116
DOWNS, William W		2	104	**DRIVER,** Clarence		2	105
DOWSE, F		3	82	**DRIVER,** George		3	82
DOWSELL, Richard Henry	P	2	104	**DRIVER,** Henry		1	116
DOWSETT, Arthur		2	105	**DRIVER,** Jacob William		4	48
DOWSON, George Charles		4	48	**DROLET,** Narcisse Edouard		1	116
DOWSON, William H		2	105	**DROUGHT,** Charles Frederic	P	2	105
DOYLE, A		3	82	**DROVER,** Charles Peacock	P	4	48
DOYLE, A		3	82	**DROVER,** John Edgar James	P	3	83
DOYLE, Edward		2	105	**DRUITT,** Everard Joseph	P	1	117
DOYLE, Francis Hubert	P	2	105	**DRUMMOND,** David Robert		2	105
DOYLE, J		3	82	**DRUMMOND,** Eric Grey	P	1	117
DOYLE, J		3	82	**DRUMMOND,** Frederick John		1	117
DOYLE, J		3	82	**DRUMMOND,** H		3	83

Name	Photo	Part No.	Page No.
DRUMMOND, J		3	83
DRUMMOND, T		2	105
DRUMMOND, William	P	1	117
DRUMMOND, William Boyd		2	105
DRURY, H P		3	83
DRURY, Harry		3	83
DRURY, J		3	83
DRURY, W		3	83
DRYDEN, Ernest		5	50
DRYDEN, George Henry	P	2	105
DRYDEN, J		2	105
DRYSDALE, Alexander	P	3	83
DRYSDALE, Samuel		2	105
DRYSDALE, W		2	105
DRYSDALE, William	P	2	105
DUBBIN, Ernest Lawrence		5	50
DUBERLY, Vernon Conrad	P	3	83
DUBOIS, Latimer Ridley		4	49
DUBOIS, Oliver Cromwell		4	49
DUCAT, Richard		1	117
DUCK, Albert Edwin		1	117
DUCK, Edward		1	117
DUCK, Ernest Hillman	P	2	105
DUCKENFIELD, Francis Harold		4	49
DUCKETT, James Thomas		1	117
DUCKHAM, Merton		5	50
DUCKLES, Leonard Butler		4	49
DUCKWORK, John		2	106
DUCKWORTH, Eric		2	106
DUCKWORTH, Joseph		2	106
DUCKWORTH, Walter		4	49
DUCKWORTH, William	P	5	50
DUDDERIDGE, Herbert Orlando		3	83
DUDDRIDGE, Albert John	P	3	83
DUDDY, Frank		1	117
DUDDY, Henry		2	106
DUDDY, William	P	2	106
DUDLEY, Bernard John Charleton	P	3	83
DUDLEY, Charles Leonard		2	106
DUDLEY, David	P	1	117
DUDLEY, Harry Pemberton		3	83
DUDLEY, John Edward		1	117
DUDLEY, Leonard Grey	P	1	117
DUDLEY, Robert		4	49
DUDLEY, Thomas Michael	P	2	106
DUDMAN, E		3	83
DUFF, Adrian Grant		2	106
DUFF, Beauchamp Oswald		2	106
DUFF, Beauchamp Patrick	P	2	106
DUFF, David Cumming		3	83
DUFF, Hugh John	P	5	51
DUFF, J		2	106
DUFF, Sir Robert George Vivian		2	106
DUFF, William	P	3	83
DUFFIELD, Ernest E		2	106
DUFFIELD, Oscar Sydney		3	84
DUFFIELD, William		1	117
DUFFUS, John		4	49
DUFFUS, Thomas Edward	P	1	118
DUFFY, B		4	49
DUFFY, F		2	106
DUFFY, H		2	106
DUGAN, George Cleaver	P	2	106
DUGDALE, Richard William		5	51
DUGGAN, A F B		3	84

Name	Photo	Part No.	Page No.
DUGGAN, Con	P	1	118
DUGGAN, G W		3	84
DUGGAN, George Grant	P	1	118
DUGGAN, John Rowsell	P	1	118
DUGGAN, Patrick	P	1	118
DUGGINS, Frank Howard		2	106
DUGGINS, Norman William		2	107
DUGGINS, Sidney John		2	107
DUGMORE, J		3	84
DUGUID, William George	P	4	49
DUKE, Barry Pevensey		2	107
DUKE, J		3	84
DUKE, Ramsay		5	51
DUKE, Richard Thomas		4	49
DUKE, S		3	84
DUKE, S		3	84
DUKE, Thomas		2	107
DUKE, Thomas		4	49
DUKE, William	P	1	118
DUMAS, Charles Derrick	P	3	84
DUMBELL, Leslie Sydney	P	3	84
DUMMA, James		1	118
DUMPER, F H		3	84
DUMPHY, J		3	84
DUN, Leslie Finlay		2	107
DUNBAR, Alexander Cobb		2	107
DUNBAR, Francis Grant		1	118
DUNBAR, J		2	107
DUNBAR, John Maxwell		1	118
DUNBAR, Norman James		5	51
DUNBAVAND, Hubert	P	2	107
DUNCALF, Arthur		5	51
DUNCAN, Albert Henry		2	107
DUNCAN, Albert Robert		5	51
DUNCAN, Alexander John Farquharson	P	4	49
DUNCAN, Alexander Robertson		1	118
DUNCAN, David Mcleod		3	84
DUNCAN, Edward Francis		4	49
DUNCAN, Ernest F		2	107
DUNCAN, George		1	118
DUNCAN, J		3	84
DUNCAN, J A		2	107
DUNCAN, James		2	107
DUNCAN, James		3	84
DUNCAN, James		3	84
DUNCAN, John		3	84
DUNCAN, John		4	49
DUNCAN, John	P	5	51
DUNCAN, John Hopkirk		1	118
DUNCAN, Joseph Henry		2	107
DUNCAN, Kenneth William Allan		5	51
DUNCAN, Neil Ferguson	P	2	107
DUNCAN, Robert	P	3	84
DUNCAN, Robert Gordon Campbell	P	4	49
DUNCAN, Stuart		1	118
DUNCAN, Walter Durie		3	84
DUNCAN, William Charles		3	84
DUNCAN, William Hardy		3	84
DUNCAN, William Proctor	P	3	84
DUNCANSON, R		2	107
DUNCOMBE, H		3	84
DUNDAS, Cecil Henry	P	1	118
DUNDAS, David George Minden	P	4	50
DUNDAS, Hon. Kenneth Robert	P	1	119
DUNFORD, B		3	84

Name	Photo	Part No.	Page No.
DYER, Sydney Beresford Hope		4	50
DYER, Thomas		2	109
DYER, W		3	86
DYER, W C		3	86
DYER, Walter		1	121
DYER, William		2	109
DYKE, Francis Hart		3	86
DYKE, George Walker		1	121
DYKE, H H		3	86
DYKE, Walter Ball		4	50
DYKE, William George		5	52
DYKES, Alfred Mcnair	P	1	121
DYKES, T		3	86
DYKES, William Henry		4	50
DYMOCK, William Duncan		3	86
DYMOND, Richard Henry Albert		5	52
DYNES, Albert		1	122
DYSON, Cecil Venn	P	1	122
DYSON, E C		3	86
DYSON, Edward		2	109
DYSON, W		3	86
EADE, Oliver		3	86
EADE, Reginald John		1	122
EADE, Sidney		2	109
EADE, William John		4	50
EADES, George William		2	109
EADES, Herbert		2	109
EADES, William George		1	122
EADIE, James N		2	109
EADY, John		1	122
EADY, Thomas	P	3	86
EAGAR, Francis Russell	P	1	122
EAGLES, Charles Edward Campbell		4	50
EAGLES, George Sawyer		3	86
EAGLETON, John Ronaldson		4	50
EAGLETON, Samuel Thomas		3	86
EAGLETON, Thomas		3	86
EAGLING, E		3	86
EAKIN, Herbert Stuart Chambers		2	109
EALAND, Arthur Noel		4	51
EALAND, Frederick John Arthur		2	109
EALES, Frank		5	52
EALES, Frederick Thomas		5	52
EAMAN, Alfred		1	122
EAMES, Thomas Bates	P	3	86
EARDLEY-WILMOT, Frederick Lawrence	P	1	381
EARDLEY-WILMOT, Gerald Howard		2	317
EARDLEY-WILMOT, Gerald Howard		4	239
EARL, Alfred Ernest		2	109
EARL, Stephen		1	122
EARLS, C P		3	86
EARNEY, Harry		4	51
EARNSHAW, Fred	P	4	51
EARNSHAW, John Etches	P	2	109
EARNSHAW, Walter	P	4	51
EARP, Joseph Alfred		4	51
EASEY, H		3	86
EASON, E		3	86
EASON, Edward Stanley		4	51
EASON, Jesse Herbert		1	122
EASON, Sampson	P	1	122
EAST, Alfred Charles		1	122
EAST, Alfred Tomlin	P	2	110
EAST, George	P	1	122
EAST, Hubert James		2	110

Name	Photo	Part No.	Page No.
EAST, Lionel William Pellew		5	52
EASTERBROOK, William Thomas		1	122
EASTERBROOKS, Albert David		2	110
EASTERLING, Frederick		2	110
EASTHAM, G		3	86
EASTHOPE, Edward Donald		2	110
EASTLAKE, Frank Wotton	P	2	110
EASTLOW, E		3	86
EASTON, Andrew John	P	3	87
EASTON, J		3	87
EASTON, John		2	110
EASTON, Stewart Macalister	P	2	110
EASTOP, Wallis E A		2	110
EASTWOOD, Charles Edmund		2	110
EASTWOOD, Frank Molyneux		2	110
EASTWOOD, Gad		4	51
EASTWOOD, Richard Gordon		5	52
EASTWOOD, Ronald		3	87
EATON, Arthur Ernest Wilson		1	122
EATON, Arthur Thomas		1	122
EATON, George Hubert		4	51
EATON, Harold		3	87
EATON, Herbert		2	110
EATON, James		3	87
EATON, Samuel Edward		5	52
EATON, W		3	87
EATWELL, J H		2	110
EAVES, Alfred Thomas	P	3	87
EAVES, Ernest Charles		2	110
EBDEN, Sydney Charles	P	4	51
EBSARY, Frederick Ernest		1	122
EBY, Alexander Ralph	P	1	122
ECCLES, Charles		3	87
ECCLES, Francis		3	87
ECCLES, Frederick William		2	110
ECCLES, John Dennison	P	2	110
ECCLESHARE, Thomas Bernard		1	122
ECKERT, John J G		2	110
EDBROOKE, Frank Thomas		1	122
EDDISON, James	P	1	122
EDDISON, John Radley	P	1	122
EDDLESTON, Albert		4	51
EDE, Edwin William	P	5	52
EDE, Wallace		2	110
EDEN, Albert E		2	110
EDEN, John		2	110
EDEN, Robert James		1	123
EDGAR, John Hammond	P	2	110
EDGAR, William Francis	P	4	51
EDGE, Frederick Charles		1	123
EDGE, Thomas		2	111
EDGE, Thomas John		5	52
EDGECOMBE, George		2	111
EDGES, Philip		2	111
EDGEWORTH, Wilfred Henry		3	87
EDGINTON, Robert Walter Laurence	P	1	123
EDIKER, James		2	111
EDINBURGH, Alfred Charles	P	3	87
EDLMANN, Ernest Elliot	P	1	123
EDMENSON, Thomas		2	111
EDMOND, Alfred Thomas		1	123
EDMOND, Robert Duthie		3	87
EDMOND, Seaward Richard		1	123
EDMOND-JENKINS, William Hart	P	2	183
EDMONDS, A		3	87

Name	Photo	Part No.	Page No.
EDMONDS, Arthur John		2	111
EDMONDS, Herbert John		5	52
EDMONDS, John		2	111
EDMONDS, Joseph Leonard		1	123
EDMONDSON, Cyril Arthur	P	3	87
EDMONDSON, G H		3	87
EDMONDSTON, Robert Stuart		4	51
EDMONDSTON, William George		4	51
EDMONSTON, Edward W		2	111
EDMONSTONE, William John		5	52
EDMUNDS, John	P	5	52
EDMUNDS, Melbourne	P	5	52
EDMUNDS, William	P	5	53
EDSELL, George Alfred	P	1	123
EDWARD, Frank	P	3	87
EDWARDES, C J		3	88
EDWARDES, J		2	111
EDWARDS, A		2	111
EDWARDS, Albert		1	123
EDWARDS, Albert		2	111
EDWARDS, Albert George		1	123
EDWARDS, Alfred Joseph	P	2	111
EDWARDS, C		3	88
EDWARDS, Charles	P	2	111
EDWARDS, Charles		2	111
EDWARDS, Charles Edwin		5	53
EDWARDS, Charles Ernest	P	5	53
EDWARDS, Charles J		2	111
EDWARDS, Charles James		2	111
EDWARDS, Edward Ernest	P	4	51
EDWARDS, Edward Ledger		4	52
EDWARDS, Edwin Allen James		2	111
EDWARDS, Eric Lea Priestley		1	123
EDWARDS, Eric Wilson	P	3	88
EDWARDS, Ernest Irving		1	123
EDWARDS, Ernest Victor		4	52
EDWARDS, Frank Glencairn De Burgh		2	111
EDWARDS, Frank Thomas		1	123
EDWARDS, Frederick		1	123
EDWARDS, George		1	123
EDWARDS, George Thomas		1	123
EDWARDS, Harold Thorne	P	1	124
EDWARDS, Harri Willis	P	3	88
EDWARDS, Harry		1	124
EDWARDS, Harry	P	3	88
EDWARDS, Henry		2	111
EDWARDS, Herbert		4	52
EDWARDS, Herbert Martin Charles		1	124
EDWARDS, J		2	111
EDWARDS, J		3	88
EDWARDS, J		3	88
EDWARDS, J H		2	111
EDWARDS, J S		3	88
EDWARDS, James		2	111
EDWARDS, John Arthur	P	5	53
EDWARDS, John Edward		1	124
EDWARDS, John Eric		4	52
EDWARDS, John Henry		3	88
EDWARDS, John Ivon Jones		5	53
EDWARDS, Joseph		5	53
EDWARDS, Philip Arthur	P	2	111
EDWARDS, R		3	88
EDWARDS, Richard		1	124
EDWARDS, Robert Amor	P	5	53
EDWARDS, Robert Garnet Chawner		1	124
EDWARDS, Robert Jarman		4	52
EDWARDS, Sidney Stevens	P	5	53
EDWARDS, T		3	88
EDWARDS, Thomas Frederick		5	53
EDWARDS, W		3	88
EDWARDS, W		3	88
EDWARDS, Walter		3	88
EDWARDS, Walter Thomas		4	52
EDWARDS, William	P	1	124
EDWARDS, William		1	124
EDWARDS, William		3	88
EDWARDS, William Gladstone	P	4	52
EDWARDS, William Henry		1	124
EDWARDS, William Joseph		1	124
EDWARDS, William Victor		3	88
EDWARDSON, Richard		2	111
EELES, F		3	88
EFEMEY, Albert George		3	88
EFFORD, Cecil		2	111
EGAN, E		3	88
EGAN, P		3	88
EGAN, Stephen		2	111
EGERTON, Arthur George Edward	P	2	111
EGERTON, Arthur Oswald	P	2	112
EGERTON, Bertram Gustavus		3	88
EGERTON, Charles Alfred		3	88
EGERTON, Philip John		2	112
EGERTON, Robert Randle		2	112
EGERTON, Rowland Le Berward		1	124
EGERTON-WARBURTON, Piers (Peter)	P	1	366
EGGAN, William		2	112
EGGAR, W		3	88
EGGENTON, W		3	88
EGGINTON, E G		3	88
EGGLETON, C M		3	88
EGGLETON, Charles	P	5	53
EGGLETON, Charles S		2	112
EGGLETON, William Horace		2	112
EGLINGTON, Robert Cecil		1	124
EITKEN, George	P	3	88
ELAND, Reginald George Walton		3	88
ELD, Arthur William	P	3	89
ELDER, Charles	P	1	124
ELDER, Edward Henry	P	5	53
ELDER, James Jarvis		5	53
ELDER, R		3	89
ELDER, Robert		2	112
ELDERKIN, John Victor		3	89
ELDERKIN, Robert Richard		3	89
ELDRED, John Sturgess		2	112
ELDRIDGE, A		3	89
ELDRIDGE, Albert		2	112
ELDRIDGE, John		2	112
ELDRIDGE, Percy E		2	112
ELDRIDGE, Thomas Henry		1	124
ELEMENT, Henry		1	124
ELEY, Albert Edward		1	124
ELGIN, Robert		2	112
ELION, Andrew Ernest		2	112
ELIOT, Peter Douglas Colin	P	3	89
ELIOT, William Laurence		2	112
ELIOTT, Hugh Russell		2	112
ELIOTT-LOCKHART, Percy Clare		1	229
ELITO, Antoine		1	124
ELKIN, J		3	89

Name	Photo	Part No.	Page No.	Name	Photo	Part No.	Page No.
ELKINGTON, H		3	89	ELLIS, Edmund Albert		1	125
ELKINS, William James		1	124	ELLIS, Ernest George		4	52
ELLACOTT, Alexander Cameron	P	3	89	ELLIS, F		2	113
ELLARBY, Charles Edward		4	52	ELLIS, F A		2	113
ELLARD, J		3	89	ELLIS, Frederick		2	113
ELLAWAY, Alfred Henry		1	124	ELLIS, Geoffrey Philip	P	5	54
ELLEN, E		3	89	ELLIS, George A		2	113
ELLEN, Eric Adrian		3	89	ELLIS, George E		2	113
ELLEN, Frank A		2	112	ELLIS, George Willis		1	125
ELLEN, Harry John		5	54	ELLIS, J		3	90
ELLEN, Wilfrid Victor		4	52	ELLIS, J		3	90
ELLENDER, Richard Stanley		1	124	ELLIS, J		3	90
ELLERY, Jack		3	89	ELLIS, James Clive	P	4	52
ELLERY, Thomas Cecil Percy	P	2	112	ELLIS, John Richard	P	3	90
ELLEWAY, William Richard	P	5	54	ELLIS, John Thomas		1	125
ELLICE, Alexander		3	89	ELLIS, Judson Harold	P	1	125
ELLICE, Andrew Robert		3	89	ELLIS, Leonard		1	125
ELLICE, William		3	89	ELLIS, Martin Lawford		3	90
ELLINGHAM, Edgar		5	54	ELLIS, R		3	90
ELLINGHAM, F		3	89	ELLIS, Robert		2	113
ELLINGHAM, William Albert Henry		1	124	ELLIS, S		3	90
ELLINGTON, G		3	90	ELLIS, Stanley Venn		3	90
ELLIOT, Francis Hall		5	54	ELLIS, T		3	90
ELLIOT, Gavin William Esmond	P	3	90	ELLIS, T		3	90
ELLIOT, Gladstone		5	54	ELLIS, W		3	91
ELLIOT, Henry Grattan		2	112	ELLIS, W		3	91
ELLIOT, James		1	124	ELLIS, W F		3	91
ELLIOT, John Amyand	P	1	124	ELLIS, Walter		4	52
ELLIOT, John Lindsay		3	90	ELLIS, Wilfred		2	113
ELLIOT, Matthew Taylor		1	124	ELLIS, Wilfred Kirkpatrick Bramwell		4	52
ELLIOT, Thomas	P	1	124	ELLIS, William E		2	113
ELLIOTT, A		2	112	ELLIS, Yvo Lempriere	P	2	113
ELLIOTT, A		3	90	ELLISON, Edward		3	91
ELLIOTT, Arthur		2	112	ELLISON, H		3	91
ELLIOTT, Charles Arthur Boileau		3	90	ELLISON, J		3	91
ELLIOTT, Douglas Arthur		4	52	ELLISON, Joseph		3	91
ELLIOTT, Eustace Trehane	P	3	90	ELLISON, Michael Hubert Bertram		3	91
ELLIOTT, Francis		3	90	ELLISON, R		3	91
ELLIOTT, Frederick John		1	124	ELLISON, Reginald	P	1	125
ELLIOTT, George Keith	P	5	54	ELLISON, Robert	P	1	125
ELLIOTT, George William	P	1	124	ELLISON, T H J		3	91
ELLIOTT, George William		3	90	ELLISON, Theodore Tarleton	P	2	113
ELLIOTT, Henry		1	124	ELLISON, Tom		3	91
ELLIOTT, J		3	90	ELLISTON, Arthur Edward		1	125
ELLIOTT, J		3	90	ELLOT, William		1	125
ELLIOTT, James	P	2	112	ELLSWORTH, Ernest Malvern		1	125
ELLIOTT, James		5	54	ELLSWORTH, James	P	1	125
ELLIOTT, James Harold	P	2	112	ELLWOOD, Charles Hugh	P	1	125
ELLIOTT, John		1	124	ELLWOOD, Robert		5	54
ELLIOTT, Leonard Kirkby		3	90	ELLWOOD, Thomas		3	91
ELLIOTT, Philip Lloyd		2	112	ELMER, John William		4	52
ELLIOTT, Reginald William Sidney		2	112	ELMER, Joseph Henry		1	125
ELLIOTT, Richard		4	52	ELMER, Walter Henry		4	52
ELLIOTT, Richard John		5	54	ELMORE, A		3	91
ELLIOTT, Walter		3	90	ELMORE, W		3	91
ELLIS, A		2	112	ELMS, A R		3	91
ELLIS, Alfred		2	112	ELMS, Bartlett C		2	113
ELLIS, Basil Frederick		2	112	ELMS, George Alfred		2	113
ELLIS, Basil Herbert	P	1	125	ELMSLIE, Kenward Wallace		2	113
ELLIS, C		3	90	ELPHICK, R		3	91
ELLIS, Cecil Arthur Ager		2	112	ELPHINSTONE, George Adam		5	54
ELLIS, Cecil Douglas	P	2	112	ELRICK, W		3	91
ELLIS, Charles		2	113	ELRINGTON, Gerard Gordon Clement	P	1	125
ELLIS, Charles James		2	113	ELSEY, Harry	P	2	113
ELLIS, Charles Trevitt		2	113	ELSON, Edwin Arthur		4	52

Name	Photo	Part No.	Page No.
ELSON, Edwin Arthur	P	5	54
ELSON, George Edwards		1	125
ELSTON, John		2	113
ELSTON, William H		2	113
ELSTONE, Frederick Harold	P	2	113
ELTON, A E		3	91
ELTON, Gordon Daubeny Gresley	P	4	53
ELTON, Thomas		2	113
ELTRINGHAM, John William		3	91
ELVES, Thomas		1	125
ELVIN, B		3	91
ELWELL, Alexander		2	113
ELWELL, Alfred		4	53
ELWIN, Frank Harold	P	1	125
EMBLING, E		3	91
EMERY, Charles		4	53
EMERY, Frederick	P	3	91
EMERY, Percy Edward		3	91
EMERY, William James		1	125
EMMERSON, Henry Hetherington	P	3	91
EMMERSON, Walter		1	125
EMMERTON, Alfred		2	113
EMMETT, Alfred Harry		2	113
EMMETT, Robert George		2	113
EMMETT, Thomas	P	3	91
EMMITT, George Edward		4	53
EMMOTT, John Barlow		1	125
EMMS, John William Andrew		5	54
EMPSALL, Jack		5	54
EMPSON, Richard William Henry Macartney	P	1	126
EMPTAGE, George William		1	126
EMSLEY, John Alfred		5	55
EMSLEY, Samuel Edward		2	113
EMSLIE, W		3	91
EMSLIE, William A		2	113
ENDER, Arthur P		2	113
ENFIELD, Charles John		1	126
ENGLAND, Albert		5	55
ENGLAND, Arthur		2	113
ENGLAND, Herbert Harry		3	91
ENGLAND, Nicholas		5	55
ENGLAND, Raymond		2	113
ENGLAND, T		3	91
ENSOR, Ernest Edwin James	P	5	55
ENSOR, Henry George		5	55
ENSOR, William Alfred	P	5	55
ENTICKNAP, John	P	3	92
ENTICKNAPP, Frank		2	113
ENTWISTLE, Albert Herbert		4	53
ENTWISTLE, Benjamin		1	126
ENTWISTLE, Charles A		2	113
ENTWISTLE, John		4	53
ENTWISTLE, John Maurice Binley	P	5	55
ENTWISTLE, Joseph		5	55
ENTWISTLE, Richard		3	92
EOGAN, J F		3	92
EPPS, H		3	92
EPPS, John Frederick		4	53
EPPS, William John		1	126
ERSKINE, Donald		2	113
ESCREET, Albert		2	114
ESDAILE, Arthur James	P	5	55
ESHELLEY, John Charles		3	92
ESPIE, David		2	114
ESPLIN, D		3	92

Name	Photo	Part No.	Page No.
ESSERY, Albert Edward		3	92
ESSON, William Philip		5	55
ESTHERBY, John		2	114
ETCHELLS, Walter J		2	114
ETCHES, John	P	4	53
ETHERINGTON, Henry		2	114
ETHERINGTON, William J		2	114
ETHERTON, Charles Edward		1	126
ETHERTON, Henry John		1	126
ETRIDGE, Charles Herbert	P	5	55
ETRIDGE, Frederick	P	5	55
ETTLES, David		3	92
EVAN-JONES, Hilary Gresford	P	1	210
EVANS, A		2	114
EVANS, A		3	92
EVANS, A G		3	92
EVANS, Alexander Easson	P	1	126
EVANS, Alfred	P	4	53
EVANS, Arthur	P	1	126
EVANS, Arthur Leslie	P	4	53
EVANS, Augustus Alexander		5	55
EVANS, C		3	92
EVANS, Charlie		4	53
EVANS, Daniel Brookes		4	54
EVANS, David John	P	3	92
EVANS, Douglas Lane		3	92
EVANS, E		3	92
EVANS, E		3	92
EVANS, Edward		1	126
EVANS, Edward		4	54
EVANS, Edward Frank		1	126
EVANS, Edwin Stanley		2	114
EVANS, Ernest Edward		2	114
EVANS, Evan James	P	3	92
EVANS, F		3	92
EVANS, F W		3	92
EVANS, Frederick G		2	114
EVANS, Frew Ferguson		4	54
EVANS, Geoffrey Maynard	P	3	92
EVANS, George		5	55
EVANS, George Rhys		5	56
EVANS, Goronwy		3	92
EVANS, Harry John		3	92
EVANS, Herbert Clyde		1	126
EVANS, J		3	92
EVANS, J		3	92
EVANS, James		1	126
EVANS, James	P	1	126
EVANS, James Wright		1	126
EVANS, Jesse		4	54
EVANS, John		2	114
EVANS, John Ernest		5	56
EVANS, John Ewart	P	5	56
EVANS, John Michael Winter		2	114
EVANS, John Michael Winter		3	92
EVANS, John Trevor	P	3	92
EVANS, John Wynne	P	5	56
EVANS, Leonard George		3	93
EVANS, Meredith		3	93
EVANS, Neville Vernon		3	93
EVANS, Octavius		4	54
EVANS, Phillip	P	2	114
EVANS, Raymond	P	3	93
EVANS, Richard Douglas		3	93
EVANS, Richard William		2	114

Name	Photo	Part No.	Page No.
EVANS, Robert Henry		3	93
EVANS, Samuel		2	114
EVANS, Samuel John	P	2	114
EVANS, Simon Davies	P	5	56
EVANS, T		3	93
EVANS, Thomas		3	93
EVANS, Thomas Hatfield	P	1	127
EVANS, Timothy Idwal Hope		3	93
EVANS, V		3	93
EVANS, W		3	93
EVANS, William		2	114
EVANS, William	P	3	93
EVANS, William Alfred		1	127
EVANS, William Harkness	P	5	56
EVANS, William Herbert	P	1	127
EVANS, William James		1	127
EVASON, William Dodd		1	127
EVATT, George Raleigh Kerr	P	1	127
EVELEGH, Rosslyn Curzon		2	114
EVEN, Donald		2	114
EVENDEN, Charles W		2	114
EVENDEN, Henry		3	93
EVENS, G B		2	114
EVENS, Henry John		4	54
EVERALL, Edward Henry		1	127
EVERALL, R J		3	93
EVERALL, William Arthur		2	114
EVEREST, Arthur		2	114
EVEREST, Arthur		2	114
EVEREST, J		2	114
EVERETT, Edmund		2	114
EVERETT, Edmund		4	54
EVERETT, F A		3	93
EVERETT, J		3	93
EVERETT, Thomas James William		3	93
EVERINGHAM, Guy	P	3	94
EVERINGHAM, Robin	P	3	94
EVERSON, S		3	94
EVERTON, Thomas William		2	114
EVILL, Chetwode Percy		5	56
EWAN, George	P	5	56
EWAN, Harry Stevenson		4	54
EWART, James	P	3	94
EWART, Victor Alexander	P	2	114
EWART, William Bisset		2	114
EWBANK, John Walter	P	3	94
EWBANK, Leonard	P	3	94
EWELL, Leslie		1	127
EWEN, Alexander Peter		4	54
EWEN, Ernest Cecil		1	127
EWING, Douglas Ramsay	P	3	94
EWING, J		2	114
EWINS, Alexander	P	2	115
EXALL, Albert		2	115
EXLEY, Frederick		4	54
EXLEY, George Allan	P	3	94
EYERS, William James		1	127
EYEVAL, John Alexander		5	56
EYKYN, Gilbert Davidson Pitt	P	1	127
EYLES, D		3	94
EYRE, Frederick Richard		5	56
EYRE, John		1	127
EYRE, William	P	1	127
EYRES, Edward Frank		3	95
EYRES, Henry Tarrant		5	56
EZARD, Herbert Henry		3	95
FABER, Victor Edmund	P	4	54
FACER, T W		3	95
FACH, Arthur	P	5	56
FADE, Harold		1	127
FAGAN, J		3	95
FAGEN, Thomas		4	54
FAGG, Albert		1	127
FAGG, Albert Arthur		3	95
FAGG, W		3	95
FAHEY, M		3	95
FAHMY, Eric Percival	P	4	54
FAHMY, Eric Percival	P	5	56
FAIR, J		3	95
FAIR, James Gerald	P	3	95
FAIR, John		2	115
FAIR, Roy Nichols		1	128
FAIRBAIRN, J F		3	95
FAIRBRASS, G		3	95
FAIRCHILD, Edward James		1	128
FAIRCLOUGH, J		3	95
FAIRCLOUGH, John	P	1	128
FAIRES, William		1	128
FAIRLEY, Gilbert		3	95
FAIRLEY, Gilbert		4	54
FAIRLEY, James Fairburn	P	2	115
FAIRLEY, James Fairburn		4	54
FAIRLEY, James Fairweather		5	57
FAIRLIE, Frank		2	115
FAIRLIE, John Ogilvy	P	2	115
FAIRLIE, Walter		3	95
FAIRLIE, William		2	115
FAIRS, Ernest William	P	1	128
FAIRS, Walter		2	115
FAIRWEATHER, George		1	128
FAIRWEATHER, Henry		3	95
FAIRWEATHER, James Burdett (Alias Burdett)		3	95
FAIRWEATHER, John	P	1	128
FAIRWEATHER, Percy Reeves		2	115
FAITHFUL, Eric		2	115
FAITHFULL, Francis William Alexander	P	2	115
FALCONER, Alexander Harrold		3	95
FALCONER, Drew	P	5	57
FALCONER, John		2	115
FALCONER, William		2	115
FALCONER, William		2	115
FALCONER, William Meek	P	2	115
FALK, Charles		2	115
FALKARD, William Charles		5	57
FALKINER, Frederick Ewen Baldwin		3	95
FALKINER, George Stride		3	95
FALKNER, Henry Frederic Noel	P	2	115
FALLOWS, A		3	95
FANNING, Frederick		2	115
FARADAY, J		3	95
FARDELL, Hubert George Henry		1	128
FAREBROTHER, George H		3	95
FAREBROTHER, Leicester	P	3	95
FAREHAM, G		3	95
FAREY, W		2	115
FARLEY, Martha Sabina		5	57
FARLEY, W A		3	95
FARLIE, Edgar J		3	95
FARLING, William		2	115
FARMAN, Thomas Henry		3	95

Name	Photo	Part No.	Page No.
FENWICK, Basil Middleton	P	1	131
FENWICK, Frederick Richard William		1	131
FEREDAY, Thomas Harold		1	131
FERG, Edward Charles	P	1	131
FERGUSON, Andrew		4	55
FERGUSON, Charles J		2	117
FERGUSON, D		2	117
FERGUSON, David Turner		5	57
FERGUSON, Donald		3	97
FERGUSON, Gordon Scott		2	117
FERGUSON, J		2	117
FERGUSON, J		2	118
FERGUSON, J		2	118
FERGUSON, J		2	118
FERGUSON, James		1	131
FERGUSON, James		2	118
FERGUSON, James		2	118
FERGUSON, James Mcgregor		5	57
FERGUSON, James Mckee	P	5	58
FERGUSON, John	P	1	131
FERGUSON, John	P	4	55
FERGUSON, John	P	4	55
FERGUSON, John Mortimer	P	2	118
FERGUSON, Joseph		3	97
FERGUSON, Joseph		3	97
FERGUSON, Matthew		1	131
FERGUSON, Peter		1	131
FERGUSON, Peter	P	3	97
FERGUSON, Richard Martin		4	55
FERGUSON, Robert		1	131
FERGUSON, Robert	P	5	58
FERGUSON, William		1	131
FERGUSON, William		1	131
FERGUSON, William		2	118
FERGUSON, William Bruce		4	55
FERGUSSON, Fitzjames Shillington	P	4	55
FERGUSSON, James Adam Hamilton	P	1	131
FERGUSSON, Robert Frank	P	1	131
FERISH, C		2	118
FERNANDES, Dudley Luis De Tavora		2	118
FERNIE, William		5	58
FERNS, Harold Johnson		1	131
FERNS, S G		3	97
FERRAND, Herbert Harold	P	1	131
FERRAR, Walter Hughes		2	118
FERRIER, Gilbert Colin Cunninghame		2	118
FERRIER, John Pearson Douglas	P	5	58
FERRIS, Alfred William		3	97
FERRIS, Cornelius Percy Sparling		1	131
FERRIS, R		3	98
FERRIS, S		3	98
FERRY, John		2	118
FESTER, William Ernest		1	132
FETHERSTONE, Ross Lea		1	132
FEWSTER, Albert		2	118
FEWTRELL, Henry Ernest		4	56
FEWTRELL, Sydney Thomas Arthur	P	5	58
FFIELD, Bernard Osborne	P	1	132
FFITCH, Harry Herbert	P	1	132
FIDDES, James William Dick		1	132
FIDLER, Carel Watt	P	3	98
FIELD, Arthur Clarence Henley	P	3	98
FIELD, Charles Cecil		3	98
FIELD, Edward Arthur		2	118
FIELD, Edward William		1	132

Name	Photo	Part No.	Page No.
FIELD, Edwin		2	118
FIELD, Francis Henry		1	132
FIELD, Frederic Alan Victor		3	98
FIELD, Frederick		2	118
FIELD, Frederick James		4	56
FIELD, George Henry		3	98
FIELD, Henry		2	118
FIELD, Herbert F		2	118
FIELD, John William	P	4	56
FIELD, Oliver	P	2	118
FIELD, Robert Alister	P	3	98
FIELD, Stephen	P	1	132
FIELDER, Albert Edward		1	132
FIELDER, George William		1	132
FIELDING, Herbert Hilton	P	3	98
FIELDING, Joshua		3	98
FIELDS, Charles H		2	118
FIGG, Walter George		3	99
FILBY, Walter Alfred		3	99
FILLEUL, Leonard Amauri	P	1	132
FILLINGHAM, Reginald John	P	5	58
FILMER, Harry William		4	56
FINCH, Edward		2	118
FINCH, Edward Terence Doyne	P	1	132
FINCH, Frederick R		2	118
FINCH, Herbert Marshall	P	2	118
FINCH, Leonard Edward	P	1	132
FINCH, Philip John		2	119
FINCH, Philip John	P	5	58
FINCH, Sydney George		1	132
FINCH, W J		3	99
FINCHLEY, Arthur Ernest		2	119
FINDLAY, Cyril Olney		3	99
FINDLAY, David Jaffrey	P	5	58
FINDLAY, George Halliday		1	133
FINDLAY, Herbert	P	3	99
FINDLAY, John Leighton	P	5	58
FINDLAY, Neil Douglas	P	1	133
FINDLAY, Robert Scott	P	2	119
FINDLAY, Roland	P	5	58
FINEGAN, Joseph Patrick		3	99
FINES, George William	P	1	133
FINK, Gordon	P	1	133
FINK, Sydney		3	99
FINLAY, Edward Norman Alison	P	3	99
FINLAY, Edward Norman Alison		4	56
FINLAY, Eric Lionel	P	3	99
FINLAY, Frederick		1	133
FINLAY, James Cowans		2	119
FINLAY, Robert Christie		1	133
FINLAYSON, A		4	56
FINLAYSON, Alexander Dunlop	P	3	99
FINLAYSON, Charles Tullock		1	133
FINLAYSON, George Russell		1	133
FINLAYSON, Malcolm Groat		5	59
FINLEY, F		4	56
FINLEY, James Frederick		2	119
FINN, Edward		5	59
FINN, S		2	119
FINNEGAN, Robert Thompson	P	5	59
FINNETT, Henry Charles	P	1	133
FINNIE, Alexander		2	119
FINNIGAN, J		2	119
FINNIGAN, James		1	133
FINNIGAN, William		1	133

Name	Photo	Part No.	Page No.
FORTH, William Harry		2	124
FORTUNE, Henry George		5	61
FORTUNE, James	P	1	139
FORTUNE, W W		3	105
FORWARD, George T		2	124
FORWELL, William Lyon		5	61
FOSKETT, Joseph George		4	58
FOSSEY, Alfred		5	62
FOSSEY, O		3	105
FOSTER, Archibald Courtenay Hayes	P	1	139
FOSTER, Arthur Cedric	P	1	140
FOSTER, Cecil William		4	58
FOSTER, Charles Clifford	P	5	62
FOSTER, Christopher John		3	105
FOSTER, David		1	140
FOSTER, Edward	P	3	105
FOSTER, Frank		3	105
FOSTER, Frank Cyril		4	58
FOSTER, Frederick		1	140
FOSTER, Frederick William		3	105
FOSTER, George	P	4	58
FOSTER, Heaton	P	5	62
FOSTER, Herbert Charles	P	5	62
FOSTER, Herbert Knollys	P	1	140
FOSTER, James		2	124
FOSTER, James Graham		4	58
FOSTER, John		1	140
FOSTER, John Thomas	P	1	140
FOSTER, Laurence Talbot Lisle	P	1	140
FOSTER, Leonard	P	2	124
FOSTER, Ralph	P	2	124
FOSTER, Robert	P	1	140
FOSTER, Robert Elliot		3	106
FOSTER, Stephen		5	62
FOSTER, Thomas H		5	62
FOSTER, Thomas Richard		2	124
FOSTER, W		3	106
FOSTER, Walter		4	59
FOSTER, Walter Francis		3	106
FOSTER, William	P	1	140
FOSTER, William Augustus Portman		2	124
FOSTER, William John		2	124
FOTHERINGHAM, Alexander Boyne	P	1	140
FOUCAR, Clement Auguste	P	1	140
FOULGER, Charles Frederick		2	124
FOULGER, William A		2	124
FOULKES, Herbert		1	140
FOULKS, Henry Samuel		2	124
FOULSTONE, C N		3	106
FOUND, John		1	140
FOURNIER, Emile		1	140
FOWKE, Mansergh Cuthbert		2	124
FOWKE, William Robert		2	124
FOWLER, Cecil Dashwood Milman	P	2	124
FOWLER, Charles William		2	124
FOWLER, Christopher Richard	P	1	140
FOWLER, G Herbert		2	124
FOWLER, George	P	1	141
FOWLER, George Arthur		3	106
FOWLER, Harry Victor		3	106
FOWLER, Theodore Humphrey		1	141
FOWLER, Walter Frank	P	5	62
FOWLER, William		1	141
FOWLER, William		2	124
FOWLER, William		3	106

Name	Photo	Part No.	Page No.
FOWLER, William Bruce		3	106
FOWLER, William Henry	P	1	141
FOWLER, William James	P	5	62
FOWLES, Reginald Lawrence	P	3	106
FOWLING, Bertie Evelyn		1	141
FOWLOW, Richard	P	1	141
FOX, A E		2	124
FOX, Alfred	P	2	125
FOX, Arthur		5	62
FOX, Charles Alexander Newcome	P	4	59
FOX, Charles Leonard		3	106
FOX, D R		2	125
FOX, Douglas Charles	P	3	106
FOX, Francis Nevil Wilson		3	106
FOX, Frank Herbert	P	4	59
FOX, Fred	P	3	106
FOX, Frederick Donald	P	2	125
FOX, H C T		3	106
FOX, Haniel Morriss		3	106
FOX, Harry		1	141
FOX, Harry Edwin		1	141
FOX, Henry		4	59
FOX, John		1	141
FOX, M		2	125
FOX, Maurice Arthur		1	141
FOX, Thomas Noel		5	62
FOX, Thomas William		2	125
FOX, V		2	125
FOX, Walter Henry	P	1	141
FOX, Wilfrid Armstrong		1	141
FOX, William		1	141
FOX, William		2	125
FOX, William Alfred		1	141
FOXELL, Frederick James		1	141
FOXEN, Thomas George		3	106
FOXON, E E		2	125
FOXTON, James		1	141
FOXWELL, Cyril Henry Rowland		4	59
FOY, David		2	125
FOY, Martin Victor		2	125
FOYER, William		1	141
FRADLEY, Harry		2	125
FRAIL, John		2	125
FRAIL, Walter		2	125
FRAME, Andrew		2	125
FRAME, James		3	106
FRAMPTON, John Guy		5	62
FRAMPTON, John Howard		2	125
FRAMPTON, John Thomas		1	141
FRAMPTON, Joseph Henry		1	141
FRAMPTON, Walter John	P	1	141
FRANCE, Arthur Alderson		3	106
FRANCE, Gordon		3	106
FRANCE, Herbert		3	106
FRANCIS, Arthur	P	1	141
FRANCIS, Arthur Burdett	P	3	106
FRANCIS, Basil Hugh		1	141
FRANCIS, Charles J		2	125
FRANCIS, Ernest Edward		4	59
FRANCIS, Franklin Herbert	P	2	125
FRANCIS, Gilbert Bryan	P	1	141
FRANCIS, Henry William	P	1	142
FRANCIS, James Thomas		1	142
FRANCIS, John	P	1	142
FRANCIS, John		1	142

Name	Photo	Part No.	Page No.	Name	Photo	Part No.	Page No.
FRIEND, Harry Edwin		1	144	FULLER, Leslie John		2	129
FRIEND, Joseph Bertie		5	63	FULLER, Lionel Henry	P	2	129
FRIER, Charles		2	128	FULLER, Thomas	P	1	145
FRITH, Herbert		2	128	FULLER, William John		1	145
FRITH, John Felix		2	128	FULLERTON, George		5	64
FRITH, Stephen Arthur		5	63	FULLICK, Robert Stanley		1	145
FRITZ, W A		2	128	FULLWOOD, William		5	64
FRIZELL, Richard Alexander		4	60	FULTON, Andrew		2	129
FRODSHAM, William Thomas	P	3	108	FULTON, David Munroe	P	5	64
FROGGATT, Alexander		1	144	FUNNELL, Arthur		2	129
FROST, Arthur William		4	60	FUNNELL, C E		3	108
FROST, Bertie Cyril		3	108	FUNNELL, Ernest		2	129
FROST, Charles Dale	P	2	128	FUNNELL, Ernest E		2	129
FROST, Colin Blomfield		5	63	FUNNELL, Stephen		2	129
FROST, Edmund Lionel	P	1	144	FUNNELL, Thomas Edward		1	145
FROST, Eric George	P	3	108	FUREY, Cecil Herbert		2	129
FROST, Evelyn Fairfax Meadows	P	2	128	FUREY, Ignatius		1	145
FROST, George Maurice		5	63	FURLEY, Robert Basil	P	2	129
FROST, Gerard Garton Stacy	P	1	144	FURLONG, Philip James	P	5	64
FROST, Hilton Brown		2	128	FURMIDGE, James Henry		4	60
FROST, John		2	128	FURNEAUX, Philip Templer		2	129
FROST, K T		2	128	FURNELL, A		3	108
FROST, Kenneth	P	1	144	FURNESS, Arthur		1	145
FROST, Percy	P	5	63	FURNESS, B		3	108
FROST, Thomas		2	128	FURNESS, Frederick		4	60
FROUD, George		3	108	FURNISS, Evelyn Oswald	P	3	108
FRY, Alfred Harold	P	2	128	FURNIVAL, Walter George John	P	3	108
FRY, Edwin Harries Sargood		4	60	FURPHY, George Henry		1	145
FRY, Frederick George		5	64	FURSE, George Armand	P	1	145
FRY, Horace		1	145	FURSEY, Edward		2	129
FRY, James		1	145	FURZE, Frederic	P	3	108
FRY, John Campbell		3	108	FURZE, Henry Charles		2	129
FRY, Joseph Huish		3	108	FUTERS, Norman Ratcliffe		5	64
FRY, Leslie Harrington	P	5	64	FUTRILL, Charles		1	145
FRY, Thomas		2	128	FUTTER, Frank Charles		1	146
FRY, Walter Charles	P	2	128	FUTTER, James		4	60
FRY, William Benjamin		4	60	FUTTER, Walter		4	60
FRY, William Henry	P	3	108	FYALL, Andrew	P	5	64
FRYATT, Thomas		3	108	FYALL, John Cunningham Knight	P	5	64
FRYER, Anthony Thomas	P	2	128	FYFE, Douglas John		4	60
FRYER, Edwin Samuel	P	1	145	FYFE, William Quentin		5	64
FRYER, Ernest George	P	1	145	FYFFE, J		2	129
FRYER, Norman Moody		1	145	FYFFE, T		2	129
FRYER, Thomas		2	128	FYFIELD, James		1	146
FUCHSBALG, Maurice Marcelle	P	1	145	FYLES, David		4	60
FUDGE, Walter		2	128	FYLES, Henry	P	4	60
FUGE, Thomas Robertes	P	5	64	FYSH, Alfred William		5	65
FUGGLES, H W		2	128	FYSH, Charles Edward		4	60
FULCHER, Bernard Vincent		2	128	FYSH, William		1	146
FULCHER, Frederick		1	145	FYSHE, Francis	P	1	146
FULCHER, Hugh		2	128	FYSON, Oliver		1	146
FULFORD, Horace		2	128	GABB, William Harold		2	129
FULFORD, William Ira	P	1	145	GABBETT, Edmond Poole		1	146
FULLARTON, J		2	128	GABELL, James		1	146
FULLER, Alfred E		2	128	GABRIEL, Stewart Arkcoll	P	3	108
FULLER, Claud Liddle	P	2	128	GADSEN, Walter Samuel		1	146
FULLER, Colin Melville		1	145	GAFFNEY, J		2	129
FULLER, E		3	108	GAFFNEY, J		3	108
FULLER, Frank Alexander	P	1	145	GAFFNEY, James		2	129
FULLER, H W		3	108	GAFFNEY, Leon Arthur	P	1	146
FULLER, Harry		1	145	GAGE, Alfred		1	146
FULLER, James		1	145	GAGE, Charles		5	65
FULLER, John Henry Middleton		2	128	GAGE, John Stewart Moore	P	4	60
FULLER, John Severn		5	64	GAIGER, Arthur Alfred		1	146
FULLER, Leonard	P	1	145	GAILEY, Edward Joseph		1	146

Name	Photo	Part No.	Page No.
GAILLARD, Lucien Raoul D'etainville	P	2	129
GAINES, G		3	108
GAINEY, Samuel		2	129
GAIR, Thomas		3	108
GAISFORD, Lionel		2	129
GAITLEY, Arthur		1	146
GAITSKELL, Cyril Egremont		2	129
GALBRAITH, Archibald		3	109
GALBRAITH, Donald		3	109
GALBRAITH, Donald James Findlay		1	146
GALE, C D W		2	129
GALE, G		3	109
GALE, G S		3	109
GALE, George	P	3	109
GALE, Marmaduke Henry Littledale	P	1	146
GALL, Frederick		4	61
GALLACHER, David	P	2	129
GALLACHER, J		3	109
GALLACHER, P		2	129
GALLAGHER, George Loftus		3	109
GALLAGHER, J		3	109
GALLAGHER, M		3	109
GALLAGHER, Michael		2	129
GALLAGHER, Thomas		5	65
GALLAGHER, William Augustine	P	1	146
GALLAHGER, J		3	109
GALLANT, Herbert		2	129
GALLANT, Joseph	P	1	146
GALLARD, William Henry Edward		3	109
GALLERY, John Richard	P	1	146
GALLIVAN, H		3	109
GALLOCHER, P		2	129
GALLON, William Clavering	P	2	129
GALLOWAY, Alexander Tevendale		5	65
GALLOWAY, Archibald Wilson		1	146
GALLOWAY, George David		2	129
GALLOWAY, J		3	109
GALLOWAY, J		3	109
GALLOWAY, John		2	130
GALLOWAY, John		4	61
GALLYER, William R		2	130
GALPIN, Harold Ernest Sydney		1	147
GALPIN, William Frank	P	1	147
GALTON, Theodore Hugh		2	130
GALVIN, William		5	65
GALWAY, J		3	109
GAMAGE, Benjamin		2	130
GAMBLE, Edward	P	4	61
GAMBLE, Frank William		2	130
GAMBLE, James		1	147
GAMBLE, Joseph	P	4	61
GAMBLE, Ralph Dominic	P	4	61
GAMBLE, Richard Maurice Brooks	P	1	147
GAMBLE, Richard Sumner	P	1	147
GAMBRILL, John		1	147
GAME, Frank Cyril		5	65
GAMINARA, Emmanuel Enrique	P	2	130
GAMLIN, William Harold	P	4	61
GAMMON, George William		1	147
GAMMON, Harry		1	147
GAMMON, Richard Thomas		3	109
GAMMON, William Stanley Argyle	P	1	147
GAMMONS, Samuel		3	109
GANDAR, Bertram James		1	147
GANDE, A		2	130

Name	Photo	Part No.	Page No.
GANDER, Reginald William Joseph		4	61
GANDY, Charles		5	65
GANDY, Frederick George	P	1	147
GANDY, Herbert Howard	P	5	65
GANE, Henry		2	130
GANT, Alfred James		2	130
GANT, Charles		4	61
GANT, Henry	P	1	147
GANT, Reginald		2	130
GANT, Samuel	P	5	65
GANT, Wilfred		2	130
GANTLE, A		2	133
GARBUTT, Charles William		1	147
GARD, Alfred William		1	147
GARD, Stephen Alfred		2	130
GARDEN, John Alexander		4	61
GARDEN, Norman Macleod	P	2	130
GARDENNER, John Vernon	P	5	65
GARDINER, Alec	P	1	147
GARDINER, Alexander Anson		3	109
GARDINER, Andrew	P	1	148
GARDINER, Archibald Macalister	P	3	109
GARDINER, Cecil William		4	61
GARDINER, Eric William		4	61
GARDINER, Ernest Frederic (Eric)	P	1	148
GARDINER, Fred		1	148
GARDINER, George Archibald Victor		4	61
GARDINER, H		3	109
GARDINER, Herbert	P	4	62
GARDINER, J		3	109
GARDINER, J S B		3	109
GARDINER, James		2	130
GARDINER, John Philip	P	1	148
GARDINER, John Slater		4	62
GARDINER, Lewis		1	148
GARDINER, Paul Wrey		4	62
GARDINER, Percy Henry		1	148
GARDINER, R		3	109
GARDINER, W J		2	130
GARDINER, Walter Arthur		1	148
GARDINER, William		4	62
GARDNER, Albert		3	109
GARDNER, Alfred John	P	5	65
GARDNER, Caldwell		3	109
GARDNER, Charles Robert		4	62
GARDNER, F		3	109
GARDNER, Frederick Albert		1	148
GARDNER, Frederick Thomas		2	130
GARDNER, G		3	109
GARDNER, G F		3	109
GARDNER, George		2	130
GARDNER, George Cumming	P	2	130
GARDNER, George Samuel	P	5	65
GARDNER, Godfrey Derman	P	4	62
GARDNER, H		3	109
GARDNER, Henry Patrick		1	148
GARDNER, J		3	109
GARDNER, J T		3	109
GARDNER, James		5	65
GARDNER, John		1	148
GARDNER, John	P	2	130
GARDNER, John Harrison		5	65
GARDNER, Robert Macgregor Stewart	P	1	148
GARDNER, Sidney		4	62
GARDNER, Thomas		2	130

Name	Photo	Part No.	Page No.
GARDNER, W		3	109
GARDNER, Walter Evershed	P	3	110
GARFIT, Thomas Noel Cheney	P	1	148
GARLAND, Christopher Oscar		2	130
GARLICK, J		3	110
GARLING, Frederick Hubert		4	62
GARNER, Frank Albert	P	3	110
GARNER, Frederick		5	65
GARNER, George		2	130
GARNER, Harold		4	62
GARNER, Joseph		4	62
GARNESS, W		3	110
GARNETT, Claude Lionel	P	2	130
GARNETT, Egerton	P	5	65
GARNETT, Ivan William	P	2	130
GARNETT, Jerry Knowles		2	131
GARNETT, Kenneth Gordon	P	3	110
GARNETT, Philip Nigel		2	131
GARNETT, William Hubert Stuart	P	3	110
GARNETT-BOTFIELD, Alfred Clulow Fitzgerald	P	1	43
GARNETT-BOTFIELD, Charles Sidney	P	1	43
GARNIER, John Warren	P	1	148
GARNONS WILLIAMS, Alexander Aylmer Curtis	P	4	237
GARRARD, A		3	110
GARRARD, Edward Burdett		3	110
GARRATT, William		3	110
GARRAWAY, Leonard		5	66
GARRETT, A E		3	110
GARRETT, Albert Isaac		1	149
GARRETT, G		3	110
GARRETT, S		3	111
GARRETT, Walter George	P	1	149
GARRETT, William Sydney		1	149
GARRIE (ALIAS MCGARRIE), James W		2	131
GARROD, Albert C		5	66
GARROD, Alfred Noel	P	2	131
GARROD, Arthur James		1	149
GARROD, Basil Rahera		5	66
GARROD, Charles Valentine		1	149
GARROD, L H		3	111
GARROD, Roland Percival	P	1	149
GARROD, Thomas Martin	P	2	131
GARROWAY, Alfred Henry		1	149
GARSIA, Oliver Dunham Melville		2	131
GARSIDE, Jack		5	66
GARSTANG, Charles Harropp	P	5	66
GARSTIN, Charles William North		2	131
GARSTIN, Denys Norman	P	5	66
GARSTIN, William Fortescue Colborne		3	111
GARTON, Herbert Westlake		3	111
GARTON, William James		4	62
GARVEY, J		3	111
GARVIE, Edwin Stanley		2	131
GARVIE, Peter Thomas	P	3	111
GARVIE, William		5	66
GARWOOD, Alfred Joseph	P	5	66
GARWOOD, Bertram	P	1	149
GARWOOD, J		3	111
GASBY, S		3	111
GASCOIGNE, Archibald		2	131
GASCOIGNE, H		3	111
GASCOIGNE, T		3	111
GASCOYNE, George Frederick		5	66

Name	Photo	Part No.	Page No.
GASCOYNE-CECIL, Rupert Edward	P	1	75
GASKELL, David Lyndsay Stranack	P	2	131
GASKELL, Holbrook Lance	P	3	111
GASKELL, James		5	66
GASTON, James		5	66
GATACRE, John Kirwan		2	131
GATELEY, Arnold Walter		5	67
GATER, Walter Frederick		1	149
GATES, Charles William		4	62
GATES, Frederick John		1	149
GATES, Richard Thomas	P	2	131
GATES, William		1	149
GATH, Charles Henry		2	131
GATHERCOLE, Charles Henry		2	131
GATHORNE-HARDY, Alfred Cecil	P	2	158
GATLEY, James		4	62
GATRELL, W		2	131
GATWOOD, Arnold Walter		4	62
GAUGHAN, James		1	149
GAULD, Alexander Wilson		4	62
GAUNT, Cecil		1	149
GAUNT, Frederick	P	2	131
GAUNT, George Alfred		2	131
GAUNT, Kenneth Macfarlane		2	131
GAUTREY, George William		1	149
GAUTREY, Thomas Arthur		1	149
GAVIN, Neil Murphy	P	2	132
GAVIN, P		3	111
GAVIN, Peter		2	132
GAWAN-TAYLOR, Francis	P	1	347
GAWLER, George Victor		1	149
GAWTHORN, James Edward	P	3	111
GEALL, C		3	111
GEAR, George Edward		5	67
GEARD, A		3	111
GEARD, Frederick John Parsons	P	1	149
GEARE, William Duncan		3	111
GEAREY, Albert Edward		5	67
GEAREY, Edward		2	132
GEAREY, Frederick James		2	132
GEARING, Alfred		1	149
GEARY, Alfred Thomas		4	62
GEARY, Joseph Ashmore	P	2	132
GEATON, William Christopher		3	111
GEBBIE, James Francis Roy		2	132
GEDDES, A		3	111
GEDDES, Alexander		4	62
GEDDES, Andrew Brown	P	4	62
GEDDES, Arthur Alexander	P	2	132
GEDDES, Augustus David	P	1	149
GEDDES, Charles Falconer		3	111
GEDDES, Robert		2	132
GEDDES, William		1	149
GEDDES, William Murray	P	2	132
GEDDIE, John		5	67
GEDGE, Cecil Bertie	P	2	132
GEDGE, Joseph Theodore	P	2	133
GEDGE, Peter	P	2	133
GEE, Frederick William Thomas		1	149
GEE, James Henry		2	133
GEE, Robert Francis Mclean	P	1	149
GEE, Stephen John	P	2	133
GEE, William		2	133
GEE, William Heathcote		3	111
GEERE, Cecil		3	111

Name	Photo	Part No.	Page No.	Name	Photo	Part No.	Page No.
GELL, Christopher Stowell		3	111	GIBBS, Walter Edward		4	63
GELLYER, George Peabody	P	1	182	GIBBS, William		1	151
GELSON, John George		2	133	GIBBS, William Charles		1	151
GEMMELL, James Brown Richardson		3	111	GIBNEY, Hugh		2	134
GEMMELL, Paul William		5	67	GIBSON, Albert Edward		1	151
GENERY, Hugh Thomas Watson		1	150	GIBSON, Albert Edward		2	134
GENT, Edward		1	150	GIBSON, Alexander		2	134
GENTLE, Charles Frederick	P	2	133	GIBSON, Alexander	P	4	63
GEOGHEGAN, James Randolph		2	133	GIBSON, Alexander	P	4	63
GEOGHEGAN, Stannus		5	67	GIBSON, Andrew		2	134
GEORGE, Alec	P	1	150	GIBSON, Athol Thomas		2	134
GEORGE, Athelstane Key Durance		2	133	GIBSON, Charles Methuen		5	67
GEORGE, Bertie Aaron		1	150	GIBSON, Daniel		2	134
GEORGE, Charles Richard	P	2	133	GIBSON, Edward Telford		2	134
GEORGE, Ernest Frederick	P	1	150	GIBSON, F		3	112
GEORGE, Ernest Harry	P	2	133	GIBSON, Francis Malloch	P	2	134
GEORGE, Frederick Ralph		2	133	GIBSON, Fred		4	63
GEORGE, J		3	112	GIBSON, G		3	112
GEORGE, J		3	112	GIBSON, G		3	112
GEORGE, John Low		3	112	GIBSON, H		3	112
GEORGE, Maxim		1	150	GIBSON, Harry		4	63
GEORGE, William F		2	133	GIBSON, Ifor Griffiths		5	67
GERMAN, Thomas		1	150	GIBSON, James Guthrie		5	67
GERMINE, Ernest Wilfred		5	67	GIBSON, John		1	151
GERRANS, Christopher Davies		1	150	GIBSON, John		4	63
GERRARD, George Henry		4	62	GIBSON, John E		2	135
GERRARD, Harry Vernon		2	133	GIBSON, Joseph		2	135
GERRARD, John	P	4	63	GIBSON, Mungo Campbell	P	1	151
GERRARD, Samuel	P	2	133	GIBSON, Peter		4	63
GERRARD, Samuel		2	134	GIBSON, R		2	135
GERRARD, Thomas		2	134	GIBSON, Reginald		2	135
GERRARD, W		3	112	GIBSON, Robert		1	151
GERRED, Joseph James	P	4	63	GIBSON, Robert		2	135
GERRIE, Charles Edward	P	5	67	GIBSON, Robert	P	4	63
GERRIE, Harry Copland	P	2	134	GIBSON, T		3	112
GERRISH, Frank		1	150	GIBSON, W		2	135
GERRY, Albert John	P	1	150	GIBSON, William		2	135
GETHING, Hugh Bagnall	P	1	150	GIBSON-CRAIG, Sir Archibald Charles		2	83
GIBB, Albert		2	134	GIDDINGS, M W		3	112
GIBB, Alexander		3	112	GIDLEY, Gerald Edgar		4	63
GIBB, Lawrence Michael		3	112	GIDLOW, T		3	112
GIBB, William Alexander	P	1	150	GIDMAN, Fred		4	63
GIBB, William James	P	1	150	GIDNEY, Edwin	P	1	151
GIBBARD, William		1	150	GIFFARD, Robert		2	135
GIBB-FEILD, William	P	3	97	GIFFORD, George Edward		1	151
GIBBIN, Albert Edward	P	2	134	GIFFORD, James Henry		2	135
GIBBINS, Henry Edward		1	150	GIGG, Henry Albert		1	151
GIBBINS, John		1	150	GILBANK, Charles		1	151
GIBBINS, William Robert		3	112	GILBANKS, Richard Parker	P	2	135
GIBBONS, Charles		1	150	GILBERT, Albert		2	135
GIBBONS, Charles William Crowne	P	1	151	GILBERT, Alfred		2	135
GIBBONS, Harry William		3	112	GILBERT, Bertram Thomas Chesterton	P	3	112
GIBBONS, J		3	112	GILBERT, Charles		2	135
GIBBONS, J		3	112	GILBERT, Charles Henry		3	112
GIBBONS, R		3	112	GILBERT, Frank		2	135
GIBBS, Albert		3	112	GILBERT, G S		3	112
GIBBS, Albert Walter		1	151	GILBERT, Gilbert Garnet		4	63
GIBBS, Alfred		1	151	GILBERT, H		3	112
GIBBS, E De L		3	112	GILBERT, James William	P	1	151
GIBBS, Ernest		1	151	GILBERT, John Henry		5	67
GIBBS, Ivan Richard	P	2	134	GILBERT, Leslie Spencer	P	4	64
GIBBS, Leslie George		3	112	GILBERT, Nelson		1	151
GIBBS, Noel Martin	P	2	134	GILBERT, W		3	112
GIBBS, Percival Seaman		4	63	GILBERT, Walter		2	135
GIBBS, Ronald Charles Melbourne	P	1	151	GILBERT, Wilfred Valentine	P	1	151

Name	Photo	Part No.	Page No.	Name	Photo	Part No.	Page No.
GILBERT-JOHNS, William		5	95	GILLESPIE, Robert		2	136
GILBERTSON, A H		3	112	GILLESPIE, Thomas		2	136
GILBERTSON, Richard		3	112	GILLESPIE, Thomas Cunningham	P	1	152
GILBEY, Caleb J		2	135	GILLESPIE, William John		1	153
GILBEY, Eric	P	1	151	GILLESPIE, William Robert Beauchamp	P	3	113
GILBEY, William		2	135	GILLETT, Albert Edward		2	136
GILBEY, William Edward		1	152	GILLETT, William John		2	136
GILBRIDE, James		4	64	GILLHAM, Benjamin		1	153
GILBRIDE, Thomas		1	152	GILLHAM, Cyril Henry		5	68
GILBY, G		3	112	GILLIAT, Cecil Glendower Percival		2	136
GILCHRIST, Hugh		3	112	GILLIAT, Otho Claude Skipwith		2	136
GILCHRIST, Ian Edward	P	2	135	GILLIAT, Robert Vincent	P	5	68
GILCHRIST, Ivan Hamilton Learmonth	P	2	135	GILLIAT-SMITH, Arthur		4	191
GILCHRIST, John Anderson		2	135	GILLIES, David Alexander		4	64
GILCHRIST, Malcolm Mcniven	P	3	112	GILLIES, James		3	113
GILCHRIST, Robert Crooks	P	1	152	GILLIES, James Taylor		5	68
GILCHRIST, T		2	135	GILLINGHAM, Frank		1	153
GILDER, Tom Norman		5	67	GILLIS, J		3	113
GILDERDALE, John Edward		2	135	GILLMAN, Angus George		3	113
GILDERTHORP, Harry Stanley	P	1	152	GILLON, J		2	136
GILES, Albert Arthur	P	4	64	GILLORAY, C		3	113
GILES, Albert G		2	135	GILLS, George		1	153
GILES, Charles Innes		5	67	GILMARTIN, M		3	113
GILES, Edward		3	113	GILMORE, J		3	113
GILES, Frank Eric William	P	3	113	GILMORE, Stephen		5	68
GILES, Frank William		1	152	GILMORE, Thomas		5	68
GILES, James		1	152	GILMOUR, H		3	113
GILES, John		2	135	GILMOUR, H		3	113
GILES, Sidney		1	152	GILMOUR, Walter Ernest		3	113
GILES, Sidney Duncan		1	152	GILPIN, Albert John		3	113
GILES, Sydney George	P	4	64	GILROY, William Charles		5	68
GILFILLAN, John Alfred Alison		1	152	GILYARD, Ernest William		4	64
GILHAM, Henry		1	152	GINDER, William Frank		4	64
GILHOOLY, James	P	2	135	GINGELL, H		3	113
GILKISON, Dugald Stewart		2	135	GINGELL, R		3	113
GILKISON, James David		2	135	GINN, John		3	113
GILL, Bernard		3	113	GINNIFER, G		3	113
GILL, Charles Treverbyn	P	4	64	GIPPS, Reginald Nigel		2	136
GILL, Edmund		4	64	GIRARDOT, Paul Chancourt	P	1	153
GILL, Ellis Sibley		5	67	GIRLING, Charles John	P	2	136
GILL, Frederick William		1	152	GIRLING, Stephen Eastaugh		5	68
GILL, George		2	135	GIRLING, Theodore Augustus		5	68
GILL, George		3	113	GIROUX, Theodore	P	1	153
GILL, George Robert		1	152	GISBY, Edgar Ewart		3	114
GILL, Sidney Alec		2	135	GISPERT, Modesto Arthur	P	4	64
GILL, Stanley		3	113	GIVEN, Maurice		5	68
GILL, Thomas		4	64	GIVENS, Gilbert	P	5	68
GILL, Worsley		3	113	GIVENS, Thomas		2	136
GILLAM, Cecil Thomas		1	152	GIVENS, William Norris	P	5	68
GILLAM, William Frederick		3	113	GLADDISH, Edward		1	153
GILLAN, James		2	136	GLADMAN, James		2	136
GILLANDERS, George Hamilton		2	136	GLADMAN, John Owen	P	1	153
GILLARD, Thomas James	P	3	113	GLADSTONE, William Glynne Charles	P	1	153
GILLARD, William James		1	152	GLADWELL, John Jeffery		3	114
GILLESPIE, Alexander Douglas	P	1	152	GLADWELL, William Henry		3	114
GILLESPIE, Alexander Douglas		2	136	GLADWIN, Arthur George		5	68
GILLESPIE, Andrew		1	153	GLADWIN, Ralph Hamilton Fane		2	136
GILLESPIE, Arthur Neil		2	136	GLANDFIELD, Albert Victor		3	114
GILLESPIE, Charles	P	2	136	GLANDFIELD, Albert Victor		4	64
GILLESPIE, E		2	136	GLANFIELD, J		3	114
GILLESPIE, Franklin Macaulay	P	1	152	GLANVILL, Ernest Mure		2	136
GILLESPIE, Fred Joseph	P	5	67	GLANVILLE, Albert Andrew		1	153
GILLESPIE, James	P	2	136	GLANVILLE, Frederick C		2	136
GILLESPIE, John Gordon		3	113	GLANVILLE, John Harry		3	114
GILLESPIE, Norman Alexander	P	1	152	GLASGOW, Henry Macdonald		3	114

Name	Photo	Part No.	Page No.
GLASS, Ernest George		1	153
GLASS, Ernest Graham	P	1	153
GLASS, James Walter		2	136
GLASS, Robert	P	4	64
GLASS, William		1	154
GLAYZER, Sidney E		2	137
GLAZEBROOK, Henry		1	154
GLEDHILL, Norman		2	137
GLEESON, William		4	65
GLEGG, Arthur Livingstone	P	1	154
GLEGG, Robert	P	2	137
GLEN, J		2	137
GLEN, William	P	1	154
GLENISTER, William Montague		2	137
GLENNON, Thomas Henry		3	114
GLEW, Aubrey Edmund	P	2	137
GLIBBERY, William		3	114
GLIDDON, Frank Charles		1	154
GLIDDON, Maurice	P	3	114
GLITHRO, Frank William		1	154
GLOAG, Alexander Hoy		5	68
GLORNEY, Ernest Edward	P	2	137
GLOSBY, James		2	138
GLOSSOP, Ernest Edward	P	1	154
GLOSTER, A E		3	114
GLOSTER, Henry Colpoys	P	1	154
GLOSTER, James David		5	68
GLOVER, Francis Luther		1	154
GLOVER, George Martin	P	2	137
GLOVER, H		3	114
GLOVER, Harry	P	3	114
GLOVER, Harvey		3	114
GLOVER, J		2	137
GLOVER, John		3	114
GLOVER, N R		2	137
GLOVER, Richard Bowie Gaskell	P	2	137
GLOVER, Thomas		2	137
GLYN, Richard Spencer		2	137
GOACHER, Stephen Frank		1	154
GOADBY, John Clifton		5	68
GOATER, John Robert		1	154
GOBBEY, John		2	137
GOBLE, Albert Edward		1	154
GOBY, William		1	154
GODDARD, Albert		2	137
GODDARD, Albert Bertie		1	154
GODDARD, Arthur Hawkins	P	1	154
GODDARD, Frank		3	114
GODDARD, H		3	114
GODDARD, James		1	154
GODDARD, James		1	154
GODDARD, John		2	137
GODDARD, Reginald Stanley	P	3	114
GODDARD, S		3	114
GODDARD, S		3	114
GODDARD, Thomas		1	154
GODDARD, William		1	154
GODDEN, Arthur Henry Griffiths		1	154
GODDEN, E E		3	114
GODFERY, Ernest Herbert		1	154
GODFREE, John		1	154
GODFREY, Arthur Pole	P	3	114
GODFREY, David	P	2	137
GODFREY, Edward Baker	P	3	115
GODFREY, Ernest		2	137

Name	Photo	Part No.	Page No.
GODFREY, Frederick		1	154
GODFREY, Frederick (Dan)		3	115
GODFREY, George Arthur Henry (Harry)	P	2	138
GODFREY, John		2	138
GODFREY, John Leslie	P	5	69
GODFREY, William		2	138
GODFREY-FAUSSETT, Owen Godfrey		2	117
GODIN, Moise	P	1	154
GODRICH, William		2	138
GODSAL, Alan	P	1	154
GODSALL, A		3	115
GODWARD, Eric James	P	1	155
GODWIN, Ernest William	P	5	69
GODWIN, Frederick Mark		2	138
GODWIN, Harold North	P	3	115
GODWIN, Philip Edgar	P	2	138
GODWIN, Robert		5	69
GODWIN, Sidney William	P	2	138
GOFF, C H		2	138
GOFF, Henry Albert		4	65
GOFFE, William Reginald		3	115
GOFFIN, Herbert Cullis	P	1	155
GOGGS, Frank	P	1	155
GOLDBAUM, Harry	P	1	155
GOLDBERG, Parris		2	138
GOLDER, A		3	115
GOLDER, Reginald James		4	65
GOLDER, William	P	5	69
GOLDFINCH, George John		2	138
GOLDIE, A		2	138
GOLDIE, Andrew		2	138
GOLDIE, Barre Herbert		1	155
GOLDING, Eden Charles		5	69
GOLDING, Lawford Hymus	P	2	138
GOLDING, T J	P	4	65
GOLDING, Thomas Harold		5	69
GOLDING, William		2	138
GOLDING, William Richard		1	155
GOLDSACK, John George William		4	65
GOLDSMID, Sydney Alexander	P	1	155
GOLDSMID-STERN-SALOMONS, David Reginald Harman Phillip	P	2	268
GOLDSMITH, Bertie Hurr	P	1	155
GOLDSMITH, Frank		2	138
GOLDSMITH, Frank		5	69
GOLDSMITH, G		3	115
GOLDSMITH, George Thomas		3	115
GOLDSMITH, John		4	65
GOLDSMITH, Thomas Mark	P	1	155
GOLDSMITH, Walter Thomas		2	138
GOLDSMITH, William C		2	138
GOLDSTON, Lionel Emanuel	P	1	155
GOLDSTONE, C E		3	115
GOLDSTONE, Leonard		5	69
GOLDSWORTHY, Alfred Ernest		1	155
GOLDTHORP, Frank	P	2	138
GOLIGHTLY, George Frederick		3	115
GOLIGHTLY, William		1	155
GOLLAN, R		3	115
GOLLICK, G		3	115
GOLLOP, Alphonso		1	155
GOLPHIN, John Renner	P	1	155
GOMES, Manoel Antonio	P	1	156
GOMM, E H		2	138
GOMM, Edward T		2	138

Name	Photo	Part No.	Page No.
GOMME, Henry		2	138
GONELLA, Joseph William	P	1	156
GOOCH, A		2	138
GOOCH, Alfred		1	156
GOOCH, Geoffrey Fulthorpe	P	5	69
GOOCH, P		3	115
GOOD, William Burnett		3	115
GOODACRE, W H		3	115
GOODAIR, Hugh John		1	156
GOODALE, James Frederic		5	69
GOODALL, Clarence William		3	115
GOODALL, F		3	115
GOODALL, G		3	115
GOODALL, J		3	115
GOODALL, R		3	115
GOODBODY, Henry Edgar		1	156
GOODBURN, John James		1	156
GOODCHILD, Frank		1	156
GOODCHILD, John William		1	156
GOODE, Alan Samuel		3	115
GOODE, Eric Ralf	P	1	156
GOODE, Gerald		2	138
GOODE, Gordon Powell	P	1	156
GOODE, T		3	115
GOODE, William Edward		1	156
GOODEN, Bertie Levi	P	4	65
GOODES, George Leonard	P	2	138
GOODEVE, Lionel	P	2	139
GOODFELLOW, Arthur James	P	2	139
GOODFELLOW, Arthur Victor		4	65
GOODFELLOW, Eric Hector	P	5	69
GOODFELLOW, James Dunn		4	65
GOODFELLOW, James Gordon	P	5	69
GOODFELLOW, Walter Tom Fyfe		5	70
GOODGER, Fred William		2	139
GOODGER, Frederick William		3	115
GOODGER, H		3	115
GOODHART, Eric John	P	1	156
GOODHEW, Thomas Henry		1	156
GOODIER, E		2	139
GOODILL, George		2	139
GOODINGS, John		1	156
GOODLAKE, G		3	115
GOODMAN, Arthur Ernest	P	2	139
GOODMAN, Douglas		3	116
GOODMAN, R		2	139
GOODMAN, Thomas		4	65
GOODMAN, W		2	139
GOODREAD, John		2	139
GOODREAN, George Henry		1	156
GOODRICH, James		1	156
GOODRICK, William		2	139
GOODRIGHT, G H		3	116
GOODRUM, Frederick Springthorpe	P	5	70
GOODSELL, Charles Lewis	P	1	156
GOODSELL, Percy	P	1	157
GOODSHIP, Sidney W		2	139
GOODSHIP, William		1	157
GOODSON, Harold Walter	P	5	70
GOODSTON, Charles J C A	P	5	70
GOODWILLIE, John		5	70
GOODWIN, A		3	116
GOODWIN, A E		3	116
GOODWIN, Bransby William		5	70
GOODWIN, Eric Lindsey		3	116

Name	Photo	Part No.	Page No.
GOODWIN, G		3	116
GOODWIN, G H H		3	116
GOODWIN, Harold James	P	3	116
GOODWIN, J A		3	116
GOODWIN, John		2	139
GOODWIN, John Henry		1	157
GOODWIN, Rupert George		5	70
GOODWIN, Seymour Thomas	P	4	65
GOODWIN, Sidney Alfred		1	157
GOODWIN, T		3	116
GOODWRIGHT, Frederick		2	139
GOODY, Walter		4	65
GOODYER, Charles		2	139
GOOM, Norman		3	116
GOOSEY, William Coleman		3	116
GORBEY, Frank Reuben	P	1	157
GORDON, Alexander	P	1	157
GORDON, Alexander John Maxwell	P	4	65
GORDON, Bertie	P	4	65
GORDON, Charles Cecil	P	4	65
GORDON, Charles James Donald Simpson		3	116
GORDON, Cosmo George		2	139
GORDON, David Burns		2	139
GORDON, Donald		2	139
GORDON, Eldred Pottinger		2	139
GORDON, Elizabeth Marjorie		3	116
GORDON, George Duff	P	1	157
GORDON, George F		2	139
GORDON, Gerard Montague	P	4	66
GORDON, James		3	116
GORDON, James Frederick		2	139
GORDON, James Thom	P	4	66
GORDON, James William Nugent	P	1	157
GORDON, John		2	139
GORDON, John		3	116
GORDON, John Fraser	P	5	70
GORDON, John Frederick Strathearn		2	139
GORDON, John Shearer	P	2	139
GORDON, Joseph		1	157
GORDON, Lewis	P	2	140
GORDON, Lockhart Brown		3	116
GORDON, Peter		2	140
GORDON, Peter Davidson		4	66
GORDON, Reginald Glegg		4	66
GORDON, Robert		2	140
GORDON, Robert Eddington		2	140
GORDON, Robert Frederick		1	157
GORDON, Robert Norman		2	140
GORDON, Ronald Steuart		2	140
GORDON, Sidney Eustace Laing	P	1	157
GORDON, W		3	116
GORDON, Walter		2	140
GORDON, William James		1	157
GORDON GRAY, Robert Maxwell	P	5	73
GORDON-DUFF, Lachlan		2	106
GORDON-HUGHES, Gordon Stonhouse (Dick)	P	1	197
GORDON-WALKER, Charles Nigel	P	1	363
GORE, George		3	116
GORE, Gerard Ribton		2	140
GORE, H		3	116
GORE, Sydney Kingston	P	1	157
GORE, William	P	2	140
GORE-BROWNE, Eric Anthony Rollo	P	5	24
GORE-BROWNE, Harold Rollo	P	5	24
GORE-LANGTON, Montagu Vernon	P	2	197

Name	Photo	Part No.	Page No.
GORHAM, Edward Henry		2	140
GORING, Edward		2	140
GORMAN, Andrew Joseph		2	140
GORMAN, Charles John		1	157
GORMAN, Gerald Francis	P	4	66
GORMAN, James Toland		1	157
GORMAN, Michael	P	1	157
GORMAN, Sidney H		2	140
GORMAN, T		3	116
GORMAN, T		3	116
GORMAN, William Albert		3	116
GORMERLEY, David		2	140
GORMLEY, John		2	140
GORRIE, James		2	140
GORRIE, John Alexander	P	2	140
GORRINGE, Edward		2	140
GORRINGE, Mervyn Hugh Egerton	P	4	66
GORRY, J		3	116
GORST, Eric William		2	140
GORTON, George W		2	140
GOSLIN, Henry		2	140
GOSLING, Ernest Alfred		1	157
GOSLING, John		1	157
GOSLING, John		1	157
GOSLING, Walter Samuel		4	66
GOSNELL, Alfred John		2	140
GOSS, Ernest		1	157
GOSS, Henry Thomas		1	157
GOSS, James		4	66
GOSS, Leonard Sidney		4	66
GOSS, Raymond George Frederick	P	2	140
GOSS, W		3	116
GOSSEDGE, John Stanley		3	116
GOSSER, Percival George		2	141
GOSSET, William Beresford		2	141
GOTCH, Duncan Hepburn	P	1	158
GOTCH, Roby Myddleton	P	4	66
GOTT, Charles		2	141
GOUDIE, Alexander Currie		3	116
GOUDIE, Humphrey Blaikie		3	116
GOUDIE, T		2	141
GOUGH, Bertie Vincent	P	4	67
GOUGH, Eric John Fletcher	P	1	158
GOUGH, George Edward		3	117
GOUGH, George Henry Waldron	P	5	70
GOUGH, J		2	141
GOUGH, John Bloomfield		2	141
GOUGH, John Edmond	P	1	158
GOUGH, John Noel	P	5	71
GOUGH, Owen		2	141
GOUGH, Richard		1	158
GOUGH, William George		5	71
GOULD, A		3	117
GOULD, Albert Stanley		1	158
GOULD, Arthur Edmund	P	2	141
GOULD, Arthur Edmund		4	67
GOULD, Arthur Robert		2	141
GOULD, C		3	117
GOULD, Chalkley Vivian	P	3	117
GOULD, Claude		1	158
GOULD, G		3	117
GOULD, Harry		2	141
GOULD, John		1	158
GOULD, John Mills		1	158
GOULD, Lionel Bertram		1	158

Name	Photo	Part No.	Page No.
GOULD, R		2	141
GOULD, Richard Walter		1	158
GOULD, Robert Stephen		1	158
GOULD, Roland		1	158
GOULD, T		3	117
GOULDEN, Frank		2	141
GOULDEN, Frederick Guy		2	141
GOULDER, Harry	P	4	67
GOULDING, George William		2	141
GOULDING, J		3	117
GOULDING, Stanley John	P	2	141
GOULDSBROUGH, Allen		5	71
GOULDSBURY, Henry Cullen	P	3	117
GOURLAY, Alexander Smith Forrest	P	5	71
GOURLAY, William Norris	P	4	67
GOURLEY, Joseph H		2	141
GOVE, Andrew	P	4	67
GOVER, Frederick Thomas		1	158
GOVER, George		3	117
GOVER, R J		3	117
GOVER, William		2	141
GOVER, William	P	5	71
GOVIER, William James		3	117
GOW, Roderic Charles Alister		3	117
GOW, William Kenneth		2	141
GOWANS, Louis Mcleod		2	141
GOWEN, Walter George		3	117
GOWER, Arthur Joseph		1	158
GOWER, Frank Herbert Henry		1	158
GOWERS, Walter		2	141
GOZZARD, W		3	117
GRACE, Harry		2	141
GRACE, John Leybourne		1	158
GRACE, Joseph Edward	P	5	71
GRACE, Percy		3	117
GRACE, T		3	117
GRACIE, A		2	141
GRADWELL, George Francis	P	3	117
GRADY, E		3	117
GRAEME, Lawrence Oliphant	P	3	117
GRAFTON-WIGNALL, John Dighton		3	284
GRAHAM, Adam		2	141
GRAHAM, Alan Moir		2	141
GRAHAM, Alec G M		2	141
GRAHAM, Alexander Kay		2	141
GRAHAM, Andrew	P	3	118
GRAHAM, Archibald Stuart Bullock		2	141
GRAHAM, B		3	118
GRAHAM, Bertram Robert		4	67
GRAHAM, C		3	118
GRAHAM, Colin		5	71
GRAHAM, Cyril	P	1	158
GRAHAM, David		1	158
GRAHAM, David Donald	P	5	71
GRAHAM, Donald	P	2	142
GRAHAM, Donald Hatt Noble	P	2	142
GRAHAM, Edward		3	118
GRAHAM, Frederick Ernest		5	71
GRAHAM, G		3	118
GRAHAM, George		2	142
GRAHAM, George Humphrey Irving	P	2	142
GRAHAM, George William		5	71
GRAHAM, Harry J		2	142
GRAHAM, Henry	P	1	158
GRAHAM, Herbert		2	142

Name	Photo	Part No.	Page No.	Name	Photo	Part No.	Page No.
GRAHAM, Hugh		4	67	GRANT, J		3	118
GRAHAM, J		2	142	GRANT, J		3	118
GRAHAM, J		2	142	GRANT, James		1	160
GRAHAM, J		2	142	GRANT, James Donald		5	72
GRAHAM, J		3	118	GRANT, John		2	143
GRAHAM, James		1	159	GRANT, John Philip	P	3	118
GRAHAM, James		2	142	GRANT, John Spence	P	3	118
GRAHAM, John	P	1	159	GRANT, Joseph	P	2	143
GRAHAM, John		3	118	GRANT, L A		2	144
GRAHAM, John	P	4	67	GRANT, Lawrence		2	144
GRAHAM, John Frederick	P	2	142	GRANT, Lewis Alexander	P	5	72
GRAHAM, John Frederick	P	5	71	GRANT, Moody		2	144
GRAHAM, John William	P	2	142	GRANT, Percy Kenmure		5	72
GRAHAM, Joseph Bernard		5	71	GRANT, Robert	P	4	68
GRAHAM, Kenneth Stuart	P	5	71	GRANT, Thomas		1	160
GRAHAM, Lachlan Seymour		3	118	GRANT, Thomas		1	160
GRAHAM, Malcolm Hewley	P	1	159	GRANT, Thomas Walter		4	68
GRAHAM, Malise Stewart		4	67	GRANT, William		4	68
GRAHAM, Peter		2	143	GRANT, William	P	4	68
GRAHAM, R		2	143	GRANT, William	P	5	72
GRAHAM, Robert		2	143	GRANT, William Peter	P	3	119
GRAHAM, Robert	P	3	118	GRANTHAM, Charles		2	144
GRAHAM, Robert Main		3	118	GRANTHAM, Frederick William	P	2	144
GRAHAM, T		3	118	GRANTHAM, Hugo Frederick	P	2	144
GRAHAM, T		3	118	GRANTHAM, Joshua Thomas		2	144
GRAHAM, W		3	118	GRANTHAM, William		5	72
GRAHAM, W		3	118	GRANT-SUTTIE, Archibald Ronald	P	3	261
GRAHAM, Walter Ross		2	143	GRASETT, Elliot Blair		2	144
GRAHAM, William	P	2	143	GRASS, Percy Caleb	P	3	119
GRAHAME, Francis George		4	67	GRASSICK, William Duthie		3	119
GRAHAME, John Gordon	P	1	159	GRATREX, William James Charles		5	72
GRAHAM-GILMOUR, Herbert James	P	1	153	GRATTAGE, Samuel Thomas		1	160
GRAHN, William Henry	P	4	67	GRATTON, A		2	144
GRAIG, A		2	83	GRAVES, Arthur		2	144
GRAIG, James		2	83	GRAVES, Arthur Thomas		2	144
GRAIG, John Macadam		2	83	GRAVES, E S L		2	144
GRAIG, John Walker		2	83	GRAVES, Evelyn Paget		3	119
GRAINGER, Albert Victor		1	159	GRAVES, Henry Ernest		4	68
GRAINGER, Arthur George		3	118	GRAVES, Walter Francis		2	144
GRAINGER, Charles		2	143	GRAVES-KNYFTON, Reginald Benett	P	5	102
GRAINGER, R		3	118	GRAVES-SAWLE, R C		4	178
GRAINGER, Thomas		2	143	GRAVESTOCK, Henry	P	5	72
GRAINSFORD, Henry John		2	143	GRAVETT, Charles David		1	160
GRAMSHAW, Hugh	P	2	143	GRAY, Adam Henderson	P	3	119
GRAMSHAW, Robert Wilfred Raleigh	P	1	159	GRAY, Albert John		1	160
GRANDFIELD, William Henry	P	3	118	GRAY, Charles Dixon	P	5	72
GRANDIN, Richard John	P	5	72	GRAY, Charles James Caldwell		3	119
GRANDY, Henry Drummond	P	5	72	GRAY, Charles Mann		2	144
GRANEY, John		4	67	GRAY, Charles Shortland		2	144
GRANGER, A		3	118	GRAY, Daniel	P	4	68
GRANGER, John Robert Clifford		1	159	GRAY, Duncan		3	119
GRANT, Alexander		5	72	GRAY, Frederick Colin		3	119
GRANT, Alexander Russell		3	118	GRAY, G		3	119
GRANT, David		2	143	GRAY, George		4	68
GRANT, Donald	P	2	143	GRAY, George Adam		4	68
GRANT, Duncan	P	1	159	GRAY, George Donald		3	119
GRANT, E		3	118	GRAY, Gordon Cronin	P	2	145
GRANT, Edwin Charles		5	72	GRAY, Harris Arthur William		4	68
GRANT, Ernest William	P	1	159	GRAY, Harry		3	119
GRANT, George Leonard	P	2	143	GRAY, Herbert Victor		5	73
GRANT, H		3	118	GRAY, J		3	119
GRANT, Harold Charles	P	1	159	GRAY, James	P	1	160
GRANT, Hubert Anthony		2	143	GRAY, James Bruce		5	73
GRANT, Humphrey De Butts		2	143	GRAY, James Edward		4	68
GRANT, Ian Alan William	P	3	118	GRAY, John Leslie	P	4	68

Name	Photo	Part No.	Page No.	Name	Photo	Part No.	Page No.
GRAY, John Parnwell		4	68	GREEN, F		3	119
GRAY, John William	P	4	68	GREEN, Frank Herbert		3	120
GRAY, Louis Joseph	P	4	68	GREEN, Frederick		1	161
GRAY, Mary Sutherland Brown	P	1	160	GREEN, G		3	120
GRAY, Paul Mcinnes	P	4	69	GREEN, G		3	120
GRAY, Philip		1	160	GREEN, G		3	120
GRAY, R		2	145	GREEN, G		3	120
GRAY, Ralph Sneath		2	145	GREEN, George Lawrence	P	4	69
GRAY, Robert		2	145	GREEN, Harold		3	120
GRAY, Robert		2	145	GREEN, Henry		2	145
GRAY, Robert Henry		1	160	GREEN, Henry James	P	4	70
GRAY, W		3	119	GREEN, Herbert W		2	145
GRAY, W A F		3	119	GREEN, Herbert Walter		5	73
GRAY, William	P	1	160	GREEN, Herbert William		1	161
GRAY, William		2	145	GREEN, Horace Edward		1	161
GRAY, William Douglas	P	5	73	GREEN, J		2	145
GRAY, William James	P	1	160	GREEN, J		2	145
GRAY, William Joseph		4	69	GREEN, James		3	120
GRAY, William Thomas		1	160	GREEN, James Thomas	P	1	161
GRAY, William Walter		2	145	GREEN, John Edward		1	161
GRAY-BUCHANAN, Cecil Gordon	P	1	59	GREEN, John Gustaves		4	70
GRAY-BUCHANAN, Claude	P	1	59	GREEN, John Henry		2	145
GRAY-BUCHANAN, Walter Bruce	P	1	59	GREEN, John Henry		3	120
GRAYSON, Ambrose Dixon Haldrege		2	145	GREEN, John Henry	P	4	70
GRAYSON, T		3	119	GREEN, Joseph		4	70
GRAYSTONE, A		3	119	GREEN, Malcolm Charles Andrew		2	145
GRAZEBROOK, Charles Alverey	P	1	160	GREEN, Percy		2	145
GREAR, James		1	160	GREEN, Percy Ernest		1	161
GREASLEY, Albert	P	2	145	GREEN, Percy Lewis		2	145
GREASLEY, Daniel Joseph		2	145	GREEN, Peter William		5	73
GREATHEAD, Clarence Royal	P	1	160	GREEN, R		3	120
GREATOREX, T		3	119	GREEN, Richmond Edward Ormond Lyttleton	P	3	120
GREAVES, Arthur		3	119	GREEN, Robert		2	145
GREAVES, Benjamin Herbert	P	1	160	GREEN, S		3	120
GREAVES, George Henry		3	119	GREEN, Samuel James		1	161
GREAVES, Henry		5	73	GREEN, Thomas		2	145
GREAVES, Howard Francis Linford		3	119	GREEN, Thomas Edward		4	70
GREAVES, Thomas		2	145	GREEN, Thomas Michael		1	161
GREAVES, Thomas	P	4	69	GREEN, Thomas O		2	146
GREAVES, Victor	P	4	69	GREEN, Thomas Seaman	P	3	120
GREELEY, J		3	119	GREEN, William Arnold		5	73
GREELISH, John J		2	145	GREEN, William Lambey Thorne		1	161
GREEN, A		3	119	GREEN, William Stanley		1	161
GREEN, Albert		1	160	GREEN, William Stanley		4	70
GREEN, Albert		1	160	GREENAWAY, Sidney		1	161
GREEN, Albert		2	145	GREENER, William Ernest		1	161
GREEN, Albert		2	145	GREENFIELD, Albert		2	146
GREEN, Albert		2	145	GREENFIELD, Thomas Bevil	P	2	146
GREEN, Albert John		1	160	GREENHALGH, Edward		1	161
GREEN, Arnold John	P	2	145	GREENHALGH, James Arthur	P	2	146
GREEN, Arthur		1	160	GREENHALGH, Walter		3	120
GREEN, Arthur Adelbert Lingard	P	1	161	GREENHAM, Ernest Albert		1	161
GREEN, Arthur Dawson		2	145	GREENHILL, Alexander Stewart		4	70
GREEN, Arthur Francis		4	69	GREENHILL, Douglas Sydney		3	120
GREEN, Benjamin Riley	P	2	145	GREENHILL, Frederick William Ridge		4	70
GREEN, Charles Frederick		2	145	GREENHORN, James Stewart		5	73
GREEN, Charles William		1	161	GREENLAND, Frederick John		1	161
GREEN, Clarence Alec	P	4	69	GREENLEAF, Godfrey Charles		2	146
GREEN, Claude	P	4	69	GREENSHIELDS, Thomas Edwards	P	2	146
GREEN, Clifford Whittington	P	1	161	GREENSMITH, Robert	P	4	70
GREEN, Edward James		5	73	GREENSTREET, Henry		2	146
GREEN, Edwin Charles	P	4	69	GREENSTREET, Robert George		3	121
GREEN, Ernest		1	161	GREENSTREET, Robert Smith	P	1	161
GREEN, Ernest Walter		2	145	GREENUP, John Bertram		4	70
GREEN, Evandale Crowther	P	4	69	GREENWELL, James Wiseman		2	146

Name	Photo	Part No.	Page No.
GREENWOOD, Alfred Edward		1	161
GREENWOOD, Frank	P	2	146
GREENWOOD, Fred		3	121
GREENWOOD, Frederick W		2	146
GREENWOOD, George Jesse Francis	P	1	161
GREENWOOD, Harold Sutcliffe	P	2	146
GREENWOOD, James		1	161
GREENWOOD, John Francis Bernal	P	1	161
GREENWOOD, John Thomas	P	5	73
GREENWOOD, Lancelot	P	3	121
GREENWOOD, Leonard Montague		5	73
GREENWOOD, Lewis Leonard		1	162
GREENWOOD, Robert	P	1	162
GREER, J		3	121
GREER, James Kenneth Macgregor	P	2	146
GREER, William		1	162
GREGG, John William		2	146
GREGG, John William	P	5	73
GREGG, Robert Studdert		5	73
GREGORY, Bert Walter		1	162
GREGORY, Charles Arthur	P	1	162
GREGORY, David	P	3	121
GREGORY, Ernest		1	162
GREGORY, Geoffrey Francis		2	146
GREGORY, Henry		5	74
GREGORY, James William		1	162
GREGORY, Nathaniel		1	162
GREGORY, R		3	121
GREGORY, Stephen Barnes		3	121
GREGORY, Thomas		1	162
GREGSON-ELLIS, Reginald George	P	3	91
GREIG, Archibald George		3	121
GREIG, George Anthony		2	147
GREIG, John William Henry	P	1	162
GREIG, Stewart		1	162
GREIG, W		2	147
GRENDER, Ernest H		2	147
GRENFELL, Francis Octavius	P	1	162
GRENFELL, Hon. Gerald William	P	1	162
GRENFELL, Hon. Julian Henry Francis	P	1	162
GRENFELL, Riversdale Nonus (Rivy)	P	1	163
GRESON, David Walker		1	162
GRETTON, Rupert Harold	P	2	147
GREVILL, William		2	147
GREY, George Rochfort		5	74
GREY, Gerald		1	163
GREY, J		2	147
GREY, Martin Henry		3	121
GREY, Norman	P	4	70
GREY, Patrick Riddle	P	3	121
GRIBBEN, John Marshall		5	74
GRIBBLE, Julian Royds		5	74
GRIBBON, J		2	147
GRICE, Harry		2	147
GRICE, William		2	147
GRIDLEY, Charles		2	147
GRIDLEY, Herbert A		2	147
GRIEF, Walter T		2	147
GRIERSON, Sir James Moncrieff	P	1	163
GRIEVE, Annandale Gordon	P	3	121
GRIEVE, David		2	147
GRIEVE, Harry C		2	147
GRIEVE, Nicholas Harington	P	4	70
GRIEVE, William	P	4	70
GRIEVE, William Percival	P	1	163
GRIEVE, William Porter		5	74
GRIFFIN, Albert William		4	71
GRIFFIN, Ernest John		1	163
GRIFFIN, F		3	121
GRIFFIN, John	P	2	147
GRIFFIN, William		2	147
GRIFFIN, William		2	147
GRIFFIN, William Gerald		2	147
GRIFFITH, Gerald		2	147
GRIFFITH, John Gwynne	P	1	163
GRIFFITH, Thomas Francis		1	163
GRIFFITH, Walter Stanley Currie		2	147
GRIFFITH-JONES, William Lionel Phillips		4	95
GRIFFITHS, Alexander		3	121
GRIFFITHS, Alfred		2	148
GRIFFITHS, Alfred		2	148
GRIFFITHS, Allen Rhys	P	1	163
GRIFFITHS, Arthur		2	148
GRIFFITHS, Basil Gwynne	P	1	164
GRIFFITHS, Benjamin		2	148
GRIFFITHS, David Mansel	P	2	148
GRIFFITHS, Frederick James	P	4	71
GRIFFITHS, George Henry Whitmore	P	1	164
GRIFFITHS, Henry		4	71
GRIFFITHS, Henry Hingley		5	74
GRIFFITHS, John		1	164
GRIFFITHS, Leonard		2	148
GRIFFITHS, R E		2	148
GRIFFITHS, Sidney	P	5	74
GRIFFITHS, Sidney John	P	2	148
GRIFFITHS, Walter Henry		1	164
GRIFFITHS, William		4	71
GRIFFITHS, William Arthur		5	74
GRIGG, Aaron James	P	3	121
GRIGOR, J		3	121
GRIGOR, William	P	4	71
GRIGSON, Francis Henry	P	1	164
GRILLS, Hubert John		4	71
GRIMBLE, Charles William Nelson		2	148
GRIMBLE, Walter		1	164
GRIMES, Thomas		2	148
GRIMES, Thomas George		5	74
GRIMLEY, Frank		3	121
GRIMLEY, William H		2	148
GRIMMETT, H		3	121
GRIMMETT, Thomas		3	121
GRIMSEY, Harry Steven		4	71
GRIMSHAW, Cecil Thomas Wrigley	P	1	164
GRIMSHAWE, Charles Ronald Vaughan	P	5	74
GRIMSTER, Edgar		2	148
GRIMSTER, Sidney		2	148
GRIMSTON, Horace Sylvester		2	148
GRIMWADE, Edward Ernest		3	121
GRIMWADE, George Risdon	P	2	148
GRIMWADE, Sidney Arthur	P	4	71
GRINSTEAD, Albert E		2	148
GRINSTEAD, Charles Henry		5	74
GRINT, Henry Charles		3	122
GRISBROOK, Llewellyn Alfred		3	122
GRISEWOOD, Francis	P	4	71
GRISEWOOD, George	P	4	71
GRISEWOOD, Paul	P	4	71
GRIST, John	P	4	71
GRIST, Robert George		1	164
GRITT, Arthur James Philip		3	122

Name	Photo	Part No.	Page No.		Name	Photo	Part No.	Page No.
GROMETT, Charles	P	1	164		GUNNER, Charles		2	149
GRONOW, Arthur		4	71		GUNNING, G		3	123
GROOM, Stephen Spurrell		2	148		GUNNING, John		3	123
GROOM, William Sydney		1	164		GUNTER, Henry Thomas		1	166
GROOME, Edward Alfred		5	74		GUNZBURG, Baron Alexis De	P	2	149
GROOME, Frank	P	1	164		GURDEN, William		1	166
GROOME, Stanley George	P	1	164		GURDON, Philip Norman		3	123
GROSVENOR, Arthur William		3	122		GURNEY, Bernard Frank	P	1	166
GROUND, Francis William		3	122		GURR, John Henry	P	1	166
GROUT, Thomas		4	72		GURR, Stephen		1	166
GROVE, Basil Sidney Ernest		3	122		GURRIN, Reginald Wells		3	123
GROVE, Charles Henry		2	148		GUSH, Archibald Walter	P	5	75
GROVE, John Archibald		5	74		GUSH, Charlie Cleaver	P	5	75
GROVER, Harry Cecil		3	122		GUTHERIDGE, John Frederick		4	72
GROVES, Francis Neville	P	1	165		GUTHERSON, Robert		4	72
GROVES, George		1	165		GUTHRIE, Archibald		2	149
GROVES, George		1	165		GUTHRIE, Edmund Robert		2	149
GROVES, Richard Ernest	P	5	74		GUTHRIE, Edward Percy Malcolm	P	2	149
GROVES, Robert Harry	P	3	122		GUTHRIE, George Webb		2	149
GROVES, Thomas		2	148		GUTHRIE, Hector Maclennan		2	149
GROWNS, Alfred John Thomas		3	122		GUTHRIE, John	P	5	75
GRUBB, Lawrence Ernest Pelham		2	148		GUTHRIE, John Mack	P	5	75
GRUBB, Walter Bousfield Watkins	P	1	165		GUTHRIE, Robert Forman	P	2	150
GRUBB, William Edward Kemp		4	72		GUTHRIE, Thomas Mack	P	2	150
GRUCHY, Arthur Gordon	P	1	165		GUTHRIE, William	P	4	72
GRUCHY, Frank Le Maistre		2	149		GUTHRIE, William Campbell		1	166
GRUNDY, Edwin Bosworth	P	4	72		GUTHRIE, William Lovie		4	72
GRUNDY, Geoffrey Stewart	P	1	165		GUY, Arthur Charles John		1	166
GRUNDY, George Edward	P	1	165		GUY, Benjamin F		4	72
GRUNDY, Thomas		1	165		GUY, Charles Philip		2	150
GRYLLS, Desse Edgar		1	165		GUY, Edmund Henry Ewart		5	75
GUBBY, John Arthur		2	149		GUY, Harry Albert		1	166
GUDGEON, John Thomas	P	2	149		GUY, J		2	150
GUERAN, William		2	149		GUY, William		1	166
GUERIN, C		3	122		GWILLIAM, S		4	72
GUERNSEY, Heneage Creville Finch Lord	P	1	165		GWILT, John	P	2	150
GUESS, Edward A		2	149		GWILYN, John	P	2	150
GUESS, Frederick J		2	149		GWYDIR, The Very Rev. Canon Robert Basil	P	1	166
GUEST, John Eric Cox	P	5	74		GWYER, Alexander Grant		2	150
GUEST, Richard Thomas		1	165		GWYNNE, Albert Edward		3	123
GUEST, Sunny Frank		1	165		GWYNNE, John Fitzgerald	P	1	166
GUEST, Thomas		5	75		GWYNNE, Owen Perrott	P	1	166
GUIEL, Arthur		2	149		GWYNNE, Thomas Henry	P	2	150
GUILD, William Forbes	P	3	122		GWYTHER, J H		3	123
GUILFORD, William Henry	P	3	122		GYE, Alexander Hugh		3	123
GUILL, Raymond James		1	165		GYLE, Ernest Woods	P	5	75
GUISE, Reginald Edward	P	5	75		GYLES, John Herman		3	123
GULLAND, A A		2	149		HABBLETT, Harold		1	167
GULLAND, Reginald Glover Ker		2	149		HABERSHON, Kenneth Rees		4	72
GULLIFORD, William		4	72		HABGOOD, A J		4	72
GULLY, J T		3	122		HACK, Charles Edward	P	1	167
GUMBRELL, Charles Edward Leopold		1	165		HACK, H		4	72
GUMMER, Basil Austin		3	122		HACK, Mary Ileene		5	76
GUMMER, Frank Edward		1	165		HACKER, Alfred John		2	150
GUMMER, Reginald Henry	P	5	75		HACKER, Arthur Alfred		1	167
GUMMER, Stanley	P	4	72		HACKETT, A		2	150
GUNN, Alexander		3	123		HACKETT, Arthur		3	123
GUNN, Arthur		2	149		HACKETT, Charles William		2	150
GUNN, Charlie		4	72		HACKETT, Ernest Wilfred		2	150
GUNN, Frederick		1	165		HACKETT, Harold		2	150
GUNN, John Alexander		3	123		HACKETT, James		2	150
GUNN, John Angus		1	166		HACKETT, John Henry		1	167
GUNN, John Hedley	P	1	166		HACKETT, Percy James		2	150
GUNN, Peter	P	1	166		HACKETT, William		2	150
GUNN, W		4	72		HADDEN, Evans	P	3	123

Name	Photo	Part No.	Page No.	Name	Photo	Part No.	Page No.
HADDEN, John		4	72	HALE, Joseph		3	124
HADDEN, John Duncan		2	150	HALE, Stuart Anthony		3	124
HADDEN, John Hazlett Millar	P	2	150	HALES, Alfred		4	73
HADDEN, William Lumsden		2	150	HALES, William Clifford	P	3	124
HADDOCK, David		3	123	HALEY, R A		2	152
HADDOCK, William		2	150	HALEY, Richard Ernest		1	167
HADDOCK, William		2	150	HALEY, W		3	124
HADDON, Albert Ernest		3	123	HALFACRE, Francis Henry	P	4	73
HADDON, Harold Esmond	P	2	151	HALFACRE, Henry		1	167
HADDON, Joseph Manning		4	72	HALFORD, Alfred Robert Widdows		2	152
HADDON, Walter	P	2	151	HALFORD, W F V		3	124
HADDRILL, Harry Charles		2	151	HALIBURTON, Borthwick		1	167
HADFIELD, H		3	123	HALKERSTON, John		4	73
HADFIELD, Wilfrid John Mackenzie	P	1	167	HALKERSTON, William		4	73
HADLEY, Alfred Thomas		1	167	HALKETT, Alexander Laing		3	124
HADLEY, Charles Frederick	P	2	151	HALL, A		3	125
HADLEY, William Albert	P	2	151	HALL, A		3	125
HADLOW, Albert		2	151	HALL, A W		3	125
HADLOW, Joseph James William		2	151	HALL, Albert		1	168
HADMAN, A		2	151	HALL, Albert George		2	152
HADOW, Erland Godfrey		3	123	HALL, Alexander Percy		4	73
HADRILL, Arthur William		2	151	HALL, Alfred H		2	152
HAEFFNER, Frederick Wilfred	P	2	151	HALL, Alfred Henry		5	76
HAGAN, Henry		2	151	HALL, Archie Clyde	P	1	168
HAGGAN, J		4	72	HALL, Arthur		1	168
HAGGAR, Harry Douglas Fox	P	3	123	HALL, Arthur Frank		4	73
HAGGAR, Harry Douglas Fox		4	72	HALL, Arthur Gordon	P	1	168
HAGGARD, Mark		2	151	HALL, Bruce		2	152
HAGGART, D		3	124	HALL, Burton Howard		1	168
HAGGART, Robert Alexander		2	151	HALL, C B		3	125
HAGGARTY, Patrick		1	167	HALL, Charles		2	152
HAGGARTY, Robert		2	151	HALL, Charles Edward	P	2	152
HAGGERTY, James		2	151	HALL, Charles Henry		2	152
HAGGERTY, P		3	124	HALL, Charles Sidney	P	3	125
HAGGIE, George Esmond	P	3	124	HALL, E E		3	125
HAGUE, H		3	124	HALL, E T		3	125
HAGUE, James		1	167	HALL, E W		2	152
HAGUE, Owen Carsley Frederic	P	1	167	HALL, E W		3	125
HAIDEN, Trew	P	3	124	HALL, Edward		1	168
HAIG, Archibald Malcolm	P	5	76	HALL, Ernest Albert		1	168
HAIGH, Arthur Gordon		3	124	HALL, Ernest Edward		2	152
HAIGH, Charles Roderick		2	151	HALL, Ernest James		3	125
HAIGH, Harold		5	76	HALL, F H		3	125
HAIGH, J		3	124	HALL, Frederick		1	168
HAIGH, John Harry		1	167	HALL, Frederick C		2	152
HAIGH, Percy Samuel Francis	P	3	124	HALL, Frederick Dobson		2	152
HAILSTONE, George Rupert	P	5	76	HALL, G W		3	125
HAIN, Edward	P	2	152	HALL, George		3	125
HAINES, Albert Edward		2	152	HALL, George		3	125
HAINES, Alexander Crichton Cooper	P	1	167	HALL, George		4	73
HAINES, Herbert Henry	P	3	124	HALL, George		4	73
HAINES, O		3	124	HALL, George Henry		4	73
HAINES, Percy W		2	152	HALL, George Walter		1	168
HAINES, R E		3	124	HALL, George William		1	168
HAINES, William Richard		2	152	HALL, Gerald Percy	P	1	168
HAINS, Cyril Lalande	P	4	73	HALL, Harry Frank		1	168
HAINSWORTH, A		3	124	HALL, Henry		1	168
HAIRSINE, Owen	P	3	124	HALL, Henry Joseph		1	168
HAKE, Ormond George	P	2	152	HALL, Herbert		2	152
HALCOP, C		3	124	HALL, Humphrey Evans		2	152
HALDANE, Robert Patrick	P	1	167	HALL, J		3	125
HALDENBY, Albert		2	152	HALL, J		3	125
HALE, C R H		3	124	HALL, John		4	73
HALE, Frederick Thomas	P	1	167	HALL, John Edward Kenyon		2	152
HALE, George Garibaldi		2	152	HALL, John Frederick		1	168

Name	Photo	Part No.	Page No.	Name	Photo	Part No.	Page No.
HALL, John Gilbert	P	4	73	HALSALL, Thomas Albert Edward		5	77
HALL, John Tannahill		4	73	HALSE, Albert William	P	5	77
HALL, Joseph		3	125	HALSEY, Eric Charles		3	125
HALL, Norman De Havilland		3	125	HALSEY, John		1	169
HALL, Percy Montague Cameron	P	4	73	HALSTEAD, Arthur Frederick	P	1	169
HALL, Peveril Austin		5	76	HALSTEAD, G H		3	125
HALL, Robert		5	76	HAMBLETT, Philip		4	74
HALL, S		3	125	HAMBLIN, Cecil Claude		2	153
HALL, Samuel		3	125	HAMBRIDGE, Harry George		2	153
HALL, Simeon		2	152	HAMBRIDGE, William	P	1	169
HALL, Stanley Byron		5	76	HAMELL, Arthur		2	153
HALL, Sydney Albert		1	168	HAMELL, John G		2	153
HALL, T		3	125	HAMER, Arthur Derrick		5	77
HALL, Thomas		2	152	HAMER, Hubert James Tudor	P	1	169
HALL, Thomas Allison		1	168	HAMER, William Shadrach		1	169
HALL, Thomas Charles		5	76	HAMILL, Joseph P		2	153
HALL, Thomas Howard		1	168	HAMILTON, Andrew		4	74
HALL, Thomas Lambert	P	2	152	HAMILTON, Archibald Samuel	P	2	153
HALL, Thomas Peter Moubray		5	76	HAMILTON, Arthur Leslie		5	77
HALL, Vincent John Baird	P	2	152	HAMILTON, Benjamin Charles		4	74
HALL, W		3	125	HAMILTON, Bernard St. George		3	125
HALL, W		3	125	HAMILTON, Cecil Fife Pryce		2	154
HALL, Walter Charles Nelson		1	168	HAMILTON, Charles		1	169
HALL, Wilfred Leslie	P	3	125	HAMILTON, David Beattie	P	2	154
HALL, Wilfred Rodenhurst	P	4	74	HAMILTON, Edward Leon		2	154
HALL, William		1	168	HAMILTON, F		3	125
HALL, William Alexander		5	76	HAMILTON, Frederick Charles		1	169
HALL, William Frederick		1	168	HAMILTON, Gavin		3	125
HALLAM, Charles		4	74	HAMILTON, Herbert James		4	74
HALLAM, Horace George Searle		4	74	HAMILTON, Herbert Otho		2	154
HALLAM, John		2	153	HAMILTON, Hubert Arthur	P	2	154
HALLAM, N		3	125	HAMILTON, Hubert Ion Wetherall		2	154
HALLAM, W		3	125	HAMILTON, J		3	126
HALLAM, Walter	P	1	168	HAMILTON, J A		3	126
HALLAN, Rowland		1	168	HAMILTON, James		2	154
HALLAS, Frederick		2	153	HAMILTON, John George		1	169
HALLAS, R		2	153	HAMILTON, Leslie William Robert	P	2	154
HALLASEY, Henry Robert		5	76	HAMILTON, Lord Arthur John		2	153
HALLER, John Henry Lyle	P	1	168	HAMILTON, Mervyn James		2	154
HALLETT, Arthur		1	169	HAMILTON, P		3	126
HALLETT, G J		3	125	HAMILTON, Pybus William	P	4	74
HALLETT, H R		3	125	HAMILTON, Robert James		2	154
HALLETT, Theo Bennett	P	1	169	HAMILTON, Robert James	P	4	74
HALLETT, Walter		2	153	HAMILTON, Robert John		1	169
HALLETT, William		1	169	HAMILTON, Robert Peat		1	169
HALLEY, David Bowie		5	76	HAMILTON, The Hon. Leslie D'henin		2	154
HALLEY, Henry W		2	153	HAMILTON, William		2	154
HALLIDAY, A		3	125	HAMILTON, William		3	126
HALLIDAY, David		4	74	HAMILTON-DALRYMPLE, John Raphael	P	2	91
HALLIDAY, James		2	153	HAMILTON-JOHNSTON, Douglas Charles	P	2	185
HALLIDAY, James Storey		1	169	HAMLYN, Arthur Franklin		2	155
HALLIDAY, John		2	153	HAMLYN, Wilfrid Stephen	P	3	126
HALLIDAY, John Alexander	P	1	169	HAMM, William George		3	126
HALLIDAY, Joseph Harrison	P	2	153	HAMMANS, Arthur John Spencer		3	126
HALLIMAN, M		3	125	HAMMERTON, George John	P	2	155
HALLIWELL, Fred	P	4	74	HAMMERTON, Leslie Turrall		2	155
HALLIWELL, George	P	4	74	HAMMERTON, R P		2	155
HALLIWELL, George Nowell	P	2	153	HAMMERTON, William		2	155
HALLOWES, Rupert Price	P	5	76	HAMMET, John		2	155
HALLS, Frederick William		4	74	HAMMETT, Conrad		5	77
HALLS, Harry Wilfred	P	2	153	HAMMICK, Eustace		5	77
HALLS, Walter George		3	125	HAMMICK, Stephen Frederick	P	2	155
HALLWARD, Kenneth Leslie	P	2	153	HAMMOND, Arthur Claude		2	155
HALLWORTH, Cecil Arthur		5	77	HAMMOND, Dick	P	5	77
HALSALL, Edward	P	1	169	HAMMOND, Frederick		1	170

Name	Photo	Part No.	Page No.
HAMMOND, George Thomas		1	170
HAMMOND, Gilbert Philip	P	1	170
HAMMOND, Harry		1	170
HAMMOND, Henry		2	155
HAMMOND, Henry		5	77
HAMMOND, J		3	126
HAMMOND, James	P	5	77
HAMMOND, John Maxmilian		3	126
HAMMOND, Mark		1	170
HAMMOND, Richard	P	5	77
HAMMOND, Samuel Henry		1	170
HAMMOND, Shirley		2	155
HAMMOND, Sidney Charles		3	126
HAMMOND, T		3	126
HAMMOND, Thomas Verran		1	170
HAMMOND, W		3	126
HAMMOND, W G		3	126
HAMMOND, W H		3	126
HAMPE-VINCENT, Percival Campbell		4	220
HAMPSON, Samuel		2	155
HAMPTON, Albert		2	155
HAMPTON, Alexander		4	74
HAMPTON, Charles Spencer		2	155
HAMPTON, Thomas		2	155
HAMS, Frederick John	P	4	75
HANBRIDGE, George		2	155
HANBURY-TRACEY, Hon. Felix Charles Hubert	P	1	353
HANBY, James William		2	155
HANCOCK, A		3	126
HANCOCK, Albert Edward		1	170
HANCOCK, Charles William		1	170
HANCOCK, Ernest William		1	170
HANCOCK, G T		3	126
HANCOCK, George		2	155
HANCOCK, Hugh Frederick George		2	155
HANCOCK, James		3	126
HANCOCK, John		1	170
HANCOCK, John		2	156
HANCOCK, Owen Samuel		5	77
HANCOCK, Ralph Escott	P	1	170
HANCOCK, Ralph Longhurst	P	3	126
HANCOCK, T		3	126
HANCOCK, Walter	P	1	170
HANCOCKS, William		4	75
HANCOX, William J		2	156
HAND, Leonard E		2	156
HANDAWAY, Terence		2	156
HANDFIELD, Charles Reginald		1	170
HANDFORD, E R		3	126
HANDFORD, Everard Francis Sale	P	2	156
HANDFORD, Henry Basil Strutt	P	2	156
HANDLEY, Bernard Watson	P	4	75
HANDLEY, John William		4	75
HANDLEY, S		3	126
HANDLEY, Thomas Frederick James		1	170
HANDLEY, Tom		3	126
HANDLEY, W		3	126
HANDS, Arthur		1	170
HANDS, Frederick		3	126
HANDS, George		2	156
HANDS, George Bertram		4	75
HANDYSIDE, George		1	170
HANES, George		1	170
HANEY, P		3	127

Name	Photo	Part No.	Page No.
HANKIN, A		3	127
HANKIN, Charles		4	75
HANKINSON, Harry		1	170
HANKS, Albert		2	156
HANKS, Richard Hubert	P	2	156
HANLEY, Herbert		2	156
HANLEY, J		3	127
HANLEY, John Malby	P	2	156
HANLON, William		1	170
HANN, F		3	127
HANN, Granville A		2	156
HANNA, David Wishart		3	127
HANNA, J		3	127
HANNA, John Weir		1	170
HANNAFORD, Charles W		2	156
HANNAFORD, Reginald George		3	127
HANNAM, George Frederick		5	78
HANNAN, Henry Monteith	P	1	170
HANNAN, J M		3	127
HANNAN, James Maxwell A (Max	P	5	78
HANNAN, Joseph William		3	127
HANNARD, Albert		2	156
HANNAY, D		2	156
HANNIS, James		3	127
HANNON, Henry Edward Percy	P	2	156
HANNYNGTON, John Arthur		5	78
HANRAHAM, D		3	127
HANRAHAN, Thomas Frederick	P	1	171
HANRALTY, Thomas		2	156
HANSELL, Robert Stanley	P	3	127
HANSEN, Elwin	P	1	171
HANSEN, William George	P	3	127
HANSFORD, Albert John		4	75
HANSFORD, H		3	127
HANSFORD, William George Edward		1	171
HANSON, Archibald	P	5	78
HANSON, Ernest		1	171
HANSON, William James		2	156
HANTON, John Clifton	P	2	156
HARBIDGE, Geoffrey Victor		4	75
HARBORD, Stephen Gordon		3	127
HARBORNE, R T		3	127
HARDACRE, Arthur		1	171
HARDAKER, William		2	157
HARDCASTLE, E		2	157
HARDCASTLE, E		3	127
HARDCASTLE, James		4	75
HARDCASTLE, John Thomas		3	127
HARDEN, Allan Humphrey	P	1	171
HARDEN, Arthur James Victor	P	2	157
HARDEN, Richard Townley		5	78
HARDES, John	P	1	171
HARDIE, George		2	157
HARDIE, Gordon		2	157
HARDIE, James		2	157
HARDIE, Lewis John		3	127
HARDIE, Thomas Adams		4	75
HARDIE, William James		2	157
HARDING, A		3	127
HARDING, Alfred		1	171
HARDING, Alfred Robert Francis	P	2	157
HARDING, Arthur Basil Baverstock		4	75
HARDING, Arthur Dennis		2	157
HARDING, Benjamin Charles		3	127
HARDING, Bernard		2	157

Name	Photo	Part No.	Page No.
HARDING, C A G		3	127
HARDING, Charles	P	2	157
HARDING, Charles		2	157
HARDING, Charles Edward		3	127
HARDING, Ernest Frank	P	1	171
HARDING, Frank R		2	157
HARDING, G		3	127
HARDING, George		1	171
HARDING, George William		5	78
HARDING, Harold		2	157
HARDING, Harry		1	171
HARDING, Jack Maynard		2	157
HARDING, John		2	157
HARDING, John Samuel	P	2	157
HARDING, Lionel Cox	P	1	171
HARDING, Percy		1	171
HARDING, Richard	P	3	127
HARDING, Robert Denis Stewart		2	158
HARDING, Stanley Cuthbert	P	1	172
HARDING, Stanley Whittall	P	5	78
HARDING, W		3	127
HARDING, Wilfrid John	P	4	75
HARDING, William Leslie		3	127
HARDINGE, Patrick Robert		3	127
HARDINGE, The Hon. Edward Charles		2	158
HARDISTY, Wilfred		1	172
HARDMAN, Edward		5	78
HARDMAN, Frederick Mcmahon		2	158
HARDMAN, George		1	172
HARDMAN, Harry		3	128
HARDON, David Gilston		5	78
HARDS, E W		3	128
HARDWICK, Nathaniel Charles	P	3	128
HARDWICK, Richard Oliver	P	3	128
HARDY, A		3	128
HARDY, Albert Henry		5	78
HARDY, Alfred		2	158
HARDY, Frederick Percy		2	158
HARDY, J		3	128
HARDY, Leonard Basil	P	1	172
HARDY, R		3	128
HARDY, R		3	128
HARDY, R		3	128
HARDY, Ralph Miller		5	78
HARDY, Richard John		1	172
HARDY, T		3	128
HARDY, T A		3	128
HARDY, Victor Harriott	P	1	172
HARDY, William Frank		1	172
HARDYMAN, John Hay Maitland		5	78
HARE, A		3	128
HARE, Albert Henry		1	172
HARE, Ernest Vivian		3	128
HARE, Harry Vivian		2	158
HARE, John		3	128
HARE, Wilfrid John	P	3	128
HAREWOOD, George		1	172
HARGATE, James Albert		3	128
HARGRAVE, Geoffrey Lewis	P	1	172
HARGRAVES, Joseph		5	79
HARGREAVES, A		3	128
HARGREAVES, Alan Enyveton		2	158
HARGREAVES, Frederick John		4	75
HARGREAVES, Harold		2	158
HARGREAVES, Harry		1	172

Name	Photo	Part No.	Page No.
HARGREAVES, J		2	158
HARGREAVES, James Harold	P	3	128
HARGREAVES, James Henry		5	79
HARGREAVES, Joseph		2	158
HARGREAVES, Leopold Reginald		2	158
HARGREAVES, Ralph Walter		4	75
HARGREAVES, Robert		1	172
HARGREAVES, William		3	128
HARINGTON, Herbert Biernacki		2	158
HARKER, A		3	128
HARKER, William		1	172
HARKNESS, Charles		2	158
HARLAND, Eustace William	P	4	75
HARLAND, Harold		4	75
HARLAND, J		2	158
HARLAND, Reginald Wickham		1	172
HARLAND, William James		1	172
HARLAND, William Thomas		1	172
HARLE, Richard John Patterson		3	128
HARLEN, Percy		2	158
HARLEY, Charles		2	158
HARLEY, George Alexander		1	172
HARLEY, George Melven	P	2	158
HARLEY, George Walter		4	76
HARLEY, John	P	2	158
HARLEY, Thomas		3	128
HARLING, William James		1	172
HARLOCK, George		2	158
HARLOW, Thomas Henry		1	172
HARMAN, Charles Edward	P	1	172
HARMAN, Edwin William		5	79
HARMAN, George Malcolm Nixon	P	1	172
HARMAN, Herbert Reginald	P	1	173
HARMAN, James Henry Thomas		5	79
HARMAN, John Bower		1	173
HARMAN, Joseph		5	79
HARMAN, Robert Sydney	P	4	76
HARMER, Alfred		2	159
HARMER, Charles		2	159
HARMER, Ernest		2	159
HARMER, Frank		2	159
HARMER, Frederick H		2	159
HARMER, Herbert Henry		5	79
HARMER, Horace William		1	173
HARNDEN, Herbert J		2	159
HARNETT, Frederick E		2	159
HARNEY, John		1	173
HARPER, A		3	128
HARPER, A G		3	128
HARPER, Alan Gordon		3	128
HARPER, Alexander Simpson	P	3	129
HARPER, Andrew Coutts Findlay		3	129
HARPER, Charles		2	159
HARPER, Ernest Magowan		2	159
HARPER, F		3	129
HARPER, Frederick Will		2	159
HARPER, George		2	159
HARPER, George Edward		1	173
HARPER, George Hall		4	76
HARPER, James Albion Noble		5	79
HARPER, John	P	2	159
HARPER, John		2	159
HARPER, Joseph		2	159
HARPER, Lancelot Leslie		3	129
HARPER, Robert		3	129

Name	Photo	Part No.	Page No.
HARPER, William James		1	173
HARPER, William Percival Joseph		1	173
HARPER, William Samuel	P	3	129
HARPS, E		3	129
HARRADINE, Albert Arthur		4	76
HARRADINE, Frederick Charles		3	129
HARRAP, Benjamin Norman	P	2	159
HARRELL, Herbert William		1	173
HARRIES, Eric Guy	P	1	173
HARRIES, John Elvet	P	4	76
HARRIES, Robert Henry		5	79
HARRIES, S		3	129
HARRIES, William Meurig	P	2	159
HARRIES, William Reginald		3	129
HARRIMAN, Thomas		2	159
HARRINGTON, A		3	129
HARRINGTON, Edgar		2	159
HARRINGTON, John Joseph	P	1	173
HARRINGTON, Leonard Mark		2	159
HARRINGTON, Philip William	P	3	129
HARRINGTON, Theodore Jack		2	159
HARRIS, Albert		2	159
HARRIS, Albert James		4	76
HARRIS, Alfred		2	159
HARRIS, Alfred Henry		1	173
HARRIS, Antrobus Taft		3	129
HARRIS, Arthur		1	173
HARRIS, Bertram Page		1	173
HARRIS, C		3	129
HARRIS, Charles Cecil		3	129
HARRIS, Charles Edwin		1	173
HARRIS, D		3	129
HARRIS, David Rixon		3	129
HARRIS, Douglas Morris Henry	P	3	130
HARRIS, E		3	130
HARRIS, Edward		3	130
HARRIS, Ernest		2	159
HARRIS, Ernest Edward		3	130
HARRIS, Ernest George		1	173
HARRIS, F		3	130
HARRIS, Frank		2	159
HARRIS, Frank Walter	P	3	130
HARRIS, Frederick Albert		1	173
HARRIS, George		1	173
HARRIS, George Henry		4	76
HARRIS, Henry John		1	173
HARRIS, Henry R		2	159
HARRIS, Herbert Joseph		3	130
HARRIS, Hubert Alfred		3	130
HARRIS, J		3	130
HARRIS, J		3	130
HARRIS, J		3	130
HARRIS, J		3	130
HARRIS, J		3	130
HARRIS, John		2	160
HARRIS, John Auguste Emile	P	1	173
HARRIS, John Bertram		5	79
HARRIS, John Frederick		1	173
HARRIS, John Henry		3	130
HARRIS, John Henry		4	76
HARRIS, Joseph	P	2	160
HARRIS, Joseph	P	5	79
HARRIS, Joseph Walter		1	173
HARRIS, L G		2	160
HARRIS, Lancelot Graham	P	1	174

Name	Photo	Part No.	Page No.
HARRIS, Leonard James		2	160
HARRIS, Leslie George Hamlyn		2	160
HARRIS, Macdonald		2	160
HARRIS, Norman	P	1	174
HARRIS, Norman Elton	P	1	174
HARRIS, R		3	130
HARRIS, Richard		2	160
HARRIS, Richard Arthur		2	160
HARRIS, Richard Henry		4	76
HARRIS, T		3	130
HARRIS, V		3	130
HARRIS, Waldron		1	174
HARRIS, William		1	174
HARRIS, William		3	130
HARRIS, William Charles		1	174
HARRIS, William E		2	160
HARRIS, William Henry		1	174
HARRIS, William Robert	P	5	79
HARRIS, William Thomas		1	174
HARRIS-ARUNDELL, John D'auvergne	P	1	11
HARRISON, A		3	130
HARRISON, A		3	130
HARRISON, A W		3	130
HARRISON, Alfred		1	174
HARRISON, Cecil Eustace	P	1	174
HARRISON, Charles Benjamin		2	160
HARRISON, Charles Brewster		1	174
HARRISON, Charlton Cyril	P	3	130
HARRISON, Chillion Booth		1	174
HARRISON, Cyril Cazalet		2	160
HARRISON, E		3	130
HARRISON, Edward Ernest	P	2	160
HARRISON, Edward Rainsford		5	79
HARRISON, F		3	130
HARRISON, Frank		2	160
HARRISON, Fred	P	1	174
HARRISON, Fred Swaine	P	4	76
HARRISON, Fred William		3	130
HARRISON, G		3	130
HARRISON, Garland Brooking		5	79
HARRISON, Geoffrey		4	76
HARRISON, George Edward		2	160
HARRISON, George Mercer		4	76
HARRISON, Godfrey Bousfield		2	160
HARRISON, H		3	130
HARRISON, Henry		1	175
HARRISON, Henry Hayward		2	160
HARRISON, Herbert Jarvis		2	160
HARRISON, Herbert Laurence		3	131
HARRISON, Hibbert Charles		3	131
HARRISON, J O		3	131
HARRISON, James		1	175
HARRISON, James Rudolph		4	76
HARRISON, John		2	160
HARRISON, John		2	160
HARRISON, John		3	131
HARRISON, John	P	4	76
HARRISON, John Bailey		1	175
HARRISON, Leonard John	P	1	175
HARRISON, Lionel Joseph Briggs		4	76
HARRISON, Percy Pool		3	131
HARRISON, Ronald Sinclair	P	2	160
HARRISON, Ronald Sinclair		4	76
HARRISON, Samuel		3	131
HARRISON, Sidney		2	160

Name	Photo	Part No.	Page No.	Name	Photo	Part No.	Page No.
HARRISON, T		3	131	**HARTLEY,** Joseph		4	77
HARRISON, Thomas		1	175	**HARTLEY,** W		3	131
HARRISON, Walter Bernard		3	131	**HARTLEY,** W H		2	161
HARRISON, Wilfrid		4	77	**HARTLEY,** William Cecil		4	77
HARRISON, William	P	2	160	**HARTMAN,** Emily		5	80
HARRISON, William		4	77	**HART-MCHARG,** William Frederick Richard	P	1	235
HARRISON, William		4	77	**HARTNELL,** Cuthbert	P	1	175
HARRISON, William		5	79	**HARTNOLL,** Hugh Peter	P	1	175
HARRISON, William George		1	175	**HARTRIDGE,** Francis Henry		1	175
HARRISON, William George		1	175	**HARTWELL,** Barry		2	161
HARRISS, Augustus Henry		5	79	**HARTWELL,** Ernest George		2	161
HARRISS, R B		3	131	**HARVEY,** Alexander Scott		4	77
HARROD, R		3	131	**HARVEY,** Bernard Matheson	P	1	175
HARROP, H		3	131	**HARVEY,** Charles Lewis	P	4	77
HARROP, Herbert		2	160	**HARVEY,** Charles Milne	P	2	162
HARROW, William Albert		5	79	**HARVEY,** Christopher Edwin	P	1	175
HARSANT, Austin Frederick		5	80	**HARVEY,** Douglas Lennox		2	162
HARSANT, John Grange		2	160	**HARVEY,** Emmanuel		1	175
HART, A H		3	131	**HARVEY,** Frederick James	P	2	162
HART, Alfred	P	4	77	**HARVEY,** Gerald Franklin		2	162
HART, Alfred J		2	160	**HARVEY,** Herbert William		2	162
HART, Arthur Reginald		3	131	**HARVEY,** J		3	131
HART, Bertram Welby	P	2	160	**HARVEY,** John Gourlay		2	162
HART, Cecil James Welby	P	2	161	**HARVEY,** John Laurence		5	80
HART, Charles Crowther		3	131	**HARVEY,** Joseph Victor	P	1	175
HART, Edward		2	161	**HARVEY,** Leslie		1	175
HART, Edward		2	161	**HARVEY,** Richard Ernle		2	162
HART, Edward John		1	175	**HARVEY,** Richard Prentice		1	175
HART, Ernest		2	161	**HARVEY,** Rollo D'aubigne		2	162
HART, Ernest George		5	80	**HARVEY,** S		3	131
HART, Frederick John		1	175	**HARVEY,** Thomas Macnair	P	4	77
HART, George		2	161	**HARVEY,** W		3	131
HART, George		2	161	**HARVEY,** Walter William		2	162
HART, George Albert	P	4	77	**HARVEY,** Wickham Leathes	P	1	176
HART, H		3	131	**HARVEY,** William		1	176
HART, Harold George		1	175	**HARVEY,** William Edward		1	176
HART, Harry Thomas		2	161	**HARVEY,** William Edward		1	176
HART, Horace Arthur	P	2	161	**HARVEY,** William Henry Heard		5	80
HART, Horace Cecil	P	1	175	**HARVIE,** Eric Fulton	P	5	80
HART, J		2	161	**HARVIE,** James		4	77
HART, James		2	161	**HARVIE,** Stuart Mclaren	P	5	80
HART, John		2	161	**HARWOOD,** Arthur Edmund		1	176
HART, John		2	161	**HARWOOD,** E G		3	131
HART, John James		2	161	**HARWOOD,** George Thomas		4	77
HART, Laurence George		2	161	**HARWOOD,** Randal John		3	131
HART, Phillip		2	161	**HARWOOD,** W		3	131
HART, Raphael		4	77	**HARWOOD,** William		1	176
HART, Robert Henry		5	80	**HASDELL,** G		3	131
HART, Stephen Henry	P	2	161	**HASELER,** William Hereward		3	131
HART, T		3	131	**HASKELL,** Ernest Bone	P	1	176
HART, Thomas		2	161	**HASKELL,** Frank		1	176
HART, William		2	161	**HASKELL,** Harry James Payne	P	1	176
HART, William C		2	161	**HASKELL,** W E		3	131
HART-DAVIES, Ivan Beauclerk		3	74	**HASKEY,** S		3	131
HARTE, James		4	77	**HASLAM,** Charles Stanley	P	3	131
HARTFORD, Hugh Irving St. John		2	161	**HASLAM,** Robert		4	78
HARTFREE, Ernest Bertram	P	2	161	**HASLER,** Julian	P	1	176
HARTLAND, Frederick G		3	131	**HASLETT,** Alfred George		3	131
HARTLAND, George		2	161	**HASLETT,** James Holmes	P	1	176
HARTLAND, J		3	131	**HASLUCK,** Sidney Vandyke	P	1	176
HARTLAND, Robert Thomas		5	80	**HASSALL,** T		3	131
HARTLAND, William Edmond		2	161	**HASSAN,** P		3	131
HARTLEY, A		3	131	**HASTIE,** James		4	78
HARTLEY, Frank	P	2	161	**HASTIE,** R		3	131
HARTLEY, John		2	161	**HASTINGS,** Charles		1	177

91

Name	Photo	Part No.	Page No.
HAYES, W		3	133
HAYES, William		5	81
HAYES, William Ernest	P	4	79
HAYES-SADLER, Edwin John Berkeley		4	175
HAYES-SADLER, Ernest Reginald		4	175
HAYHOE, John Charles	P	5	81
HAYHOW, R J		3	133
HAYHURST, John		5	81
HAYLES, Edward		1	179
HAYLLAR, William Reginald		3	133
HAYMAN, Alfred George	P	3	133
HAYMAN, C		3	133
HAYMAN, D		2	163
HAYMAN, James George	P	1	179
HAYMAN, William Muir	P	3	133
HAYMES, Albert		1	179
HAYNES, Arthur		2	163
HAYNES, C		3	133
HAYNES, C T		3	133
HAYNES, Charles Thomas		2	163
HAYNES, Ernest George		1	179
HAYNES, Frederick		2	163
HAYNES, Henry Agular		1	179
HAYNES, R		3	133
HAYNES, William		4	79
HAYNTON, George		2	163
HAYSMAN, Richard Ewart	P	4	79
HAYTER, Alexander James		4	79
HAYTER, Arthur Humphrey		5	81
HAYTER, Cyril	P	1	179
HAYTER, George Alfred		1	179
HAYTHORNTHWAITE, Rycharde Mead	P	1	179
HAYTOR, Hugh Clervaux		2	67
HAYWARD, Arthur Charles	P	1	179
HAYWARD, Bertram George		2	163
HAYWARD, Charles Oswald	P	2	164
HAYWARD, George		2	164
HAYWARD, Harry		1	180
HAYWARD, Henry		3	133
HAYWARD, Milward Cecil	P	3	133
HAYWARD, Thomas Alexander		1	180
HAYWARD, Thomas Charles		5	81
HAYWARD, Thomas Western		2	164
HAY-WEBB, Allan Bonville		2	308
HAYWOOD, Frederick F		2	164
HAZEL, Dudley		5	81
HAZEL, John Thomas	P	1	180
HAZELDEN, F G		3	133
HAZELDEN, James		1	180
HAZELL, Stanley Ernest Bowyer	P	2	164
HAZELTON, John Douglas		4	79
HAZZELDINE, F		3	133
HEACHER, William		2	164
HEACOCK, Joseph		5	81
HEAD, Alfred G		2	164
HEAD, Frederick George		2	164
HEAD, George Frederick	P	1	180
HEAD, Joseph		2	164
HEAD, Mark		2	164
HEAD, Reginald	P	1	180
HEAD, Richard		5	81
HEAD, William Arthur	P	1	180
HEADLEY, Harold		5	81
HEADLEY, Lorimer	P	5	81
HEAL, W R		3	133

Name	Photo	Part No.	Page No.
HEAL, William Francis		1	180
HEALD, W		3	133
HEALD, William Margetson		4	79
HEALE, Cecil Harry	P	4	79
HEALEY, Arthur Thomas		2	164
HEALEY, E		3	133
HEALEY, Fred		4	79
HEALEY, J		3	133
HEALEY, Peter John		2	164
HEALY, Maurice Kevin		3	133
HEALY, Patrick		2	164
HEALY, Richard M		3	133
HEALY, Thomas	P	1	180
HEALY, Thomas		2	164
HEANEY, A A		2	164
HEANEY, Albert Bouchier Bussell		3	133
HEANEY, Paul Otren		2	164
HEAP, John Hartland	P	2	164
HEAP, S		3	133
HEAPE, Brian Ruston	P	3	133
HEARD, Arthur Reginald		4	79
HEARD, Edward Terence		4	79
HEARD, Harold Edward		5	81
HEARD, John Hooper		4	79
HEARD, Robert Henry Warren	P	5	81
HEARN, C W		2	164
HEARN, Charles James		1	180
HEARN, Edgar Frank		1	180
HEARN, F		3	134
HEARN, G W		3	134
HEARN, Henry John		4	79
HEARN, James Samuel		1	180
HEARN, John Stanley		3	134
HEARN, Robert Cecil	P	5	82
HEARNE, T		3	134
HEARSON, George Neville		4	79
HEARSON, Richard Philip		4	79
HEASMAN, Frank E		2	164
HEASMAN, J		3	134
HEASTE, William		2	164
HEASTMAN, John Edward	P	1	180
HEATER, C F		3	134
HEATH, A J H		3	134
HEATH, Albert Arthur	P	1	180
HEATH, Albert Gordon	P	5	82
HEATH, Alfred James		1	180
HEATH, Ernest Alfred		2	164
HEATH, Ernest John		3	134
HEATH, Eustace Nelson	P	4	80
HEATH, Frederick		2	164
HEATH, Gerald Coussmaker	P	1	180
HEATH, J W		3	134
HEATH, John		5	82
HEATH, John Roland	P	4	80
HEATH, R L		3	134
HEATH, Voltelin Percy	P	1	180
HEATH, W		3	134
HEATHCOTE, Thomas William	P	5	82
HEATHCOTE, W		3	134
HEATHER, Charles		2	164
HEATHER, Douglas William		2	164
HEATHER, James William		2	164
HEATHER, Robert J		2	164
HEATHWAITE, T		3	134
HEATLY, Henry Francis	P	1	181

Name	Photo	Part No.	Page No.
HEATON, Evelyn	P	1	181
HEATON, Harold Sinclair	P	4	80
HEATON, Harry Barclay		5	82
HEATON, William		1	181
HEAVEN, Norman Edwin	P	4	80
HEBDITCH, Laurance Hubert		5	82
HEBELER, Roland Stuart	P	3	134
HEDDING, James Lawrence		3	134
HEDEN, Alfred Howard	P	1	181
HEDGE, Leonard Augustus	P	1	181
HEDGECOCK, John Henry		2	164
HEDGES, Frank Arthur		4	80
HEDGES, Harry		3	134
HEDGES, Henry Thomas		1	181
HEDGES, Herbert		1	181
HEDGES, John		2	164
HEDGES, Noel Victor		4	80
HEDGES, Ronald Egerton		1	181
HEDGLEY, Thomas Edward		3	134
HEDLEY, Rowland		4	80
HEDLEY, William		4	80
HEDLEY, William James	P	3	134
HEELEY, Arnold		1	181
HEENAN, Michael Cornelius		4	80
HEFFERNAN, William Patrick	P	1	181
HEFFRON, Stanley George		2	164
HEFFRON, Thomas James		2	164
HEGARTY, Dennis		1	181
HEGGIE, Thomas		2	164
HEIGHAM-PLUMPTRE, Leslie Grantham		4	159
HEILBRON, Victor Israel		3	134
HEINEMANN, John Walter		3	134
HELDMAN, Harry Randolph		2	165
HELLIWELL, Joseph Grant	P	1	181
HELLYER, James		1	182
HELLYER, Sidney Hannaford	P	1	182
HELME, Alfred		2	165
HELME, Guy Masterman	P	3	134
HELME, Harold Lutwyche		2	165
HELME, Robert Barnard	P	3	134
HELMORE, Stanley Thomas John	P	4	80
HELPS, Frank Bovett	P	1	182
HELSDON, Harold Leofrie		4	80
HELYAR, Maurice Howard	P	1	182
HELYER, Richard		3	134
HEMING, Charles Leonard Parlett	P	3	134
HEMMETT, John		2	165
HEMMING, Frederick Thomas		1	182
HEMMING, Harry		3	135
HEMMINGS, Algernon Envlyn		2	165
HEMMINGS, E		3	135
HEMMINGS, James		2	165
HEMP, A		3	135
HEMPHILL, Richard Patrick	P	3	135
HEMSLEY, Spencer Harold		5	82
HEMSWORTH, F		3	135
HENBEST, Wilfrid Walter		4	80
HENCHER, Joseph		1	182
HENDER, John Henry		1	183
HENDERSON, A		3	135
HENDERSON, Alec Stewart	P	1	183
HENDERSON, Alexander Rennie		2	165
HENDERSON, Alfred Cecil	P	1	183
HENDERSON, Arthur	P	5	82
HENDERSON, Arthur Francis		2	165
HENDERSON, Charles Edward Piercy		3	135
HENDERSON, David Kinnaird		3	135
HENDERSON, G		3	135
HENDERSON, G		3	135
HENDERSON, George	P	3	135
HENDERSON, George	P	5	82
HENDERSON, George		5	82
HENDERSON, Harry William		3	135
HENDERSON, Henry		2	165
HENDERSON, Hugh		2	165
HENDERSON, John		4	80
HENDERSON, John Mcluckie	P	1	183
HENDERSON, Matthew		2	165
HENDERSON, Norman William Arthur		2	165
HENDERSON, Raymond Montgomerie Hume		2	165
HENDERSON, Robert	P	3	135
HENDERSON, Robert Henry		1	183
HENDERSON, S		3	135
HENDERSON, Stewart		3	135
HENDERSON, W		3	135
HENDERSON, William	P	2	165
HENDERSON, William		5	82
HENDERSON, William Alexander		2	165
HENDERSON, William George		3	135
HENDERSON, William Slater		1	183
HENDERSON-BEGG, John	P	2	25
HENDERSON-BEGG, Robert	P	2	25
HENDERSON-HAMILTON, Charles Campbell		2	155
HENDERSON-HAMILTON, James Campbell		2	155
HENDLEY, Charles Thomas		3	135
HENDLEY, Charles Thomas		4	81
HENDRA, Charles		2	165
HENDRY, Alexander		4	81
HENDRY, Alistair	P	4	81
HENDRY, H		2	165
HENDRY, Jack Walker	P	4	81
HENDRY, John		2	165
HENDRY, W G		3	135
HENLEY, Frank		1	183
HENLEY, Frank		1	183
HENLEY, George Charles		1	183
HENNA, Alfred		5	82
HENNESSEY, B		3	136
HENNESSEY, G H		3	136
HENNESSY, Ivan Thomas		1	183
HENNEY, Herbert Norman	P	3	136
HENNING, William Albert	P	3	136
HENNIS, Henry		2	165
HENON, William R		3	136
HENRICK, Wilfred		2	165
HENRIQUES, Philip Brydges Gutterez		2	165
HENRIQUES, Ronald Lucas Quixano		2	165
HENRY, Arthur Bagnall	P	4	81
HENRY, Bertie		5	82
HENRY, Charles Burrell		1	183
HENRY, Claude		2	165
HENRY, Frank		1	183
HENRY, J		3	136
HENRY, J T		3	136
HENRY, James Alfred		4	81
HENRY, John Mitchell		5	83
HENRY, Joseph		1	183
HENRY, P		2	165
HENRY, Walter		1	183
HENRY, William	P	5	83

Name	Photo	Part No.	Page No.
HENSELEIT, Frederick		1	183
HENSHALL, W		3	136
HENSHAW, Robert		4	81
HENSHAW, W		3	136
HENSHAW, William Frederick	P	1	183
HENSLEY, Wilfrid Henry		4	81
HENSON, Herbert Edward		1	183
HENSON, Leonard	P	1	183
HENSON, Stanley Benskin	P	1	183
HENSTOCK, Kenneth Parnell		2	165
HENTHORN, James Henry		5	83
HENTY, Arthur Frank	P	3	136
HENWOOD, Harry James		5	83
HENWOOD, W		3	136
HEPBURN, Archibald James	P	1	183
HEPBURN, Arthur Jacobs	P	4	81
HEPBURN, Malcolm Arnold		2	165
HEPBURN, William Duncan	P	2	165
HEPINSTALL, George	P	1	183
HEPPLES, F		3	136
HEPPLESTONE, John William		4	81
HEPTINSTALL, A W		2	166
HEPWORTH, Percy		1	183
HERALD, Thomas		3	136
HERAUD, Charles P		5	83
HERBERT, Albert	P	4	81
HERBERT, Arthur E		2	166
HERBERT, Benjamin Charles Esmond	P	4	81
HERBERT, Charles	P	4	81
HERBERT, Ernest		1	183
HERBERT, Frederick Daniel		1	183
HERBERT, H A		2	166
HERBERT, Henry		2	166
HERBERT, Henry Robert		2	166
HERBERT, J		3	136
HERBERT, Reginald	P	4	82
HERBERT, Richard Thomas		4	82
HERBERT, S		3	136
HERBERT, S		3	136
HERBERT, Thomas William Percy	P	3	136
HERBERT, W		2	166
HERD, George	P	5	83
HERD, Horace Falkland		2	166
HERDMAN, Arthur Widdrington		1	183
HERINGTON, Percy Godfrey	P	3	136
HERION, Arthur		1	184
HERION, George		2	166
HERITAGE, Herbert Frank	P	3	136
HERLIHY, Sidney Holloway	P	3	136
HERLING, George Milward		5	83
HERN, Thomas Henry		2	166
HERN, William Henry		1	184
HERON, David	P	3	137
HERON, William		1	184
HERRETT, A F		3	137
HERRICK, Arthur Desmond		4	82
HERRICK, Harry Eustace		5	83
HERRIDGE, W		3	137
HERRIDGE, W G		3	137
HERRIDGE, William		1	184
HERRING, Edward Edgar	P	1	184
HERRING, Norman Hamilton		3	137
HERRINGHAM, Geoffrey Wilmot		2	166
HERRON, Walter Fitzroy	P	2	166
HERVEY, Douglas Frederick	P	5	83
HESELTINE, Reginald		2	166
HESKETT, John	P	5	83
HESOM, A H		3	137
HESSELL, Walter		2	166
HESSEY, W		3	137
HESTER, William Henry		1	184
HETHERINGTON, Geoffrey Nevill		4	82
HETHERINGTON, John	P	4	82
HETHERINGTON, John Robert	P	1	184
HETHERINGTON, R		3	137
HETHERINGTON, Thomas		2	166
HETHERINGTON, William Robertson		5	83
HEUMANN, Richard	P	2	166
HEUSTON, Frank	P	2	166
HEUSTON, Frederic Gibson	P	2	166
HEWARD, George Henry	P	4	82
HEWAT, Anthony Morris Coats		2	166
HEWENS, Frederick Armatage	P	5	83
HEWER, Charles William	P	4	82
HEWETSON, George Hayton		1	184
HEWETT, Edward John Vincent	P	4	82
HEWETT, F D A		3	137
HEWETT, John Edward	P	1	184
HEWETT, W R		3	137
HEWISH, Richard James	P	4	82
HEWIT, Walter		5	83
HEWITSON, George		3	137
HEWITT, Charles Robert		5	83
HEWITT, Cyril Ernest		4	82
HEWITT, Denis George Wyldbore	P	3	137
HEWITT, Ernest		3	137
HEWITT, Ernest Henry	P	1	184
HEWITT, Guy Stevenson		4	82
HEWITT, H		3	137
HEWITT, James Francis	P	1	184
HEWITT, John James		5	84
HEWITT, Robert		1	184
HEWITT, William George	P	1	184
HEWKLEY, Francis Paget	P	3	137
HEWLETT, Wilfred Arthur		1	184
HEWLETT, William		5	84
HEWSON, Wilfred John	P	5	84
HEXT, Frank		4	82
HEYCOCK, John Ivor		3	137
HEYNES, Dudley Hugo		4	83
HEYS, Arthur		1	184
HEYS, James Henry	P	4	83
HEYWOOD, John		3	137
HEYWOOD, Thomas	P	4	83
HEYWORTH, Heyworth Potter Lawrence	P	1	184
HEYWORTH, Wilfred Alexander	P	3	137
HIBBERD, G A W		3	137
HIBBERT, J		3	137
HIBBERT, Septimus	P	1	184
HIBBERT, William		2	166
HICHENS, William Thomas		3	137
HICKES, Robert Ian Alexander		5	84
HICKEY, C		3	138
HICKEY, J		3	138
HICKEY, J		3	138
HICKLIN, Harold		4	83
HICKLING, Edward Robert Eyre	P	1	184
HICKLING, Frederick William		2	166
HICKLING, William Charles		1	185
HICKMAN, Ernest John		2	166

Name	Photo	Part No.	Page No.
HICKMOTT, Stephen		2	166
HICKS, Basil Perrin	P	2	166
HICKS, Charles Hubert		4	83
HICKS, Frederick Richard	P	1	185
HICKS, James Thomas William		1	185
HICKS, John George	P	2	166
HICKS, W G		3	138
HICKS, Walter Gerald	P	1	185
HICKSON, Reginald Davies		3	138
HIDDING, James Lawrence		5	84
HIDER, Henry W		2	167
HIEB, Daniel		2	167
HIGGINBOTTOM, Frank		1	185
HIGGINBOTTOM, Thomas		1	185
HIGGINS, E		3	138
HIGGINS, Frederic		1	185
HIGGINS, Frederick William		2	167
HIGGINS, Harry		1	185
HIGGINS, Henry		3	138
HIGGINS, Herbert Henry		2	167
HIGGINS, J		3	138
HIGGINS, J		3	138
HIGGINS, M		3	138
HIGGINS, S R		3	138
HIGGINSON, Alfred		2	167
HIGGINSON, Alfred Sidney Denman		2	167
HIGGS, Alfred		2	167
HIGGS, Charles		1	185
HIGGS, John Edmund		5	84
HIGGS, Joseph		5	84
HIGGS, Tom		2	167
HIGH, George Henry		1	185
HIGHAM, Albert		2	167
HIGHAMS, Ernest Edward		3	138
HIGHAN, E		3	138
HIGHGATE, Thomas J		2	167
HIGINBOTHAM, George Mowat		2	167
HILBERT, Horace Ernest		2	167
HILDER, Rowland E		2	167
HILDERSLEY, James		2	167
HILDITCH, Richard	P	2	167
HILDYARD, Nona Mildred	P	1	185
HILDYARD, Robert Aubrey	P	5	84
HILES, William Henry		3	138
HILES, William James		3	138
HILEY, Herbert		1	185
HILL, A		3	138
HILL, A		3	138
HILL, Albert		1	185
HILL, Albert		2	167
HILL, Albert		2	167
HILL, Arthur		5	84
HILL, Arthur Lionel	P	2	167
HILL, Beresford Winnington		3	138
HILL, Brian Edward	P	5	84
HILL, C		3	138
HILL, Charles Haydock	P	1	185
HILL, Charles William John		1	185
HILL, E		3	138
HILL, E W		3	138
HILL, Edwin		5	84
HILL, Ernest George		4	83
HILL, F		2	167
HILL, Francis		5	84
HILL, George		1	185
HILL, George Allen	P	2	167
HILL, George F		2	167
HILL, George Payne	P	1	185
HILL, Gerard Leader	P	3	138
HILL, Harry		3	138
HILL, Henry		2	167
HILL, Henry William		5	84
HILL, Isaac		2	167
HILL, John		4	83
HILL, John		4	83
HILL, Leonard Augustus	P	1	185
HILL, Leslie Brownlow	P	1	186
HILL, R		3	138
HILL, Reginald Edward		3	138
HILL, T		3	138
HILL, Thomas Wynne		4	83
HILL, Victor Gordon		4	83
HILL, W		3	138
HILL, W T		3	138
HILL, Walter Edward	P	1	186
HILL, Walter Frederick John		3	138
HILL, William		2	167
HILL, William Dudley	P	1	186
HILL, William Thomas	P	5	84
HILLAND, Joseph		1	186
HILLERNS, Hero Wilhelm Oswald		3	138
HILLIER, Albert		3	138
HILLIER, Albert		3	138
HILLIER, C		2	167
HILLIER, C		3	138
HILLIER, Ernest Alfred	P	1	186
HILLIER, Frederick		3	138
HILLIER, John		3	139
HILLIER, William George		4	83
HILLIGER, T		2	167
HILLINGSWORTH, John		2	167
HILLIS, James Herbert		1	186
HILLIS, Samuel Denys	P	1	186
HILLS, Alfred Elkins		5	84
HILLS, Alfred Thomas		1	186
HILLS, Benjamin		2	167
HILLS, F		3	139
HILLS, Frederick		1	186
HILLS, Herbert Walter		5	84
HILLS, J E		2	167
HILLS, John George		2	167
HILLS, William Jesse		1	186
HILLSDON, Claude Stedman George	P	2	167
HILL-TREVOR, Hillyar George Edwin		4	215
HILLYEAR, Jesse		3	139
HILLYER, Arthur George Henry	P	3	139
HILLYER, Thomas James Selby	P	1	186
HILSON, George William		1	186
HILTON, Dennis S		2	167
HILTON, Henry Denne		2	167
HILTON, Herbert Philip		1	186
HILTON, John William		5	85
HILTON, Thomas		1	186
HILTON, W		3	139
HILTON, William Ernest		1	186
HIMSWORTH, J E		3	139
HINCKESMAN, John William	P	3	139
HINCKS, Bertram		3	139
HINCKSLIFF, Charles		2	168
HIND, William Abraham Little		5	85

Name	Photo	Part No.	Page No.
HINDE, Kenneth	P	3	139
HINDES, H		3	139
HINDLE, H		2	168
HINDLEY, John		5	85
HINDLEY, Muir Robert		4	83
HINDMARSH, Albert	P	1	186
HINDSLEY, Eric	P	3	139
HINE, Augustus		4	83
HINE, S C		3	139
HINES, George Henry		2	168
HINES, William John		2	168
HINGSTON, Frederic Leonard		1	187
HINGSTON, George Bennett	P	2	168
HINKLEY, Thomas Joseph		2	168
HINMAN, Arthur Gurr	P	1	187
HINNELL, Thomas Squier		4	83
HINSON, Oliver Fred		1	187
HINTON, Ernest Henry		1	187
HINTON, Sidney Arthur		1	187
HINVES, Alfred Edmund		1	187
HINVES, Arthur Henry	P	3	139
HIPKINS, Frederick Wystan		5	85
HIPKISS, J A		3	139
HIPPISLEY, Harold Edwin	P	1	187
HIPWELL, Edward John		2	168
HIRD, Christopher M		4	84
HIRONS, M E		3	139
HIRST, Edward		1	187
HIRST, Gerald William	P	3	139
HIRST, Haydn		3	139
HISCOCKS, Sydney		3	140
HISCOX, A		2	168
HISCOX, Thomas Andrew		1	187
HISLOP, Frederick Laurence	P	3	140
HITCHCOCK, Edward William		1	187
HITCHEN, Arthur Benjamin	P	1	187
HITCHIN, George Robert	P	3	140
HITCHINGS, George Walter	P	3	140
HITCHINS, Alfred George		5	85
HITCHINS, Henry William Ernest	P	1	187
HOAD, Henry James William		1	188
HOAD, Percy Ewart		1	188
HOARE, Fred		4	84
HOARE, Gerard Croft		4	84
HOARE, James		2	168
HOARE, James		5	85
HOARE, Thomas		1	188
HOARE, William Henry		1	188
HOBAN, William		1	188
HOBBS, Alfred Herbert		1	188
HOBBS, Ernest James		4	84
HOBBS, Frank Matthew	P	1	188
HOBBS, Gerald Parker	P	3	140
HOBBS, Herbert		1	188
HOBBS, James Beesley	P	2	168
HOBBS, James William Biggs		1	188
HOBBS, John	P	1	188
HOBBS, Joseph Levine		1	188
HOBBS, Sydney Louis	P	3	140
HOBBS, William George		2	168
HOBDEN, Charles Frank	P	2	168
HOBLYN, Walter Frederick		2	168
HOBSON, Alan Faber		4	84
HOBSON, Andrew John Hay		4	84
HOBSON, George		2	168

Name	Photo	Part No.	Page No.
HOBSON, Herbert		5	85
HOBSON, Horace		2	168
HOBSON, Leslie Faber		4	84
HOBSON, Owen Ellis	P	5	85
HOCKEY, Henry Albert		5	85
HOCKEY, James		3	140
HOCKIN, George Chamberlain	P	2	168
HOCKING, Francis James	P	1	188
HOCKING, William John	P	1	189
HOCKNELL, Thomas		2	168
HODDEN, Henry Ernest		1	189
HODDER, Edward George		2	169
HODDINETT, William Giles		2	169
HODGE, Andrew Buckland		3	140
HODGE, Dorrien Edward Grose		1	189
HODGE, Frederick		2	169
HODGE, George		3	140
HODGE, John		2	169
HODGE, Percy		2	169
HODGES, Arthur		2	169
HODGES, George Walter		5	85
HODGES, Harold		1	189
HODGES, Harold Wardale	P	1	189
HODGES, Henry Burden	P	1	189
HODGES, Henry Thomas		1	189
HODGES, Herbert James Gordon		2	169
HODGES, Howard Frederick		2	169
HODGES, James Eli		5	85
HODGES, John Cyril	P	3	140
HODGES, Ray Bowen	P	2	169
HODGES, Samuel Joseph		5	85
HODGES, Tom		3	141
HODGES, W J		2	169
HODGES, William Benjamin	P	2	169
HODGES, William Edward		4	84
HODGES, William H		2	169
HODGES, William Sydney		1	189
HODGINS, Richard		4	84
HODGKINSON, A		2	169
HODGKINSON, Geoffrey Still		3	141
HODGKINSON, Hannes Gerald		3	141
HODGKINSON, James Hartley		5	85
HODGKINSON, John Francis	P	1	189
HODGKINSON, Joseph		5	85
HODGKINSON, Morris		5	85
HODGKINSON, Samuel Charles Lindsey	P	1	189
HODGSON, Albert Edward		5	85
HODGSON, Arthur Dawson		3	141
HODGSON, Cyril Francis		3	141
HODGSON, Francis Faith	P	1	189
HODGSON, Francis Herbert	P	5	85
HODGSON, Frederick		1	189
HODGSON, Geoffrey Mitchell	P	1	189
HODGSON, George Graham	P	1	189
HODGSON, Philip Ormiston	P	1	190
HODGSON, Reginald Drury		4	84
HODGSON, Richard Eveleigh	P	5	86
HODGSON, Robert	P	1	190
HODGSON, W		2	169
HODKINSON, Charles William		5	86
HODSDON, Harry		1	190
HODSOLL, George Bertram Pollock	P	1	190
HODSON, Daniel		1	190
HODSON, Edward Wilfrid	P	1	190
HODSON, Harold		5	86

Name	Photo	Part No.	Page No.
HODSON, Harold Edgar		4	84
HODSON, Hubert Bernard	P	1	190
HODSON, Robert		1	190
HOFFE, Thomas Mitchell		3	141
HOFFMAN, Francis Edward Charles		1	190
HOGAN, Arthur Edward		2	169
HOGAN, Charles Alec		5	86
HOGAN, John		1	190
HOGAN, Robert Garrett Roche	P	1	190
HOGBEN, Henry Francis Thomas	P	2	169
HOGG, Adam		2	169
HOGG, Albert George William	P	1	191
HOGG, Andrew		1	191
HOGG, Charles William		2	169
HOGG, Edward		2	169
HOGG, Frank Alexander		5	86
HOGG, Frederick		2	169
HOGG, George F		2	169
HOGG, George William	P	2	169
HOGG, Harry Paul	P	1	191
HOGG, Ian Graham		1	191
HOGG, Ivan Dayrell Meredith	P	1	191
HOGG, James		1	191
HOGG, James Hutchison	P	4	84
HOGG, Robin Cavers	P	3	141
HOGG, Thomas	P	2	169
HOGG, Thomas William		5	86
HOGG, William		4	84
HOGG, William James		5	86
HOGGARTH, J		3	141
HOGGINS, Arthur		2	169
HOLBECH, David		3	141
HOLBECH, William Hugh		1	191
HOLBROOK, George Lodwig	P	4	84
HOLBROOK, Henry George		1	191
HOLBROOK, James		5	86
HOLDBROOK, Joseph		1	191
HOLDEN, Albert George		4	84
HOLDEN, Charles		2	169
HOLDEN, G H		3	141
HOLDEN, Harry		2	169
HOLDEN, J D		2	169
HOLDEN, Richard		2	169
HOLDEN, Taylor		2	169
HOLDEN, Vernon		5	86
HOLDER, George Stephen		1	191
HOLDING, Frank	P	1	191
HOLDING, Samuel	P	2	169
HOLDING, William		2	169
HOLDRON, Harold Douglas		3	141
HOLDSWORTH, C		3	141
HOLDSWORTH, Henry Bernard	P	5	86
HOLDSWORTH, Thomas		3	141
HOLE, A		3	141
HOLFORD, Alfred Frederick		1	191
HOLGATE, Charles Harold		2	169
HOLGATE, William Lawson	P	3	141
HOLLAMBY, Albert Edward	P	1	191
HOLLAND, Alfred		4	85
HOLLAND, Edward George		2	169
HOLLAND, Edward Matthew	P	2	170
HOLLAND, Edwin Charles		5	86
HOLLAND, Ernest	P	4	85
HOLLAND, Frank Davenport	P	1	191
HOLLAND, Frederick		2	170

Name	Photo	Part No.	Page No.
HOLLAND, George Percival	P	4	85
HOLLAND, H		2	170
HOLLAND, Henry		2	170
HOLLAND, Henry Charles		5	86
HOLLAND, John William		1	192
HOLLAND, Joseph		1	192
HOLLAND, Thomas Welsby	P	4	85
HOLLAND, W A		3	141
HOLLAND, William Henry		4	85
HOLLAND, William Lennox Farquharson	P	3	141
HOLLAS, A		2	170
HOLLAS, John Henry		4	85
HOLLAS, William		2	170
HOLLEBON, William George		3	142
HOLLETT, W J		3	142
HOLLICK, Arthur		2	170
HOLLICK, Walter Stanley	P	1	192
HOLLIDAY, William		3	142
HOLLIGAN, David		2	170
HOLLINGDALE, Jesse		3	142
HOLLINGS, A		3	142
HOLLINGS, William		2	170
HOLLINGSWORTH, John		2	170
HOLLINGWORTH, George		1	192
HOLLINGWORTH, Herbert Bartlett	P	5	86
HOLLIS, Arthur		2	170
HOLLIS, Arthur Reginald		5	86
HOLLIS, G		2	170
HOLLIWELL, Charles William		3	142
HOLLORAN, John		2	170
HOLLOWAY, Alfred Cart	P	5	87
HOLLOWAY, Herbert James	P	2	170
HOLLOWAY, Victor James		3	142
HOLMAN, Francis William		1	192
HOLMAN, Frank		5	87
HOLMAN, Frederick Pendennis		5	87
HOLME, Alexander Charles	P	1	192
HOLME, Bertram Lester		3	142
HOLME, Ronald Henry Paull	P	1	192
HOLMES, Albert		2	170
HOLMES, Arthur Edward		4	85
HOLMES, Balaam		2	170
HOLMES, Bryan Hanby	P	5	87
HOLMES, Cecil Crampton	P	1	192
HOLMES, Cyril Ernest Jackson		3	142
HOLMES, Edwin Frederick		4	85
HOLMES, Francis Lennox	P	1	192
HOLMES, Frederick Henry		1	192
HOLMES, George Francis Edwin	P	3	142
HOLMES, Harold		5	87
HOLMES, Harry		3	142
HOLMES, Henry Ball	P	2	170
HOLMES, John Alexander	P	3	142
HOLMES, John Henry		3	142
HOLMES, Joseph		1	192
HOLMES, Louis Gordon	P	1	192
HOLMES, Matthew William		5	87
HOLMES, Oswald Matthews		3	142
HOLMES, Robert		1	192
HOLMES, Victor		3	142
HOLMES, William		1	192
HOLMES, William		3	143
HOLMES, William Dumbleton	P	3	143
HOLMES, William Edward	P	3	143
HOLMES, William John		3	143

Name	Photo	Part No.	Page No.
HOLMES, William Percy		5	87
HOLMWOOD, Frederick Ambrose John		5	87
HOLNESS, T G		2	170
HOLROYD, John George		1	192
HOLROYD, John Othic	P	4	85
HOLROYD, Wilfrid Hugh	P	4	85
HOLSGROVE, James		2	170
HOLT, Cecil William		1	192
HOLT, Clement		2	170
HOLT, Harold Ainsworth		3	143
HOLT, John Edmund		4	85
HOLT, Kenneth Thomas William	P	4	85
HOLT, William Leslie	P	4	85
HOLTBY, Arthur William	P	1	193
HOLTHAM, George		4	85
HOLTHAM, William Frederick		4	86
HOLTOM, George		3	143
HOLTON, Frederick		2	170
HOLTON, Reginald Clifford		4	86
HOLTON, Thomas		3	143
HOMEWOOD, Stephen John		2	170
HOMEWOOD, William Albert Henry		3	143
HOMEWOOD, William Lewis	P	4	86
HONAN, Matthew		4	86
HONE, Ernest Frederick		5	87
HONE, Harry		5	87
HONE, Herbert		5	87
HONEY, Albert Tom	P	1	193
HONEY, Alec Cowper	P	4	86
HONEY, Geoffrey Henry Le Sueur	P	2	170
HONEY, Herbert		1	193
HONEYBALL, Clifford Bruce		3	143
HONEYBOURNE, Sidney Edward		4	86
HONEYMAN, Edward		2	170
HONEYMAN, Walter Bailie		5	87
HONEYWILL, Herbert Cecil		1	193
HONEYWILL, Stanley Ross	P	5	87
HONOR, James Thomas		2	170
HONOUR, Reginald Alexander		5	87
HOOD, Archie	P	2	170
HOOD, Charles Christopher		3	143
HOOD, Christopher Thomas		1	193
HOOD, George		1	193
HOOD, John Thomas		1	193
HOOD, Johnstone Latto	P	3	143
HOOD, Lewis Reginald		1	193
HOOD, Robert		2	171
HOOD, Stuart Clink	P	1	193
HOOD, William		2	171
HOODLESS, Thomas		5	87
HOOK, George		2	171
HOOK, Horace		2	171
HOOKE, Alfred Douglas	P	5	87
HOOKE, John Huon	P	1	193
HOOKER, Albert Victor	P	5	88
HOOKER, Alfred		1	193
HOOKER, Henry George		1	193
HOOKER, Stanley Harrison		3	143
HOOKHAM, Henry Charles		1	193
HOOKHAM, James		1	193
HOOKHAM, William		1	193
HOOKWAY, Joseph James		5	88
HOOLE, Leonard Alexander		4	86
HOOLEY, Basil Terah	P	5	88
HOOLEY, James		5	88

Name	Photo	Part No.	Page No.
HOOLIGAN, J		4	86
HOOPER, Albert Edward		3	143
HOOPER, Charles Winsmore	P	2	171
HOOPER, David		1	193
HOOPER, David Ernest	P	1	193
HOOPER, Francis William		5	88
HOOPER, Frederick Arthur		2	171
HOOPER, Frederick John	P	2	171
HOOPER, George Albert		1	193
HOOPER, H		3	143
HOOPER, John Hamilton Morriss		4	86
HOOPER, Joseph		1	193
HOOPER, Thomas	P	2	171
HOOPER, Thomas Edward		1	193
HOOPER, Thomas Henry		1	193
HOOPER, Walter Thomas		3	143
HOOPER, Walter William		1	193
HOOPER, William		4	86
HOOPER, William Richard	P	5	88
HOOPS, Harry Albert Mostyn	P	4	86
HOPCRAFT, Arthur William		1	193
HOPE, Bertie Fred		2	171
HOPE, David Wilkinson		3	144
HOPE, John		2	171
HOPE, John		5	88
HOPE, Reginald Addison		3	144
HOPE, Samuel	P	3	144
HOPE, W R		3	144
HOPE, William		1	193
HOPE, William Edward		4	86
HOPE, William Hayhurst	P	4	86
HOPE-JOHNSTONE, William Gordon Tollemache	P	1	208
HOPER, Ern Sydney Joseph		1	193
HOPEY, Edmund Eugene	P	1	193
HOPKINS, Albert Edwin		3	144
HOPKINS, Charles Edwin		1	194
HOPKINS, Frederick Charles	P	4	86
HOPKINS, J		2	171
HOPKINS, Jack		1	194
HOPKINS, John G		2	171
HOPKINS, Stanley Charles		2	171
HOPKINS, Walter	P	4	87
HOPKINSON, Charles Wilfrid		4	87
HOPKINSON, John William		5	88
HOPKINSON, Rudolph Cecil		3	144
HOPLEY, Geoffrey William Vander Byl		2	171
HOPLEY, Herbert	P	1	194
HOPPER, George		1	194
HOPPER, Henry Edward		2	171
HOPPER, Jerry		1	194
HOPPER, Raymond		4	87
HOPPER, William		1	194
HOPPS, Hugh James	P	2	171
HOPPS, William Leonard	P	2	171
HOPSON, Joseph Alfred	P	2	172
HOPTON, Guy William		1	194
HOPTON, Tom Francis		1	194
HORASTEAD, Fred		2	172
HORDERN, Cedric	P	1	194
HORE, William Courtenay		1	194
HORGAN, J		3	144
HORLICK, Gerald Nolekin	P	4	87
HORLOCK, John Harry		4	87
HORN, Henry Adrian	P	1	194

Name	Photo	Part No.	Page No.
HORN, James		1	194
HORN, James Frederick		1	194
HORN, Robert		4	87
HORNBLOW, Frederick		2	172
HORNBY, Cecil Geoffrey		5	88
HORNBY, Sethenos Gomer		5	88
HORNE, Andrew	P	3	144
HORNE, David Douglas	P	3	144
HORNE, George Charles	P	1	194
HORNE, Harry		2	172
HORNE, James Law	P	2	172
HORNE, John Morrison		1	194
HORNE, Stanley Frank		1	194
HORNER, C		3	144
HORNER, Frederick William Charlton		2	172
HORNER, Garrett		2	172
HORNER, H A		3	144
HORNER, Joseph Richard	P	1	195
HORNEY, William Henry		1	195
HORNSBY, George		2	172
HORNSBY, Robert		4	87
HORRELL, Albert Ernest		2	172
HORRELL, Thomas William		1	195
HORRILL, Ernest John		3	144
HORSBURGH, G		2	172
HORSBURGH, William Brown		2	172
HORSCROFT, Charles		2	172
HORSEY, Albert		5	88
HORSEY, Arthur		5	88
HORSEY, Walter Edward		5	88
HORSFALL, Alfred Garnett	P	4	87
HORSFALL, Henry Francis Coghlan	P	2	172
HORSFALL, William		5	88
HORSFIELD, Frank		3	144
HORSFIELD, Harold		3	144
HORSLEY, Harry Matthew		1	195
HORSLEY, Henry Edmund		1	195
HORSMAN, William		4	87
HORSNELL, William Thomas		5	88
HORT, Courtenay Randall	P	3	144
HORTON, Albert Edward		1	195
HORTON, Albert Edward		3	144
HORTON, Alfred James	P	2	172
HORTON, Charles T		2	172
HORTON, Colin Charles		4	87
HORTON, Francis		2	172
HORTON, Francis King	P	3	145
HORTON, George		1	193
HORTON, Harold Frederick		4	87
HORTON, Reggie		2	172
HORTON, William		2	172
HORTON, William		2	172
HOSIE, William John		1	195
HOSKEN, Albert Newton		5	88
HOSKIN, Charles Leonard	P	5	89
HOSKIN, Frank		3	145
HOSKING, F		3	145
HOSKINS, George		2	172
HOSKINS, George Charles		2	172
HOSKINS, H F		3	145
HOSKINS, Harry G		2	173
HOSKINS, Harry Smith		4	87
HOSKINS, Walter E		2	173
HOSKYNS, Henry Charles Walter	P	2	173
HOSMER, Philip Charles		5	89

Name	Photo	Part No.	Page No.
HOSTE, George Michael	P	2	173
HOTCHKIN, Lambert Annesley		3	145
HOTCHKIS, Gilbert	P	3	145
HOUGH, Thomas Albert		5	89
HOUGHAN, Edward Joseph		1	195
HOUGHTON, Albert		3	145
HOUGHTON, Albert Henry		3	145
HOUGHTON, Arthur Hamilton		4	87
HOUGHTON, Charles Henry		4	87
HOUGHTON, Frederick Joseph	P	5	89
HOUGHTON, John		5	89
HOUGHTON, Percy		1	195
HOUGHTON, Percy		5	89
HOULDSWORTH, William Gilbert	P	1	195
HOURSTON, David William	P	4	88
HOUSE, Ernest Edward	P	1	195
HOUSE, Frederick C		2	173
HOUSE, John Robert		1	195
HOUSE, Malcolm Hutchinson		3	145
HOUSE, Robert		2	173
HOUSEGO, Edward George		1	195
HOUSLEY, Harry John		1	195
HOUSTON, Archibald	P	2	173
HOUSTON, G		2	173
HOUSTON, James		1	195
HOUSTON, T		2	173
HOUSTOUN-BOSWALL, Sir George Reginald	P	2	34
HOVELL, George Woodward	P	2	173
HOWARD, A R		4	88
HOWARD, Charles Arthur		2	173
HOWARD, Cyril James	P	1	195
HOWARD, Dennis Brook	P	4	88
HOWARD, Ernest Guy		1	195
HOWARD, George M		2	173
HOWARD, George William		1	195
HOWARD, Henry Charles Mowbray		2	173
HOWARD, Herbert Richard		1	195
HOWARD, James John		1	195
HOWARD, John		1	195
HOWARD, John Alfred Carter		3	145
HOWARD, Joseph	P	1	195
HOWARD, Robert		4	88
HOWARD, Thomas		2	173
HOWARD, Thomas James		1	195
HOWARD, Walter Olanda		5	89
HOWARD, William		4	88
HOWARTH, John	P	3	145
HOWAT, David Watson	P	5	89
HOWAT, William Wyllie		3	145
HOWATT, Herbert		1	195
HOWATT, James	P	2	173
HOWE, Claude Arthur		4	88
HOWE, Cyril		4	88
HOWE, Ernest James Cowell		1	195
HOWE, Walter		4	88
HOWELL, Alfred		5	89
HOWELL, Charles Joseph		3	145
HOWELL, Frank		5	89
HOWELL, James		2	174
HOWELL, James William		3	145
HOWELL, Richard Laban		4	88
HOWELL, Walter Richard		2	174
HOWELLS, Courtney Philip		5	89
HOWELLS, Francis Henry		4	88
HOWELLS, John Wesley		3	145

Name	Photo	Part No.	Page No.
HOWELLS, Wilfred J		3	145
HOWES, A		4	88
HOWES, Albert Edward		1	195
HOWES, Herbert Arthur		1	195
HOWES, John Henry		1	195
HOWIE, John		5	89
HOWIE, William		2	174
HOWIE, William Gladstone	P	2	174
HOWIESON, Alexander		2	174
HOWIS, Frederick Samuel		4	88
HOWLAND, Stanley Herbert		2	174
HOWLETT, James		3	145
HOWLING, John Matthew		1	195
HOWORTH, William James		5	89
HOWSON, George Rowland Paget		3	145
HOY, John Alfred		1	195
HOYE, James		1	195
HOYES, Fred		3	146
HOYLAND, Godfrey Algernon	P	5	89
HOYLAND, John		1	195
HOYLE, Basil William Edmund	P	2	174
HOYLE, Harold		3	146
HOYLE, Walter Maynard		3	146
HOYLES, Ernest		4	88
HOYLES, George		4	88
HOYLES, Richard		4	88
HOYTE, Raymond Wilson		5	90
HRAUDA-ROWDER, Guy Walter		2	265
HUBBARD, Adrian George	P	4	89
HUBBARD, Ernest Arthur		4	89
HUBBARD, Ernest William	P	4	89
HUBBARD, Fred	P	1	196
HUBBARD, Frederick George	P	2	174
HUBBARD, George		2	174
HUBBARD, J G		3	146
HUBBARD, Richard		2	174
HUBBARD, Thomas		2	174
HUBBARD, Walter Hugh	P	2	174
HUBBARD, William		1	196
HUBBERSTEY, John		2	174
HUBBLE, Henry Cornelius		5	90
HUBIE-AXE, William Cecil		1	196
HUCKSTEP, James Thomas		1	196
HUDDART, Cuthbert Edmund Arnold	P	3	146
HUDLESTON, Harold Robert	P	3	146
HUDSON, Adam		1	196
HUDSON, Albert		2	174
HUDSON, Arthur		1	196
HUDSON, Arthur Cyril	P	4	89
HUDSON, Claude G		2	174
HUDSON, Edward Stanley	P	3	146
HUDSON, Francis Parker		5	90
HUDSON, Frederick Cattell	P	1	196
HUDSON, Frederick George		1	196
HUDSON, Frederick James		3	146
HUDSON, George Arthur		4	89
HUDSON, J		3	146
HUDSON, J		3	146
HUDSON, John William Willoughby		2	174
HUDSON, Robert Denis	P	2	174
HUDSON, Thomas		1	196
HUDSON, Thomas Ernest	P	1	196
HUDSON, Thomas Ernest		5	90
HUDSON, W		2	174
HUDSPITH, Harold Baron	P	1	196

Name	Photo	Part No.	Page No.
HUFFINGTON, Thomas		4	89
HUFTON, B		3	146
HUGGARD, Alan		2	174
HUGGARD, Charles Evan		2	174
HUGGETT, Maurice		1	196
HUGGINS, Albert		1	196
HUGGINS, Percy Henry	P	2	175
HUGGINS, Peter William		1	196
HUGGLESTONE, Alfred Henry	P	3	146
HUGGLESTONE, William Thomas	P	3	146
HUGHES, Albert Victor		4	89
HUGHES, Alfred W		2	175
HUGHES, Ben		4	89
HUGHES, Bernard		5	90
HUGHES, Burroughes Maurice	P	2	175
HUGHES, Charles		1	196
HUGHES, Charles Edmund		5	90
HUGHES, Charles William		2	175
HUGHES, Chester		2	175
HUGHES, David		5	90
HUGHES, Edward Reginald Graham	P	2	175
HUGHES, Evan Owen		4	89
HUGHES, Frederick		2	175
HUGHES, Frederick Benjamin		5	90
HUGHES, Frederick Royce		5	90
HUGHES, George		2	175
HUGHES, George William		1	196
HUGHES, Guy Wiley		1	196
HUGHES, Henry James		2	175
HUGHES, Henry John		1	196
HUGHES, Henry Ledsome		4	89
HUGHES, Irvin John	P	5	90
HUGHES, J		2	175
HUGHES, James		4	89
HUGHES, John		5	90
HUGHES, John Edward		5	90
HUGHES, Joseph		1	196
HUGHES, Joseph		2	175
HUGHES, Joseph William		1	196
HUGHES, Lewis		2	175
HUGHES, Lionel		1	196
HUGHES, Lionel Holford	P	1	196
HUGHES, Patrick		2	175
HUGHES, Pryce		1	196
HUGHES, Robert T		2	175
HUGHES, Ronald Baskerville		3	146
HUGHES, Sidney Isaac	P	1	196
HUGHES, Sidney Russell		5	90
HUGHES, Thomas		2	175
HUGHES, Thomas	P	3	146
HUGHES, Thomas		4	89
HUGHES, Thomas Hector		1	197
HUGHES, Thomas Joseph		1	196
HUGHES, Victor Henry		3	146
HUGHES, W		3	147
HUGHES, W G		3	147
HUGHES, Wallace John		1	197
HUGHES, William		2	175
HUGHES, William		2	175
HUGHES, William Barton		4	89
HUGHES, William Edward		4	89
HUGHES, William George		4	89
HUGHES, William John	P	2	175
HUGHES, William John		4	89
HUGHES, William Jones	P	4	89

Name	Photo	Part No.	Page No.
HUGHES, William Marshall		4	89
HUGHES-DAVIES, Arthur Gwynne		5	44
HUGHES-HUGHES, William Montagu		2	175
HUGHSON, Robert	P	4	90
HUGO, Lawrence William Albert	P	1	197
HULBERT, George Dodgson	P	5	90
HULBERT, Harold John	P	1	197
HULEATT, Francis Hugh		4	90
HULL, John		2	175
HULM, Wynne Odyerne		2	175
HULME, Sidney		1	197
HULME, Wilfrid		5	90
HULSE, Alfred Benjamin		3	147
HULSTON, Edwin Herbert		5	90
HUMBERSTONE, Daniel Walter	P	4	90
HUMBERSTONE, Edward J		2	175
HUMBERSTONE, Herbert S		2	176
HUMBLE-CROFTS, Cyril Mitford	P	2	85
HUMBLES, Arthur		2	176
HUMBY, Frederick Alfred		5	91
HUME, Alfred James		5	91
HUME, Arthur Grenville		1	197
HUME, David		2	176
HUME, Isaac		1	197
HUME, John Douglas	P	3	147
HUME, William Henry		2	176
HUMFREY, William Knox	P	1	197
HUMM, William		2	176
HUMPHREY, Albert		1	197
HUMPHREY, Albert		2	176
HUMPHREY, Charles		2	176
HUMPHREY, Edmund William Alfred	P	1	197
HUMPHREY, Ernest		2	176
HUMPHREY, George Thomas		2	176
HUMPHREY, Herbert Wheatley		3	147
HUMPHREY, Herbert William		3	147
HUMPHREY, Ichval Machno		5	91
HUMPHREY, Joseph Herbert		4	90
HUMPHREY, William		2	176
HUMPHREY-DAVY, Darrel Nelson O'neale		3	75
HUMPHREYS, Alfred		2	176
HUMPHREYS, Alfred		4	90
HUMPHREYS, Cornelius C		2	176
HUMPHREYS, George Geoffrey Pendergast	P	1	197
HUMPHREYS, John Edward		2	176
HUMPHREYS, John Theodore Gordon		3	147
HUMPHREYS, John Thomas		1	197
HUMPHREYS, William E		2	176
HUMPHRIES, Ernest Vernon		5	91
HUMPHRIES, George Charles		2	176
HUMPHRIES, George Willis	P	1	197
HUMPHRIES, Herbert James		3	147
HUNGERFORD, Albert		2	176
HUNNIBELL, Job Sydney		3	147
HUNT, Albert		1	198
HUNT, Albert Edward		3	147
HUNT, Alfred		3	147
HUNT, Alfred Edward	P	1	198
HUNT, Alfred J		2	176
HUNT, Charles		2	176
HUNT, Edward J		2	176
HUNT, Frank Ernest	P	1	198
HUNT, Fred		3	147
HUNT, Frederick		5	91
HUNT, George Henry		1	198

Name	Photo	Part No.	Page No.
HUNT, Harry		1	198
HUNT, Henry Rainford	P	3	147
HUNT, Herbert W		2	176
HUNT, James		5	91
HUNT, James John		2	176
HUNT, Percy Henry Hart	P	1	198
HUNT, Richard H		2	176
HUNT, Roger Victor Cecil	P	5	91
HUNT, Samuel		5	91
HUNT, Thomas		2	176
HUNT, William Thomas	P	4	90
HUNTER, Albert H		2	176
HUNTER, Bentley Moore	P	3	147
HUNTER, David		2	176
HUNTER, Eric Hamilton	P	2	176
HUNTER, George Rupert		1	198
HUNTER, Hugh	P	1	198
HUNTER, J		2	176
HUNTER, James Andrew	P	1	198
HUNTER, John George	P	1	198
HUNTER, Leslie	P	1	198
HUNTER, Martin		4	90
HUNTER, Melville Adrian Cecil	P	2	176
HUNTER, Robert		1	198
HUNTER, Thomas Hannah	P	2	176
HUNTER, Thomas Vicars	P	4	90
HUNTER, William		2	176
HUNTER, William Boyle	P	3	147
HUNTINGTON, Ernest Henry		3	147
HUNTINGTON, William	P	4	90
HUNTLEY, Alfred Chiswell		3	147
HURCOCK, Joseph James	P	3	147
HURD, Ernest Nigel		5	91
HURDEN, James		2	176
HURLBERT, Rexford	P	1	198
HURLEY, Ernest F		2	176
HURLEY, J		2	176
HURLEY, J		3	148
HURLEY, John James		2	176
HURLEY, R		3	148
HURLL, Henry George		4	90
HURLUCK, William Vincent		4	90
HURN, Frederick John		5	91
HURRELL, Albert		5	91
HURRELL, Edward		2	176
HURST, Albert		2	176
HURST, Alfred Richard		3	148
HURST, Francis		2	176
HURST, George Henry		2	176
HURST, Hubert Edward		2	176
HURSTBOURNE (HIRSCHBEIN), Walter Hirsch	P	3	148
HURST-BROWN, Dudley		1	56
HURT, George William		1	198
HURT, Seymour Frederick Auckland Albert		1	199
HUSBAND, Donald Irons	P	3	148
HUSBAND, Herbert Barry	P	1	199
HUSBAND, Joseph Sim	P	4	90
HUSBAND, Peter Ross	P	3	148
HUSBANDS, Clifford Charles		3	148
HUSKINSON, Charles Robert		1	199
HUSSELL, Alfred Peter		4	91
HUSSEY, Edmund Thornber	P	3	148
HUSSEY, George William	P	4	91
HUSSEY, Harold Edward		3	148

Name	Photo	Part No.	Page No.
HUSSEY, James William		1	199
HUSSEY, Thomas Joseph		1	199
HUTCHEON, Keith		2	176
HUTCHESON, Gordon James		4	91
HUTCHESON, James	P	3	148
HUTCHESON, John	P	1	199
HUTCHINGS, Robert Sidney		1	199
HUTCHINS, Thomas Arthur	P	1	199
HUTCHINS, Wilfred Arthur		2	176
HUTCHINSON, Alfred Richard		1	199
HUTCHINSON, Anthony Christopher Campbell		5	91
HUTCHINSON, Cecil Dunbar	P	4	91
HUTCHINSON, Cecil Leigh	P	3	148
HUTCHINSON, Charles		4	91
HUTCHINSON, Duncan Frank		3	149
HUTCHINSON, Henry Ernest		1	199
HUTCHINSON, John		3	149
HUTCHINSON, John Cayley		2	177
HUTCHINSON, John Thomas		2	177
HUTCHINSON, Lionel Clyde	P	1	199
HUTCHINSON, Robert Greenwood		1	199
HUTCHINSON, Thomas		3	149
HUTCHINSON, Thomas H		2	177
HUTCHINSON, William John	P	3	149
HUTCHISON, Alexander		2	177
HUTCHISON, Alexander		2	177
HUTCHISON, David		2	177
HUTCHISON, E		2	177
HUTCHISON, John		2	177
HUTCHISON, Robert Hamilton		2	177
HUTCHISON, Thomas Walter	P	2	177
HUTH, Austin Henry	P	1	199
HUTSON, George W		2	177
HUTT, Harold Vernon	P	1	199
HUTT, John Charles		5	91
HUTTON, A		2	177
HUTTON, George		1	199
HUTTON, Ian Campbell	P	1	199
HUTTON, John Barnabas		2	177
HUTTON, Lorne De Hutton	P	5	91
HUTTON, Rev. Sydney Frederick	P	2	177
HUTTON, Robert	P	5	91
HUTTON-SQUIRE, Robert Henry Edmund	P	4	195
HUXHAM, William Spencer	P	3	149
HUXTABLE, E W		3	149
HYATT, Charles		2	177
HYBART, John	P	3	149
HYDE, Charles Sidney		5	91
HYDE, Charles Stuart	P	2	177
HYDE, Edgar		2	177
HYDE, Ernest		2	177
HYDE, Eustace Emil	P	2	177
HYDE, George Thomas		2	177
HYDE, James Charles	P	3	149
HYDE, Samuel		3	149
HYDER, Alfred William		5	91
HYDER, Jack Heathcote		5	92
HYDON, Charles Henry		5	92
HYDON, Charles John		5	92
HYLAND, Edwin		2	177
HYLAND, John Edward	P	1	200
HYLAND, William		2	177
HYMERS, Thomas H		2	178
HYND, Henry		4	91
HYNDS, William	P	2	178

Name	Photo	Part No.	Page No.
HYNE, Henry		2	178
HYNES, James		1	200
HYNES, James Joseph	P	1	200
HYSLOP, Robert Edward	P	3	149
IDDON, W		3	149
IDE, J		3	149
ILES, John Owen	P	2	178
ILES, Thomas Ernest		2	178
ILES, W		3	149
ILIFF, Henry		3	149
ILIFFE, G		3	149
ILLETT, Francis C		2	178
ILLINGWORTH, Albert Edward		5	92
ILLINGWORTH, Frederick William		5	92
ILLINGWORTH, Harry Oakden		3	149
ILLINSWORTH, J		3	150
ILSLEY, John George		2	178
IMLAH, Lewis		4	91
IMRIE, David		4	91
IMRIE, George Wilfred		2	178
IMRIE, James		5	92
IMRIE, James Walter	P	1	200
IMS, Robert Thomas	P	1	200
INCE, Charles Edward		5	92
INCHES, James		2	178
INDGE, Frederick T		2	178
INESON, Ernest		3	150
INGATE, Joseph		3	150
INGATE, Walter William		1	200
INGHAM, John Thomas		1	200
INGHAM, Richard Francis		2	178
INGHAM, S		2	178
INGHAM, S		3	150
INGHAM, Thomas		3	150
INGLE, Percy		2	178
INGLES, Alexander Wighton		1	200
INGLES-CHAMBERLAYNE, Rupert Henry	P	1	76
INGLESON, Albert Sidney	P	4	91
INGLIS, Andrew	P	5	92
INGLIS, Charles North Dalrymple	P	1	200
INGLIS, David	P	1	200
INGLIS, G		3	150
INGLIS, James Malcolm		5	92
INGLIS, John		3	150
INGLIS, W		2	178
INGLIS, William		3	150
INGRAM, C H		3	150
INGRAM, E		3	150
INGRAM, Ernest Frank		2	178
INGRAM, Frank		2	178
INGRAM, Frederick James		1	201
INGRAM, G J		3	150
INGRAM, George		1	201
INGRAM, Gordon		4	91
INGRAM, James		1	201
INGRAM, R		3	150
INGRAM, Walter		1	201
INGRAM, William		2	178
INGRAM, William Alexander	P	3	150
INGRAM, William Bradley	P	2	178
INGRAM, William Henry		1	201
INGRAM, William Henry		2	178
INGRAM, William John		2	178
INGREY, Frederick George		4	91
INKPEN, Percy		2	178

Name	Photo	Part No.	Page No.
INMAN (ALIAS FARMER), George Charles		2	178
INNES, Alexander Berowald	P	1	201
INNES, Daniel Cottier		1	201
INNES, Frederick Arthur		3	150
INNES, George B R		2	178
INNES, Henry Pembroke	P	5	92
INNES, Ian Charles	P	1	201
INNES, J		3	150
INNES, James Brydon		2	178
INNES, James Ian	P	1	201
INNES, John	P	1	201
INNES, John		4	91
INNES, Peter Douglas		2	178
INNES, Robert Prentice	P	5	92
INNES, William Bowie	P	3	150
INNES HOPKINS, Castell Percy		1	194
INNES HOPKINS, Charles Randolph	P	1	194
INNES HOPKINS, James Randolph	P	1	194
INNOCENT, James Alfred		1	201
INSKIP, R		3	150
INSTONE, Leonard Frederick	P	1	201
IONIDES, Ambrose Constantine	P	2	178
IONIDES, Theodore Alexander	P	3	150
IREDALE, Harold		2	179
IRELAN, John A		2	179
IRELAND, G		3	150
IRELAND, J		3	150
IRELAND, James Mclaren		4	91
IRELAND, John		5	92
IRELAND, Ralph	P	3	150
IRELAND, Thomas B		3	150
IRELAND, William		1	201
IRELAND, William Johnston	P	4	91
IRISH, Leonard		2	179
IRONMONGER, Frank Charles		2	179
IRONS, Ernest		1	201
IRONSIDE, Alexander Adie		5	92
IRONSIDE, C		3	151
IRONSIDE, James		3	151
IRONSIDE, Robert Stewart	P	1	201
IRVEN, Walter James		1	201
IRVINE, A		3	151
IRVINE, Christopher Theodore Corrie		1	201
IRVINE, Daniel	P	2	179
IRVINE, Francis Duncan	P	1	201
IRVINE, Harold		2	179
IRVINE, J		2	179
IRVINE, J		3	151
IRVINE, James Forbes		2	179
IRVINE, John		5	92
IRVINE, Stannus Charles Edward		1	202
IRVINE, Walter		2	179
IRVINE, William		1	202
IRVING, Albert		4	91
IRVING, Archibald Denys		5	92
IRVING, Eric Cecil		2	179
IRVING, Harold James	P	5	93
IRVING, James		5	93
IRVING, John Victor		1	202
IRVING, William Charles		1	202
IRWIN, Charles Patrick Michael		3	151
IRWIN, G		3	151
IRWIN, George		1	202
IRWIN, Philip Henry York	P	2	179
ISAAC, Hopkin	P	1	202
ISAACS, Alfred		1	202
ISAACS, Henry		2	179
ISAACS, Henry Roland	P	3	151
ISDALE, John		2	179
ISON, Arthur Ernest	P	2	179
ISON, Charles Albert		2	179
ISTED, William	P	1	202
IVE, David	P	1	202
IVES, Arthur		2	179
IVES, E H		3	151
IVES, William Henry		1	202
IVINS, John Herbert	P	1	202
IVINSON, Thomas Edward		5	93
IZZARD, William		1	202
JACK, Alexander		2	179
JACK, C		3	151
JACK, James Charles	P	5	93
JACK, James Hutcheson		2	179
JACK, John		2	179
JACK, William		2	179
JACKMAN, Albert Edward		1	202
JACKMAN, Frank Charles	P	3	151
JACKMAN, P		3	151
JACKSON, Albert Sadler		2	179
JACKSON, Arthur		2	180
JACKSON, Arthur Graham		4	91
JACKSON, C		3	151
JACKSON, Claude Stewart		3	151
JACKSON, Clifford York	P	2	180
JACKSON, E		3	151
JACKSON, Edgar Amphibal	P	2	180
JACKSON, Edward		2	180
JACKSON, Edward A G		2	180
JACKSON, Edward Cecil		5	93
JACKSON, Edward Phillips	P	1	202
JACKSON, F A		3	151
JACKSON, Francis Leonard Hunter	P	3	151
JACKSON, Frederick James	P	1	202
JACKSON, G		3	151
JACKSON, George		3	151
JACKSON, George		5	93
JACKSON, George Conway		2	180
JACKSON, George Covell		3	151
JACKSON, George Olaf Damian Ceadda	P	3	151
JACKSON, George William	P	2	180
JACKSON, Herbert Meynell	P	3	152
JACKSON, Howard Maurice	P	2	180
JACKSON, Hugo Anthony Launcelot Ceadda	P	3	152
JACKSON, J		2	180
JACKSON, J		3	152
JACKSON, J		3	152
JACKSON, J		3	152
JACKSON, J		3	152
JACKSON, J J		3	152
JACKSON, James Battle		4	92
JACKSON, John		1	202
JACKSON, John		3	152
JACKSON, John		3	152
JACKSON, John David		5	93
JACKSON, John George		1	202
JACKSON, John Henry		2	180
JACKSON, John Montague Hammick		2	180
JACKSON, Joshua Graham	P	1	202
JACKSON, L		3	152
JACKSON, Maurice		5	93

Name	Photo	Part No.	Page No.	Name	Photo	Part No.	Page No.
JAYES, George William		1	204	JENKINS, William		3	155
JAYNES, A		3	154	JENKINS, William Havelock		4	93
JEAL, A D		3	154	JENKINS, William Joseph	P	4	93
JEAL, Percy Albert		4	93	JENKINSON, J		3	155
JEAL, Walter		3	154	JENKINSON, John		2	183
JEAL, William James Charles		4	93	JENKINSON, John Banks	P	1	205
JEAYES, Henry Laurence	P	3	154	JENKINSON, John Dennis		3	155
JEBB, J		3	154	JENKINSON, William Royle		2	183
JEBBETT, Frank Arnold		3	154	JENKS, George Vale		5	94
JEFFARES, Reginald Isaac	P	3	154	JENNER, G H		3	155
JEFFCOCK, Stephen		2	182	JENNER, J T		3	155
JEFFEREYES, C		3	154	JENNER, Robert		2	183
JEFFERIES, Edgar Bartholomew		5	94	JENNER, William C		2	183
JEFFERIES, Thomas Henry		2	182	JENNINGS, A R		2	183
JEFFERS, William		5	94	JENNINGS, Albert Victor		2	183
JEFFERSON, George William		1	204	JENNINGS, Alfred G		5	94
JEFFERSON, Ingleby Stuart		3	154	JENNINGS, Allen William Mark		1	205
JEFFERY, Arthur		2	182	JENNINGS, Arnold Simkin		5	94
JEFFERY, Claud Giffard		1	205	JENNINGS, Arthur		1	205
JEFFERY, F W		3	154	JENNINGS, Basil Spencer	P	2	183
JEFFERY, John James	P	3	154	JENNINGS, Charles Albany	P	4	93
JEFFERY, Robert Berry		1	205	JENNINGS, Frederick		1	205
JEFFERY, William Allen		1	205	JENNINGS, Frederick		3	155
JEFFORD, Leonard Laurence Morden		4	93	JENNINGS, Frederick Sinclair Wills	P	1	205
JEFFREY, James Binning		5	94	JENNINGS, G		3	155
JEFFREY, John	P	1	205	JENNINGS, Hugh Cotter		3	155
JEFFREYS, Albert		2	182	JENNINGS, J		3	155
JEFFREYS, Arthur		3	154	JENNINGS, J P		3	155
JEFFRIES, Harold John Fotheringham		2	182	JENNINGS, James		1	205
JEFFRIES, Herbert John		1	205	JENNINGS, James		2	184
JEFFRIES, Sidney		5	94	JENNINGS, John Gilderdale		2	184
JEFFRIES, William Richard	P	2	182	JENNINGS, Joseph		2	184
JEFFS, Albert		3	154	JENNINGS, Percy Frederick		3	155
JELF, Charles Gordon		2	182	JENNINGS, Reginald John	P	1	205
JELF, L		3	154	JENNINGS, Richard Louis		1	205
JELLEY, Harold George		2	182	JENNINGS, Richard T		5	95
JELLY, A R		3	154	JENNINGS, Richard William		3	155
JEMMETT-BROWNE, Anthony Edward		2	44	JENNINGS, Thomas		2	184
JENINGS, George Pierse Creagh		1	205	JENNINGS, William		1	205
JENKIN, Archibald George	P	2	183	JENNINGS, William Henry		4	93
JENKINS, A		3	154	JENOURE, George Ethelread		1	205
JENKINS, A		3	154	JEPHSON, John Noble	P	1	206
JENKINS, Alexander		3	154	JEPPS, E C		2	184
JENKINS, Alfred		5	94	JEPSON, Sydney Stephen		4	93
JENKINS, Arthur Cyril		3	154	JEREMIAH, David John		3	155
JENKINS, Arthur Lewis		4	93	JEREMY, F		3	155
JENKINS, Charles	P	4	93	JEREMY, Thomas		2	184
JENKINS, Cyril Frank Bingham	P	3	154	JEROME, John William		1	206
JENKINS, Daniel Morley		2	183	JEROME, Ralph Charles	P	1	206
JENKINS, David Roy		3	155	JEROME, W H		3	155
JENKINS, Edward		2	183	JERRAM, Harry Escombe Ravenhill		1	206
JENKINS, Ernest Joseph		3	155	JERRED, Frank		1	206
JENKINS, G		3	155	JERROM, H H		3	155
JENKINS, George Reginald	P	2	183	JESSE, Robert Turville		1	206
JENKINS, J T		3	155	JESSOL, George		2	184
JENKINS, James		3	155	JESSOP, Napier Arnott	P	1	206
JENKINS, John		3	155	JESSUP, H		2	184
JENKINS, John Reginald	P	1	205	JESSUP, John Richard		5	95
JENKINS, Leonard Ellerm		4	93	JEWELL, Arthur William		3	155
JENKINS, Richard Borlase	P	2	183	JEWELL, Dudley Mark Hayward	P	2	184
JENKINS, Robert		1	205	JEWELL, Edward Herbert	P	2	184
JENKINS, Sidney Royston		3	155	JEWELL, William		2	184
JENKINS, Sydney Randell	P	2	183	JEWITT, Frederick		2	184
JENKINS, Thomas James Morris		2	183	JEWSON, F T		3	155
JENKINS, Walter		1	205	JIGGLE, Cyril Victor	P	5	95

Name	Photo	Part No.	Page No.
JOB, Bernard Craig Keble	P	1	206
JOBBINS, Thomas Arthur		1	206
JOBERNS, Edward	P	3	155
JOBERNS, William	P	3	155
JOBES, Robert		2	184
JOBSON, Herbert		2	184
JOE, David Smith		4	93
JOEL, John Hugh		3	155
JOHANNESSEN, Peter Hans		5	95
JOHN, Thomas		5	95
JOHN, William	P	3	156
JOHNINGS, William Henry		2	184
JOHNS, Alfred T		3	156
JOHNS, Arthur Philip	P	3	156
JOHNS, Bernard Digby		3	156
JOHNS, Charles Edward		3	156
JOHNS, Frank George		2	184
JOHNS, Thomas Frederick		4	93
JOHNSON, A		2	184
JOHNSON, Albert		1	206
JOHNSON, Albert		4	93
JOHNSON, Albert Chapman	P	1	206
JOHNSON, Alfred Arthur		1	206
JOHNSON, Alfred Thomas		2	184
JOHNSON, Arthur		2	184
JOHNSON, Arthur Graham	P	3	156
JOHNSON, Arthur William	P	4	94
JOHNSON, C E		3	156
JOHNSON, Charles Edwin		4	94
JOHNSON, D		3	156
JOHNSON, Daniel		2	184
JOHNSON, David		1	206
JOHNSON, David		4	94
JOHNSON, Donald Fredric Goold		4	94
JOHNSON, E T		3	156
JOHNSON, Edward	P	5	95
JOHNSON, Edwin Ernest		3	156
JOHNSON, Ernest David		5	95
JOHNSON, Ernest H		2	184
JOHNSON, Frederick		2	184
JOHNSON, Frederick		2	184
JOHNSON, Frederick		2	184
JOHNSON, Frederick	P	2	184
JOHNSON, Frederick John		4	94
JOHNSON, Frederick Miller	P	2	184
JOHNSON, G J		3	156
JOHNSON, George		2	185
JOHNSON, George		2	185
JOHNSON, George Albert William		1	206
JOHNSON, George Gumbrell		1	206
JOHNSON, Gilbert Ernest	P	4	94
JOHNSON, H		3	156
JOHNSON, H E		3	156
JOHNSON, Herbert Lewis	P	5	95
JOHNSON, Herbert William		1	206
JOHNSON, J		3	156
JOHNSON, J		3	156
JOHNSON, J		3	156
JOHNSON, James		3	156
JOHNSON, James Henry		2	185
JOHNSON, John		1	206
JOHNSON, John L		2	185
JOHNSON, John Mervyn		2	185
JOHNSON, John Thomas	P	3	156
JOHNSON, John William		2	185

Name	Photo	Part No.	Page No.
JOHNSON, Joseph		1	206
JOHNSON, Joseph		4	94
JOHNSON, Joseph J		5	95
JOHNSON, Leslie Nethercote		3	156
JOHNSON, Luther Vincent Burgoyne	P	1	206
JOHNSON, Maurice Richard Wheatley	P	5	95
JOHNSON, Philip Norman	P	5	95
JOHNSON, Ralph		3	156
JOHNSON, Rayner Harvey	P	5	95
JOHNSON, Richard Digby	P	1	207
JOHNSON, Robert		2	185
JOHNSON, Robert Warren	P	1	207
JOHNSON, Rodney Richard		3	157
JOHNSON, Ronald		4	94
JOHNSON, T		3	157
JOHNSON, Thomas		1	207
JOHNSON, Thomas		1	207
JOHNSON, Thomas Allan		5	96
JOHNSON, Thomas Arthur James		4	94
JOHNSON, Thomas Colwell		5	96
JOHNSON, Thomas P		2	185
JOHNSON, Thomas W		2	185
JOHNSON, Vernon Dockery	P	5	96
JOHNSON, W		2	185
JOHNSON, W		3	157
JOHNSON, W J		3	157
JOHNSON, Walter		1	207
JOHNSON, Walter		1	207
JOHNSON, Wilfred Ernest		2	185
JOHNSON, Wilfrid Lloyd	P	5	96
JOHNSON, William		2	185
JOHNSON, William George		1	207
JOHNSON, William Henry		1	207
JOHNSTON, Alexander		3	157
JOHNSTON, Allan Todd		3	157
JOHNSTON, Andrew Yuill	P	3	157
JOHNSTON, Bruce Allen	P	1	207
JOHNSTON, Charles		2	185
JOHNSTON, Christopher		2	185
JOHNSTON, Dempter		2	185
JOHNSTON, Evans Clement Stuart	P	3	157
JOHNSTON, G		3	157
JOHNSTON, George Albert		1	207
JOHNSTON, George Braidford		2	185
JOHNSTON, Henry		5	96
JOHNSTON, J		2	185
JOHNSTON, J		3	157
JOHNSTON, James		2	185
JOHNSTON, James Barlow		5	96
JOHNSTON, James Cecil	P	1	207
JOHNSTON, James Hogarth	P	1	207
JOHNSTON, John D		2	185
JOHNSTON, John Lyonel Lukin	P	3	157
JOHNSTON, John Stuart		2	185
JOHNSTON, John Thomas	P	3	157
JOHNSTON, Landel	P	5	96
JOHNSTON, P		2	185
JOHNSTON, Peter Linskill		2	185
JOHNSTON, Reuben John		1	208
JOHNSTON, Robert		1	208
JOHNSTON, Robert		3	157
JOHNSTON, Robert		4	94
JOHNSTON, Thomas		2	185
JOHNSTON, William		1	208
JOHNSTON, William		1	208

Name	Photo	Part No.	Page No.
JOHNSTON, William		2	185
JOHNSTON, William Henry	P	1	208
JOHNSTON, William Tordiff	P	3	157
JOHNSTONE, Alexander		3	157
JOHNSTONE, Arthur Charles		2	185
JOHNSTONE, B E		2	185
JOHNSTONE, E		2	185
JOHNSTONE, G		2	185
JOHNSTONE, G		2	185
JOHNSTONE, J		2	185
JOHNSTONE, J		3	157
JOHNSTONE, J		3	157
JOHNSTONE, M W		3	157
JOHNSTONE, Miller	P	1	208
JOHNSTONE, Peter		1	208
JOHNSTONE, Peter		2	185
JOHNSTONE, Rupert Bertram		2	186
JOHNSTONE, Samuel	P	5	96
JOHNSTONE, T		2	186
JOHNSTONE, Thomas		2	186
JOHNSTONE, W		2	186
JOHNSTONE, W		3	157
JOHNSTONE, William		1	208
JOHNSTONE, William		1	208
JOHNSTONE, William		2	186
JOHNYS, Arthur G		2	186
JOINT, Robert James		3	157
JOLIFFE, John		1	208
JOLLEY, John Andrew Benjamin		2	186
JOLLIE, John		2	186
JOLLIFF, John		1	208
JOLLIFFE, William James		1	208
JOLLY, Ernest Robert		3	157
JOLLY, John		2	186
JOLLY, Robert	P	3	158
JOLLY, William J		2	186
JONES, A		3	158
JONES, A		3	158
JONES, A		3	158
JONES, A		3	158
JONES, A		3	158
JONES, A		3	158
JONES, A A		3	158
JONES, A F P		3	158
JONES, A H		3	158
JONES, A S		3	158
JONES, A W		2	186
JONES, Adrian Herbert	P	1	208
JONES, Alan Stoakes	P	4	94
JONES, Albert Edward		2	186
JONES, Albert Henry		5	96
JONES, Alfred Benjamin Cockerill	P	5	96
JONES, Alfred Edward		1	208
JONES, Alfred Poole	P	1	208
JONES, Archibald Edward		3	158
JONES, Arthur		1	208
JONES, Arthur Vernon	P	5	97
JONES, Arthur William		1	208
JONES, Arthur Wynn	P	1	208
JONES, Basil Gordon Dawes	P	3	158
JONES, Bryan John		5	97
JONES, C		3	158
JONES, C		3	158
JONES, C B		3	158
JONES, C J		3	158

Name	Photo	Part No.	Page No.
JONES, Charles		1	208
JONES, Charles Taylor	P	2	186
JONES, Clarence William		4	94
JONES, David Bowen		4	94
JONES, David George		2	186
JONES, David Jonah Davies		4	94
JONES, Douglas Llewellyn		3	158
JONES, E		3	158
JONES, E		3	158
JONES, E E		3	158
JONES, Edward		2	186
JONES, Edward		2	186
JONES, Edward		4	94
JONES, Edward		5	97
JONES, Edward Vincent		2	186
JONES, Edwin		1	209
JONES, Edwin M		2	186
JONES, Emrys		2	186
JONES, Eric Arthur Owen	P	3	158
JONES, Ernest		2	186
JONES, Ernest		4	94
JONES, Ernest David	P	1	208
JONES, Ernest Edward		2	186
JONES, F		2	186
JONES, F		3	158
JONES, F		3	158
JONES, F		3	158
JONES, F P		3	158
JONES, Felix Ernest	P	3	158
JONES, Fenn		1	209
JONES, Francis George	P	1	209
JONES, Francis Maynard Harvey	P	3	158
JONES, Francis Thomas		3	158
JONES, Frank Reginald	P	2	186
JONES, Fred	P	1	209
JONES, Frederick	P	3	159
JONES, Frederick		3	159
JONES, Frederick Charles		1	209
JONES, Frederick Charles		2	186
JONES, Frederick Owen	P	2	186
JONES, Frederick Walwyn		3	159
JONES, G		3	159
JONES, G		3	159
JONES, G E		3	159
JONES, George		2	186
JONES, George		2	186
JONES, George		2	186
JONES, George	P	5	97
JONES, George Alfred		2	186
JONES, George Frederick		1	209
JONES, George Frederick		4	95
JONES, George Henry		4	95
JONES, George Thomas		3	159
JONES, George William		1	209
JONES, Gerald Adrian Disney		4	95
JONES, Gower	P	2	187
JONES, Gwillim Jenkin	P	3	159
JONES, Gwilym Arthur Tegid		4	95
JONES, Gwilym Thomas		3	159
JONES, H		3	159
JONES, Harry		1	209
JONES, Harry		5	97
JONES, Harry Dukinfield		1	209
JONES, Harry Leonard		3	159
JONES, Henry Ashcroft		2	187

Name	Photo	Part No.	Page No.
JOYCE, E		3	161
JOYCE, F		3	161
JOYCE, J U		3	161
JOYCE, Leui Harold		1	211
JUDD, Albert		2	188
JUDD, W		3	161
JUDD, William Henry		3	161
JUDE, E D		3	161
JUDGE, Albert		5	98
JUDGE, Charles Henry		5	98
JUDGE, Frederick David	P	1	211
JUDGE, J		3	161
JUKES, A G S		3	161
JUKES, J		3	161
JUKES, Ronald Worthington	P	1	211
JULIETTE, Philip		1	211
JULIN, Thomas Fawcett		1	211
JUPE, Bruce Dunning		1	211
JUPP, Alfred		2	188
JUPP, George		1	211
JUPP, Henry George	P	3	161
JUPP, T		3	161
JUPP, Wilfrid J		2	188
JURGENS, Sydney George		2	188
JURY, William		1	211
JUSTICE, Maurice		1	211
JUSTICE, Percy Harold	P	1	211
KADWELL, William		1	211
KAIN, Stanley		1	211
KAIN, W		3	161
KAINES, A		3	161
KALLAWAY, Edgar	P	1	211
KANE, Charles		1	212
KANE, J		3	161
KANE, Samuel		2	188
KANE, W J		3	161
KAUGHTON, George		2	188
KAVANAGH, Thomas Joseph Cuthbert		1	212
KAVANEY, J W		3	161
KAY, Alexander		3	161
KAY, Andrew Drennan	P	3	162
KAY, G M		3	162
KAY, H J		4	96
KAY, Henry		5	98
KAY, Maurice John		5	98
KAY, Robert Murray		4	96
KAYE, James		2	188
KAYE, Levi		4	96
KAYE, William Fairlie	P	3	162
KAYNES, Reginald Genvy		4	96
KAY-SHUTTLEWORTH, The Hon Edward James	P	5	151
KAY-SHUTTLEWORTH, The Hon Lawrence Ughtred	P	5	151
KAYSS, John Harvey Bainbridge	P	4	96
KAYWOOD, Thomas		2	188
KEABLE, Joseph William		1	212
KEAM, George James		1	212
KEAN, Charles		2	188
KEAN, John Herdman	P	3	162
KEARNEY, Thomas James		4	96
KEARNS, Alfred		2	188
KEARON, Patrick		4	96
KEARSLEY, Frederick		3	162
KEARSLEY, W		3	162

Name	Photo	Part No.	Page No.
KEATES, Arthur Sydney	P	1	212
KEATES, Ernest		2	188
KEATES, Reginald		1	212
KEATES, Richard John	P	4	96
KEATES, Thomas Trancer		1	212
KEATING, Alfred		2	188
KEATING, Joseph		4	96
KEATING, T		3	162
KEATING, Thomas		2	188
KEATINGS, J		2	188
KEATLEY, Henry		2	188
KEATS, William Mark		5	98
KEAY, James Gordon	P	3	162
KEAY-FALCONER, William	P	1	128
KEDDIE, Alfred		2	188
KEDGE, Frederick		2	188
KEEBLE, Philip John		5	98
KEEBLE, R E		3	162
KEEBLE, William		5	98
KEECH, George Christopher	P	2	188
KEEDWELL, George	P	4	96
KEEFE, E		3	162
KEEFE, Thomas		5	98
KEEGAN, Michael John		5	98
KEEGAN, W		2	188
KEEGEN, J J		3	162
KEELAN, John		1	212
KEELER, Sidney		1	212
KEELEY, William Lester		5	98
KEELING, E		3	162
KEEN, E		2	188
KEEN, Fred		1	212
KEEN, Harry Douglas		4	97
KEEN, Leonard		2	188
KEEN, Thomas William		4	97
KEEN, W		3	162
KEEN, W C H		3	162
KEEN, W E		3	162
KEENE, Edward		1	212
KEENE, Frederick Charles		2	188
KEENE, Oswald Rees		1	212
KEENLYSIDE, Cecil Alexander Headlam	P	1	212
KEENLYSIDE, Guy Francis Headlam		1	212
KEEP, Albert Edward		5	98
KEEPAX, W		3	162
KEER, George		3	162
KEERS, Joseph		4	97
KEETON, Walter Thomas		2	188
KEEVIL, Frederick Charles		3	162
KEIGHT, Joseph		1	212
KEIGHTLEY, Joseph Albert		3	162
KEIGHTLEY, N		3	162
KEIGHTLEY, Philip Charles Russell		5	98
KEIGHTON, Michael Joseph		2	188
KEIL, Alexander Peter Maclennan	P	2	188
KEILANS, Frederick	P	2	188
KEILEY, Donald Frazer		4	97
KEIR, Alexander George	P	4	97
KEIR, James Bertram	P	4	97
KEIR, John	P	4	97
KEITH, C		2	188
KEKEWICH, Arthur St. John Mackintosh	P	2	188
KELL, Robert		5	98
KELL, W T		3	162
KELLAS, Arthur	P	1	212

Name	Photo	Part No.	Page No.	Name	Photo	Part No.	Page No.
KELLEHER, Christopher		1	212	KEMP, William		4	97
KELLEHER, John		2	189	KEMP, William Meadows	P	2	189
KELLEY, George		1	212	KEMPSTER, Alec Albert Dresden	P	2	189
KELLIE, Esmond Lawrence	P	1	212	KEMPSTER, John Douglas		1	213
KELLIE, John Patterson	P	3	162	KEMPSTER, W H		3	163
KELLIE, T		3	162	KEMPSTON, James Campbell		3	163
KELLY, Amos J		2	189	KEMPTHORNE, Harold Sampson	P	4	97
KELLY, Arthur		1	212	KEMPTON, Harry Leonard		1	213
KELLY, B D		3	162	KEMPTON, Thomas	P	3	163
KELLY, Cecil Godfrey Bernard		5	98	KEMSLEY, William Charles Henry	P	1	213
KELLY, D		3	162	KENDALL, Harry A		2	190
KELLY, Daniel		5	98	KENDALL, Jesse		1	213
KELLY, David		2	189	KENDRICK, Haden Mostyn		3	163
KELLY, Dennis		2	189	KENDRICK, John Edward		2	190
KELLY, E		3	162	KENNA, Albert Reginald		2	190
KELLY, F		2	189	KENNARD, Arthur	P	1	213
KELLY, Harry Holdsworth	P	1	212	KENNARD, E		3	163
KELLY, J		2	189	KENNARD, Edward		2	190
KELLY, J		3	162	KENNARD, James		2	190
KELLY, J		3	162	KENNARD, Leonard John		3	163
KELLY, J		3	163	KENNARD, S		3	164
KELLY, James		2	189	KENNARD, Stanley Charles		1	213
KELLY, James	P	2	189	KENNAWAY, Arthur Lewis	P	5	99
KELLY, John		4	97	KENNEDY, A		3	164
KELLY, John Joseph		5	98	KENNEDY, A		3	164
KELLY, Joseph		2	189	KENNEDY, Adam		2	190
KELLY, Joseph Francis	P	3	163	KENNEDY, Alexander		2	190
KELLY, P		3	163	KENNEDY, Anthony		2	190
KELLY, Philip James		3	163	KENNEDY, Arthur Herbert	P	4	97
KELLY, R		2	189	KENNEDY, Arthur St. Clair	P	1	213
KELLY, R		3	163	KENNEDY, Charles Seccombe Craufurd	P	2	190
KELLY, Reginald		4	97	KENNEDY, Douglas Maitland	P	5	99
KELLY, Robert Edward		2	189	KENNEDY, Duncan Cameron	P	2	190
KELLY, S		3	163	KENNEDY, Ernest Ebenezer		2	190
KELLY, T		3	163	KENNEDY, George		2	190
KELLY, Thomas		1	213	KENNEDY, George		2	190
KELLY, Thomas		5	99	KENNEDY, Harold		2	190
KELLY, W		3	163	KENNEDY, Hugh	P	2	190
KELLY, W		4	97	KENNEDY, James	P	2	190
KELLY, William		5	99	KENNEDY, James		5	99
KELMAN, William		4	97	KENNEDY, John Edwin	P	2	190
KELSEY, Albert		2	189	KENNEDY, John Horace	P	1	213
KELSEY, John		2	189	KENNEDY, John Murray Stewart	P	2	191
KELSO, Archibald		2	189	KENNEDY, John Pitt		1	213
KELSON, Ernest Richard		4	97	KENNEDY, M		3	164
KELWAY-BAMBER, Claude Herschel	P	2	17	KENNEDY, R		3	164
KELYNACK, Richard Henry	P	3	163	KENNEDY, R T		3	164
KEMISH, George Richard		5	99	KENNEDY, Rev. Edmund John	P	2	190
KEMP, Alan Forster		3	163	KENNEDY, Ronald Bayly Craven		4	98
KEMP, Albert Henry		3	163	KENNEDY, S Lancelot	P	3	164
KEMP, Alfred		1	213	KENNEDY, T		3	164
KEMP, Alfred Charles		2	189	KENNEDY, William	P	3	164
KEMP, Arthur	P	1	213	KENNEDY, William Robert		2	191
KEMP, Ernest Charles		3	163	KENNEL, John Henry	P	1	213
KEMP, Frank		2	189	KENNETT, Percy William		4	98
KEMP, Frederick Owen	P	2	189	KENNETT, Percy William Bishop	P	1	213
KEMP, George	P	3	163	KENNEY, Joseph Edward		3	164
KEMP, H		3	163	KENNINGLEY, C		3	164
KEMP, Horace		5	99	KENNY, A		3	164
KEMP, J A		3	163	KENNY, Cecil John	P	4	98
KEMP, J E		3	163	KENNY, Francis Joseph Leo		3	164
KEMP, James		2	189	KENNY, James		2	191
KEMP, John Bain		3	163	KENNY, James Samuel		5	99
KEMP, Richard John		5	99	KENNY, W		3	164
KEMP, Sydney		1	213	KENSETT, Frank		2	191

Name	Photo	Part No.	Page No.	Name	Photo	Part No.	Page No.
KIRK, James	P	4	100	KNIGHT, William		2	195
KIRK, James		4	100	KNIGHT, William		2	195
KIRK, John Wilfred		2	194	KNIGHTLEY, W		3	167
KIRK, Joseph		2	194	KNIGHTON, Georbge Henry		5	102
KIRK, Randal	P	1	217	KNIGHTON, Gerald Godfrey	P	3	167
KIRK, W H		3	167	KNIGHTS-SMITH, Bernard Arthur	P	2	280
KIRKALDY, David		2	194	KNOCKER, Arthur Paget	P	1	217
KIRKBY, Bertram James		1	216	KNOTT, Frederick William		3	167
KIRKHAM, Samuel	P	4	100	KNOTT, Henry		1	217
KIRKLAND, Frederick William	P	3	167	KNOWERS, Harold James	P	2	195
KIRKLAND, John		5	102	KNOWERS, Percy Albert Edward	P	2	195
KIRKLAND, Thomas Lindsay		1	217	KNOWLE, Donald		5	102
KIRKMAN, Henry James		3	167	KNOWLES, Arthur Yalden		3	167
KIRKPATRICK, Alexander Douglas	P	1	217	KNOWLES, Edward Henry		5	102
KIRKPATRICK, Cecil Alexander St. John		2	194	KNOWLES, Harry		4	101
KIRKPATRICK, Charles		2	194	KNOWLES, John		2	195
KIRKPATRICK, John Crighton		4	101	KNOWLES, John Albert		2	195
KIRKPATRICK, R William		4	101	KNOWLES, Jonathan Edward		1	217
KIRKPATRICK, William F		2	194	KNOWLES, Leonard		5	102
KIRKWOOD, Thomas		2	194	KNOWLES, Stephen	P	2	195
KIRTLAND, W		3	167	KNOWLES, William Alfred		1	217
KIRWAN, Phillip		2	194	KNOWLES, William Harold		4	101
KITCHEN, George Rowland		4	101	KNOWLES, William Henry		3	167
KITCHEN, Walker Wilson		4	101	KNOX, Charles A		2	195
KITCHENER, Alfred		2	194	KNOX, Herbert		2	195
KITCHENER, John Henry		2	194	KNOX, J		3	167
KITCHING, Abner Percival		1	217	KNOX, James		3	167
KITCHING, George Allenby	P	4	101	KNOX, John		2	195
KITCHING, W		3	167	KNOX, Ralph		1	217
KITE, Charles Joseph		2	194	KNOX, William		2	195
KITSON, A E		3	167	KNOX, William Gordon		5	102
KITSON, Jack		4	101	KNUTTON, Thomas		2	195
KITTLE, C E		3	167	KOCH, William James	P	1	217
KITTLE, Hugh James		3	167	KOSH, Harry J		2	195
KIVER, Hubert William	P	3	167	KREUTER, Francais		5	102
KLEMANTASKI, Louis Arthur	P	2	194	KUFF, George Edward		2	195
KLEMP, Albert		4	101	KYAD, Joseph		2	195
KLEMP, Charles Thomas		4	101	KYD, Frank Proctor	P	2	196
KLITZ, Evelyn Anthony		1	217	KYDD, Chester Bishop		3	167
KLOOS, Sidney Albert Edward		1	217	KYDD, James Phillip		1	217
KNAGGS, John William		4	101	KYDD, John William Albert		4	101
KNELL, Edward		5	102	KYLE, Robert Bruce		1	217
KNIGHT, A		3	167	KYLE, Thomas		3	168
KNIGHT, Albert Alfred		1	217	KYLES, David		2	196
KNIGHT, Albert E P		2	195	KYNOCH, Colin Smith	P	1	217
KNIGHT, Arthur Henry		4	101	KYRKE-SMITH, Arthur Kyrke		4	191
KNIGHT, Charles T		2	195	KYTE, Frederick Charles		1	217
KNIGHT, Charles William		3	167	LA PASTURE, Charles Edward Mary			
KNIGHT, Francis Ernest		3	167	(Count De La Pasture)		2	197
KNIGHT, Frederick Gilbert	P	4	101	LACAITA, Francis Charles		4	101
KNIGHT, George Stephen		5	102	LACEY, Charles		1	217
KNIGHT, Harry		2	195	LACEY, George		1	218
KNIGHT, Henry Arthur		1	217	LACEY, R		2	196
KNIGHT, Henry Charles		1	217	LACK, Arthur E		2	196
KNIGHT, John	P	4	101	LACK, Percy Edmund		1	218
KNIGHT, John Hall	P	2	195	LACY, Francis Prior	P	1	218
KNIGHT, John Peake	P	2	195	LACY, Frederick		1	218
KNIGHT, Joseph		1	217	LADD, Ernest William		1	218
KNIGHT, Phillip		3	167	LADD, Robert John		1	218
KNIGHT, Stephen		1	217	LADDS, Frederick		1	218
KNIGHT, Thomas		1	217	LAFONE, Claude Alexander	P	1	218
KNIGHT, Thomas	P	2	195	LAFONTAINE, Fernand Emile Louis		3	168
KNIGHT, W		2	195	LAIDLAW, Charles Glass Playfair	P	1	218
KNIGHT, Walter		2	195	LAIDLAW, Douglas		4	102
KNIGHT, Walter Alfred Francis		4	101	LAIDLAW, James Brownlee	P	5	102

Name	Photo	Part No.	Page No.	Name	Photo	Part No.	Page No.
LANGFORD, Wallace		1	219	**LAUDER,** Richard		4	104
LANGFORD, William John		3	169	**LAUDER,** Stanislaus Joseph	P	1	220
LANGHAM, Walter George		5	103	**LAUDY,** Victor Spencer Harold		5	104
LANGHAM, William Frederick	P	1	219	**LAURANCE,** Herbert		4	105
LANGLANDS, Alan	P	1	220	**LAURENCE,** Andrew		1	220
LANGLEY, Charles George		4	103	**LAURENCE,** Edward James	P	1	220
LANGLEY, E		3	169	**LAURIE,** Nathaniel John		1	220
LANGLEY, William		1	220	**LAURISCH,** Frederick William	P	3	170
LANGRIDGE, Francis Bertram		1	220	**LAURISTON,** Robert		4	105
LANGRIDGE, Frederick Hansford		4	103	**LAVERACK,** Ernest Clyde		4	105
LANGRIDGE, Frederick M G		2	197	**LAVERTY,** Daniel		1	220
LANGRISH, Arthur Charles		4	104	**LAVERY,** J		3	170
LANGRISH, Henry William		1	220	**LAVERY,** P		2	197
LANGSDALE, William Anthony	P	5	103	**LAW,** Alfred		3	170
LANGSFORD, Tosti	P	3	170	**LAW,** C W		3	170
LANGSTAFF, Rupert Alwyn	P	3	170	**LAW,** D		3	170
LANGSTON, A		2	197	**LAW,** Frederick		2	197
LANGSTON, Charles		2	197	**LAW,** Harry		2	197
LANGSTRETT, Edmund		4	104	**LAW,** Henry Milner		4	105
LANGSWORTHY, Frederick		2	197	**LAW,** John Douglas		4	105
LANGTHORNE, Frank		2	197	**LAW,** John Thomas		1	220
LANGTHORP, Thomas Arthur		4	104	**LAW,** Paul		1	220
LANGTRY, W		2	197	**LAW,** Percy Peacock		1	220
LANGWORTH, Harold Samuel		3	170	**LAW,** Stanley	P	5	104
LANGWORTHY, William Southmead		4	104	**LAW,** T		3	170
LANKEMAN, F		3	170	**LAW,** Thomas Pakenham	P	1	220
LANSLEY, William		1	220	**LAW,** William Frederick D		2	197
LANSLEY, William George	P	4	104	**LAW,** William Henry George		2	197
LANSOM, Gerald		4	104	**LAW,** William Leslie		4	105
LANSOM, Leonard		4	104	**LAWES,** Charles Gilbert	P	3	171
LAPISH, Charles	P	3	170	**LAWES,** Frederick John	P	1	220
LARBY, Horace Frederick	P	3	170	**LAWES,** Herbert William John		2	197
LARBY, Walter		1	220	**LAWFORD,** John G		2	197
LARDNER, Roderick Donald		1	220	**LAWLER,** Peter		4	105
LARGE, Eustace Ernest	P	4	104	**LAWLER,** R		3	171
LARK, A F		3	170	**LAWRENCE,** A		3	171
LARK, Arthur Frank		2	197	**LAWRENCE,** Albert		2	197
LARK, George Arnold		4	104	**LAWRENCE,** Albert Jesse		2	197
LARKHAM, A P		3	170	**LAWRENCE,** Albert Robert		4	105
LARKIN, Alfred Basil	P	4	104	**LAWRENCE,** Cecil Henry John		4	105
LARKIN, S J		3	170	**LAWRENCE,** Charles Samuel		1	220
LARKING, Charles Alfred		1	220	**LAWRENCE,** Chas. Edward		1	220
LARKINS, Robert Downie		4	104	**LAWRENCE,** Christopher Hal	P	1	220
LARKMAN, James		3	170	**LAWRENCE,** Edgar Ernest Albert		1	220
LARNER, Ernest William		4	104	**LAWRENCE,** Edward A		2	197
LARNER, Robert William		4	104	**LAWRENCE,** George Albert		1	221
LARRARD, H		3	170	**LAWRENCE,** George Morgan		4	105
LARSON, Oken Frank		1	220	**LAWRENCE,** Henry		2	197
LARVIN, James	P	1	220	**LAWRENCE,** Henry		4	105
LASCELLES, Guy Ernest	P	4	104	**LAWRENCE,** Henry Ernest		2	197
LASHBROOK, Henry Charles		1	220	**LAWRENCE,** J		3	171
LASKEY, Geoffrey Arthur	P	3	170	**LAWRENCE,** J H		3	171
LASLETT, Frank Roland		1	220	**LAWRENCE,** James		2	197
LASSETTER, Arthur J		2	197	**LAWRENCE,** John	P	2	197
LAST, George		4	104	**LAWRENCE,** John Arthur		4	105
LAST, W		3	170	**LAWRENCE,** Leonard Alfred		2	197
LATHAM, Charles Edward		1	220	**LAWRENCE,** Malcolm Eyton	P	1	221
LATHAM, E		3	170	**LAWRENCE,** Thomas Greenfield		4	105
LATHAM, James		3	170	**LAWRENCE,** W C		3	171
LATHAM, John Thomas		2	197	**LAWRENCE,** William		1	221
LATHAM, Percy George		2	197	**LAWRENCE,** William		2	197
LATTA, Charles Keith	P	1	220	**LAWRIE,** David Orman		4	105
LATTA, Robert William Campbell		5	103	**LAWRIE,** Ernest Norman	P	1	221
LATTIEFF, Joseph		2	197	**LAWRIE,** James Black		1	221
LATTO, G		3	170	**LAWRIE,** T		2	197

Name	Photo	Part No.	Page No.
LAWRIE, William Greig		4	105
LAWRY, Arthur		3	171
LAWS, Alfred William		2	197
LAWS, John		2	197
LAWS, Philip Umfreville	P	4	105
LAWSON, Alexander		2	197
LAWSON, Arthur Cyril		4	106
LAWSON, Cecil D N		2	197
LAWSON, Cecil Thomas	P	3	171
LAWSON, Frederick George		2	197
LAWSON, Frederick Henry	P	1	221
LAWSON, H		2	197
LAWSON, Harry Norfolk		2	197
LAWSON, Henry Heaton		4	106
LAWSON, Joseph Percy	P	2	198
LAWSON, Peter		5	104
LAWSON, Reginald Hugh		2	198
LAWSON, W		3	171
LAWSON, W		3	171
LAWSON, William		1	221
LAWSON, William		2	198
LAWSON, William		2	198
LAWSON-SMITH, John	P	1	333
LAWSON-SMITH, Thomas Edward	P	1	333
LAWTON, J		2	198
LAWTON, James Cecil		3	171
LAWTON, Joseph Sydney		1	221
LAWTON, Leonard		3	171
LAWTON, Thomas Parr	P	5	104
LAWTON, William		1	221
LAWTON, William Victor		4	106
LAY, Isaac		2	198
LAYARD, Peter Clement		4	106
LAYCOCK, G		3	171
LAYDON, William		1	221
LAYLAND, George James		4	106
LAYTON, C E		3	171
LAYTON, Cecil William John		4	106
LAYTON, Frank Thomas		1	221
LAYTON, Frederick Oliver		4	106
LAYTON, Roland Churchill		4	106
LAYZELL, Kenneth Bernard	P	5	104
LAZELL, Walter Joseph		3	171
LAZENBY, A H		3	171
LAZENBY, Arthur		1	221
LAZENBY, Harry		4	106
LE BLOND, J		3	172
LE BRUN, Chris.		1	222
LE FLEMING, Lawrence Julius		4	108
LE MARCHAND, John Wharton Jones	P	1	224
LE MARCHAND, Louis St. Gratien	P	1	224
LE MASURIER, Alfred Clive	P	1	224
LE MASURIER, John Edward		1	224
LE MAY, Algernon Edward		4	108
LE PAGE, Edmond John		1	225
LE SUEUR, Clement George	P	1	225
LE VESCONTE, John Thomas		1	225
LEA, G		3	171
LEA, Thomas Lampit		1	221
LEACH, Albert John		4	106
LEACH, Edward Savory Wykeham		4	106
LEACH, F C		3	171
LEACH, Frederick Charles		4	106
LEACH, Gerald Kemball		1	221
LEACH, James John		4	106

Name	Photo	Part No.	Page No.
LEACH, Thomas Herbert	P	2	198
LEACH, William Frank		5	104
LEADBEATER, Alexander	P	3	171
LEADBETTER, Walter	P	4	106
LEADER, Benjamin Eastlake	P	3	171
LEADER, Francis William Mowbray	P	1	221
LEAFE, Frederick Foster		4	106
LEAH, Edward Francis	P	3	171
LEAHY, H C		3	172
LEAHY, J		3	172
LEAHY, J		3	172
LEAK, Reginald	P	2	198
LEAKE, C		3	172
LEAKE, Eric Larkin Wheadon	P	2	198
LEAKE, George Dalton	P	2	198
LEAKES, Bertram Alfred		1	221
LEAL, A J F		3	172
LEAL, J		3	172
LEAMAN, Henry		2	198
LEAMAN, Joseph Herbert		1	221
LEAMAN, Mark Reginald	P	5	104
LEAR, James		2	198
LEARY, A		3	172
LEARY, J		3	172
LEARY, Thomas		1	221
LEASON, Herbert Joseph		4	106
LEATHER, Christopher	P	1	221
LEATHER, Edward Wilberforce	P	1	221
LEATHER, Ernest Arthur	P	1	222
LEATHER, John Francis		5	104
LEATHERBARROW, F		3	172
LEATHERDALE, Alan Richard		3	172
LEATHERDALE, Donald Ryan		3	172
LEATHWOOD, John Pearson		1	222
LEAVER, Thomas William		4	106
LEAVEY, M		3	172
LEAVEY, Thomas Charles		4	107
LEAY, Arthur	P	4	107
LECHMERE, Nicholas George Berwick		2	198
LECKENBY, Harry	P	5	104
LECKIE, Malcolm	P	1	222
LECKY, John Rupert Frederick	P	2	198
LEDBITTER, Herbert Peter	P	3	172
LEDGARD, A		3	172
LEDGER, Frederick		1	222
LEDGER, Raymond Kirwood	P	1	222
LEDIARD, Francis	P	1	222
LEDINGHAM, Thomas Mark		5	105
LEDINGHEM, George Murray		4	107
LEDSHAM, Frank		2	198
LEDSHAM, Lawrence		2	198
LEE, A		3	172
LEE, A R		3	172
LEE, Albert Alfred	P	1	222
LEE, Alexander Charles		4	107
LEE, Alfred James		4	107
LEE, Carlton		5	105
LEE, Charles		1	222
LEE, Charles		1	222
LEE, Charles Harold	P	5	105
LEE, Edgar Charles		3	172
LEE, Edwin William		5	105
LEE, F R		3	172
LEE, Frederick Gurdon Driffield	P	4	107
LEE, G		3	172

Name	Photo	Part No.	Page No.
LEE, George	P	3	172
LEE, George Francis		1	222
LEE, Harry		2	198
LEE, Harry		5	105
LEE, J		2	199
LEE, J		3	172
LEE, James		2	199
LEE, James Clifford	P	3	172
LEE, John Mitchell	P	2	199
LEE, Joseph	P	4	107
LEE, Joseph	P	5	105
LEE, L		3	172
LEE, Lennox Cleland Lee		1	222
LEE, Lewis (Dick)	P	1	222
LEE, Noel		2	199
LEE, Reginald Alias Thomas	P	1	222
LEE, Richard Henry Driffield	P	4	107
LEE, Robert T H V		3	172
LEE, S		3	172
LEE, W		3	172
LEE, W H		3	172
LEE, Walter	P	5	105
LEE, William		1	222
LEE, William		2	199
LEE, William Ervine		4	107
LEE, William George Ellis		4	107
LEECH, Robert Edward Holt		5	105
LEECH, Thomas Edwin		2	199
LEECH, William Leonard Boghurst	P	1	222
LEEDHAM, William		2	199
LEEK, Herbert Arthur		2	199
LEEK, William		1	222
LEEKE, Charles	P	2	199
LEEKE, Ralph Henry	P	2	199
LEE-LEE, Lennox Cleland	P	2	199
LEES, Charles		4	107
LEES, Charles Fletcher Stafford	P	2	199
LEES, Edmund Hastings Harcourt	P	1	223
LEES, Eric Brown	P	5	105
LEES, Harry		5	105
LEES, J		3	172
LEES, Percy Beresford		1	223
LEES, Ritchie		4	107
LEES, Robert		4	107
LEES, Thomas Prior	P	1	223
LEES, William		2	199
LEES, William Robert	P	4	107
LEESE, Francis Henry	P	5	105
LEESON, Arthur Gerald		4	107
LEFROY, Bertram Perceval	P	2	199
LEFTLY, H R		3	172
LEGARD, Reginald John		2	200
LEGATE, Frank		4	108
LEGG, Alexander Hendry		4	108
LEGG, George Alfred John	P	4	108
LEGG, P		3	172
LEGGAT, William	P	1	223
LEGGATT, Charles Frederick		4	108
LEGGATT, Edward		1	223
LEGGATT, George Frederick		5	105
LEGGE, John Maurice		2	200
LEGGE, Ronald George	P	1	223
LEGGE, Stafford Henry		1	223
LEGGE-BOURKE, Nigel Walter Henry		2	35
LEGGETT, Alan Randall Aufrere	P	1	223
LEGGETT, Eric Henry Goodwin		3	172
LEGGETT, G F		3	173
LEGGETT, George		1	223
LEGGETT, George		1	223
LEGGETT, W		3	173
LEGGETT, Wilfred Noel		3	173
LEICESTER, Donovan Nicholas	P	3	173
LEIGH, Albert Edward		1	223
LEIGH, Chandos	P	1	223
LEIGH, Charles		1	223
LEIGH, Edward	P	1	224
LEIGH, Edward Henry	P	1	224
LEIGH, H		3	173
LEIGH, Harry Tunstill		5	105
LEIGH, Percy Lempriere	P	2	200
LEIGH, T		3	173
LEIGH, Thomas Horatio Alfred	P	1	224
LEIGH-BENNETT, Arthur	P	1	30
LEIGH-PEMBERTON, Thomas Edward Geoffrey	P	1	286
LEIGHTON, Roland Aubrey	P	2	200
LEIPER, Andrew		2	200
LEIPER, George		4	108
LEIPER, James		2	200
LEIPER, James		2	200
LEIPER, James		4	108
LEIPER, John		2	200
LEISHMAN, Archibald		2	200
LEISHMAN, John		2	200
LEISHMAN, Robert	P	4	108
LEISHMAN, Thomas	P	4	108
LEITCH, Archibald Niven		5	105
LEITCH, James		2	200
LEIVERS, John Robinson		1	224
LEMERCIER, W G		3	173
LEMM, J		3	173
LEMMON, Montague Hague	P	1	225
LEMMON, R		3	173
LEMON, James Charles		4	108
LEMON, John Edward		1	225
LENCH, James Sydney		1	225
LENCH, Joseph Henry	P	2	200
LENGTHORN, Thomas		2	200
LENIHAN, Albert George		2	200
LENNARD, Joseph Marlow		3	173
LENNARD, Samuel Frederic	P	3	173
LENNARD, W H		3	173
LENNIE, William		4	108
LENNON, J		3	173
LEONARD, Albert		2	201
LEONARD, Alfred		1	225
LEONARD, Francis Patrick Mapletoft		3	173
LEONARD, Thomas		1	225
LEONARD, Thomas		2	201
LEONARD, W R		3	173
LERRY, Hubert James		4	108
LESLIE, Alexander Henry		4	109
LESLIE, William Kinnear		4	109
LESTER, J		2	201
LESTER, John		1	225
LESTER, William		2	201
LETCHFORD, Victor Amos		2	201
LETFORD, W		3	173
LETFORD, William Edward		1	225
LETHBRIDGE, Frank		2	201

Name	Photo	Part No.	Page No.
LOCKETT, R		3	175
LOCKEY, Ernest William		4	113
LOCKEY, Thomas Knox		4	113
LOCKHART, Alan Ross		4	113
LOCKHART, George Barclay		5	107
LOCKIE, Thomas Corbett		5	107
LOCKLEY, William		4	113
LOCKSMORE, Richard James		1	229
LOCKWOOD, H		3	175
LOCKWOOD, Hector Ernest		5	107
LOCKWOOD, John Reginald		4	113
LOCKWOOD, Mark		1	229
LODER, Edwin		4	113
LODGE, A F		3	175
LODGE, Bernard Grime	P	3	175
LODGE, Henry William		5	107
LODGE, Jack Fred		5	107
LODWICK, John Thornton	P	2	204
LOFT, Alma James		1	229
LOFT, Stanley		2	204
LOFTS, Bernard	P	1	229
LOFTS, James		1	229
LOFTUS, Frank Leslie	P	3	175
LOFTUS, M		3	176
LOGAN, Crawford Jack	P	4	113
LOGAN, Edward Townshend	P	2	204
LOGAN, Hugh		5	107
LOGAN, J		3	176
LOGAN, James Aird		1	229
LOGAN, John		1	229
LOGAN, John Stewart		4	113
LOGAN, Preston		2	204
LOGAN, Roland Octavius		2	205
LOGAN, Samuel James		2	205
LOGAN, William		2	205
LOGGIE, Keith William Thomas	P	3	176
LOGIE, John		3	176
LOMAS, R		3	176
LOMAX, Gerald David	P	1	229
LOMAX, Harry	P	1	229
LONEY, Thomas Gow	P	2	205
LONEY, William Thomas		4	113
LONG, A		3	176
LONG, Alfred R		2	205
LONG, Austin Theodore		4	113
LONG, Charles Albert Joseph		5	107
LONG, Edward William Valentine		5	107
LONG, Frank		5	107
LONG, Frederick Reginald	P	5	108
LONG, Frederick Richard Randolph		1	229
LONG, James		2	205
LONG, John Edward		1	229
LONG, S		3	176
LONG, Stewart Shacroft		1	229
LONG, William		2	205
LONGBOURNE, Hugh Richard	P	3	176
LONGBOURNE, William Louis Jennings	P	1	229
LONGDEN, A		3	176
LONGDEN, Ernest William		5	108
LONGDEN, Frederick Cecil		5	108
LONGDON, Harry	P	2	205
LONGFELLOW, Joseph		5	108
LONGFIELD, Leonard Gaunt		4	113
LONGFIELD, Percy		4	113
LONGHURST, Charles		1	229

Name	Photo	Part No.	Page No.
LONG-INNES, Selwyn		2	178
LONGLEY, H		2	205
LONGMAN, Frederick	P	1	229
LONGMAN, George Eveleigh		4	113
LONGMOOR, James		2	205
LONGMORE, Cyril Raymond		4	113
LONG-PRICE, Cecil Evelyn	P	2	254
LONGSDON, Alfred Allen	P	1	229
LONGSHAW, Arthur		4	113
LONGWORTH, R		3	176
LONIE, Alexander Duncan		3	176
LONSDALE, Arthur Carr Glyn	P	1	230
LONSDALE, David		1	230
LONSDALE, Edwin	P	5	108
LOOK, John Leopold	P	5	108
LOOKER, G T		3	176
LOONEY, Walter Kissack	P	4	113
LOOS, Cecil George Bertram	P	1	230
LOOSELY, W		3	176
LORAM, Allen		1	230
LORD, Arthur		3	176
LORD, F		3	176
LORD, George		1	230
LORD, Herbert		1	230
LORD, William Herbert		1	230
LORING, Charles Buxton		2	205
LORING, George Frederick		2	205
LORING, Robert Nele		2	205
LORING, Walter Latham		2	205
LORING, William	P	2	205
LOTHIAN, Harry	P	4	113
LOTHIAN, Norman Bruce	P	3	176
LOTT, James Onslow		4	114
LOUCH, Thomas	P	1	230
LOUD, George Edward	P	4	114
LOUDOUN-SHAND, Stewart Walter		3	243
LOUGHRAN, Alexander		3	176
LOVATT, T		3	176
LOVATT, William Henry Turner		1	230
LOVE, Albert C		2	206
LOVE, Charles Goode Landels		4	114
LOVE, Herbert Henry		2	206
LOVE, Robert		4	114
LOVE, Robert Parker		4	114
LOVE, W		3	176
LOVEBAND, Lionel William	P	4	114
LOVEDAY, Arthur Edward	P	1	230
LOVEDAY, Frederick Walter	P	5	108
LOVEITT, T H		3	176
LOVEJOY, Charles Frederick	P	5	108
LOVELL, Augustus William		4	114
LOVELL, F		3	176
LOVELL, J		3	176
LOVELL, Reginald		2	206
LOVELL, William Henry	P	4	114
LOW, Andrew Leslie		1	230
LOW, Charles Hay		4	114
LOW, David	P	1	230
LOW, George		4	114
LOW, George Morrison	P	5	108
LOW, Howard St.John		4	114
LOW, James		2	206
LOW, John	P	4	114
LOW, Robert Thomas		1	230
LOW, William Thomas	P	2	206

Name	Photo	Part No.	Page No.
LYNCH, Peter		2	207
LYNCH, Reginald Francis	P	5	109
LYNCH, Thomas		3	177
LYNDEN, John Henry	P	1	231
LYNDSELL, Philip		1	231
LYNES, Bertie Frederick		1	231
LYNESS, Harold		3	177
LYNN, Ernest		1	231
LYNN, Frederick		3	178
LYNN, Frederick Charles		2	207
LYON, Albert Edward		1	231
LYON, Alexander Muir		4	116
LYON, John James	P	1	231
LYON, Robert Mair	P	1	231
LYONS, A		3	178
LYONS, Ernest		1	232
LYONS, J		3	178
LYONS, L		3	178
LYONS, William		5	109
LYSTER, John		2	207
LYTTLE, David John Albert	P	1	232
MACADAM, Thomas Theodore		4	116
MACALPINE-DOWNIE, James Robert		5	50
MACANDREW, William Forsyth		3	178
MACARTHUR, Alaster		3	178
MACARTHUR, James Gray		2	207
MACARTHUR, Neil		2	207
MACATEER, John		1	232
MACAULAY, Bruce Wallace	P	4	116
MACAULAY, Donald		5	109
MACAULAY, Frederic Charles		3	178
MACAULAY, Horace	P	4	116
MACAULAY, William Hope		4	116
MACAUSLAN, John	P	2	208
MACAUSLAND, Oliver Babington	P	1	232
MACBEAN, Alexander		2	208
MACBEAN, Duncan Gillies Forbes	P	1	232
MACBEY, George Monro	P	4	116
MACBRAYNE, John Burns	P	2	208
MACCABE, Robert Maxwell	P	1	232
MACCABEE, William Ernest	P	1	232
MACCALLUM, Archie Currie Macqueen	P	2	208
MACCASKILL, John		4	117
MACCOLL, Malcolm Graeme		4	117
MACCORMICK, Alexander Campbell	P	2	209
MACCULLOCH, Iain Hugh	P	2	210
MACCUNN, Francis John		2	210
MACDERMOT, Hugh Maurice		2	210
MACDIARMID, Duncan Campbell	P	4	117
MACDONALD, Alfred		2	211
MACDONALD, Allan		2	211
MACDONALD, Angus Macgillivray		5	110
MACDONALD, Archibald		1	233
MACDONALD, Archibald		2	211
MACDONALD, C		3	179
MACDONALD, Colin		2	211
MACDONALD, D		3	179
MACDONALD, David Johnston	P	4	118
MACDONALD, Donald		4	118
MACDONALD, Donald	P	5	110
MACDONALD, Donald Campbell	P	2	211
MACDONALD, Evan Ronald Horatio Keith	P	1	234
MACDONALD, Hugh		5	110
MACDONALD, Hugh Mackenzie	P	4	118
MACDONALD, James		1	234
MACDONALD, James		2	211
MACDONALD, James	P	4	118
MACDONALD, James Shaw Rose	P	4	118
MACDONALD, John	P	2	211
MACDONALD, John		3	179
MACDONALD, John		4	118
MACDONALD, John Archibald Millar		5	110
MACDONALD, John Doran	P	5	111
MACDONALD, John Fraser	P	2	211
MACDONALD, John Robert		4	119
MACDONALD, John Row Mackenzie	P	5	111
MACDONALD, Kenneth Campbell	P	3	179
MACDONALD, Kenneth Norman		4	119
MACDONALD, Murdo Dan		4	119
MACDONALD, R		3	179
MACDONALD, Rev. Charles Gordon	P	1	234
MACDONALD, Robert		2	211
MACDONALD, Ronald		4	119
MACDONALD, Rouallan		2	211
MACDONALD, The Honourable Ronald Ian		5	111
MACDONALD, W G		3	179
MACDONALD, William		2	211
MACDONALD, William Francis	P	5	111
MACDONELL, Alastair Somerled	P	2	211
MACDOUGALL, David Graham Mather		4	119
MACDOUGALL, Donald		3	179
MACDOUGALL, Peter M		2	212
MACDOUGALL, Stewart Dunsmore	P	4	119
MACDUFF, Alexander		1	234
MACE, Edwin Charles	P	3	179
MACE, James		1	234
MACE, William James		4	119
MACECHERN, Hector George	P	4	119
MACER, Walter George	P	5	111
MACEY, Frederick George		2	212
MACEY, James William		3	180
MACEY, Sydney Charles		2	212
MACEY, U		3	180
MACFARLAND, George Adams		4	120
MACFARLANE, David		4	120
MACFARLANE, Ian		4	120
MACFARLANE, James		2	212
MACFARLANE, John Shephard	P	1	234
MACFARLANE, Robert Craig	P	1	235
MACFARLANE, Ronald Wallace		3	180
MACFARLANE-GRIEVE, Alwyn Ronald		4	70
MACFIE, Claud William	P	1	235
MACGILLIVRAY, Angus		4	120
MACGILLIVRAY, Archibald		2	212
MACGREGOR, Benjamin		4	120
MACGREGOR, Cortlandt Richard		1	235
MACGREGOR, Donald Alastair	P	2	212
MACGREGOR, Ian Ross		5	112
MACGREGOR, James Hamilton		3	181
MACGREGOR, Kenneth Cortlandt		1	235
MACGREGOR, Robert John		5	112
MACGUIRE, D J		3	181
MACHIN, Charles	P	1	236
MACHRAY, William	P	3	181
MACILROY, Thomas Shanks		4	121
MACILWAIN, Alexander Spears		5	113
MACINNES, Donald	P	5	113
MACINTYRE, Donald	P	3	181
MACINTYRE, Hugh		4	121
MACINTYRE, Thomas W		3	182

Name	Photo	Part No.	Page No.
MACIVER, Donald		2	213
MACK, Arthur Paston		4	121
MACK, Fred		1	236
MACK, J		3	181
MACK, James William		1	236
MACK, Robert	P	3	182
MACK, Thomas	P	3	182
MACK, William Bell		1	236
MACKAIN, James Fergus	P	1	236
MACKAY, Alastair Sutton	P	1	236
MACKAY, Alexander Herbert Robins		4	121
MACKAY, Alexander Kinnison		2	213
MACKAY, Arnold Langley		3	182
MACKAY, Colin		5	113
MACKAY, George		1	236
MACKAY, Gordon		4	121
MACKAY, Hamish Strathy		5	113
MACKAY, Hubert Coleman		2	213
MACKAY, Ian	P	4	121
MACKAY, Ian Forbes		2	213
MACKAY, J		3	182
MACKAY, James		2	213
MACKAY, John		1	236
MACKAY, Kenneth Scott	P	2	213
MACKAY, Norman Nicolson	P	2	213
MACKAY, Samuel Francis Henderson		4	121
MACKAY, Walter Edward		1	236
MACKAY-COGHILL, Hugh	P	2	74
MACKELLER, Hugh		5	113
MACKENNA, John Norman	P	2	214
MACKENZIE, Alexander		4	122
MACKENZIE, Alexdria George		2	214
MACKENZIE, Colin Landseer	P	1	236
MACKENZIE, Cortlandt Graham Gordon	P	1	236
MACKENZIE, F R		3	182
MACKENZIE, George Alexander	P	4	122
MACKENZIE, George Thomas		4	122
MACKENZIE, Gordon Alxander Gordon	P	1	236
MACKENZIE, J		2	214
MACKENZIE, James	P	1	236
MACKENZIE, James		1	237
MACKENZIE, James		3	182
MACKENZIE, James		5	113
MACKENZIE, John		2	214
MACKENZIE, Keith Bethune	P	1	237
MACKENZIE, Kenneth		1	237
MACKENZIE, Lynedoch Archibald	P	2	214
MACKENZIE, Percy Melville	P	5	113
MACKENZIE, Thomson		5	113
MACKENZIE, Ulric	P	4	122
MACKENZIE OF DOLPHINTON, Kenneth		5	113
MACKEOWN, John Harold		5	114
MACKERCHER, Alexander Robert		5	114
MACKEY, Harry		1	237
MACKIE, Albert George Rutherford	P	3	182
MACKIE, Alfred		4	122
MACKIE, Andrew		2	214
MACKIE, D		3	182
MACKIE, J		3	182
MACKIE, James		4	122
MACKIE, John	P	3	182
MACKIE, John		4	122
MACKIE, P		2	215
MACKIE, Peter		2	215
MACKIE, Peter Isbister		4	122
MACKIE, Reginald Ernest	P	1	237
MACKIE, Robert		3	182
MACKIE, Robert Cole		1	237
MACKIE, Thomas Brebner		5	114
MACKIE, William		4	122
MACKINNON, Charles		1	237
MACKINTOSH, Donald		4	123
MACKINTOSH, Edward		2	215
MACKINTOSH, Garden Hepburn	P	2	215
MACKINTOSH, James Donald		5	114
MACKINTOSH, James Lawton		1	237
MACKINTOSH, John		2	215
MACKINTOSH, John Lachlan		3	182
MACKINTOSH, Malcolm Macphail		4	123
MACKINTOSH, Neil		4	123
MACKINTOSH, W H		3	182
MACKIRDY, Peter Mackay		1	237
MACKIRDY, Robert Fingland		1	237
MACKLIN, Alfred Henry		1	237
MACKRELL, Thomas		1	237
MACKRIDGE, Ralf Leslie	P	5	114
MACKWORTH, Francis Julian Audley	P	1	237
MACLACHLAN, David Corson	P	4	123
MACLACHLAN, Paul		4	123
MACLAGAN, James		5	114
MACLAGAN, James Graham		5	114
MACLAGAN, Philip Whiteside		5	114
MACLAREN, Charles Alexander		4	123
MACLAREN, James Algie	P	3	183
MACLAURIN, John Henry	P	5	114
MACLAVERTY, Colin Johnstone	P	3	183
MACLEAN, Alistair Allan	P	1	238
MACLEAN, Andrew De Vere		1	238
MACLEAN, Angus Robert		1	238
MACLEAN, C		2	216
MACLEAN, Malcolm		5	115
MACLEAN, William	P	5	115
MACLEAY, George Cameron	P	2	216
MACLEHOSE, Norman Crawford	P	1	238
MACLELLAN, Joseph Taylor		5	115
MACLELLAN, Lewis		5	115
MACLELLAN, Malcolm	P	4	123
MACLENNAN, Iain Donald Forrest	P	4	123
MACLENNAN, Ian Douglas	P	1	238
MACLENNAN, John	P	4	124
MACLENNAN, John Ernest	P	5	115
MACLENNAN, Kenneth		2	216
MACLENNAN, Ronald		2	216
MACLEOD, Alastair Roderick	P	1	238
MACLEOD, Angus		4	124
MACLEOD, David Ferguson		1	239
MACLEOD, David John		4	124
MACLEOD, Ian Breac	P	1	239
MACLEOD, John		4	124
MACLEOD, John Roderick		5	115
MACLEOD, Torquil Harry Lionel	P	1	239
MACLEOD, William Patrick		5	115
MACLINDEN, John		2	216
MACMAHON, Herbert Henry		3	183
MACMAHON, J		4	124
MACMILLAN, Alexander Phillips		4	124
MACMILLAN, Ian	P	4	124
MACMILLAN, James Alexander		5	115
MACMILLAN, Peter Christie	P	2	216
MACMILLAN, William M'call	P	4	124

Name	Photo	Part No.	Page No.
MACMURCHIE, John Stuart		5	115
MACNAB, Donald Angus	P	3	184
MACNAB, George		4	124
MACNAMARA, George	P	3	184
MACNAUGHTON, Alexander	P	5	116
MACNAUGHTON, John D	P	5	116
MACNEECE, James Douglas Gaussen	P	2	216
MACNEILL, William Mackinnon	P	1	239
MACNICOL, Horatius Bonar	P	1	239
MACNIVEN, Robert		1	239
MACPHERSON, Duncan		4	125
MACPHERSON, Duncan Stuart Ross	P	1	240
MACPHERSON, George M		5	116
MACPHERSON, James Charles Brewster	P	5	116
MACPHERSON, James Gordon		4	125
MACPHERSON, John	P	1	240
MACPHERSON, John Cook	P	2	217
MACPHERSON, Robert David		3	185
MACPHERSON, Robert Nasmyth	P	3	185
MACRAE, Alexander	P	5	116
MACRAE, Alexander Campbell		5	116
MACRAE, Alexander Nicolson	P	5	116
MACRAE, Donald		2	217
MACRAE, George Pitt Taylor	P	3	185
MACRAE, Ivor Alexander	P	1	240
MACRAE, John Alexander	P	4	125
MACRAE, John Nigel		5	117
MACRAE, Kenneth Charles Ernest	P	1	240
MACRAE, Norman Farquhar	P	3	185
MACRAE, Peter		4	125
MACRAE, Victor Charles James		1	240
MACREIGHT, Arthur William James	P	1	240
MACROW, Herbert		2	217
MACRURY, John Alexander	P	5	117
MACSWAN, Angus	P	1	240
MACTAGGART, Murdoch Archibald	P	3	185
MACWHINNIE, Norman Henry	P	1	241
MACWHIRTER, James Alexander	P	5	117
MACWILLIAM, James Julian Gordon	P	1	241
MADDAMS, Charles Francis		5	117
MADDANS, Frederick		1	241
MADDEN, Clarence William Crawford		4	126
MADDEN, Gerald Hugh Charles	P	2	218
MADDEN, John	P	2	218
MADDEN, John Aldwin	P	5	117
MADDEN, Thomas Hylton	P	1	241
MADDEN, William Henry	P	4	126
MADDEVER, Robert William Diggory		4	126
MADDISON, Alfred		1	241
MADDOCK, Thomas Henry		1	241
MADDRA, John Osborne		4	126
MADELEY, Claude Neville	P	4	126
MADGETT, William Stephen	P	4	126
MADIGAN, James Francis Joseph		1	241
MADLEY, Frank Herbert	P	2	218
MAFFUNIADES, Alexis Ectos	P	4	126
MAGEE, Richard Edward		1	241
MAGGS, William Jesse Reginald		4	127
MAGIHON, D		2	218
MAGIHON, W		3	186
MAGILL, Hugh		1	241
MAGNAY, John Christopher Frederick		4	127
MAGNAY, Philip	P	3	186
MAGNIAC, Erskine		4	127
MAGNIAC, Meredith		4	127
MAGRATH, Beauchamp Henry Butler	P	3	186
MAGRATH, Charles William Graham	P	5	117
MAGUIRE, Charles		1	241
MAGUIRE, David Miller		3	186
MAGUIRE, John	P	3	186
MAGUIRE, M		2	218
MAHAFFY, Samuel	P	4	127
MAHON, A W J		3	186
MAHONEY, William		1	241
MAHONY, Frederick Henry	P	1	242
MAHONY, James		2	218
MAHONY, James	P	3	186
MAHY, J. Le Page		3	186
MAIDMENT, Francis Samuel		4	127
MAILLEY, Martin	P	2	218
MAILLEY, Thomas		2	218
MAIN, James Edward	P	5	117
MAIN, John		5	117
MAINE, Joseph Leslie		1	242
MAINPRISE, Bertie Wilmot	P	3	186
MAINWARING, John		3	186
MAINWOOD, William Richard		1	242
MAIR, John		1	242
MAIR, Thomas	P	2	218
MAIRS, Alexander		1	242
MAIRS, James		4	127
MAISEY, Frank Douglas		1	242
MAISEY, Walter Srafford		1	242
MAIT, Albert		2	218
MAITLAND, A		3	186
MAITLAND, Alexander	P	4	127
MAITLAND, Alexander Mclean		5	117
MAITLAND, Arthur James		5	118
MAITLAND, R		2	218
MAITLAND, Robert		5	118
MAITLAND, William Ebenezer	P	2	218
MAITLAND-ADDISON, Alec Crichton		2	2
MAITLAND-MAKGILL-CRICHTON, Charles Julian	P	2	84
MAJOR, Eric Cyril		4	127
MAJOR, John		2	219
MAKEHAM, Ernest	P	4	128
MAKEHAM, Ernest	P	5	118
MAKIN, George		2	219
MAKIN, Joshua		4	128
MAKINS, Geoffrey		2	219
MAKINS, Hugh		2	219
MAKINSON, Robert		3	186
MALARKIE, John		2	219
MALCOLM, A		2	219
MALCOLM, Archibald Houlder		5	118
MALCOLM, George John	P	3	186
MALCOLM, James (Hamish) Waddell	P	1	242
MALCOLM, Pulteney	P	5	118
MALCOLM, William		4	128
MALET, Hugh Arthur Grenville	P	1	242
MALKIN, Percy		1	242
MALLAM, Clifford Angus		5	118
MALLARD, Harry		4	128
MALLEN, Donald Miller		5	118
MALLEY, H		3	187
MALLINS, Claude Joseph O'conor	P	1	242
MALLINSON, George Thomas		4	128
MALLON, Robert		2	219
MALONEY, T		3	187

Name	Photo	Part No.	Page No.
MALONEY, William		2	219
MALYEN, E A		3	187
MANCER, Arthur James		1	242
MANCEY, A G		3	187
MANDERS, John		2	219
MANDERS, Neville	P	1	243
MANDS, Thomas		4	128
MANGAN, J		3	187
MANLEY, Alfred		4	128
MANLEY, C F		3	187
MANLEY, David Henry George	P	3	187
MANLEY, Herbert John	P	1	243
MANLEY, John Dundas	P	1	243
MANN, A		4	128
MANN, Alexander James(Hamish)	P	3	187
MANN, Bernard Joseph		5	118
MANN, Bertram		2	219
MANN, Ernest		4	128
MANN, Ernest Walter Charles		1	243
MANN, George Cyril Stanley	P	3	187
MANN, Howard William		1	243
MANN, James Emil Hubert		4	128
MANN, John		5	118
MANN, P		4	128
MANN, Reuben		1	243
MANN, Stanley Walter	P	3	187
MANN, Thomas		2	219
MANN, W J		3	187
MANN, William Horace		1	243
MANN, William Thomas		4	128
MANNERING, Arthur Lidstone		1	243
MANNERING, R R		3	187
MANNERS, B		3	187
MANNERS-SMITH, Frederick	P	1	333
MANNING, Alfred		1	243
MANNING, E		2	219
MANNING, Frank		2	219
MANNING, Henry		2	219
MANNING, J		3	187
MANNING, L		3	187
MANSELL, J		3	188
MANSELL, J		4	128
MANSELL, James		2	219
MANSEL-PLEYDELL, Edmund Morton	P	1	291
MANSERGH, John Loftus Otway	P	2	219
MANSFIELD, John Richard		1	243
MANSFIELD, Thomas Richard		1	243
MANSFIELD, William		1	243
MANSON, Alexander		3	188
MANSON, Eric Douglas		4	128
MANSON, Magnus Murray	P	1	243
MANT, Walter		2	219
MANT, William		1	243
MANTELL, George Frederick		2	219
MANTELL, Herbert Thomas		2	219
MANTLE, Alexander		4	128
MANTLE, W		2	219
MANUEL, Hugh Leslie		4	128
MANUEL, Thomas		3	188
MANVILLE, Henry		2	219
MAPLESTONE, James William		1	243
MAPLEY, Alfred James		2	219
MAPP, Charles Reginald	P	5	118
MAPPLETHORPE, Claude	P	1	243
MARCHANT, Albert Edward		4	128

Name	Photo	Part No.	Page No.
MARCHANT, Charles Frederick Blizard	P	3	188
MARCHANT, George Albert		5	118
MARCHANT, Hugh Stephen	P	2	219
MARCHANT, William Goodwin		5	118
MARCHANT, William Joseph		4	128
MARCHBANKS, James Robert Williamson		2	219
MARCHETTI, Alec	P	2	219
MARCHETTI, Eustie	P	2	219
MARCHMENT, G H		3	188
MARDELL, Charles Henry		3	188
MARDELL, Edward		1	243
MARDELL, William Thomas		4	128
MARDEN, Frederick William		2	219
MARDEN, Land Gerald		3	188
MARES, Bertram George	P	2	219
MARGARY, S G		3	188
MARGERISON, Arthur		4	128
MARGESSON, Anthony Robert	P	3	188
MARGETTS, Percy Alexander		2	220
MARINER, Thomas		2	220
MARJORIBANKS, D		3	188
MARJORIBANKS, David		3	188
MARKAM, Henry C		2	220
MARKER, Raymond John	P	1	243
MARKHAM, Allan		1	244
MARKHAM, Ernest Frederick		5	118
MARKHAM, John Addis		1	244
MARKIE, M		2	220
MARKILLIE, Edgar John	P	1	244
MARKILLIE, Ernest Stuart	P	1	244
MARKLEW, F		2	220
MARKLEY, Walter Eric		2	220
MARKQUICK, Arthur Christian		1	244
MARKS, Arthur Sampson		5	118
MARKS, Harry		2	220
MARKWICK, Joseph William		5	119
MARLER, Albert Walter		1	244
MARLER, Ernest Henry Herbert	P	5	119
MARLEY, William		2	220
MARLEY, William	P	3	188
MARLOW, Albert Charles	P	5	119
MARLOW, Percy		4	129
MARLOWE, Cecil Arthur		5	119
MARMION, M		2	220
MARNEY, Evelyn		2	220
MARNIE, J C		3	188
MARQUER, Toussaint Marys		1	244
MARQUIS, Duncan		4	129
MARR, Ainslie	P	4	129
MARR, Alexander David		2	220
MARR, Alexander Murray		5	119
MARR, George Edward		2	220
MARR, James		4	129
MARR, Joseph		2	220
MARRAN, Frank		2	220
MARRIOTT, Arthur Pelham		4	129
MARRIOTT, C		3	188
MARRIOTT, Frederick Ernest		2	220
MARRIOTT, H		3	188
MARRIOTT, H E		3	188
MARRIOTT, Hugh Digby		2	220
MARRIOTT, Richard Henry		3	188
MARRIOTT-DODINGTON, Thomas	P	4	47
MARRIS, Alan Barrington	P	2	220
MARROW, Edward Armfield	P	1	244

Name	Photo	Part No.	Page No.
MARRS, David		2	220
MARSDEN, Ernest		2	220
MARSDEN, Harold		5	119
MARSDEN, John Horace		4	129
MARSDEN, Thomas	P	4	129
MARSDEN, William Gordon	P	5	119
MARSH, Albert George		2	220
MARSH, Alfred		2	220
MARSH, Arthur		1	244
MARSH, Bertie		2	220
MARSH, Cecil Frank		1	244
MARSH, Douglas Charles Earle	P	4	129
MARSH, E T		3	188
MARSH, Edward		2	220
MARSH, F		3	188
MARSH, F E M		3	188
MARSH, Frederick	P	5	119
MARSH, Frederick George		2	220
MARSH, Frederick James		4	129
MARSH, Frederick William		2	220
MARSH, Henry Herbert Stanley	P	1	244
MARSH, J		2	220
MARSH, J T		3	188
MARSH, John Lockwood	P	2	220
MARSH, Robert Henry		3	188
MARSH, Robert Neville Caldecot		3	188
MARSH, W G		3	188
MARSH, W J		3	188
MARSH, Walter James		2	220
MARSH, William		5	119
MARSHALL, Albert Edward	P	3	188
MARSHALL, Albert Frank		1	244
MARSHALL, Alexander Balfour		2	220
MARSHALL, Alfred Edgar George		3	188
MARSHALL, Alfred Ernest		1	244
MARSHALL, Allan Gow	P	3	189
MARSHALL, Arthur		1	244
MARSHALL, Arthur Norris		3	189
MARSHALL, Arthur Raymond		4	129
MARSHALL, Arthur William		2	220
MARSHALL, Augustus De La Pere	P	1	244
MARSHALL, Charles Devereux		5	119
MARSHALL, Charles William		4	129
MARSHALL, Clifford Hammond		4	129
MARSHALL, D R		3	189
MARSHALL, Edward		2	220
MARSHALL, Edward Leslie		5	119
MARSHALL, Eric James	P	2	221
MARSHALL, Evelyn Saffrey	P	1	244
MARSHALL, Francis William		2	221
MARSHALL, Frank		2	221
MARSHALL, Frederick G		2	221
MARSHALL, Frederick George		2	221
MARSHALL, George		2	221
MARSHALL, George Dallas		5	119
MARSHALL, George Frederick	P	1	245
MARSHALL, George Garth	P	1	245
MARSHALL, George Henry		2	221
MARSHALL, H		3	189
MARSHALL, H		3	189
MARSHALL, Harold		3	189
MARSHALL, Horace		2	221
MARSHALL, Isaiah		1	245
MARSHALL, J		3	189
MARSHALL, James	P	3	189

Name	Photo	Part No.	Page No.
MARSHALL, Jenner Stephen Chance	P	1	245
MARSHALL, John		2	221
MARSHALL, John		2	221
MARSHALL, John		2	221
MARSHALL, John Edward	P	1	245
MARSHALL, L		3	189
MARSHALL, Percy Stanley Thomas		1	245
MARSHALL, Philip Spencer	P	3	189
MARSHALL, Robert		3	189
MARSHALL, Roger	P	1	245
MARSHALL, S G		3	189
MARSHALL, Thomas	P	4	129
MARSHALL, Tom		4	129
MARSHALL, W H		3	189
MARSHALL, Walter John		5	119
MARSHALL, William Albert		4	130
MARSHALL, William Harry		5	120
MARSHALL-LEWIS, Frank	P	5	106
MARSHAM-TOWNSHEND, Ferdinand	P	2	298
MARSON, Herbert		1	245
MARSON, John Charles	P	1	245
MARSTON, Frank		2	221
MARSTON, Horace		3	189
MARSTON, Percy Ingram		4	130
MARTELL, Brice Selwyn		4	130
MARTEN, Charles Peter	P	3	189
MARTEN, Henry Humphrey		2	221
MARTIN, Alan Stewart		4	130
MARTIN, Albert Henry	P	1	246
MARTIN, Alfred		3	190
MARTIN, Arthur James Samuel		5	120
MARTIN, Arthur Lynd	P	3	190
MARTIN, Arthur Thomas		1	246
MARTIN, Aylmer Richard Sancton	P	1	246
MARTIN, B T		3	190
MARTIN, Basil Cuthbert Danvers	P	1	246
MARTIN, C		3	190
MARTIN, C F		5	120
MARTIN, Cecil Hampson	P	2	221
MARTIN, Cecil T		3	190
MARTIN, Cecil Taylor	P	1	246
MARTIN, Charles		1	246
MARTIN, Charles Edward John		1	246
MARTIN, Charles Herbert George	P	1	246
MARTIN, Cyril Arthur	P	2	221
MARTIN, Francis Albert		2	221
MARTIN, Francis Duke	P	3	190
MARTIN, Francis Henry		5	120
MARTIN, Frank		3	190
MARTIN, Frank Charles		5	120
MARTIN, Fred		4	130
MARTIN, Frederick		2	221
MARTIN, G		3	190
MARTIN, G C		3	190
MARTIN, George		2	221
MARTIN, H		2	221
MARTIN, Harold Thornhill	P	5	120
MARTIN, Harry		3	190
MARTIN, Harry		4	130
MARTIN, Herbert Edward		1	246
MARTIN, Herbert William		4	130
MARTIN, J		2	221
MARTIN, J		2	221
MARTIN, James		2	221
MARTIN, John		1	246

Name	Photo	Part No.	Page No.	Name	Photo	Part No.	Page No.
MARTIN, John		2	221	MASON, Peter	P	3	191
MARTIN, John		2	221	MASON, T		2	222
MARTIN, John		4	130	MASON, T		3	191
MARTIN, John Kingsley Lunn	P	2	221	MASON, Theophilus	P	1	247
MARTIN, John William		1	246	MASON, Walter		2	222
MARTIN, Joseph Edward		1	246	MASON, Walter Trower		1	247
MARTIN, Lawrence Henry		5	120	MASON, William		1	247
MARTIN, Lionel Arthur	P	5	120	MASON, William John		2	222
MARTIN, P		3	190	MASSAM, Harold		2	222
MARTIN, Peter Mcewan		4	130	MASSEY, Charles Thomas		1	247
MARTIN, R		2	221	MASSEY, R		3	191
MARTIN, R		2	221	MASSEY, W		3	191
MARTIN, Robert		4	130	MASSIE, John Hamon	P	1	247
MARTIN, S		3	190	MASTER, Charles Lionel	P	1	248
MARTIN, T		3	190	MASTERS, Geoffrey	P	5	120
MARTIN, W		2	221	MASTERS, J A		3	191
MARTIN, Wilfred John		4	130	MASTERS, J H		2	222
MARTIN, William		1	246	MASTERS, Trevor Monro Hoare		1	248
MARTIN, William		4	130	MASTERSON, A G		3	191
MARTIN, William Gerald	P	3	190	MATCHETT, Thomas		2	222
MARTIN, William Herbert	P	1	246	MATES, Thomas George		2	222
MARTINDALE, Albert		2	221	MATHER, Edward William	P	2	222
MARTINDALE, Edwin Featherstone		4	130	MATHER, James	P	1	248
MARTINDALE, John Bell		4	130	MATHER, John Kearsley		1	248
MARTINDALE, Richard		5	120	MATHER, John Wilfrid		2	222
MARTINGALE, John		2	221	MATHER, Joseph	P	3	191
MARTYN, Edward Thomas		1	247	MATHERRON, Edward John		1	248
MARTYN, Lancelot Sidney	P	3	190	MATHERS, William Henry	P	5	120
MARTYR, John Francis		2	221	MATHESON, Archibald Angus	P	5	120
MARVIN, Henry		1	247	MATHESON, Claud Bruce		3	191
MARYAN, Ernest		2	222	MATHESON, David		4	131
MASEFIELD, Robert	P	1	247	MATHESON, John Hugh	P	4	131
MASH, William Henry		4	130	MATHESON, John Roderick Fletcher		1	248
MASHAM, Frederick Henry		4	130	MATHESON, Neil		3	191
MASHFORD, Cyril Claude		4	131	MATHESON, Roderick		2	222
MASKELL, L		3	190	MATHEWS, Alfred Felton	P	1	248
MASLEN, Charles Aaron		3	190	MATHEWS, Arnold	P	2	222
MASLEN, George Alfred		4	131	MATHEWS, Frank		2	222
MASLEN, N		3	190	MATHEWS, Henry		2	222
MASLIN, Sidney		2	222	MATHEWS, John		2	222
MASON, A		2	222	MATHIESON, Donald		2	222
MASON, Albert	P	3	190	MATHIESON, Thomas Alexander	P	5	120
MASON, Albert Edward		1	247	MATHURN, John		1	248
MASON, Albert Edward		2	222	MATHWIN, Douglas Gatecliff	P	1	248
MASON, Albert H		2	222	MATON, E T		3	191
MASON, Andrew Nimmo		1	247	MATRAVERS, George		1	248
MASON, Arthur	P	1	247	MATSON, Andrew George Shand		3	191
MASON, Arthur Humfrey		2	222	MATSON, Clifford		1	248
MASON, Arthur Pelham	P	4	131	MATTEY, Charles Percival	P	3	191
MASON, Arthur Walton	P	3	190	MATTHEW, William		2	222
MASON, C		2	222	MATTHEW, William	P	4	131
MASON, Charles	P	4	131	MATTHEWS, Ambrose Simeon		2	222
MASON, Edward	P	1	247	MATTHEWS, Arthur Thomas	P	3	191
MASON, George		1	247	MATTHEWS, Arthur William		2	222
MASON, George		3	191	MATTHEWS, C E		3	191
MASON, Gerald Francis		4	131	MATTHEWS, Charles Henry	P	1	248
MASON, Gilbert		4	131	MATTHEWS, Charles Samuel	P	5	121
MASON, Harry		2	222	MATTHEWS, David		2	222
MASON, Henry Thomas		1	247	MATTHEWS, E		3	191
MASON, J W		3	191	MATTHEWS, E C		3	191
MASON, James		1	247	MATTHEWS, F		3	191
MASON, James John		4	131	MATTHEWS, Francis		1	248
MASON, John		1	247	MATTHEWS, Frank		1	249
MASON, John		1	247	MATTHEWS, Frank George	P	1	249
MASON, John Norman	P	5	120	MATTHEWS, Harold Carey	P	1	249

Name	Photo	Part No.	Page No.
MATTHEWS, John		4	131
MATTHEWS, John Andrew	P	4	131
MATTHEWS, Sydney Arthur		5	121
MATTHEWS, T		3	191
MATTHEWS, W		3	191
MATTHEWS, William Charles		3	191
MATTHEWS, William Charles		3	191
MATTHEWSON, F E		3	191
MAUDE, John William Ashley		3	191
MAUDSLEY, Harry Dean		4	131
MAUGER, E		3	191
MAUGHAN, John		1	249
MAUGHAN, John		3	191
MAUGHAN, John William Richard		5	121
MAULE, Robert	P	1	249
MAULEVERER, Claude Du Pre Stansfield Mauleverer Gowan	P	5	121
MAUNDER, Leonard		1	249
MAUNDERS, L		3	191
MAUNSELL, Douglas Slade		4	131
MAUNSELL, George Wyndham		3	192
MAURICE, Francis Dennison	P	1	249
MAVOR, John Alexander		5	121
MAVOR, Robert George Innes	P	4	132
MAW, William Francis		1	249
MAXEY, Charles Pulley	P	2	222
MAXFIELD, Hugh		5	121
MAXIM, Ernest Frederick		4	132
MAXTED, Alfred John		2	222
MAXTED, Thomas		1	249
MAXWELL, (Alias Roberts) Bertram Jesse	P	1	249
MAXWELL, A		3	192
MAXWELL, Aymer Edward	P	1	249
MAXWELL, Bertram Jesse		5	121
MAXWELL, David		4	132
MAXWELL, Harley Hyslop		5	121
MAXWELL, J		2	222
MAXWELL, John		4	132
MAXWELL, Peter		5	121
MAXWELL, Power Macmurrough		3	192
MAXWELL, Thomas		3	192
MAXWELL, Thomas Morrison		4	132
MAXWELL, William		3	192
MAXWELL, William Francis John	P	2	222
MAXWELL, William Gardner		5	121
MAXWELL, William Martin	P	2	223
MAXWELL-STUART, Alfred Joseph		4	202
MAXWELL-STUART, Edmund Joseph		4	202
MAXWELL-STUART, Henry Joseph		4	202
MAXWELL-STUART, Joseph Joachim		4	202
MAY, C H		2	223
MAY, Edward Thomas		1	249
MAY, Frank Jubilee		1	249
MAY, George		5	121
MAY, George Neville	P	4	132
MAY, H		2	223
MAY, J		2	223
MAY, J		3	192
MAY, J		3	192
MAY, John		1	249
MAY, John	P	5	121
MAY, John Edward		1	249
MAY, Sidney Charles		1	249
MAY, W		3	192
MAY, W H		3	192

Name	Photo	Part No.	Page No.
MAY, Walter J		2	223
MAY, William		1	249
MAY, William		3	192
MAY, William James		5	121
MAY, William Richard		1	249
MAYATT, Charles William		4	132
MAYBE, F		3	192
MAYBERY, Richard Aveline	P	5	122
MAYCOCK, George		1	249
MAYCOCK, H J		3	192
MAYCOCK, Henry George		4	132
MAYES, Albert George		4	132
MAYES, Ernest Harry		4	132
MAYGAR, Edgar Leslie Cecil Willis Walker		4	132
MAYHEW, Edwin		2	223
MAYHEW, Kenneth Spurling		5	122
MAYLIN, Frederick Francis		1	249
MAYLOTT, Harold		2	223
MAYNARD, Daniel		1	249
MAYNARD, Hugh Charles	P	3	192
MAYNARD, John Wilmot	P	1	249
MAYNE, Frederick Robert		4	132
MAYNE, W		4	132
MAYO, Arthur Cyril		4	132
MAYO, George Patrick		1	249
MAYO, William		2	223
MAYS, Septimus		4	132
MAYSON, Robert		2	223
MAZZIE, L		4	132
MCADAM, David Gray		2	207
MCADAM, Thomas		2	207
MCADOO, Thomas John		3	178
MCAFEE, Lewis Alexander	P	2	207
MCALEA, B		3	178
MCALEVY, P		2	207
MCALL, Thomas Boyle		5	109
MCALLAN, George Herbert		5	109
MCALLION, P		3	178
MCALLISTER, Andrew		1	232
MCALLISTER, Eneas		2	207
MCALLISTER, T		3	178
MCALLISTER, William		2	207
MCALPINE, John		2	207
MCANDREW, Stewart		5	109
MCANEY, Patrick		5	109
MCARTHUR, A		3	178
MCARTHUR, C		3	178
MCARTHUR, Donald		2	207
MCARTHUR, James Falconer	P	4	116
MCATEER, James		2	208
MCAULAY, A		3	178
MCAULEY, D		3	178
MCAUSLAN, John	P	2	208
MCAVOY, Robert		2	208
MCBAIN, A		3	178
MCBAIN, John Mortimer	P	2	208
MCBARNET, Edward James		2	208
MCBARROW, John		2	208
MCBEATH, William		3	178
MCBRIDE, Edward Joseph		2	208
MCBRIDE, Gilbert		1	232
MCBRIDE, Henry T		3	178
MCBRIDE, Joseph		2	208
MCBRIDE, P		3	178
MCBRIDE, William Wilson		4	116

Name	Photo	Part No.	Page No.	Name	Photo	Part No.	Page No.
MCBROOM, Andrew Irvine	P	4	116	MCCORMAC, Michael		2	209
MCCABE, J		2	208	MCCORMAC, Samuel		2	209
MCCABE, John		2	208	MCCORMACK, J		3	178
MCCABE, Joseph	P	1	232	MCCORMACK, John		1	233
MCCABE, M		2	208	MCCORMACK, M		3	178
MCCABE, William		2	208	MCCORMACK, R		3	178
MCCABE, William		2	208	MCCORMACK, Thomas Frederick		5	110
MCCAFFERTY, J		2	208	MCCORMICK, Frank		1	233
MCCALL, Robert James	P	1	232	MCCOSKIE, J		3	178
MCCALL, T		3	178	MCCOURT, Cyril Douglas		3	178
MCCALL, Walter Douglas		2	208	MCCOURT, J		2	209
MCCALLIE, Douglas		2	208	MCCOURT, T		2	209
MCCALLUM, Andrew		3	178	MCCRACKEN, Benjamin Brayshaw Victor	P	3	179
MCCALLUM, D		2	208	MCCRACKEN, Samuel		2	209
MCCALLUM, George		3	178	MCCRAE, George		1	240
MCCALLUM, Malcolm Cochrane	P	3	178	MCCRAE, Patrick		2	209
MCCALLUM, W		2	208	MCCRAITH, Bernard	P	5	110
MCCALLUM, W		3	178	MCCRAITH, Vincent Francis Joseph Ignatius	P	2	210
MCCANN, Frank Richard		1	232	MCCRAW, Gordon Mcallister		4	117
MCCANN, Joseph		2	208	MCCREA, J H		3	179
MCCANN, P		3	178	MCCREADIE, T		3	179
MCCANN, T		3	178	MCCREADIL, Charles		1	233
MCCARLIE, John		2	208	MCCREADY, George		2	210
MCCAROGHER, John Ommanney		1	232	MCCREATH, Andrew Berghaus	P	4	117
MCCARTEN, William James Daniel		1	233	MCCROA, William		2	210
MCCARTER, John Wylie		4	116	MCCRORY, Thomas		3	179
MCCARTHY, C		3	178	MCCUISH, A		3	179
MCCARTHY, Denis	P	1	233	MCCULLAGH, George David	P	4	117
MCCARTHY, George		1	233	MCCULLOCH, Alexander	P	5	110
MCCARTHY, George William		2	209	MCCULLOCH, Daniel		2	210
MCCARTHY, J		3	178	MCCULLOCH, George Gordon Duncan		4	117
MCCARTHY, J		3	178	MCCULLOCH, M		2	210
MCCARTHY, Jerry Joseph	P	1	233	MCCULLOCH, M		2	210
MCCARTHY, Timothy		3	178	MCCULLOCH, Malcolm		2	210
MCCARTHY, Wilfred Cyril	P	1	233	MCCULLOCH, Robert Squince	P	3	179
MCCARTNEY, Joseph Donkin		1	233	MCCULLOCH, Victor		4	117
MCCARTY, Martin		1	233	MCCULLOUGH, A		3	179
MCCASKELL, Donald	P	5	109	MCCULLY, Frederick	P	2	210
MCCASKILL, A		2	209	MCCULLY, William James Holly	P	2	210
MCCAUGHERTY, David		1	233	MCCURDIE, Archibald	P	4	117
MCCAUSLAND, Arthur John Kennedy	P	2	209	MCCURRACH, William		4	117
MCCAY, Thomas Fulton		4	117	MCCUTCHEON, J		3	179
MCCELLAND, Sidney		1	233	MCDADE, H		3	179
MCCELLAND, Thomas	P	1	233	MCDADE, James		2	210
MCCLARENCE, James	P	2	209	MCDAID, Alexander		2	210
MCCLEAN, James Henry		4	117	MCDEAN, W		3	179
MCCLELLAND, Charles Steen	P	1	233	MCDERMOTT, Alfred George		5	110
MCCLELLAND, D		3	178	MCDERMOTT, Frederick Aylward	P	1	233
MCCLELLAND, L		3	178	MCDERMOTT, M		3	179
MCCLELLAND, William Alan		4	117	MCDIARMID, Hugh		3	179
MCCLOSKEY, Jack Montague	P	4	117	MCDIARMID, Kenneth	P	1	233
MCCLURE, Alan Robert	P	2	209	MCDIARMID, William		2	210
MCCLURE, David Pollock	P	2	209	MCDONALD, A		2	210
MCCLUSKEY, Alfred John	P	1	233	MCDONALD, A		2	211
MCCLUSKEY, John		2	209	MCDONALD, A		3	179
MCCOLGAN, Robert		2	209	MCDONALD, Albert		4	118
MCCOMB, Hugh		1	233	MCDONALD, Alexander	P	2	211
MCCONNACHIE, Robert		4	117	MCDONALD, Alexander Auld		5	110
MCCONNEL, G		2	209	MCDONALD, Alexander Tom Clark		1	233
MCCONNELL, Adam		5	109	MCDONALD, Allan		4	118
MCCONNELL, P		2	209	MCDONALD, Andrew		3	179
MCCONNELL, Primrose		5	110	MCDONALD, Angus		1	233
MCCONNELL, Robert N		2	209	MCDONALD, Archibaid		1	233
MCCONVILLE, J		3	178	MCDONALD, D		3	179
MCCORKINDALE, J		2	209	MCDONALD, Donald		1	234

Name	Photo	Part No.	Page No.	Name	Photo	Part No.	Page No.
MCDONALD, George	P	1	234	MCFARLANE, James	P	4	120
MCDONALD, George		5	110	MCFARLANE, Thomas		2	212
MCDONALD, George Duffus		1	234	MCFARLANE, William		1	235
MCDONALD, H		3	179	MCFEAT, John		3	180
MCDONALD, J		2	211	MCGEACHIE, James Anderson	P	1	235
MCDONALD, J		3	179	MCGECHIE, John		2	212
MCDONALD, James		1	234	MCGEE, James Michael		1	235
MCDONALD, James		4	118	MCGEOCH, William		3	180
MCDONALD, James Alexander		4	118	MCGIBBON, William Patrick		4	120
MCDONALD, John		2	211	MCGILL, G		2	212
MCDONALD, John		2	211	MCGILL, George Thomas		4	120
MCDONALD, John		2	211	MCGILL, John		4	120
MCDONALD, John		2	211	MCGILL, Robert		2	212
MCDONALD, John		4	118	MCGILL, Robert		2	212
MCDONALD, John		4	118	MCGILLIVRAY, G		2	212
MCDONALD, John Rigg		5	111	MCGINLAY, Patrick		2	212
MCDONALD, John William Scott		1	234	MCGINLEY, Francis Philip	P	2	212
MCDONALD, Kenneth Stuart	P	1	234	MCGINN, Michael		2	212
MCDONALD, Lewis		2	211	MCGINN, P		3	180
MCDONALD, Lewis		4	119	MCGINN, William		2	212
MCDONALD, Morris		2	211	MCGINNITY, Frederick		1	235
MCDONALD, Norman	P	3	179	MCGINTY, William		1	235
MCDONALD, P		4	119	MCGIRL, J		3	180
MCDONALD, Peter		2	211	MCGLADE, John	P	5	112
MCDONALD, R		2	211	MCGLASHAN, John Ewing		1	235
MCDONALD, Robert		5	111	MCGLEAD, M		3	180
MCDONALD, Roderick		2	211	MCGLENNON, J		3	180
MCDONALD, Ronald Mosse	P	1	234	MCGONAGLE, William J		2	212
MCDONALD, Thomas		2	211	MCGONEGLE, L		3	180
MCDONALD, Thomas		2	211	MCGONIGLE, David Blair		4	120
MCDONALD, Thomas		4	119	MCGOVERN, C		3	180
MCDONALD, W		2	211	MCGOWAN, C		3	180
MCDONALD, W		3	179	MCGOWAN, Edward		2	212
MCDONALD, William		2	211	MCGOWAN, F		2	212
MCDONALD, William		2	211	MCGOWAN, Sidney		4	120
MCDONELL, Angus	P	5	111	MCGOWAN, William Anthony	P	4	120
MCDONNELL, D		3	179	MCGOWN, John W		2	212
MCDONNELL, Thomas		1	234	MCGOWRAN, Joseph		2	212
MCDOUGAL, Alexander Ernest	P	4	119	MCGOWRAN, T		3	180
MCDOUGALL, A		2	212	MCGRANE, G		3	180
MCDOUGALL, Angus		4	119	MCGRATH, Frank		2	212
MCDOUGALL, James		2	212	MCGRATH, J		3	180
MCDOUGALL, William		3	179	MCGRATH, John		2	212
MCDOUGLE, George		2	212	MCGRATH, W		3	180
MCDOWELL, Ernest Victor	P	5	111	MCGREEVY, Stanley		5	112
MCEACHRAN, Charles	P	3	179	MCGREGOR, Alexander		5	112
MCELNEY, Robert Gerald	P	5	111	MCGREGOR, Andrew Smith	P	5	112
MCEVOY, Edward P		4	120	MCGREGOR, Douglas	P	3	180
MCEVOY, Michael		1	234	MCGREGOR, Ian Alexander		3	181
MCEVOY, Patrick		1	234	MCGREGOR, James	P	5	112
MCEWAN, Charles Edward		2	212	MCGREGOR, Matthew Mackay		5	112
MCEWAN, D		2	212	MCGREGOR, Samuel Begg		1	235
MCEWAN, David Grant		3	180	MCGREGOR, William		5	112
MCEWAN, John	P	2	212	MCGREGOR, William Mosley	P	3	181
MCEWAN, John		2	212	MCGREN, William J		2	212
MCEWAN, Robert		1	234	MCGUFFICK, Henry		1	235
MCEWEN, Charles R		2	212	MCGUFFIE, Alexander	P	2	212
MCEWEN, James Robert Dundas	P	2	212	MCGUIGAN, D		3	181
MCFADDEN, Robert John		3	180	MCGUILEY, Hugh		1	235
MCFADYEN, John	P	3	180	MCGUINN, M		3	181
MCFADYEN, John		5	112	MCGUINNESS, C		3	181
MCFADYEN, John Craig	P	3	180	MCGUINNESS, John		2	213
MCFADYEN, William		2	212	MCGUINNESS, Michael		1	235
MCFARLANE, Andrew		2	212	MCGUINNITY, Charles	P	2	213
MCFARLANE, James		2	212	MCGUIRE, John		2	213

Name	Photo	Part No.	Page No.	Name	Photo	Part No.	Page No.
MCGUIRE, John		2	213	MCKENZIE, Duncan		2	214
MCGUIRE, William		2	213	MCKENZIE, Duncan		2	214
MCHALE, T		3	181	MCKENZIE, Frederick Smith		4	122
MCHARDY, Alexander		4	121	MCKENZIE, George		4	122
MCHARRIE, Henry		2	213	MCKENZIE, J		2	214
MCHUGH, James		2	213	MCKENZIE, J		2	214
MCHUGH, Michael		1	236	MCKENZIE, John Victor		4	122
MCHUGH, William		4	121	MCKENZIE, John William Thorl		2	214
MCILQUHAM, James Maxwell		5	112	MCKENZIE, Kenneth Buchanan		2	214
MCILROY, Robert		2	213	MCKENZIE, R C		2	214
MCILWAINE, Arthur Arnold		3	181	MCKENZIE, Thornton	P	3	182
MCINNES, J		3	181	MCKENZIE, William	P	1	237
MCINNES, John		2	213	MCKENZIE, William		2	214
MCINNES, Robert Donald		4	121	MCKEONE, John Henry	P	5	113
MCINROY, John Blain		2	213	MCKEOWN, A		3	182
MCINTOSH, Alexander Fraser		4	121	MCKEOWN, Richard Francis		2	214
MCINTOSH, Alfred James Graham		1	236	MCKERRACHER, Charles	P	2	214
MCINTOSH, George		4	121	MCKERRELL, Martin Mungo Mure		4	122
MCINTOSH, J W		3	181	MCKERROLL, John		2	214
MCINTOSH, Laurence Scott		1	236	MCKIGNEY, A H		3	182
MCINTOSH, Robert Rae		1	236	MCKIM, Thomas Alex		2	215
MCINTYRE, Daniel David	P	3	181	MCKIMMIE, J		3	182
MCINTYRE, Donald	P	3	181	MCKINLEY, G		3	182
MCINTYRE, James Lennie		4	121	MCKINLEY, William Henry		5	114
MCINTYRE, Norman	P	5	113	MCKINNELL, Matthew		4	123
MCINTYRE, Robert		2	213	MCKINNIE, Peter	P	3	182
MCISAAC, Alexander	P	2	213	MCKINNON, Alexander		1	237
MCIVER, Donald		3	181	MCKINNON, D		3	182
MCIVER, James Noble	P	3	181	MCKINNON, Donald		5	114
MCIVER, William		2	213	MCKINNON, H		2	215
MCIVOR, R		2	213	MCKINNON, Lachlan		2	215
MCJANNET, David		5	113	MCKINNON, Roderick		2	215
MCKAY, A		2	213	MCKINSTRY, Ronald William	P	2	215
MCKAY, Daniel	P	2	213	MCLACHLAN, Duncan Mcmurchy		4	123
MCKAY, Harry	P	4	121	MCLACHLAN, James		3	182
MCKAY, James		3	182	MCLAGAN, Peter John		4	123
MCKAY, John		2	213	MCLARDIE, Archibald		2	215
MCKAY, M		3	182	MCLARDY, Henry	P	1	237
MCKAY, Peter		2	214	MCLAREN, A		3	183
MCKAY, R		2	214	MCLAREN, Eric Andrew	P	1	237
MCKAY, R		3	182	MCLAREN, Francis Walter Stafford		4	123
MCKAY, W		3	182	MCLAREN, N		2	215
MCKEAN, Matthew		2	214	MCLAREN, William	P	5	114
MCKECHNIE, A		2	214	MCLAUGHAN, Richard		2	215
MCKECHNIE, William George Ernest		1	236	MCLAUGHLIN, Edward Archibald Crofton	P	2	215
MCKEE, James		1	236	MCLAUGHLIN, Hubert Guy Bromilow	P	2	215
MCKEE, John		2	214	MCLAUGHLIN, Hubert Guy Bromilow		3	183
MCKEE, Patrick		2	214	MCLAUGHLIN, James		2	215
MCKEEVER, Bertram		2	214	MCLAUGHLIN, Thomas		2	215
MCKELLAR, J		3	182	MCLEAN, Alexander	P	5	114
MCKELVIE, Ronald		5	113	MCLEAN, Alick	P	2	215
MCKENNA, A		3	182	MCLEAN, Charles		1	238
MCKENNA, F		2	214	MCLEAN, Charles John	P	3	183
MCKENNA, F		3	182	MCLEAN, Charles William		2	216
MCKENNA, Henry	P	2	214	MCLEAN, Donald		5	115
MCKENNA, Peter		2	214	MCLEAN, George Hunter		5	115
MCKENNA, Robert		2	214	MCLEAN, H		2	216
MCKENZIE, A		2	214	MCLEAN, Harold Daniel		4	123
MCKENZIE, A		3	182	MCLEAN, Hugh		4	123
MCKENZIE, Alexander		2	214	MCLEAN, J		3	183
MCKENZIE, Alexander	P	4	122	MCLEAN, J H		3	183
MCKENZIE, Alfred Brown		5	113	MCLEAN, James		2	216
MCKENZIE, C		3	182	MCLEAN, Kenneth		5	115
MCKENZIE, Colin		2	214	MCLEAN, N		3	183
MCKENZIE, D		2	214	MCLEAN, Victor		4	123

Name	Photo	Part No.	Page No.	Name	Photo	Part No.	Page No.
MCVITIE, William Johnstone	P	2	217	MELDRUM, A		2	224
MCVITTIE, George Bertram	P	4	126	MELDRUM, Alfred		2	224
MCVITTIE, George Henry	P	1	240	MELDRUM, Andrew Cosmo		4	133
MCWHIRTER, Hugh Walter	P	1	241	MELIA, Edward		1	251
MCWILLIAM, Andrew	P	4	126	MELIA, T		4	133
MCWILLIAM, Charles Thomas	P	2	217	MELLEFONT, T		3	192
MCWILLIAMS, Christopher		4	126	MELLENFIELD, Cecil Beven	P	2	224
MCWILLIAMS, John	P	2	218	MELLES, Gordon Frank	P	5	122
MCWILLIAMS, William Harold		2	218	MELLETT, Martin		1	251
MEAD, A J		3	192	MELLING, John		5	122
MEAD, Bernard Wallace	P	1	250	MELLISH, Charles		2	224
MEAD, Christopher	P	1	250	MELLISH, Charles Herbert		1	251
MEAD, Donald Anthony	P	2	223	MELLIS-SMITH, Samuel Grant	P	4	191
MEAD, Geoffrey Phillips	P	1	250	MELLODEW, James		3	192
MEAD, George Henry		2	223	MELLOR, George Herbert		5	122
MEAD, Henry George Frederick		1	250	MELLOR, W		3	192
MEAD, John Robert Shuttleworth		2	223	MELLORS, A		3	192
MEAD, P W		3	192	MELROSE, J		2	224
MEAD, Richard James		4	132	MELSON, John Raithby	P	1	251
MEAD, Walter		2	223	MELSON, Robert	P	1	251
MEADE, Richard Gilbert Trevor		3	192	MELVILLE, Charles Potter	P	3	192
MEADON, Sydney B		2	223	MELVILLE, John Kirk		4	133
MEADOWS, Edwin Frank	P	3	192	MELVILLE, William	P	1	251
MEADOWS, Ernest		1	250	MELVIN, Robert George		2	224
MEADOWS, Fred		2	223	MEMBREY, Edward John		1	251
MEADOWS, James Horatio		1	250	MENNELL, John Richard		4	133
MEADWAY, Charles Lynford		4	133	MENZIES, Arthur John Alexander	P	4	133
MEAGEN, Lawrence J		2	223	MENZIES, David		2	224
MEAGER, Hubert Richard William	P	2	223	MENZIES, J V		2	224
MEAKIN, Herbert	P	1	250	MENZIES, Kenneth Mckenzie	P	5	122
MEAKINGS, James William	P	1	250	MERCER, Albert Richard		4	133
MEARES, Gerald Percy Sims	P	2	223	MERCER, Archibald Ariel	P	1	251
MEARNS, William Mellis	P	1	250	MERCER, E		3	193
MEARS, Francis Peel		5	122	MERCER, Edward Allan		1	251
MEARS, George		2	223	MERCER, Eric Cameron	P	1	252
MEAUTYS, Thomas Gilliat	P	1	250	MERCER, George Edward		1	252
MECHAN, David Melville		4	133	MERCER, Thomas		4	133
MECHAR, Daniel		2	223	MERCER, Waller Carpenter	P	1	252
MEDD, Alfred Wooldridge	P	4	133	MERCER, Walter F		2	224
MEDHURST, John Edwin		1	250	MERCER, William Chesley		2	224
MEDHURST, William Richard		1	250	MERCER-NAIRNE, Lord Charles George			
MEDHURST, William Richard	P	2	223	Francis	P	1	266
MEDLAND, William Harry Wilson		1	251	MERCHANT, Hubert	P	3	193
MEE, Walter Binder		5	122	MERCHANT, William		1	252
MEECHAN, John		2	224	MEREDITH, Malcolm Hereward	P	2	224
MEEDS, George		2	224	MEREDITH, William Henry	P	3	193
MEEHAN, Francis James	P	1	251	MEREDITH, William Thomas		2	224
MEEHAN, William		1	251	MERRETT, Albert John		1	252
MEEK, John Charles		4	133	MERRETT, Joseph William		1	252
MEEKAN, Samuel		2	224	MERRETT, Walter		2	224
MEEKER, Charles Edward		1	251	MERRICK, Charles		1	252
MEEKS, Bertie William		4	133	MERRICK, Thomas Edwin	P	3	193
MEEKS, William Henry		2	224	MERRIFIELD, F		3	193
MEESE, V		3	192	MERRIFIELD, William	P	2	224
MEGAW, William Cecil Kennedy	P	1	251	MERRIKIN, J		3	193
MEGSON, Robert Hargraves		4	133	MERRILEES, Stuart	P	1	252
MEHEUX, George Thomas Shelton		1	251	MERRILEES, William	P	1	252
MEHRTENS, Albert Victor		2	224	MERRIMAN, Gordon	P	1	252
MEIGHAN, C		3	192	MERRIMAN, John		2	225
MEIKLE, Archibald		2	224	MERRIMAN, W		3	193
MEIKLE, James Heggie		2	224	MERRITT, Cecil Mack	P	1	252
MEIKLEJOHN, Kenneth Forbes	P	1	251	MERRITT, Henry		1	252
MEIKLE-JONES, Bertie Wallace		5	122	MERRITT, Percy George		3	193
MEIN, Dudley Gerald		5	122	MERSON, Alexander		2	225
MEIN, George Frederick Coore	P	2	224	MESS, A		2	225

Name	Photo	Part No.	Page No.
MESSAGE, Edgar		1	252
MESSAM, John William		1	252
MESSENGER, W E F		3	193
MESSENGER, Wilfrid Chaundler	P	3	193
METCALFE, John Claude		5	122
METCALFE, Richard		1	252
METCALFE, William Miles		4	133
METCALFE-SMITH, Bertram Cecil	P	4	191
METHERALL, H		3	193
METHUEN, St. John Arthur Paul	P	4	133
METHUEN, William		1	252
MEW, Roland	P	4	133
MEYER-GRIFFITH, Harold Walter Gooch	P	2	147
MEYERS, M		3	193
M'GAW, William		4	120
M'GHEE, James Cuthbert		5	112
MICHAEL, E		3	193
MICHELSEN, Arthur Conrad		4	133
MICHIE, John	P	3	193
MICHIE, Joseph		3	193
MICHIE, William Alexander		5	122
MICKELS, Thomas Edward		1	252
MIDDLEBROOK, T		3	193
MIDDLECOTE, George Albert		5	123
MIDDLEDITCH, Archibald Milne		2	225
MIDDLEDITCH, Arnold Warden		2	225
MIDDLEMISS, Thomas Elmslie		4	134
MIDDLETON, Arnold	P	4	134
MIDDLETON, Frank		2	225
MIDDLETON, George		2	225
MIDDLETON, Jacob	P	4	134
MIDDLETON, James		4	134
MIDDLETON, John	P	3	193
MIDDLETON, John Liddle	P	1	252
MIDDLETON, Matthew		3	193
MIDDLETON, Theodore Henry		2	225
MIDDLETON, W C		3	193
MIDGLEY, John Geoffrey		3	193
MIDMER, Harry George		1	253
MIELL, Charles Frederick		1	253
MIFOND, A		3	193
MIGHALL, Cecil Charles Newman	P	1	253
MILBANK, Frederick George		4	134
MILBURN, J E		3	193
MILBURN, William Hedley	P	3	194
MILDENHALL, H		3	194
MILEHAM, Fred George		2	225
MILES, Archie		2	225
MILES, Charles		2	225
MILES, David	P	1	253
MILES, Ernest Henry		4	134
MILES, Frank		5	123
MILES, Thomas		2	225
MILES, William Douglas		2	225
MILES, William John		4	134
MILEY, John		1	253
MILEY, Miles		2	225
MILGATE, Percy Lilley James	P	2	225
MILL, James Davidson	P	2	225
MILLAR, Arthur James	P	1	253
MILLAR, Arthur Liberty		4	134
MILLAR, David Bogie	P	5	123
MILLAR, Edward Chaytor	P	2	225
MILLAR, Henry Alfred		4	134
MILLAR, Ian Andrew	P	3	194

Name	Photo	Part No.	Page No.
MILLAR, John		4	134
MILLAR, John James		1	253
MILLAR, John Pitcairn		5	123
MILLAR, John Trotter	P	1	253
MILLAR, Robert Gordon	P	3	194
MILLAR, Thomas		2	225
MILLARD, Albert Edward		4	134
MILLBANK, B		3	194
MILLEN, C		3	194
MILLEN, Wilfrid	P	5	123
MILLER, A		3	194
MILLER, Alexander	P	1	253
MILLER, Andrew		4	134
MILLER, Andrew		5	123
MILLER, Arthur William		1	253
MILLER, Bert		2	225
MILLER, C H		3	194
MILLER, Charles		4	134
MILLER, Charles L		2	225
MILLER, Cyril William	P	2	225
MILLER, Edward		1	253
MILLER, Edward Minty		3	194
MILLER, Ernest Charles William		1	253
MILLER, Ernest Cyril	P	1	253
MILLER, F		3	194
MILLER, Francis John	P	2	225
MILLER, Frederick		3	194
MILLER, G		3	194
MILLER, George		2	225
MILLER, Godfrey Lyall		1	253
MILLER, H		3	194
MILLER, Harry		1	253
MILLER, Inglis Francis Rowley	P	1	253
MILLER, J		3	194
MILLER, James		2	225
MILLER, James		4	134
MILLER, James		4	134
MILLER, John		1	253
MILLER, John		2	226
MILLER, Lionel		1	253
MILLER, Matthew William Barclay	P	2	226
MILLER, R		3	194
MILLER, R		3	194
MILLER, Ralph Marillier		5	123
MILLER, Rex De Hochepied Marillier		5	123
MILLER, Richard Leslie		1	253
MILLER, Robert	P	4	134
MILLER, Robert Grattan	P	2	226
MILLER, Thomas	P	5	123
MILLER, Thomas James		1	253
MILLER, Thomas Murray	P	3	194
MILLER, Tom Drysdale	P	2	226
MILLER, W		3	194
MILLER, W		3	194
MILLER, W C		3	194
MILLER, Walter		1	253
MILLER, Walter Roy		5	123
MILLER, Wilfrid	P	3	194
MILLER, Wilfrid		4	135
MILLER, William		2	226
MILLER, William		2	226
MILLER, William Edward		2	226
MILLER, William Reginald Francis	P	3	194
MILLER-STIRLING, Edward George Bradshaw		3	258

Name	Photo	Part No.	Page No.
MILLERWOOD, George Thomas		4	135
MILLETT, Arthur	P	1	253
MILLETT, Frederick		1	254
MILLETT, M		3	194
MILLGATE, Ernest		2	226
MILLGATE, Thomas W		2	226
MILLIGAN, Alastair	P	3	194
MILLIGAN, Arthur		2	226
MILLIGAN, David		2	226
MILLIN, Charles		2	226
MILLINGTON, George Ernest		1	254
MILLINGTON, Herbert Hugh	P	1	254
MILLMAN, Percy Edward		4	135
MILLMAN, Richard Henry		4	135
MILLS, A		3	194
MILLS, Alfred Joseph		5	123
MILLS, Andrew		3	194
MILLS, Archibald Harding		1	254
MILLS, Arthur Banes		4	135
MILLS, Charles		1	254
MILLS, Charles		2	226
MILLS, Charles Daniel		1	254
MILLS, Colin Charles		2	226
MILLS, D		2	226
MILLS, David		4	135
MILLS, Edgar Edward		5	123
MILLS, Edward George		1	254
MILLS, Ewdin		1	254
MILLS, F		4	135
MILLS, Francis J		2	226
MILLS, Frederick Henry		2	226
MILLS, George Harvey	P	1	254
MILLS, H G T		3	195
MILLS, Harold Frederick		3	195
MILLS, J		3	195
MILLS, J R		4	135
MILLS, Jesse	P	1	254
MILLS, John		1	254
MILLS, Joseph		1	254
MILLS, Joseph Henry		1	254
MILLS, Mark		1	254
MILLS, Robert George		2	226
MILLS, Robert James		3	195
MILLS, Samuel		3	195
MILLS, Sidney		2	226
MILLS, T		3	195
MILLS, Teulon Lewis		2	226
MILLS, W		3	195
MILLS, William		1	254
MILLWARD, Henry Woodvine		1	254
MILNE, A		3	195
MILNE, Albert George		5	123
MILNE, Alexander David	P	2	226
MILNE, Alexander Richard	P	3	195
MILNE, Alexander Robert	P	2	226
MILNE, Arthur William		3	195
MILNE, Douglas		5	123
MILNE, E		4	135
MILNE, Eric Sutcliffe	P	5	124
MILNE, F J		3	195
MILNE, Francis James	P	1	254
MILNE, James	P	1	254
MILNE, John		2	227
MILNE, John		4	135
MILNE, John		4	135

Name	Photo	Part No.	Page No.
MILNE, John Sangster		5	124
MILNE, John William		4	135
MILNE, Joseph	P	5	124
MILNE, Mabel Lee		4	135
MILNE, Thomas Gourley		2	227
MILNE, W		2	227
MILNE, William		1	254
MILNE, William	P	3	195
MILNE, William		4	135
MILNE, William		5	124
MILNE, William Leask		4	135
MILNER, Arthur Frederick	P	4	135
MILNER, J		3	195
MILNER, James Maurice		4	135
MILNER, John Lewis	P	1	254
MILNER, Thomas George		5	124
MILNER, Tom		2	227
MILNES, Edmund		1	254
MILNES, Herbert Albert Edwin	P	3	195
MILNES, Jesse		1	254
MILSOM, W		4	135
MILTHORPE, Walter		2	227
MILTHROPE, Herbert		4	135
MILTON, Ernest		2	227
MILTON, Frank Curtis		2	227
MILTON, H		4	135
MILTON, William Smith		4	135
MINCHINTON, Sydney Herbert		5	124
MINIHAN, Patrick		1	254
MINKS, T		3	195
MINNO, Joseph		1	254
MINNS, Walter John	P	4	135
MINTER, Frederick		1	254
MINTER, William		2	227
MINTON, J		3	195
MINTON, William		1	254
MINTY, George		3	195
MISEY, George Ernest		2	227
MISSITT, J		3	195
MISSITT, J E		3	195
MIST, Harry	P	3	195
MITCHEL, Frederick David	P	4	136
MITCHELL, Albert Charles		1	254
MITCHELL, Albert Ross		4	136
MITCHELL, Alfred		2	227
MITCHELL, Aquilla	P	5	124
MITCHELL, Arthur James		1	254
MITCHELL, Augustus James		1	254
MITCHELL, Bertie Frederick		1	254
MITCHELL, Charles		3	196
MITCHELL, Charles Carew	P	2	227
MITCHELL, Charles David		4	136
MITCHELL, Denis Stuart	P	5	124
MITCHELL, Frederick Eugene Hobart		1	254
MITCHELL, G		2	227
MITCHELL, G		3	196
MITCHELL, G H		3	196
MITCHELL, George	P	5	124
MITCHELL, George John		1	254
MITCHELL, George Mayo		5	124
MITCHELL, H J		3	196
MITCHELL, Henry D		2	227
MITCHELL, Henry Harrison	P	3	196
MITCHELL, J		2	227
MITCHELL, J		2	227

Name	Photo	Part No.	Page No.	Name	Photo	Part No.	Page No.
MITCHELL, J A		3	196	MOLLOY, Michael Vallancey	P	1	256
MITCHELL, James		2	227	MOLONEY, John Lawrence	P	1	256
MITCHELL, James Bannerman		1	255	MOLSON, Eric Elsdale	P	1	256
MITCHELL, James Campbell	P	3	196	MOLTON, Ansell Joseph		4	137
MITCHELL, James Lawson	P	4	136	MOLYNEAUX, Ian Moore		4	137
MITCHELL, John		3	196	MOLYNEUX-SEEL, Louis Edmund Harington		4	181
MITCHELL, John	P	4	136	MONAGHAN, Denis Laurence		5	125
MITCHELL, John		4	136	MONAGHAN, J		3	196
MITCHELL, John		5	124	MONCK, The Hon. Charles Henry Stanley	P	1	256
MITCHELL, John Halliburton	P	3	196	MONCKTON, Christopher	P	2	227
MITCHELL, John Monfries	P	1	255	MONCKTON, Marmaduke Henry	P	1	256
MITCHELL, Joseph Spencer	P	2	227	MONCRIEFF, James Rennie	P	4	137
MITCHELL, Peter		4	136	MONCUR, George Clark	P	1	256
MITCHELL, Peter		4	136	MONDAY, Tom	P	1	257
MITCHELL, Ralph Eric	P	5	124	MONEY, Henry Ironside	P	1	257
MITCHELL, S		2	227	MONGER, Joseph		2	227
MITCHELL, Stanley		4	136	MONILAWS, Selwyn Macgeorge	P	5	125
MITCHELL, Thomas		2	227	MONK, George Bertram Fifield	P	1	257
MITCHELL, W		2	227	MONK, Gerald Patrick De Baillou	P	2	227
MITCHELL, W		3	196	MONK, Henry William		1	257
MITCHELL, W		3	196	MONK, Oswald Frank		1	257
MITCHELL, William	P	4	136	MONKHOUSE, Robert Alexander	P	3	196
MITCHELL, William	P	5	125	MONKS, James William		2	227
MITCHELL, William Alexander	P	1	255	MONKS, Lawrence		5	125
MITCHELL, William Ford		5	125	MONKS, Stuart Cornwall	P	2	227
MITCHELL, William Holford	P	5	125	MONRO, C		3	197
MITCHENALL, William Ernest		4	136	MONSEES, Richard		2	227
MITCHINSON, John Supple		5	125	MONTAGU, Herbert Gerald	P	3	197
MITFORD, Christopher		2	227	MONTAGUE, Felix David		2	227
MITTEN, M		3	196	MONTEITH, Douglas		2	228
MITTEN, Thomas Henry		1	255	MONTEITH, George	P	2	228
MITTON, Walter		5	125	MONTEITH, Henry John Joseph	P	2	228
M'KEAN, David		2	214	MONTEITH, John Cassels	P	2	228
M'KERRELL, Neil		5	114	MONTEITH, William Neve	P	2	228
M'LENNAN, William Grant Ross		4	124	MONTFORD, Alfred Charles		4	137
M'LEOD, Alexander		5	115	MONTGOMERY, Adam	P	1	257
MOAT, W		3	196	MONTGOMERY, Neville		4	137
MOCKFORD, Herbert		4	136	MONTGOMERY, Sidney George		1	257
MOCKLER-FERRYMAN, Hugh	P	1	131	MONTGOMERY, William Sandford		4	137
MOFFAT, Archibald Skirving Woolery	P	1	255	MONTGOMERY, William Sproat	P	1	257
MOFFAT, Hugh Francis Baillie		5	125	MOODIE, Andrew Fotheringhame		2	228
MOFFAT, Robert		2	227	MOODY, A		4	137
MOFFET, John Leeson	P	1	255	MOODY, A E		4	137
MOGG, Frederick Harry		1	255	MOODY, Arthur Edward	P	3	197
MOGGRIDGE, Robert		1	255	MOODY, Douglas Whimster Keiller		2	228
MOHR, John Carl Bernharat		1	255	MOODY, Frank		2	228
MOIR, Alexander		4	136	MOODY, Frederick William		1	257
MOIR, Archibald Gifford	P	1	255	MOODY, Herbert		2	228
MOIR, Arthur Fergus	P	3	196	MOODY, J		4	137
MOIR, Charles Penny		4	136	MOODY, J R		3	197
MOIR, Denholm		2	227	MOODY, James		2	228
MOIR, George Andrew Christie		4	137	MOODY, Robert Ronald		1	257
MOIR, J		3	196	MOODY, Thomas A		2	228
MOIR, James		1	255	MOODY, Thomas John		2	228
MOIR, James	P	3	196	MOON, Albert George		2	228
MOIR, James		3	196	MOON, H		3	197
MOIR, John Andrew Alexander	P	1	255	MOON, J		3	197
MOIR, Peter		2	227	MOONEY, Edward		2	228
MOIR, William Hulten	P	3	196	MOONEY, J		2	228
MOLE, Herbert		1	255	MOONEY, J		3	197
MOLES, Charles		2	227	MOONEY, James		2	228
MOLESWORTH, Ernest Kerr		1	255	MOONEY, P		3	197
MOLINEUX, George King	P	1	256	MOONEY, P		3	197
MOLLISON, William Allan	P	5	125	MOOR, Christopher	P	1	257
MOLLOY, Charles		1	256	MOORE, A		3	197

Name	Photo	Part No.	Page No.	Name	Photo	Part No.	Page No.
MOORE, A		3	197	**MORAN,** J		3	198
MOORE, A T		3	197	**MORAN,** John Barrow		1	259
MOORE, Albert		4	137	**MORAN,** Joseph	P	1	259
MOORE, Alfred		1	258	**MORAN,** Kevin Cuthbert		5	126
MOORE, Alfred Charles		2	228	**MORAN,** T		3	198
MOORE, Alfred Thomas Oliver		4	137	**MORCOM,** John		4	138
MOORE, Anthony		1	258	**MORDAUNT,** Arthur	P	4	138
MOORE, Arthur	P	1	258	**MORETON,** Archibald Herbert	P	2	229
MOORE, Arthur		5	125	**MOREY,** J		3	198
MOORE, Charles James		1	258	**MOREY,** Leonard		2	229
MOORE, Colin Mclaughlin	P	5	126	**MORFETT,** Henry George		3	198
MOORE, Edward Hayden	P	3	197	**MORFETT,** Henry George		5	126
MOORE, Ellis Sard		4	137	**MORGAN,** Albert		1	259
MOORE, F		3	197	**MORGAN,** Albert Ernest	P	1	259
MOORE, F W		3	197	**MORGAN,** Albert Norton Proctor		2	229
MOORE, Frank Lelslie	P	1	258	**MORGAN,** Alexander		3	198
MOORE, Frederick		1	258	**MORGAN,** Alfred Lowe		3	198
MOORE, Frederick Herbert	P	5	126	**MORGAN,** Arthur		1	259
MOORE, Geoffrey	P	3	197	**MORGAN,** Arthur		2	229
MOORE, George		1	258	**MORGAN,** Arthur William Herbert	P	2	229
MOORE, H		3	197	**MORGAN,** Brinley Arthur	P	4	138
MOORE, Harold Thomas Pelham		5	126	**MORGAN,** Charles		2	229
MOORE, Henry Glanville Allen	P	1	258	**MORGAN,** Charles Bernard Francis	P	3	198
MOORE, Henry John		1	258	**MORGAN,** Charles E		2	229
MOORE, Hugh Stirling		4	137	**MORGAN,** Charles E		2	229
MOORE, J E		3	197	**MORGAN,** Edward Charles	P	1	259
MOORE, J W		3	198	**MORGAN,** Edward Compton	P	5	126
MOORE, James		2	228	**MORGAN,** Edward Stanley	P	4	138
MOORE, James		2	228	**MORGAN,** Eric Fennell Trevor		4	138
MOORE, John Alan	P	5	126	**MORGAN,** Francis Matthew		1	259
MOORE, John Fletcher	P	3	198	**MORGAN,** Fred William		3	198
MOORE, John Holmes Lyndon	P	5	126	**MORGAN,** Frederick John		2	229
MOORE, John Thomas Warren		1	258	**MORGAN,** G		3	198
MOORE, Joseph Herbert Speight		5	126	**MORGAN,** G		3	198
MOORE, P		2	228	**MORGAN,** Garland Oswald	P	4	138
MOORE, P		3	198	**MORGAN,** George	P	1	259
MOORE, Peter		5	126	**MORGAN,** George	P	3	198
MOORE, R		3	198	**MORGAN,** George Alfred Henry		5	127
MOORE, Raymond Cecil Devereux		4	137	**MORGAN,** George Henry	P	2	229
MOORE, Reginald Henry Hamilton	P	1	258	**MORGAN,** George Hungerford	P	5	127
MOORE, Richard	P	3	198	**MORGAN,** H		3	198
MOORE, Richard		5	126	**MORGAN,** H		3	198
MOORE, Richard Henry	P	5	126	**MORGAN,** Harry	P	1	259
MOORE, S		3	198	**MORGAN,** Hugh Philip		5	127
MOORE, S K		4	137	**MORGAN,** Idris		3	198
MOORE, S V		4	137	**MORGAN,** J		3	198
MOORE, T		4	137	**MORGAN,** J F		3	198
MOORE, Thomas		1	258	**MORGAN,** J G		3	198
MOORE, Thomas		1	258	**MORGAN,** James David	P	5	127
MOORE, Thomas		4	137	**MORGAN,** James Henry		3	198
MOORE, W		3	198	**MORGAN,** James Thomas		5	127
MOORE, W		4	137	**MORGAN,** L E		3	198
MOORE, Walter Frederick		4	137	**MORGAN,** Owen		4	138
MOORE, Walter William		3	198	**MORGAN,** Patrick Lawrence		5	127
MOORE, William		2	228	**MORGAN,** R E		3	198
MOORE, William		2	228	**MORGAN,** Robert William	P	1	259
MOORE, William Albert		1	258	**MORGAN,** S		3	198
MOORE, William E		2	228	**MORGAN,** Stephen Beverley	P	1	259
MOORE-ANDERSON, Walter Graham	P	1	7	**MORGAN,** T		3	198
MOOREY, John		2	228	**MORGAN,** Thomas Albert Edward		5	127
MOORHEAD, D		3	198	**MORGAN,** W		3	198
MOORHOUSE, James Henry		4	137	**MORGAN,** W J		3	198
MOORHOUSE, S		3	198	**MORGAN,** William		2	229
MOORHOUSE, William Appleyard		1	258	**MORGAN,** William		2	229
MORAN, J		2	229	**MORGAN,** William Anthony		4	138

Name	Photo	Part No.	Page No.
MORGAN, William Donal		2	229
MORGAN, William Harris		5	127
MORGAN, William John		5	127
MORGAN-GRENVILLE, The Hon. Richard George Grenville	P	1	163
MORGANS, Thomas Alfred		1	259
MORIARTY, Thomas		1	259
MORISON, Alfred James	P	3	198
MORITZ, Oscar Frank	P	2	229
MORKILL, Ronald Falshaw	P	1	259
MORLAND, Henry Alfred		1	260
MORLEY, Alexander Noel		3	198
MORLEY, Arthur F		2	229
MORLEY, David	P	3	199
MORLEY, Frederick		2	229
MORLEY, J		3	199
MORLEY, James William		2	229
MORLEY, P		3	199
MORLEY, P		3	199
MORLEY, Percy		3	199
MORLEY, T		3	199
MORNINGTON, Richard		2	229
MORONEY, C		3	199
MORONEY, Edward Francis		1	260
MORPETH, Allan	P	5	127
MORPETH, Moore	P	1	260
MORPHETT, Walter		5	127
MORPHEW, Arthur		1	260
MORPHEW, Ernest		1	260
MORPHY, Arthur Albert	P	3	199
MORRANT, Charles		2	229
MORRICE, A		3	199
MORRICE, W		3	199
MORRIS, A		3	199
MORRIS, A		3	199
MORRIS, Albert		2	229
MORRIS, Arthur		1	260
MORRIS, Arthur Edward		2	229
MORRIS, C		3	199
MORRIS, C G		3	199
MORRIS, Cecil Armstrong		2	229
MORRIS, Charles	P	5	127
MORRIS, Charles Alan Smith	P	3	199
MORRIS, Charles Frederick		2	229
MORRIS, Charles Geoffrey Noel	P	2	229
MORRIS, Charles H		2	229
MORRIS, Clive Wilson		1	260
MORRIS, Edmund Pulford		4	138
MORRIS, Edward Owen Wynne	P	2	230
MORRIS, Ernest		2	230
MORRIS, F		3	199
MORRIS, G		3	199
MORRIS, George Tod	P	4	138
MORRIS, Henry Gage	P	1	260
MORRIS, Hon. George Henry	P	1	260
MORRIS, J		3	199
MORRIS, J		3	199
MORRIS, J C		3	199
MORRIS, J S		2	230
MORRIS, J S		3	199
MORRIS, James		1	260
MORRIS, John		1	260
MORRIS, John Arthur Edwards	P	2	230
MORRIS, John Henry		2	230
MORRIS, Michael	P	3	199

Name	Photo	Part No.	Page No.
MORRIS, Michael F S		3	199
MORRIS, Rudolph		4	139
MORRIS, S		3	199
MORRIS, Sidney		3	199
MORRIS, Thomas		2	230
MORRIS, Thomas James		4	139
MORRIS, Walter Ruthin		3	199
MORRIS, William		1	260
MORRIS, William		1	260
MORRIS, William Archard Tucker	P	5	127
MORRIS, William George		4	139
MORRIS, William Henry		2	230
MORRIS, William Thomas		5	127
MORRISH, H		3	199
MORRISON, A		3	199
MORRISON, Charles Macdonald	P	2	230
MORRISON, Colquhoun Grant	P	4	139
MORRISON, Douglas St George	P	3	199
MORRISON, Edwin Duncan Rutherford	P	1	260
MORRISON, Edwin Walter	P	5	128
MORRISON, Frank John		5	128
MORRISON, Frederick Charles		1	260
MORRISON, Frederick George	P	5	128
MORRISON, George James	P	5	128
MORRISON, Gerard Humphreys	P	1	260
MORRISON, Herbert	P	3	199
MORRISON, Herbert Henry		1	260
MORRISON, J B		3	199
MORRISON, James		2	230
MORRISON, James		2	230
MORRISON, John	P	1	261
MORRISON, John Stewart	P	5	128
MORRISON, Nathaniel		5	128
MORRISON, Samuel Alexander	P	3	200
MORRISON, Stuart		4	139
MORRISON, Thomas Edmund	P	2	230
MORRISON, Vernon Macdonald		3	200
MORRISON, William		1	261
MORRISON, William		5	128
MORRISON, William Graham		2	230
MORRISON, William John		4	139
MORRITT, William Graveley	P	4	139
MORROW, Frederick Roulstone		4	139
MORROW, J S		3	200
MORROW, Robert	P	1	261
MORROW, W		3	200
MORROW, William Edward		3	200
MORROW, William Edward		4	139
MORSE, Archdale Albert		2	230
MORSE, Gordon Thomas Harcourt	P	1	261
MORSE, Gurth Stephen	P	1	261
MORSE, Thomas		5	128
MORTAR, George		1	261
MORTIMER, A E		3	200
MORTIMER, Edmund	P	2	230
MORTIMER, George Edward Hempson		4	139
MORTIMER, George Frederick		2	231
MORTIMER, Gerald Henry Walter		2	231
MORTIMER, Harry Brooks	P	1	261
MORTIMER, P		2	231
MORTIMER, Peter		4	139
MORTIMER, R		3	200
MORTIMER, Samuel		5	128
MORTIMER, William Brian	P	2	231
MORTIMER, William Henderson Thornton		5	128

Name	Photo	Part No.	Page No.	Name	Photo	Part No.	Page No.
MORTIMORE, Archer Ernest	P	2	231	MOXEY, W		3	201
MORTIMORE, Charles William		2	231	MOXON, Arthur		3	201
MORTIMORE, Edward John		2	231	MOXON, Harry	P	3	201
MORTIMORE, Eli		5	128	MOYES, Alexander Barclay		4	140
MORTIMORE, Frank Victor		4	139	MOYLE, G		3	201
MORTIMORE, Owen John		2	231	MOYNA, Edward Gerald James	P	2	231
MORTON, Edgar Douglas	P	1	261	MOZDON, Edgar Frederick		2	232
MORTON, Gordon Reid	P	4	139	M'PHERSON, James		2	217
MORTON, Henry	P	1	261	MUCHALL, George William Stewart	P	1	262
MORTON, James Fairfax Amphlett	P	1	261	MUCKLE, Thomas Edward	P	3	201
MORTON, John Sydney	P	4	140	MUDDIMAN, Oliver	P	1	262
MORTON, John William	P	3	200	MUDDLE, Joseph		2	232
MORTON, Quintin Young	P	3	200	MUDFORD, Walter		1	262
MORTON, Robert		2	231	MUDLAND, Henry John		4	140
MORTON, W		2	231	MUFF, Philip Stanley	P	5	129
MORTON, Wilfred		1	261	MUFFINIADES, Alexis Ectos	P	3	201
MORTRAM, N		3	200	MUGGRIDGE, Hubert George Cecil	P	3	201
MOSEDALE, W J		3	200	MUIR, A		2	232
MOSELEY, H		3	200	MUIR, Arthur	P	3	201
MOSLEY, H		3	200	MUIR, Charles		2	232
MOSLEY, William J		2	231	MUIR, George Chalmers		1	262
MOSMAN, Hugh	P	2	231	MUIR, George Watson	P	1	262
MOSS, Arnold Wilson	P	2	231	MUIR, William Hay		4	140
MOSS, C H		3	200	MUIRHEAD, James Graham		1	262
MOSS, George Percival		5	128	MUIRHEAD, John		4	140
MOSS, Harry		2	231	MUIRHEAD, R		2	232
MOSS, Herbert		1	262	MUIRHEAD, Robert		2	232
MOSS, Horace George		1	262	MUIRHEAD, William		2	232
MOSS, Samuel		1	262	MULADY, Alfred		1	262
MOSS, W		3	200	MULCAHY, Daniel		4	140
MOSSCROP, Allan		4	140	MULCAHY, Frederick Daniel	P	5	129
MOTH, E		3	200	MULCAHY-MORGAN, Francis Campion		2	229
MOTH, F		3	200	MULHOLLAND, Arthur		1	262
MOTHERWELL, William		3	200	MULHOLLAND, D		3	201
MOTION, Sidney Howard	P	5	128	MULHOLLAND, James		4	140
MOTRONI, Peter George	P	1	262	MULLARKEY, A J		3	201
MOTRONI, Umberto Amedie	P	1	262	MULLEN, Albert Charles		2	232
MOTT, George		1	262	MULLEN, Edward		1	262
MOTT, Henry		5	129	MULLEN, Gilbert		4	140
MOTT, Joseph		2	231	MULLEN, J		3	201
MOTTERSHALL, Herbert Stanley	P	3	200	MULLEN, P		3	201
MOTTRAM, Arthur		5	129	MULLEN, T		2	232
MOTTRAM, John Elliott		4	140	MULLEN, T		3	201
MOUCHER, Thomas Henry		1	262	MULLER, John William		3	201
MOULD, Albert Arthur	P	1	262	MULLIGAN, Alexander	P	1	262
MOULD, George William		4	140	MULLIGAN, Herbert Butler		3	201
MOULD, J S		3	200	MULLIGHAN, John		4	140
MOULDEN, John		4	140	MULLINS, Alfred		5	129
MOULDING, Percy		2	231	MULLINS, Arthur J		2	232
MOULDS, George William		2	231	MULLINS, James Brendan Lane	P	5	129
MOULL, William Daniel		1	262	MULLINS, John Ollis	P	1	262
MOULT, William		2	231	MULLISS, Walter Harry		2	232
MOULTON, Joseph Harold		3	200	MULLOY, John Thomas		1	262
MOUNT, Wallace Godfrey		2	231	MULROONEY, Thomas Martin	P	2	232
MOUNTAIN, George		1	262	MUMFORD, George		1	262
MOUNTNEY, James		3	200	MUMFORD, H		2	232
MOUTRIE, R		3	200	MUMFORD, Harry		1	262
MOUZER, Arthur		3	200	MUMFORD, Henry Walter	P	3	201
MOUZER, Frederick		3	200	MUMMERY, Alfred Ernest		2	232
MOWAT, John		2	231	MUNBY, Ernest John		1	262
MOWAT, John Maclellan	P	3	201	MUNCEY, George		2	232
MOWAT, William		4	140	MUNCKTON, Edmund James		5	129
MOWBRAY, John Leslie		4	140	MUNDAY, C		2	232
MOWBRAY, Maurice Charles		4	140	MUNDAY, Ernest Alfred		2	232
MOXEY, Charles George		1	262	MUNDAY, Herbert		4	140

Name	Photo	Part No.	Page No.	Name	Photo	Part No.	Page No.
MUNDAY, James		1	263	MURPHY, Thomas		1	263
MUNDAY, William		4	141	MURPHY, Walter Leonard		1	263
MUNDEN, William		1	263	MURRANT, William H E		2	233
MUNDY, Alfred		2	232	MURRAY, A		3	202
MUNDY, Arthur		2	232	MURRAY, Adam Blackie		2	233
MUNDY, John Henry		5	129	MURRAY, Alexander		1	263
MUNN, Duncan		1	263	MURRAY, Alexander		1	263
MUNN, George Anderson		1	263	MURRAY, Alexander	P	4	141
MUNNOCH, J		3	202	MURRAY, Alistair Ian		4	141
MUNNS, George		2	232	MURRAY, Andrew	P	2	233
MUNRO, Alexander	P	2	232	MURRAY, Andrew Currie	P	3	202
MUNRO, Angus Walter Rutherford	P	2	232	MURRAY, Angus		2	233
MUNRO, Archibald		2	232	MURRAY, Angus		4	141
MUNRO, David Sinclair		1	263	MURRAY, Arthur James		1	263
MUNRO, Donald Alexander		2	232	MURRAY, C		2	233
MUNRO, Farquhar Percival Sinclair		4	141	MURRAY, Charles John	P	1	263
MUNRO, Frederick John	P	3	202	MURRAY, David	P	3	202
MUNRO, George		5	129	MURRAY, Edward		2	233
MUNRO, H		3	202	MURRAY, Fane Wright Stapleton	P	1	264
MUNRO, J		3	202	MURRAY, Francis	P	2	233
MUNRO, James Norman		4	141	MURRAY, George		2	233
MUNRO, Lewis George		2	232	MURRAY, George		2	233
MUNRO, Norman Mcleod		3	202	MURRAY, George Adam		4	141
MUNRO, Robert William		1	263	MURRAY, Henry Berkeley	P	3	202
MUNRO, Roderick		1	263	MURRAY, Herbert Mayne		4	141
MUNRO, William		2	232	MURRAY, J		2	233
MUNRO, William Donald		3	202	MURRAY, J		2	233
MUNSTER, John Francis	P	3	202	MURRAY, J		2	233
MUNTON, Frank Boughton	P	1	263	MURRAY, J		3	203
MUNTON, S S		3	202	MURRAY, J		3	203
MURCHISON, Donald		4	141	MURRAY, James		2	233
MURDOCH, David		5	129	MURRAY, James		2	233
MURDOCH, James		5	129	MURRAY, James Brash		3	203
MURDOCH, Thomas John Carson		3	202	MURRAY, James Gerald		2	233
MURGATROYD, Walter Ernest		1	263	MURRAY, James Hamilton	P	3	203
MURIEL, Bernard John	P	2	232	MURRAY, John		2	233
MURIEL, Sidney Herbert Foster		1	263	MURRAY, John		2	233
MURISON, D B		3	202	MURRAY, John	P	3	203
MURLESS, Herbert Reginald		4	141	MURRAY, John Matthew		3	203
MURPHY, Alfred H		2	232	MURRAY, John Robertson	P	3	203
MURPHY, Cecil		2	232	MURRAY, John Thomas	P	1	264
MURPHY, Christopher Fowler	P	1	263	MURRAY, Leonard		3	203
MURPHY, Edward		2	233	MURRAY, P		3	203
MURPHY, F R		3	202	MURRAY, Patrick Maxwell	P	1	264
MURPHY, George Patrick		1	263	MURRAY, Petchell Burtt	P	1	264
MURPHY, J		3	202	MURRAY, Peter Herbert	P	3	203
MURPHY, J		3	202	MURRAY, Robert Daniel		2	233
MURPHY, James		4	141	MURRAY, Rupert Auriol Conant Gostling	P	1	264
MURPHY, Joachim	P	1	263	MURRAY, Sinclair Henderson Georgeson		2	233
MURPHY, John		1	263	MURRAY, Thomas		1	264
MURPHY, John		2	233	MURRAY, Thomas		3	203
MURPHY, John		3	202	MURRAY, Thomas H		2	233
MURPHY, John C		2	233	MURRAY, Thomas Seaforth		2	233
MURPHY, John Cornelius Matthias		1	263	MURRAY, W		3	203
MURPHY, John Francis		1	263	MURRAY, W		3	203
MURPHY, Joseph		2	233	MURRAY, Walter		1	264
MURPHY, Lawrence		2	233	MURRAY, Walter Stanley	P	1	264
MURPHY, M		3	202	MURRAY, William		5	129
MURPHY, Maurice		1	263	MURRAY, William Edward	P	1	264
MURPHY, Michael		1	263	MURRAY, William Grant		4	141
MURPHY, Michael		4	141	MURRAY, William James		4	141
MURPHY, R		3	202	MURRAY-MACGREGOR, Atholl		5	112
MURPHY, Richard Victor		5	129	MURRAY-SMITH, Arthur George		4	191
MURPHY, T		2	233	MURRELL, Edward G		2	233
MURPHY, T		3	202	MURTON, Herbert Alfred William		5	129

Name	Photo	Part No.	Page No.
MUSGRAVE, Andrew Bremner	P	1	265
MUSGROVE, William		1	265
MUSHETT, Frank		1	265
MUSK, Douglas Lionel George Roland	P	5	130
MUSK, John Aubyn Granville Strathallan	P	5	130
MUSKER, P		3	203
MUSKETT, Alfred		1	265
MUSSELL, C F		3	203
MUSSELL, Ernest S		2	233
MUSSETT, John William		1	265
MUSSETT, William Henry		1	265
MUSSO, Joseph		1	265
MUSSON, John Hardy	P	1	265
MUSTARD, Alexander		1	265
MUSTARD CHARLETON, William	P	1	78
MUSTCHIN, Joseph		2	233
MUSTOE, Phillip Joseph		4	142
MUZZALL, Frank		2	233
MUZZELL, Stanley John Herbert		4	142
MYALL, G		3	203
MYATT, J		3	203
MYDDELTON, Edward Geoffrey	P	1	265
MYER, Ernest Alex	P	1	265
MYERS, C E		3	203
MYERS, George Maurice	P	1	265
MYERS, James Wilfred		5	130
MYERS, John Flesher		4	142
MYERS, Richard Charles		4	142
MYERS, Sidney		1	265
MYHILL, Robert	P	2	233
MYLAM, Alfred Claude	P	1	265
MYLCHREEST, E		3	204
MYLES, William James	P	3	204
MYLIUS, John Kingsford		3	204
MYLNE, Euan Louis		3	204
NADIN, Arthur		4	142
NADIN, Frank		4	142
NAIRN, James		2	233
NAIRN, Walter	P	1	265
NAISBITT, George		2	233
NAISH, William Charles Gatton		1	266
NAISMITH, Andrew		2	233
NAISMITH, Percy Thomas		1	266
NANCARROW, John Vivian	P	1	266
NAPIER, Henry Lenox		2	233
NAPIER, James	P	4	142
NAPIER, Sir William Lennox		2	234
NAPIER, William		2	234
NAPIER, William		5	130
NAPPER, C W		3	204
NAPPER, Edwin		2	234
NASH, Charles Frederick Wybrow	P	4	142
NASH, Edward Radcliffe	P	1	266
NASH, Francis Henry		5	130
NASH, Francis Thomas	P	2	234
NASH, H J		3	204
NASH, Henry Whinfield		4	142
NASH, J		3	204
NASH, J		3	204
NASH, Leonard Gordon		4	142
NASH, Llewellyn Charles	P	1	266
NASH, S T		3	204
NASH, Thomas Stuart		5	130
NASH, W		3	204
NASH, William George		1	266

Name	Photo	Part No.	Page No.
NASH, William George		2	234
NASH, William Walter		5	130
NASMYTH, James Thomas Hutchinson	P	1	266
NASMYTH, John		2	234
NASON, Arthur John		2	234
NASON, John William Washington	P	3	204
NATHAN, David		4	143
NATTON, Reuben Walter	P	1	266
NAVES, Richard	P	2	234
NAYLOR, Clarence Edgar		1	267
NAYLOR, H		3	204
NAYLOR, Harry Willie		2	234
NAYLOR, Joseph		2	234
NAZARETH, John Xavier		1	267
NEAL, H B		3	204
NEAL, H H		3	204
NEAL, Harry		4	143
NEAL, Henry Joseph		1	267
NEAL, John Frederick	P	5	130
NEAL, W	P	2	234
NEAL, W		3	204
NEAL, W T		3	204
NEAL, William James		4	143
NEALE, Arthur Hill	P	2	234
NEALE, Aubrey Charles		4	143
NEALE, Colin Francis		4	143
NEALE, Edward J		2	234
NEALE, Edward W	P	5	130
NEALE, Roy Gordon King		1	267
NEALE, T		3	204
NEAME, Arthur	P	5	130
NEARS, Ernest	P	2	234
NEARY, A		3	204
NEARY, Henry Frank		1	267
NEAT, Samuel Morley Frank		3	204
NEAVE, Arundell	P	1	267
NEAVE, B R		3	204
NEAVE, Leonard Jarvis		5	130
NEAVE, W		3	204
NECK, A J		2	234
NEEDHAM, W St. C		3	204
NEEDS, Frederick Alfred		2	234
NEELY, Clive William	P	2	234
NEELY, Hugh Bertram	P	2	235
NEGUS, Albert Edward		4	143
NEGUS, George		4	143
NEIGHBOUR, Albert John		2	235
NEIGHBOUR, Sydney Richard		4	143
NEIL, Andrew Smith	P	5	130
NEILAN, Gerald Aloysius		3	204
NEILL, C		3	204
NEILL, C		3	204
NEILL, Charles		1	267
NEILL, F A		3	204
NEILL, John Thomas		1	267
NEILL, William		1	267
NEILL, William Proudfoot	P	2	235
NEILSEN, James		2	235
NEILSEN, William		2	235
NEILSON, William		1	267
NEISH, J N		3	204
NEISH, James Macpherson		5	131
NEISH, T		2	235
NEKREWES, David Smith		1	267
NELIGAN, Maurice Courtney		3	204

Name	Photo	Part No.	Page No.
NELIS, D		3	204
NELIS, James Edward Thornhill	P	1	267
NELSON, Alexander Charles	P	2	235
NELSON, David Anderson		2	235
NELSON, David Arthur	P	3	204
NELSON, Ethelbert Horatio	P	2	235
NELSON, George	P	1	267
NELSON, J		2	235
NELSON, James		2	235
NELSON, Richard James	P	2	235
NELSON, W		3	204
NELSON, William Barr	P	5	131
NEPEAN, Evan Cecil		5	131
NESBITT, J		3	204
NESBITT, Owen Hugo		2	235
NESBITT, Terence Beale	P	2	235
NESMITH, James		1	267
NESS, Gordon Stuart	P	1	267
NESS, William	P	4	143
NESSWORTHY, R		3	204
NETTLESHIP, Thomas		4	143
NEVARD, George Henry Thomas		2	235
NEVE, Basil Hovenden		1	267
NEVE, William Charles		1	267
NEVETT, Thomas Alfred	P	1	267
NEVETT, William Percy	P	1	267
NEVILE, Guy Lister		2	235
NEVILLE, G		3	204
NEVILLE, George Herbert		2	235
NEVILLE, Henry George		4	143
NEW, Alexander Herbert		1	267
NEW, C W		3	204
NEWALL, Henry		3	204
NEWALL, Jack Hainsworth Maxwell	P	2	235
NEWBERRY, James Cecil		2	235
NEWBITT, Alfred Charles		3	204
NEWBOLD, E J		3	204
NEWBOLD, T E		3	204
NEWBOLD, William		2	235
NEWBOLD, William		3	205
NEWBOULD, Sydney		5	131
NEWBROOKES, J		2	235
NEWBURY, Edward Mortimore		4	143
NEWBURY, William John		1	267
NEWBY, Charles Allan		2	236
NEWBY, George Edwin		1	267
NEWBY, J		3	205
NEWCOMBE, Thomas		1	267
NEWCOMBE, William Charles Horner		5	131
NEWELL, A		3	205
NEWELL, Charles Edward	P	2	236
NEWELL, Henry John		3	205
NEWELL, Richard Alfred Aylmer	P	2	236
NEWELL, W E		3	205
NEWELL, William George Herbert	P	4	143
NEWEY, Harry Oliver Blay	P	4	143
NEWEY, Henry		5	131
NEWHAM, Arthur John		1	267
NEWHOUSE, Matthew		5	131
NEWINGTON, Francis Reginald Hayes		4	143
NEWLAND, Frederick William		5	131
NEWLAND, Timothy		2	236
NEWLAND, William G		2	236
NEWLANDS, James		2	236
NEWLOVE, Charles		4	144

Name	Photo	Part No.	Page No.
NEWLOVE, Richard Andrew		5	131
NEWMAN, A		3	205
NEWMAN, A H		2	236
NEWMAN, Albert		2	236
NEWMAN, Alfred		2	236
NEWMAN, Alfred	P	3	205
NEWMAN, Arthur		2	236
NEWMAN, Cecil Robert		2	236
NEWMAN, Charles Henry		1	267
NEWMAN, Charles William		2	236
NEWMAN, Clement Henry		5	131
NEWMAN, Cormie Aubrey		1	267
NEWMAN, Eric Charlton		4	144
NEWMAN, Francis		1	268
NEWMAN, Frank	P	2	236
NEWMAN, H L		3	205
NEWMAN, Harry		1	268
NEWMAN, Henry		1	268
NEWMAN, Horace Frank William		4	144
NEWMAN, Horace George	P	2	236
NEWMAN, James		2	236
NEWMAN, Luke	P	3	205
NEWMAN, Nelson		2	236
NEWMAN, Richard Harry		1	268
NEWMAN, Samuel		1	268
NEWMAN, Stanley Francis		1	268
NEWMAN, Thomas Joseph		2	236
NEWMAN, W		2	236
NEWMAN, William		2	236
NEWMAN, William Grainge	P	3	205
NEWMAN, William Henry		1	268
NEWMAN, William Herbert	P	1	268
NEWMAN, William J		2	236
NEWNHAM, Alfred E		2	236
NEWPORT, Richard	P	2	236
NEWPORT, William Charles Henry		4	144
NEWPORT, William James		1	268
NEWSHAM, Charles	P	1	268
NEWSHAM, Richard		1	268
NEWSOME, Fred		3	205
NEWSOME, George Edward		2	236
NEWSOME, Reginald Horace Arthur		5	131
NEWSOME, Thomas		5	131
NEWSOME, Willie		3	205
NEWSON, Alfred John		2	236
NEWSON, F W		3	205
NEWSON, William John		2	236
NEWSTEAD, George Pope	P	1	268
NEWSUM, Clement Neill	P	3	205
NEWTH, Walter Joseph		1	268
NEWTON, Andrew		5	131
NEWTON, Arthur Leslie Garman		5	131
NEWTON, Berry William		4	144
NEWTON, Charles William	P	3	205
NEWTON, E W		3	205
NEWTON, Ernest		1	268
NEWTON, Frederick		1	268
NEWTON, George Henry		1	268
NEWTON, J		3	205
NEWTON, Richard Frederick	P	2	237
NEWTON, S		3	205
NEWTON, T		3	205
NEWTON, Thomas Henry		2	237
NEWTON, W		3	205
NEWTON, Wilfrid		3	205

Name	Photo	Part No.	Page No.	Name	Photo	Part No.	Page No.
NEWTON, William Henry		1	268	NICOL, Walter		1	270
NIBLETT, Henry		1	268	NICOLL, Alexander		2	237
NICE, Walter		4	144	NICOLL, Francis John	P	2	237
NICHOLAS, George Arthur	P	1	268	NICOLL, James Watson		5	132
NICHOLAS, Robert Stanley		1	268	NICOLL, James Watson		5	132
NICHOLL, Christopher Benoni	P	1	268	NICOLLS, Gustavus George Albert		4	144
NICHOLLS, Douglas William Arthur	P	3	205	NICOLSON, John	P	1	270
NICHOLLS, E A		3	206	NICOLSON, Paul		5	132
NICHOLLS, F		3	206	NICOLSON, Robert		4	144
NICHOLLS, Frank		5	131	NIGHTINGALE, Henry John		4	144
NICHOLLS, Frederick		2	237	NIGHTINGALE, Richard	P	2	237
NICHOLLS, G R		3	206	NIGHTINGALE, William Arthur		1	270
NICHOLLS, H		3	206	NILSON, Cecil Edgar		1	270
NICHOLLS, Harry		1	268	NIMMO, John Cumming		5	132
NICHOLLS, Henry Arthur	P	1	268	NISBET, A		3	206
NICHOLLS, Ivo Nixon		3	206	NISBET, Edward David Murray		5	133
NICHOLLS, John William Ernest		1	269	NISBET, Thomas Holmes	P	2	237
NICHOLLS, Thomas Rocliffe	P	5	132	NISBET, William		2	237
NICHOLLS, William Charles		1	269	NISBET, William Thom	P	3	206
NICHOLLS, William James		1	269	NIVEN, Alan Scott	P	4	144
NICHOLLS-JONES, Thomas Cyril	P	4	96	NIVEN, James Douglas	P	2	237
NICHOLS, Alselan Buchanan	P	5	132	NIVEN, John	P	2	237
NICHOLS, Charles		2	237	NIX, Charles John		5	133
NICHOLS, Charles	P	3	206	NIX, George	P	4	145
NICHOLS, Clifford		4	144	NIX, George	P	4	145
NICHOLS, Frank	P	3	206	NIX, Richard Walter	P	4	145
NICHOLS, Lionel Walter		4	144	NIXON, Francis Eugene Archer		1	270
NICHOLS, Walter		1	269	NIXON, Gerard Ferrers	P	1	270
NICHOLS, William Henry		1	269	NIXON, Henry Edward		2	238
NICHOLS, William James	P	5	132	NIXON, James		2	238
NICHOLSON, Arthur Knight		1	269	NIXON, John		2	238
NICHOLSON, Basil Lee	P	1	269	NIXON, John		4	145
NICHOLSON, Benjamin		5	132	NIXON, Joseph Harold		4	145
NICHOLSON, Bruce Hills	P	5	132	NIXON, William		1	270
NICHOLSON, Charles Gillan		2	237	NOAD, Percival Henry		5	133
NICHOLSON, Colin		2	237	NOAH, Frederick George Stanley		5	133
NICHOLSON, David Beveridge	P	1	269	NOAH, Henry L		5	133
NICHOLSON, Donald		3	206	NOAH, Joseph		5	133
NICHOLSON, Edward Charles		5	132	NOALL, Ernest Bertram		5	133
NICHOLSON, Edward Hills	P	5	132	NOBBS, William Robert		1	270
NICHOLSON, Eric Newzah		4	144	NOBES, C		3	206
NICHOLSON, G R		3	206	NOBLE, A J		2	238
NICHOLSON, George Crosfield Norris		3	206	NOBLE, Alexander		2	238
NICHOLSON, John Beveridge	P	1	269	NOBLE, Alexander		2	238
NICHOLSON, John Charles		1	269	NOBLE, Alfred Ernest		2	238
NICHOLSON, Lawrence Cail	P	1	269	NOBLE, Charles		5	133
NICHOLSON, Leonard Sampson	P	1	269	NOBLE, Charles Crawford	P	1	270
NICHOLSON, R		2	237	NOBLE, Charles Thomas		3	207
NICHOLSON, Randolph Renwick		5	132	NOBLE, Cornelius	P	1	270
NICHOLSON, Victor Hills	P	5	132	NOBLE, George		1	270
NICHOLSON, Walter Adams	P	3	206	NOBLE, George		1	270
NICHOLSON, Walter David	P	4	144	NOBLE, Jack Edward		1	270
NICHOLSON, William		3	206	NOBLE, James		2	238
NICKELLS, G		3	206	NOBLE, James	P	2	238
NICKLIN, George		1	269	NOBLE, Robert		1	270
NICKOLDS, H W E		3	206	NOBLE, Thomas		1	270
NICKOLLS, Ben Stanley	P	3	206	NOBLE, William		2	238
NICOL, Alexander		1	269	NOBLE, William Smyth Jackson Noble		4	145
NICOL, Charles Ashmore	P	4	144	NOCKOLDS, Owen		2	238
NICOL, Charles H		2	237	NOEL, Francis Methuen		4	145
NICOL, Frank		1	269	NOEL, Herbert Bishop		1	270
NICOL, George		2	237	NOLAN, Myles Patrick		1	270
NICOL, George		4	144	NOON, J		2	238
NICOL, Hugh John	P	1	269	NOOTT, Mervyn	P	1	270
NICOL, Robert		3	206	NORBURY, Thomas Spinks		5	133

Name	Photo	Part No.	Page No.
NORLEY, Sidney Henry		1	270
NORMAN, Albert Edmund	P	1	270
NORMAN, Arthur Henry		2	238
NORMAN, Edward		1	270
NORMAN, Ernest		2	238
NORMAN, Errington Hounsome		1	270
NORMAN, Frederick William		4	145
NORMAN, George Henry	P	2	238
NORMAN, George Phillip		3	207
NORMAN, Henry Lionel		2	238
NORMAN, J		3	207
NORMAN, James		5	133
NORMAN, John		2	238
NORMAN, Robert		1	270
NORMAN, Robert		1	270
NORMAN, Wilfred		2	238
NORMAND, Harry		2	238
NORMANLY, Martin		1	270
NORMANSELL, John	P	3	207
NORRIS, Alexander James		5	133
NORRIS, F		2	238
NORRIS, F C		3	207
NORRIS, Frederick Charles		3	207
NORRIS, George Crossley		1	270
NORRIS, Harry		2	238
NORRIS, Oswald Mark	P	1	271
NORRIS, Reginald Hayden		1	271
NORRIS, Robert		1	271
NORRIS, Robert		4	145
NORRIS, W		2	238
NORRIS, William		1	271
NORRISH, Thomas Theodore	P	2	238
NORSWORTHY, Edward Cuthbert	P	1	271
NORTH, Arthur		1	271
NORTH, Charles Napier	P	1	271
NORTH, Ernest		4	145
NORTH, Frederick Albert		1	271
NORTH, Harold Alfred	P	5	133
NORTH, Hugh Frederic	P	2	238
NORTH, William Thomas		1	271
NORTHCOTE, George Barons	P	2	239
NORTHCOTT, Albert Henry	P	1	271
NORTHCOTT, George Henry		4	145
NORTHCOTT, Henry Hans Macfarlane		4	145
NORTHCOTT, Thomas George		4	145
NORTHEY, Alfred	P	1	271
NORTHORPE, Montague Arthur	P	2	239
NORTON, C		2	239
NORTON, Eric	P	2	239
NORTON, Eric	P	3	207
NORTON, H W		3	207
NORTON, Henry Hall		3	207
NORTON, Horace John		4	145
NORTON, Leonard Stewart	P	2	239
NORTON, Richard Conyers		4	145
NORTON, William George	P	1	272
NORVAL, Alexander		4	146
NOTMAN, John		2	239
NOTT, Charles		2	239
NOTT, Charles		2	239
NOTT, Ralph		3	207
NOTTON, Harry Guy		1	272
NOURISH, Thomas Alderman	P	1	272
NOVELL, William		1	272
NOWAK, W		2	239

Name	Photo	Part No.	Page No.
NOWERS, John Anthony	P	3	207
NOYES, Claude Robert Barton		4	146
NOYSE, Francis Golding		3	207
NUNN, Arthur William		1	272
NUNN, Frank Alfred		1	272
NUNN, Frederick William		1	272
NUNN, H S		4	146
NUNN, Henry		2	239
NUNN, Herbert John		2	239
NUNN, Mervyn Henry	P	1	272
NUNNERLEY, Willson Kenwick	P	3	207
NUTCHER, Montague Cyril		1	272
NUTHALL, John Constantine		4	146
NUTLEY, Walter Ernest		4	146
NUTT, Arthur		3	207
NUTT, L		4	146
NUTTALL, Harry Norbury		4	146
NUTTALL, Ino Laurence Kennedy	P	2	239
NUTTALL, John		2	239
NUTTALL, Richard Omerod		4	146
NUTTER, Charles		2	239
NUTTER, William	P	5	133
OAKDEN, Arthur William	P	5	133
OAKDEN, Edward Ralph	P	3	207
OAKELEY, Francis Eckley	P	1	272
OAKES, Alexander Montague	P	1	272
OAKES, George		4	146
OAKES, Henry Kellett	P	2	239
OAKES, J		4	146
OAKES, James		2	240
OAKES, Orbell		1	272
OAKES, Richard		1	272
OAKES, Samuel	P	3	207
OAKLEY, Francis A G		4	146
OAKLEY, George Howard		1	272
OAKLEY, John Edward		4	146
OAKMAN, G H		3	208
OATES, Henry		2	240
OATES, John Stanley	P	4	146
OATLEY, Philip		3	208
OATWAY, Thomas William		2	240
OBBARD, Laurence Charles		2	240
O'BEIRNE, Arthur James Louis	P	4	146
O'BEIRNE, John Ingram Mullaniffe	P	4	146
O'BRIEN, Charles	P	3	208
O'BRIEN, Hugh Conor Henry	P	1	272
O'BRIEN, J J		3	208
O'BRIEN, James Joseph		1	272
O'BRIEN, John		2	240
O'BRIEN, Richard Stanton		2	240
O'BRIEN, William		2	240
O'BRIEN-BUTLER, Charles Paget		2	52
O'CALLAGHAN, Duncan Mckay Macdonald		1	273
O'CALLAGHAN, James	P	2	240
O'CALLAGHAN, John Charles	P	4	146
OCHS, Ronald Philip	P	1	273
OCKWELL, Albert Henry	P	5	133
O'CONNELL, W		3	208
O'CONNOR, J		3	208
O'CONNOR, Maurice		2	240
O'CONNOR, Samuel		2	240
O'CONNOR, T		3	208
O'CONNOR, William Turlough		4	147
ODDY, James Leslie	P	5	133
ODDY, Joseph Ethelbert		1	273

Name	Photo	Part No.	Page No.		Name	Photo	Part No.	Page No.
ODELL, Albert William		4	147		**OLIVER,** Percy Frederick		1	274
ODELL, Robert Eric	P	3	208		**OLIVER,** Richard Edward Deane		3	209
ODELL, William		3	208		**OLIVER,** Robert Kerr		4	147
ODGERS, Frederick W		2	240		**OLIVER,** Robert Young		5	134
ODGERS, Nicholas		1	273		**OLIVER,** Timothy		2	240
ODLING, Eric Robert Meade	P	1	273		**OLIVER,** Walter Herbert	P	4	147
O'DONNELL, Denis		2	240		**OLIVER,** William		5	134
O'DONNELL, J		2	240		**OLIVIER,** Jasper George	P	2	241
O'DONNELL, Martin		1	273		**OLLETT,** J B		3	209
O'DONOGHUE, Herbert Vincent Finbarr	P	5	134		**OLLEY,** Matt		1	274
O'DRISCOLL, L		2	240		**OLLIFF,** William	P	1	274
O'DRISCOLL, Laurence	P	2	240		**O'LOUGHLIN,** J		3	209
OFFER, Henry Walter		2	240		**OLSEN,** John Harold		2	241
O'FLYNN, Michael Joseph	P	4	147		**O'MALLEY,** Edward		1	274
OGDEN, Charles Fraser	P	5	134		**O'MEARA,** Leon Alfred	P	3	209
OGDEN, William G		2	240		**OMMANNEY,** Alfred Erasmus Stuart	P	2	241
OGILVIE, George Edward		5	134		**O'NEIL,** Hugh		2	241
OGILVIE, W		2	240		**O'NEILL,** Hugh Joseph	P	5	134
OGILVIE, William Edmond		2	240		**O'NEILL,** J		3	209
OGLESBY, H		3	208		**O'NEILL,** John Arthur	P	2	241
O'GRADY, Daniel		2	240		**O'NEILL,** Samuel		1	274
O'GRAM, Charles		1	273		**O'NEILL,** W		2	241
OGSTON, Alexander Lockhart		5	134		**ONIONS,** Arthur Thomas		2	241
O'HAIRE, David	P	1	273		**ONSLOW,** Arthur Gerald		2	241
O'HALLORAN, Sylvester North East		4	147		**ONSLOW,** Arthur Gerald		4	147
O'HARA, E		3	208		**ONSLOW,** Brian Walton	P	1	274
O'HARA, E		3	208		**ONSLOW,** Milo Richard Beaumont		4	147
O'HARA, Henry Desmond		1	273		**OPIE,** Arthur George		1	274
O'HARA, M		3	208		**OPIE,** William Edwin		1	274
O'HARA, Patrick		2	240		**ORD,** Charles Denton Moon	P	3	209
O'KEEFE, Joseph		2	240		**ORD,** Ord Ralph		3	209
O'KEEFE, William		2	240		**ORDE,** Herbert Walter Julian	P	2	241
O'KEEFFE, John		3	208		**ORDE,** John Barwick	P	3	209
O'KEEFFE, Thomas	P	1	273		**O'REILLY,** Fleming Pinkston		5	134
OKELL, Alan Amery	P	3	208		**ORFORD,** Charles Thomas	P	1	274
OKELL, Alan Amery		4	147		**ORFORD,** Stephen Mewburn	P	3	209
OLD, John Wright		4	147		**ORKNEY,** Robert	P	2	241
OLDBURY, Frederick		1	273		**ORLEBAR,** Robert Evelyn	P	1	275
OLDFIELD, Frank		4	147		**ORMAN,** A		2	241
OLDFIELD, Guy Christopher Ottley	P	1	273		**ORMANDY,** Alexander		2	241
OLDHAM, John Haslope	P	1	274		**ORMISTON,** Robert William		4	148
OLDHAM, John William Prince		2	240		**ORMISTON,** Uri John Baptie		4	148
OLDHAM, Leslie William Searles	P	1	274		**ORMROD,** Lawrence Moreland	P	3	210
OLDHAM, Llewellyn Harlope		2	240		**ORMROD,** Lawrence Moreland		4	148
OLDMAN, William		1	274		**ORMROD,** Oliver Hugh	P	3	210
OLDREWE, Percival		1	274		**ORMSBY,** William	P	2	241
OLDREY, Robert John Blatchford	P	1	274		**ORR,** David Cameron		4	148
OLDS, Cyril Austin		3	208		**ORR,** Jack Alexander Anderson		5	134
O'LEARY, William Felix Maccarthy		4	147		**ORR,** James Barbour	P	3	210
OLIVE, John		1	274		**ORR,** John		2	241
OLIVE, John		2	240		**ORR,** Robert Watson	P	1	275
OLIVER, A V		3	208		**ORR,** William		1	275
OLIVER, Albert J		2	240		**ORR,** William Mckay		5	134
OLIVER, Alfred		2	240		**ORROW,** Albert William		1	275
OLIVER, Alfred Charles		2	240		**ORSLER,** George Henry		1	275
OLIVER, Charles Henry		2	240		**ORTON,** James	P	1	275
OLIVER, David		4	147		**ORTON,** John Thomas		1	275
OLIVER, David Edgar		3	208		**OSBEN,** George Thomas		1	275
OLIVER, Ernest James		1	274		**OSBORNE,** A		3	210
OLIVER, Guy Bertram	P	3	208		**OSBORNE,** Albert Vincent		1	275
OLIVER, H		3	209		**OSBORNE,** Alexander Frank	P	2	241
OLIVER, J		3	209		**OSBORNE,** Brian	P	1	275
OLIVER, James		4	147		**OSBORNE,** Charles William		2	242
OLIVER, Job		2	240		**OSBORNE,** Fred		1	275
OLIVER, M G		3	209		**OSBORNE,** Frederick		1	275

Name	Photo	Part No.	Page No.
OSBORNE, George		2	242
OSBORNE, Herbert		2	242
OSBORNE, John		2	242
OSBORNE, John Alfred Victor	P	1	275
OSBORNE, John Henry		1	275
OSBORNE, Leslie Hall	P	1	275
OSBORNE, Mark Henry		3	210
OSBORNE, Maurice Godolphin		1	275
OSBORNE, Richard Henry		3	210
OSBORNE, Samuel		2	242
OSBORNE, William John	P	1	276
OSBORNE, William Thomas		5	134
OSBOURN, Sidney		2	242
OSBOURNE, G W J		3	210
OSGOOD, Thomas William		3	210
O'SHEA, John		2	242
O'SHEA, Michael John	P	1	276
OSMASTON, Oswald Camplyon Hutchinson		4	148
OSMOND, Ernest Herbert		1	276
OSMOND, Harold Coombs		1	276
OSPREY, Joseph		2	242
OSTLE, Joseph Daniel		5	134
O'SULLIVAN, Arthur Moore	P	1	276
OSWALD, William		5	134
OSWALD-HICKS, Harley Lionel Adrian		4	83
OTELLIE, William George		1	276
OTTLEY, Frederick W		2	242
OTTLEY, Geoffrey Claude Langdale		1	276
OTTLEY, John Lawrence Young		4	148
OTTLEY, Percy Crofts	P	3	210
OTTON, John William		2	242
OUCHTERLONY, John Palgrave Heathcote	P	3	210
OUSLEY, George		1	276
OUTHWAITE, G H		3	210
OUTRAM, Alexander Robert	P	3	210
OUZMAN, Albert Frederick		4	148
OVENDEN, Fred		2	242
OVENS, Charles Leonard	P	2	242
OVENS, H		3	210
OVENSTONE, T		3	211
OVERHAND, George		2	242
OVERTON, R		3	211
OVERY, William Henry		2	242
OWDEN, J		3	211
OWDEN, James		2	242
OWEN, Alfred Frederick		1	276
OWEN, B		3	211
OWEN, Charles		1	276
OWEN, Charles		1	276
OWEN, Charles		1	276
OWEN, Charles Vernon		4	148
OWEN, Edward Reid		1	276
OWEN, Ernest Haddon	P	1	276
OWEN, Frank James		1	276
OWEN, George Arthur		5	134
OWEN, George Webster		1	276
OWEN, Hugh	P	1	276
OWEN, John Owen		4	148
OWEN, Lewis Oswald		4	148
OWEN, Norman	P	5	135
OWEN, Norman Moore	P	1	276
OWEN, Philip Charles		2	242
OWEN, Richard Frank		4	148
OWEN, Thomas		1	276
OWEN, W		3	211

Name	Photo	Part No.	Page No.
OWEN, W C		3	211
OWEN, William Price	P	2	242
OWEN-JONES, Rhodri Deane	P	3	161
OWENS, Ernest	P	2	242
OWENS, Frank Arthur		4	148
OWENS, Herbert		4	148
OWENS, J		3	211
OWENS, John		2	242
OWENS, Levi George		2	242
OWENS, Robert		5	135
OWENS, William Henry		3	211
OWERS, Frank	P	4	148
OXENBRIDGE, George Herbert	P	1	277
OXENBURY, George Edward		4	148
OXFORD, E		3	211
OXFORD, F		3	211
OXFORD, Percy		2	242
OXLEY, James		2	242
OXLEY, Richard Stephen	P	4	149
OZANNE, Edward Graeme		1	277
PACK BERESFORD, Charles George	P	1	31
PACKARD, Henry Norrington	P	2	242
PACKARD, Walter Herbert		3	211
PACKER, Albert Edward Farvis		4	149
PACKER, Francis William George		4	149
PACKER, Reginald Charles	P	1	277
PACKER, Thomas A		2	242
PACKHAM, George	P	3	211
PACKMAN, Bert		4	149
PADDAY, William Hamilton	P	1	277
PADDOCK, George William		1	277
PADDY, Alfred		1	277
PADEN, W H		4	149
PADFIELD, A		3	211
PADGETT, Herbert		4	149
PADGETT, James Philip	P	3	211
PAGE, Albert		1	277
PAGE, Alfred		1	277
PAGE, David		1	277
PAGE, Dudley Alfred		4	149
PAGE, Edward		2	242
PAGE, Edward Clarence		4	149
PAGE, F		3	211
PAGE, Frank Oliver		2	242
PAGE, Frederick		1	277
PAGE, Frederick Jesse		2	242
PAGE, G P		3	211
PAGE, Herbert		3	211
PAGE, Jack		2	242
PAGE, James		2	242
PAGE, John		1	277
PAGE, Robert Edward		4	149
PAGE, Robert J		3	211
PAGE, T A		3	211
PAGE, Thomas		1	277
PAGE, William		2	242
PAGE, William Thomas		1	277
PAGE, William Willie		1	277
PAGET, George Godfrey Brandreth	P	1	277
PAGETT, F		3	211
PAICE, C		3	211
PAICE, Frank G		2	243
PAIN, Charles Ringwood		2	243
PAINE, Archibald		4	149
PAINE, Charles Percival	P	1	277

Name	Photo	Part No.	Page No.
PAINE, Charles William Stanley	P	1	277
PAINE, Sydney William	P	1	278
PAINE, Thomas Harry		1	278
PAINTER, Herbert Edward		4	149
PAINTIN, George Collis		4	149
PAINTIN, Shayler	P	1	278
PAISLEY, J		3	211
PAKENHAM, Charles John Wingfield		1	278
PAKENHAM, Robert Edward Michael		1	278
PAKENHAM, William Henry	P	1	278
PALETHORPE, Edwin Donald	P	5	135
PALFREY, A		2	243
PALFREY, George William		4	149
PALFREY, John Ellis		4	149
PALFREYMAN, B		3	211
PALFREYMAN, B		3	211
PALIN, Archibald Edwin		1	278
PALLANT, Herbert	P	1	278
PALLAS, Oscar		2	243
PALMER, Alfred Ernest H		2	243
PALMER, Allen Llewellen	P	2	243
PALMER, Arthur	P	5	135
PALMER, Arthur Frederick	P	4	149
PALMER, Cecil Howard	P	2	243
PALMER, Charles Ernest		4	149
PALMER, Charles William		4	149
PALMER, Edward H		2	243
PALMER, Edwin	P	4	150
PALMER, Ernest C		2	243
PALMER, Frederick		5	135
PALMER, Frederick Ernest		1	278
PALMER, George		1	278
PALMER, George		1	278
PALMER, George Edward		1	278
PALMER, Harry James		2	243
PALMER, Herbert		5	135
PALMER, Horace John		5	135
PALMER, James		2	243
PALMER, James Richard		4	150
PALMER, John		1	278
PALMER, John Joseph		1	278
PALMER, Leslie Cowper		4	150
PALMER, Maurice Weston	P	1	278
PALMER, Percy		4	150
PALMER, Percy Joseph		2	243
PALMER, Percy Victor	P	1	279
PALMER, Ronald William Poulton	P	1	279
PALMER, Samuel Edward		1	279
PALMER, Thomas		5	135
PALMER, William Henry Eyre Hollingworth	P	2	243
PALMES, Guy Nicholas		1	279
PANE, Ernest Cyril		2	243
PANKHURST, Charles H		2	243
PANNELL, William Francis		1	279
PANTER, William		2	243
PANTER-DOWNES, Edward Martin		2	104
PANTLAND, Robert William		1	279
PARAGREEN, Frederick Arthur		1	279
PARAMORE, T		3	211
PARBERY, Ernest		5	135
PARBURY, Frederick Nigel	P	2	243
PARDEW, Frank Arundel		4	150
PARDOE, Harry James		1	279
PARFITT, Archie Stanley Percy		4	150
PARFITT, Herbert Edward		1	279

Name	Photo	Part No.	Page No.
PARFITT, Mark		2	244
PARHAM, Frederick		1	279
PARISET, Auguste Gabriel	P	3	211
PARISH, Ernest Charles		2	244
PARISH, G		3	211
PARK, Frederick Andrew Ketchen		5	135
PARK, Hugh	P	2	244
PARK, James		2	244
PARK, James Fulton		4	150
PARK, John Alexander	P	3	211
PARK, John Frederick	P	5	135
PARK, John Rettie	P	5	135
PARK, Robert Thomson		4	150
PARK, St. John Lloyd		4	150
PARK, Thomas		2	244
PARKE, Walter Evelyn		1	279
PARKER, Alec Edward		3	211
PARKER, Arthur		1	279
PARKER, Basil Stewart	P	1	279
PARKER, Bertie Clarence		1	280
PARKER, Charles	P	5	136
PARKER, Charles William		1	280
PARKER, Claud Ernest Harington		4	150
PARKER, Cyril Edmund	P	1	280
PARKER, Edward Ernest		4	150
PARKER, Edward Joseph		2	244
PARKER, Ernest Albert		1	280
PARKER, F		3	211
PARKER, Francis Maitland Wyborn		2	244
PARKER, Frank Virland		1	280
PARKER, Frederick John Bush		1	280
PARKER, Frederick Neville	P	1	280
PARKER, George		5	136
PARKER, George Herbert		2	244
PARKER, Harry	P	1	280
PARKER, Harry Bottomley		1	280
PARKER, Jeffery Wimperis		2	244
PARKER, John		1	280
PARKER, John Thomas		4	150
PARKER, John William		1	280
PARKER, Joseph		1	280
PARKER, R		3	211
PARKER, Robert Burton	P	1	280
PARKER, Ronald Elphinstone	P	1	280
PARKER, Sydney		2	244
PARKER, Thomas		2	244
PARKER, W		2	244
PARKER, W H		3	211
PARKER, William		2	244
PARKER, William Leferre Oxley		4	150
PARKER, William Theodore		4	150
PARKES, Charles		1	280
PARKES, George		4	150
PARKES, Samuel	P	1	280
PARKIN, A		3	211
PARKIN, Ernest		2	244
PARKIN, Fred	P	4	150
PARKIN, Harold	P	2	244
PARKIN, J A		3	211
PARKIN, John Mail		3	211
PARKINGTON, Sidney Arthur	P	5	136
PARKINS, H H		3	211
PARKINSON, Albert		5	136
PARKINSON, Roy R		2	244
PARKINSON, W		3	211

Name	Photo	Part No.	Page No.
PARKS, George Edwin Harold	P	5	136
PARLETT, Alfred Edward		4	150
PARLOUR, A		3	211
PARMENTER, George		2	244
PARMENTER, J P		2	244
PARR, Arthur		1	281
PARR, Cecil		1	281
PARR, Charles		3	212
PARR, E		3	212
PARR, John		2	244
PARR, Sydney Langford		1	281
PARRETT, Charles Ernest		1	281
PARRISH, Richard		2	244
PARRISS, Walter Frederick	P	1	281
PARROTT, William		2	244
PARRY, A		3	212
PARRY, Albert Edward		5	136
PARRY, Albert Lewellyn		4	151
PARRY, Arthur Croose	P	1	281
PARRY, Benjamin		4	151
PARRY, Charles		4	151
PARRY, Frank		5	136
PARRY, G		3	212
PARRY, James Herbert		1	281
PARRY, Norman Cecil	P	1	281
PARRY, Richard		2	244
PARRY, William John		3	212
PARRY, William Thomas		4	151
PARSONS, A		3	212
PARSONS, Charles		2	245
PARSONS, Charles Francis	P	1	281
PARSONS, Desmond Clere	P	3	212
PARSONS, Edward Joseph		1	281
PARSONS, Edward William		2	245
PARSONS, Edwin Stuart Thomas		1	281
PARSONS, Eric King	P	3	212
PARSONS, Ernest		4	151
PARSONS, Fred		2	245
PARSONS, G		3	212
PARSONS, George		2	245
PARSONS, George	P	4	151
PARSONS, George Edgar		3	212
PARSONS, James Benjamin		2	245
PARSONS, Joseph Frederick Leslie	P	3	212
PARSONS, Joseph Joshua		4	151
PARSONS, Milton Frank		4	151
PARSONS, O		3	212
PARSONS, Percy		2	245
PARSONS, Robert E		2	245
PARSONS, W		3	212
PARSONS, W		3	212
PARSONS, W A		3	212
PARSONS, W C		2	245
PARSONS, W J		3	212
PARSONS, William		1	281
PARSONS, William		2	245
PARSONS, William Harry		1	281
PARTINGTON, John Bertram		3	212
PARTRIDGE, Charles Burnett	P	1	281
PARTRIDGE, Charles Henry	P	3	212
PARTRIDGE, Geoffrey Dorman	P	1	281
PARTRIDGE, George Arthur		3	212
PARTRIDGE, Henry Mears		4	151
PARTRIDGE, Thomas Josiah		1	281
PARTRIDGE, Walter		4	151
PARTRIDGE, Wilfred Issell		4	151
PASCOE, James		4	151
PASHLEY, William Stanley		4	151
PASKELL, Arthur		2	245
PASQUILL, Samuel John		2	245
PASS, H		3	212
PASSMORE, Sam	P	4	151
PASSY, De Lacy Wolrich	P	2	245
PASSY, Logan Deare	P	2	245
PATCH, Sidney Richard		2	245
PATCHETT, William Ivens		4	151
PATE, William Charles		4	151
PATEMAN, William	P	1	281
PATER, Hugh	P	3	212
PATERSON, Alastair Finlay	P	1	281
PATERSON, Andrew		2	245
PATERSON, Charles		3	212
PATERSON, Donald	P	1	281
PATERSON, Douglas William	P	4	151
PATERSON, George		4	152
PATERSON, George		4	152
PATERSON, James		4	152
PATERSON, James French	P	2	245
PATERSON, James Walter	P	4	152
PATERSON, John Agar		1	282
PATERSON, John Mclellan Stewart	P	1	282
PATERSON, Norman Keith		4	152
PATERSON, Peter		2	245
PATERSON, Richard Eadson	P	2	245
PATERSON, Robert Durward		4	152
PATERSON, W		3	212
PATIENCE, George		1	282
PATON, C		3	212
PATON, Daniel		3	212
PATON, Frederick William		4	152
PATON, George Alexander Lechmere		2	245
PATON, George Henry Tatham	P	4	152
PATON, Hugh		2	245
PATON, Hugh Dunlop	P	5	136
PATON, J		2	245
PATON, J		2	245
PATON, James		3	212
PATON, John Edward	P	1	282
PATON, Norman Giles		4	152
PATON, Peter		2	245
PATON, Peter Fleming		4	152
PATON, W		3	212
PATON, W		3	212
PATON, William		2	245
PATON, William Green		4	152
PATRICK, Francis Alexander	P	1	282
PATRICK, Fred		1	282
PATRICK, James		1	282
PATSON, William		2	245
PATTEN, Alexander		4	152
PATTEN, Edward Samuel		1	282
PATTEN, H		3	212
PATTEN, Joseph		4	152
PATTENDEN, William		2	246
PATTERSON, Alexander	P	1	282
PATTERSON, Alexander		1	282
PATTERSON, Charles Cox		4	152
PATTERSON, Cyril James		1	282
PATTERSON, George Holbrook	P	3	213
PATTERSON, Hugh Cecil	P	5	136

Name	Photo	Part No.	Page No.
PATTERSON, J		3	213
PATTERSON, John Headley		1	282
PATTERSON, Lessels Malcolm		4	152
PATTERSON, Reginald Charles		4	152
PATTERSON, S		3	213
PATTERSON, William Alexander Duncan		4	152
PATTINSON, Hugh Lee	P	1	282
PATTISON, John George	P	5	136
PATTISON, Norman Leslie		4	153
PATTISON, Ramsden John James		4	153
PATTLE, Alfred Frank		3	213
PATTLE, Ernest		1	282
PATTON, William		1	283
PAUGHER, William Andrew		1	294
PAUL, Arthur Reginald		4	153
PAUL, Gavin		1	283
PAUL, George Thomas		1	283
PAUL, John Mcneil		4	153
PAUL, O		3	213
PAUL, Richard		4	153
PAUL, Robert		1	283
PAUL, Sydney Sugg		4	153
PAUL, William Henry Bowey		1	283
PAULET, Cecil Henry	P	2	246
PAULL, Alan Drysdale	P	1	283
PAULL, F G		3	213
PAULL, Henry Baynham	P	2	246
PAUS, Oscar Lionel	P	3	213
PAVELIN, T W		3	213
PAVELY, Horace G		2	246
PAVEY, Albert Victor		3	213
PAVEY, Charles		1	283
PAVIER, William John		2	246
PAVITT, C W W		3	213
PAVITT, Stephen Arthur		1	283
PAVLOSKY, Frederick		1	283
PAXTON, Hugh		3	213
PAXTON, James		2	246
PAXTON, William	P	4	153
PAYNE, A		2	246
PAYNE, A		3	213
PAYNE, A		3	213
PAYNE, Albert		2	246
PAYNE, Albert		2	246
PAYNE, Albert G		2	246
PAYNE, Albert John		1	283
PAYNE, Arthur James		1	283
PAYNE, C A		3	213
PAYNE, Charles Geraint Christopher		1	283
PAYNE, E		3	213
PAYNE, Ernest		2	246
PAYNE, Ernest	P	3	213
PAYNE, Ernest Alfred		1	283
PAYNE, F		3	213
PAYNE, Frederick Albert		2	246
PAYNE, G		2	246
PAYNE, G		3	213
PAYNE, Harold George	P	2	246
PAYNE, Harry		2	246
PAYNE, J		3	213
PAYNE, James Humphrey Allan	P	4	153
PAYNE, John Henry		1	283
PAYNE, John James	P	1	283
PAYNE, Richard		2	246
PAYNE, Richard		4	153

Name	Photo	Part No.	Page No.
PAYNE, S		3	213
PAYNE, T G		3	213
PAYNE, W		3	213
PAYNE, Walter James	P	4	153
PAYNE, William Henry		2	246
PAYNE-GALLWEY, Frankland Maurice Hylton		3	109
PAYNE-GALLWEY, Philip Francis		1	146
PAYNTER, Charles Theodore		4	153
PAYNTER, L		3	213
PAYTON, Charles Mervyn		1	283
PAYTON, W		3	213
PEACE, Ernest S		2	246
PEACE, Henry Arthur Vernon	P	3	213
PEACE, Hubert Kirkby		1	283
PEACE, Josiah		4	153
PEACH, G		3	213
PEACH, William Henry		2	246
PEACOCK, Arthur		4	153
PEACOCK, Edward Daniel		1	283
PEACOCK, George Henry		2	246
PEACOCK, Joseph Moffat	P	1	283
PEACOCK, Richard		2	246
PEACOCK, Robert Archibald		3	213
PEAK, William		2	246
PEAKE, Cecil Gerald Wyatt	P	1	283
PEAKE, Colin	P	1	283
PEAKE, G		3	213
PEAKE, Henry Arthur Wyatt		2	246
PEAKE, Kenneth John Wyatt		2	246
PEAL, Samuel W		2	247
PEAPELL, Edward T		2	247
PEARCE, A R		3	213
PEARCE, Albert		2	247
PEARCE, Alfred	P	1	284
PEARCE, Arthur		2	247
PEARCE, B		4	153
PEARCE, Bernard Samuel		4	153
PEARCE, Charles Ambrose		4	154
PEARCE, Charles Edward		2	247
PEARCE, Dudley Hogarth	P	1	284
PEARCE, Edward Charles Henry	P	1	284
PEARCE, G		3	214
PEARCE, Geoffrey Vincent		1	284
PEARCE, George		2	247
PEARCE, George James Hunnerkin	P	3	214
PEARCE, Harold Charles		4	154
PEARCE, Harry Cecil		1	284
PEARCE, Henry F		2	247
PEARCE, Jesse		2	247
PEARCE, John Albert		1	284
PEARCE, Joseph		4	154
PEARCE, Joseph Robert		4	154
PEARCE, S		3	214
PEARCE, Thomas Edward	P	5	137
PEARCE, Walter	P	5	137
PEARCE, Walter Henry		4	154
PEARCE, William		2	247
PEARCE, William Henry Srodzinski		4	154
PEARCE, William Thomas Collier		4	154
PEARCEY, Alfred Stephen		1	284
PEARCEY, R H		3	214
PEARL, C		3	214
PEARMAN, Albert Edward		4	154
PEARMAN, E H		2	247
PEARS, A R		3	214

Name	Photo	Part No.	Page No.
PEARS, J		3	214
PEARS, Norman		4	154
PEARS, Stuart		1	284
PEARSON, A		3	214
PEARSON, Arthur Harold	P	2	247
PEARSON, C		3	214
PEARSON, C		3	214
PEARSON, C S		3	214
PEARSON, Charles Hugh	P	3	214
PEARSON, Charles Richard		2	247
PEARSON, E		3	214
PEARSON, Ernest Lemuel		4	154
PEARSON, Frank		3	214
PEARSON, Frederick Phillips	P	1	284
PEARSON, Hubert Reeve		3	214
PEARSON, John		2	247
PEARSON, John		2	247
PEARSON, John William		4	154
PEARSON, Kenneth Herbert		4	154
PEARSON, Martin Guy	P	4	154
PEARSON, R		2	247
PEARSON, Robert		2	247
PEARSON, S		2	247
PEARSON, S		3	214
PEARSON, Sydney John		1	284
PEARSON, Thomas William		4	154
PEARSON, W		3	214
PEARSON, Walter		2	247
PEARSON, William Ransome	P	1	284
PEARSON, William Robert (Alias William Clark)		2	247
PEART, George		1	284
PEART, Stanley Brace	P	1	284
PEART, Walter		2	247
PEASE, Christopher York	P	4	154
PEASE, Oswald Allen		3	214
PEASE, Oswald Allen		4	154
PEASTON, Frederick William	P	3	214
PEAT, David		5	137
PEAT, William Mcdonald		1	285
PEATE, R L		3	214
PEATTIE, David		4	154
PEAVOT, Arthur James		4	154
PEBERDY, George		2	247
PECK, A		3	214
PECK, Edwin Joseph		2	247
PECK, Frederick William		3	214
PECK, George		2	247
PECK, George Herbert		4	154
PECKER, Henry Cyril	P	1	285
PECKHAM, Bertram		1	285
PECKSON, Joseph William		1	285
PEDDEL, Sydney Edgar	P	1	285
PEDDER, Percy James		1	285
PEDEN, J		3	214
PEEBLES, A		2	247
PEEBLES, John Adair	P	5	137
PEEK, Herbert Thain		4	155
PEEL, Alan Ralph	P	1	285
PEEL, Charles Edward		2	247
PEEL, Henry Charles	P	5	137
PEEL, Robert Lloyd	P	3	214
PEEL, Walter Sidney		5	137
PEELING, Harry Courtland		1	285
PEER, J J		3	214
PEERLESS, Charles Stephen	P	2	247

Name	Photo	Part No.	Page No.
PEERS, Charles Edgar	P	4	155
PEET, Frederick William	P	3	214
PEET, John Edward Grimston	P	1	285
PEEVOR, Howard Edward		3	215
PEGDEN, Charles Frederick		4	155
PEGG, T W		4	155
PEIRCE, William Alec		4	155
PELHAM, Henry Alfred		1	285
PELHAM, Hon. Herbert Lyttleton	P	1	285
PELHAM, J		3	215
PELL, Albert Julian		4	155
PELLETT, George Albert Victor		1	286
PELLETT, Henry		2	247
PELLING, H L		3	215
PELTON, Kenneth Kemble		4	155
PEMBER, William E		2	247
PEMBERTON, Francis Percy Campbell	P	2	247
PEMBERTON, George		3	215
PEMBERTON, J		3	215
PENDALL, William Albert		1	286
PENDER, James (Hamish) Granger Geils	P	1	286
PENDERS, Joseph		2	247
PENFOLD, George Henry		1	286
PENFOLD, Jeffery Bradley (Jerry)	P	2	247
PENFOLD, Leonard		2	247
PENGELLEY, Harold		1	286
PENHALIGON, Richard Charles		3	215
PENMAN, R		2	247
PENMAN, William		1	286
PENN, Alfred Edward		1	286
PENN, Arthur	P	2	248
PENN, Joseph Lively		1	286
PENN, Lewis Sydney		1	286
PENNELLS, Charles Percy		1	286
PENNEY, John Edwin		1	286
PENNEY, Victor		5	137
PENNEY, William H		2	248
PENNINGTON, Arthur Duncan		3	215
PENNINGTON, F		3	215
PENNINGTON, T		2	248
PENNY, Henry		1	286
PENNY, Horace James		4	155
PENNY, William	P	1	286
PENNY J,		2	248
PENNYCOOK, John		2	248
PENSON, Reginald	P	1	287
PENTECOST, Leonard Denyer		4	155
PENTER, Edward Sydney		1	287
PEOVER, James William	P	4	155
PEPPER, James William Thomas		1	287
PEPPER, Wilfred Charles Vivian		4	155
PEPPIATT, J		3	215
PEPPIATT, William Henry	P	1	287
PEPPIN, W T		3	215
PEPYS, Francis	P	1	287
PEPYS, John	P	1	287
PEPYS, Reginald Whitmore	P	1	287
PERCIVAL, George		4	155
PERCIVAL, John James		5	137
PERCIVAL, William Thayer		4	155
PERCY, Algernon William	P	2	248
PERCY, Henry Edward	P	1	287
PERCY, Leonard Sidney		1	287
PERCY, Sidney		2	248
PERCY, William Reginald Minshull	P	1	287

Name	Photo	Part No.	Page No.
PHILLIPS, George		4	157
PHILLIPS, George Henry	P	1	289
PHILLIPS, Harold	P	3	217
PHILLIPS, Harold Llewelyn		4	157
PHILLIPS, Henry		1	290
PHILLIPS, Henry		2	249
PHILLIPS, Henry Bruce		4	157
PHILLIPS, J		2	249
PHILLIPS, J		3	217
PHILLIPS, J H		3	217
PHILLIPS, John		2	249
PHILLIPS, Joseph Gilbert	P	4	157
PHILLIPS, Leslie	P	2	249
PHILLIPS, O		3	217
PHILLIPS, Owen Sherwood		2	249
PHILLIPS, P		3	217
PHILLIPS, Ralph Noel		1	290
PHILLIPS, Richard Morville	P	3	217
PHILLIPS, Robert John		5	137
PHILLIPS, Stephen Arla		1	290
PHILLIPS, Sydney Vernon		3	217
PHILLIPS, Thomas Arthur		2	249
PHILLIPS, Thomas Harold	P	1	290
PHILLIPS, W F		3	217
PHILLIPS, Walter Henry Sherburn		3	217
PHILLIPS, William		1	290
PHILLIPS, William Arthur		4	157
PHILLIPS, William Howell	P	3	217
PHILLIPS, William John		3	217
PHILLIPSON, Albert		1	290
PHILLIPSON, Leo George		4	157
PHILLIS, Henry John		1	290
PHILLPOTTS, D W		3	217
PHILPOT, Godfrey	P	2	249
PHILPOTT, Horace Henry		1	290
PHILPOTT, Richard		2	249
PHILPOTT, Walter		1	290
PHIPPER, William H		2	249
PHIPPS, Edward Walter	P	2	249
PHIPPS, George Edward		4	157
PHIPPS, Russell Constantine Charles	P	3	217
PHIPPS, William Hewett		1	290
PHORSON, Douglas Stuart	P	3	217
PICKARD, J T		2	249
PICKARD, Nathaniel		2	249
PICKARD, Reginald Gilbert		3	218
PICKARD, Reginald William	P	4	157
PICKARD, Samuel		4	157
PICKARD, Walter Edward		2	249
PICKBURN, Frank		1	290
PICKEN, James		4	157
PICKERING, Basil Horace		2	249
PICKERING, Charles		4	157
PICKERING, Edward John		1	290
PICKERING, J G		3	218
PICKERING, T		2	250
PICKERING, Thomas George		1	290
PICKERSGILL, Albert Edward		1	290
PICKERSGILL, James Henry		4	157
PICKERSGILL-CUNLIFFE, John Cunliffe	P	1	103
PICKERSGILL-CUNLIFFE, John Reynolds		2	87
PICKETT, Arthur Sidney		4	157
PICKETT, Frank Ernest		4	158
PICKETT, Henry James		2	250
PICKETT, James		2	250

Name	Photo	Part No.	Page No.
PICKFORD, Thomson		4	158
PICKTHALL, John Roper		5	137
PICKUP, John Burton		2	250
PICKWELL, James E		2	250
PICTON, Ernest		3	218
PICTON-WARLOW, Arthur		4	225
PICTON-WARLOW, Wilfred	P	1	367
PIDGEON, Alfred		2	250
PIDGEON, George		4	158
PIDWELL, Charles		1	290
PIDWELL, Charles James		1	290
PIERCE, Richard Edward	P	2	250
PIERCE, Thomas George		5	137
PIERCY, H		3	218
PIERCY, Wilfrid Ashton	P	2	250
PIERSON, D		3	218
PIERSON, John Flanders	P	2	250
PIESSE, Charles James		2	250
PIGDEN, Arthur Ronald	P	1	290
PIGE, Herbert Joseph		3	218
PIGGETT, William Richard	P	5	138
PIGGOTT, Frederick Cecil Holman		4	158
PIGGOTT, J		3	218
PIGGOTT, Thomas Charles Herlec		5	138
PIGGOTT, William Frederick		4	158
PIGOT-MOODIE, Charles Alfred	P	1	257
PIGOTT, Gerald Wellesley	P	1	290
PIKE, Bert		2	250
PIKE, Charles Wightman		4	158
PIKE, Clement Everard Gregory	P	2	250
PIKE, Clifford Edric Hurstwood		4	158
PIKE, James Carey	P	2	250
PIKE, R		3	218
PIKE, S		2	250
PILBEAM, Alfred		2	250
PILBEAM, Lewis		1	290
PILBROW, Frederick Samuel		4	158
PILCHER, Thomas Percy	P	1	290
PILGRIM, William Thomas (Alias Beams)		3	218
PILKINGTON, George William		4	158
PILLAR, Samuel		1	290
PILLAR, William Henry		1	290
PILLEY, Ernest		2	250
PILLEY, Frank	P	4	158
PILLING, Walter		1	290
PIM, Mortimer	P	2	250
PIMBLETT, C		3	218
PIMM, Albert		2	250
PINCH, Thomas		2	250
PINCHES, Norman Gordon	P	2	251
PINCHIN, John Herbert	P	1	290
PINDER, Charles Nicholson		5	138
PINDRED, G		3	218
PINER, Henry John		4	158
PINFOLD, Percy C		2	251
PINK, George W		2	251
PINK, H E		3	218
PINK, Harold William	P	2	251
PINK, Joseph		1	290
PINK, Sidney Edward		1	290
PINKARD, Frank		4	158
PINKARD, S		3	218
PINKARD, Walter		4	158
PINKS, J S		2	251
PINLDEBURY, Walter		1	290

Name	Photo	Part No.	Page No.
PINN, Edwin Charles French	P	5	138
PINNEY, John Charles Adderley	P	4	158
PINNEY, Kingsley William Guy		4	158
PINNIGER, Wilfred James	P	3	218
PINTO, Harold Edward		4	158
PIPER, Edward James		1	290
PIPER, Frederick Mostyn		2	251
PIPER, George		4	158
PIPER, George M		2	251
PIPER, Malcolm		2	251
PIPER, William Henry Sage	P	5	138
PIRIE, George Matthew		5	138
PITCAIRN, Hugh Francis		4	159
PITCHER, Victor Richard Thomas		4	159
PITCHER, William George		4	159
PITCHFORD, Charles Arthur		3	218
PITCHFORD, Samuel		2	251
PITHER, James Herbert		1	290
PITKIN, Stanley		1	291
PITMAN, Horace Frank	P	5	138
PITMAN, R H E		3	218
PITT, George Robert		1	291
PITT, George Walter		2	251
PITT, Horace William		4	159
PITT, John		1	291
PITTAM, J		3	218
PITTS TUCKER, Cecil Mortimer	P	1	355
PITWOOD, H		3	218
PLANK, Frank	P	2	251
PLANK, William	P	2	251
PLANT, David		2	251
PLANT, Herbert	P	3	218
PLANT, Holford Charles Fourdrinier		4	159
PLASKETT, Herbert		4	159
PLATER, Joseph		2	251
PLATER, William John	P	1	291
PLATT, William		5	138
PLAYFAIR, Hon. Lyon George Henry Lyon	P	1	291
PLAYFAIR, Lambert	P	1	291
PLEACE, William George		1	291
PLEWIS, Oscar George		4	159
PLEYDELL-BOUVERIE, Jacob Edward	P	1	45
PLOWMAN, Charles Hugh		4	159
PLOWS, Edwin		3	218
PLUCK, William Henry	P	5	138
PLUMB, Arthur Edward		1	291
PLUMB, William		1	291
PLUMBER, George Alfred	P	5	138
PLUME, George		1	291
PLUMMER, Archibald Alfred		1	291
PLUMMER, Arthur Henry	P	1	291
PLUMMER, E		4	159
PLUMMER, L		4	159
PLUMPTON, Edward Hubert		4	159
PLUNKETT, Gerald	P	1	291
POCOCK, Alfred		2	251
POCOCK, Frank William		1	291
POCOCK, Harold Francis	P	5	138
POCOCK, Leonard		2	251
POCOCK, William Jonathan		1	292
PODD, John Edmund	P	1	292
PODMORE, Hubert		4	159
POINTER, William		1	292
POLE, George	P	2	251
POLE-CAREW, Wymond Nicholas Richard		4	26

Name	Photo	Part No.	Page No.
POLING, Charles William		1	292
POLKINGHORN, George Dennis	P	2	251
POLLARD, Arthur James		2	251
POLLARD, Clifford		1	292
POLLARD, Edward Branch	P	1	292
POLLARD, Frederick		2	251
POLLARD, Geoffrey Blemell	P	1	292
POLLARD, Herbert Edward		4	159
POLLARD, Howard		1	292
POLLARD, R		2	251
POLLARD, Robert		2	251
POLLARD, William	P	2	251
POLLEY, Alfred Charles		1	292
POLLEY, Harry	P	1	292
POLLOCK, A		2	251
POLLOCK, Frederick Robert	P	1	292
POLLOCK, Louis	P	5	138
POLLOCK, Martin Viner	P	1	292
POLLOCK, Max Kenneth		2	251
POLLOCK, Robert		2	252
POLLOCK, Walter		1	292
POLSON, D		3	218
POLSON, Donald		4	159
POLSON, Geoffrey William	P	1	292
POMEROY, Eustace Crichton		4	159
POND, Bertie		1	292
POND, William Warner		4	159
PONSFORD, Alias Jones Thomas Edward	P	1	292
PONSFORD, Ernest Ronald		2	252
PONSFORD, James William Prior	P	2	252
PONSONBY, Ashley William Neville	P	2	252
PONSONBY, Spencer Lawrence		4	159
PONSONBY, The Hon. Cyril Myles Brabazon	P	2	252
PONTEFRACT, Robert		1	292
PONTFRACT, J		2	252
PONTIN, Frederick George		4	159
PONTING, Edward Frank		5	139
POOK, Richard Thomas	P	1	293
POOL, Charles William		3	218
POOL, Ernest Charles	P	4	160
POOLE, Albert		2	252
POOLE, C H M		3	218
POOLE, Edward Bruce		1	293
POOLE, Ernest Henry		4	160
POOLE, Ernest W		4	160
POOLE, Frank		4	160
POOLE, Frederick		1	293
POOLE, George Cheadle		5	139
POOLE, H		3	218
POOLE, Harry W		2	252
POOLE, Hugh Edward Algernon	P	1	293
POOLE, J		3	218
POOLE, Robert	P	2	252
POOLE, Thomas Luke		1	293
POOLE, Walter		1	293
POOLE, William John Roland Ernest	P	3	218
POOLEY, William Henry		4	160
POOR, Albert Henry	P	1	293
POORE, J V		3	218
POPE, Alfred William Henry	P	3	218
POPE, Arthur		3	218
POPE, Arthur George	P	3	219
POPE, Cyril Montagu	P	1	293
POPE, Ernest Richard		1	293
POPE, Frank	P	3	219

Name	Photo	Part No.	Page No.	Name	Photo	Part No.	Page No.
POPE, Frederick William		1	293	POULTON, H		2	253
POPE, Henry James	P	1	293	POULTON, James	P	1	294
POPE, Herbert		1	293	POULTON, William Mitchell		1	294
POPE, J		3	219	POUND, Kenneth James	P	2	253
POPE, John		2	252	POVEY, George		1	294
POPE, John Robert Nelson		2	252	POW, George	P	2	253
POPE, Reginald Thomas Buckingham	P	1	293	POWELL, Alfred Edward	P	4	160
POPE, Walter George Henry		1	293	POWELL, Alfred Edward		5	139
POPHAM, A J		4	160	POWELL, Arthur Charles		1	294
POPPLE, Bertie		2	252	POWELL, Arthur Thomas		1	294
POPPLE, Harry		2	252	POWELL, Charles Victor		1	294
POPPLEWELL, George		2	252	POWELL, E J		3	219
POPPLEWELL, William Henry	P	5	139	POWELL, Ernest Sydney		2	253
PORT, A		2	252	POWELL, Frederick		2	253
PORT, Harry		1	293	POWELL, Frederick William		3	220
PORT, William		2	252	POWELL, George		1	294
PORTEOUS, David		3	219	POWELL, George		2	253
PORTEOUS, Dick Macdonald		1	293	POWELL, George Edward	P	1	294
PORTEOUS, Harry Morton		2	252	POWELL, Harold Osborne	P	1	294
PORTEOUS, Robert		2	252	POWELL, Harry		2	253
PORTER, A		4	160	POWELL, James Edward		2	253
PORTER, Aubrey Blackwood	P	2	252	POWELL, John		1	294
PORTER, Frederick Charles		1	293	POWELL, John W		2	253
PORTER, George Francis Lambert	P	3	219	POWELL, Rhys Campbell Ffolliott	P	1	294
PORTER, George Henry		1	293	POWELL, Richard Henry	P	3	220
PORTER, George Horsley	P	3	219	POWELL, Thomas Gerald		4	160
PORTER, Harry	P	1	293	POWELL, W O		3	220
PORTER, J		2	252	POWELL, Walter		4	160
PORTER, John Alexander	P	5	139	POWELL, William Archie		1	294
PORTER, Robert Cyril	P	2	252	POWELL, William Johnson		1	294
PORTER, Samuel		4	160	POWELL, Wilmot Frederick		2	253
PORTLOCK, Albert		2	253	POWER, G		3	220
PORTSMOUTH, C		3	219	POWER, Herbert	P	1	295
PORTWAINE, Harry		1	293	POWER, J		3	220
POSKITT, William		4	160	POWER, John Wethered		2	253
POSTANS, J		3	219	POWER, Joyce		1	295
POSTLE, John Augustine		4	160	POWER, Reginald Colin	P	2	253
POSTLETHWAITE, John Joyce	P	1	294	POWER, W		3	220
POTTER, A W		3	219	POWLEY, Walter Thomas		2	253
POTTER, Allan Paul	P	3	219	POWLING, Fred Nathan		4	160
POTTER, Archie	P	3	219	POWNALL, Allen Claude Morrison		4	160
POTTER, Arthur		4	160	POWNALL, George Harley		1	295
POTTER, Bert		1	294	POWRIE, Thomas	P	1	295
POTTER, Edmund Walter Jolit	P	2	253	POXON, Henry	P	5	139
POTTER, Frank William	P	1	294	POYNER, Alfred Ernest		2	253
POTTER, Herbert		3	219	POYNER, William Henry		2	253
POTTER, James		2	253	POYNOR, Frank John Riley		5	139
POTTER, James		5	139	POYNTER, John Jack		1	295
POTTER, John Thomas	P	5	139	POYNTON, Percy		3	220
POTTER, Maurice Henry	P	1	294	POZZI, Ian		4	160
POTTER, Reginald		4	160	POZZI, Leonard Lambert	P	2	253
POTTER, Victor James		1	294	PRANGLEY, Charles Dean		4	160
POTTER, W G		2	253	PRATER, A G		3	220
POTTER, W G E		3	219	PRATLEY, Elisha		1	295
POTTER, William Frederick		1	294	PRATT, Alfred Mason	P	1	295
POTTER, William G		2	253	PRATT, Frank Richard	P	4	161
POTTER, William John		1	294	PRATT, G		3	220
POTTER, William Wickford	P	3	219	PRATT, George		1	295
POTTERTON, Lewis John		1	294	PRATT, George Henry		4	161
POTTS, George	P	1	294	PRATT, George William		1	295
POTTS, James		4	160	PRATT, H		3	220
POUGHER, William Henry		1	294	PRATT, James Sanderson		4	161
POULSON, C F		3	219	PRATT, Joseph	P	2	254
POULTNEY, Harry		1	294	PRATT, Joseph Vernon	P	5	139
POULTON, C H		3	219	PRATT, L		3	220

Name	Photo	Part No.	Page No.
PRATT, Lionel Henry	P	1	295
PRATT, Richard Vince		5	139
PRATT, S H		3	220
PRATT, T W		3	220
PRATT, Thomas R		2	254
PRATT, W		3	220
PRATT, Walter Henry		2	254
PRATT-BARLOW, Bernhard Alexander	P	1	20
PRATTEN, Herbert		1	295
PRECIOUS, Harold		4	161
PREECE, Cecil James	P	3	220
PREECE, Charles Edwin		4	161
PREECE, Frederick John	P	1	295
PREECE, Thomas Benjamin	P	2	254
PREECE, Thomas Herbert		4	161
PREEN, Herbert	P	2	254
PRENTICE, James		4	161
PRENTICE, Joseph		1	295
PRESCOTT, Frederick John	P	1	295
PRESCOTT, Walter		2	254
PREST, A		2	254
PRESTAGE, Ralph		4	161
PRESTON, Arthur John Dillon	P	1	295
PRESTON, George Francis		1	296
PRESTON, George Thomas		1	296
PRESTON, Harold		4	161
PRESTON, Herbert Stanley	P	3	220
PRESTON, John Alec Stanley		4	161
PRESTON, Peter		3	220
PRESTON, Stanley		4	161
PRESTON, Thomas Arthur		1	296
PRESTON, Thomas Frederick		3	220
PRETSWELL, John		2	254
PRETT, Jesse		1	296
PRETTE, Anthony		5	139
PRETTY, Ernest George		2	254
PRETTY, Frederick		2	254
PRETYMAN, Frank Remington	P	3	220
PRETYMAN, Maurice William	P	3	220
PREW, Harold Edward		4	161
PRICE, Alfred		1	296
PRICE, Arthur Edward		4	161
PRICE, Charles Lempriere	P	1	296
PRICE, Charles Leonard	P	4	161
PRICE, David Leonard	P	5	139
PRICE, Edward		1	296
PRICE, Edward		1	296
PRICE, Ernest		3	220
PRICE, Evan Henry		4	161
PRICE, Frank		2	254
PRICE, Fred		4	161
PRICE, Frederick George	P	2	254
PRICE, George Bernard Locking		4	161
PRICE, George Montague		4	162
PRICE, Gordon William Bassett		4	162
PRICE, H		3	220
PRICE, J		3	221
PRICE, James		4	162
PRICE, James Salisbury		3	221
PRICE, James Thirkell		3	221
PRICE, John Edmund		5	140
PRICE, Joseph Phillips	P	3	221
PRICE, Philip Francis		1	296
PRICE, Thomas		2	254
PRICE, Thomas James		2	254

Name	Photo	Part No.	Page No.
PRICE, Victor William		5	140
PRICE, W A		3	221
PRICE, W T		3	221
PRICE, William	P	2	254
PRICE, William		2	254
PRICHARD, Arthur		2	254
PRICHARD, Arthur Douglas	P	3	221
PRICHARD, Arthur Illtyd		3	221
PRICHARD, David Thomas		2	254
PRICHARD, Edward Owen		3	221
PRICHARD, Frederick Giles	P	1	296
PRICHARD, John Thomas		2	254
PRICHARD, Joseph Arthur		2	254
PRICHARD, Rowland George	P	1	296
PRICHARD, Thomas James		4	162
PRICHARD, Thomas Lewis		1	296
PRICKETT, Lancelot		3	221
PRIDDLE, George Albert	P	3	221
PRIDDY, Charles		5	140
PRIDEAUX, Geoffrey Arthur	P	3	221
PRIDEAUX-BRUNE, Edmund Nicholas	P	4	21
PRIDHAM, Frank		4	162
PRIDMORE, Albert		5	140
PRIDMORE, Arthur Edward		5	140
PRIDMORE, George Harry	P	5	140
PRIDMORE, George William	P	1	297
PRIDMORE, John Thomas		5	140
PRIDMORE, Percy Malin		4	162
PRIEST, Aaron	P	5	140
PRIEST, Marmaduke		2	255
PRIESTLEY, B		3	221
PRIESTLEY, Charles Lacey		4	162
PRIESTLEY, John	P	3	221
PRIESTMAN, Kenneth Mallorie		3	221
PRIMMER, George William		1	297
PRIMO, John James		1	297
PRINCE, Frederick Harold	P	3	222
PRINCE, George		5	140
PRINCE, John Thomas		2	255
PRING, Bertie Charles		2	255
PRING, William Henry		1	297
PRINGLE, Leonel Graham	P	1	297
PRINGLE, Matthew		4	162
PRINTER, Charles William		4	162
PRIOR, Frederick William Walter		2	255
PRIOR, James		1	297
PRIOR, W		3	222
PRIOR, William J		2	255
PRIOR-WANDESFORDE, Christopher Butler	P	4	224
PRISMALL, Arthur	P	1	297
PRITCHARD, Edward		2	255
PRITCHARD, Isaac	P	2	255
PRITCHARD, John Leithead	P	2	255
PRITCHARD, Lindsay Douglas William	P	3	222
PRITCHARD, R		3	222
PRITCHARD, Robert Pierce		4	162
PRITCHARD, Stanley	P	4	162
PRITCHARD, William		2	255
PRITTY, George E		2	255
PROCTER, Cecil		1	297
PROCTER, Midgley		1	297
PROCTER, Stebbles William	P	3	222
PROCTER, Thomas		1	297
PROCTOR, A		3	222
PROCTOR, Alan Percy		4	162

Name	Photo	Part No.	Page No.
RAWDON, Christopher Hamer		4	165
RAWDON-HASTINGS, Edward Hugh Hastings	P	4	78
RAWDON-HASTINGS, Paulyn Charles Jr	P	4	78
RAWLES, H G		3	225
RAWLES, Percy Richard Dare		2	257
RAWLIN, Thomas		2	257
RAWLING, Wilfrid Dowse		5	140
RAWLINGS, Cecil George Sandbrook	P	1	302
RAWLINGS, Frank Henry		1	302
RAWLINGS, Joseph Eastoe		1	302
RAWLINGS, Leonard Justly	P	5	140
RAWLINS, Clifford Arthur		1	302
RAWLINS, William		4	165
RAWLINSON, A S		2	257
RAWLINSON, Curwen Vaughan	P	1	302
RAWLINSON, Guy Edward	P	4	165
RAWORTH, William Alfred	P	1	302
RAWSON, Henry		4	165
RAWSON, Lionel Reginald		3	225
RAWSTHORNE, J		3	225
RAWSTHORNE, Walter		3	225
RAY, E J		3	225
RAY, George		1	302
RAY, James Henry		1	302
RAY, Philip Oliphant	P	4	166
RAY, Richard		4	166
RAY, Wilfred		2	257
RAY, William Douglas	P	3	225
RAYBOULD, I		3	225
RAYMOND, George		2	257
RAYNER, A E		3	225
RAYNER, Charles Alfred		1	302
RAYNER, Edward	P	3	226
RAYNER, Frank		1	302
RAYNER, Harold Leslie	P	3	226
RAYNER, Hubert William		3	226
RAYNER, James		2	257
RAYNER, Owen Rupert		3	226
RAYNER, Sidney R		2	257
RAYNER, William Thomas		1	302
RAYNES, Albert Brainerd	P	1	302
RAYNES, Arthur Herbert	P	2	257
RAYNOR, Herbert		1	302
REACHER, Stanley William	P	3	226
READ, Albert Victor		4	166
READ, Arthur Beddome		4	166
READ, E		2	257
READ, Edric Hurdman		4	166
READ, Edwin		2	257
READ, Frank		2	257
READ, Fred	P	2	257
READ, Frederick William		1	302
READ, Frederick William		2	258
READ, Herbert Frank	P	3	226
READ, Richard H		2	258
READ, Walter James		3	226
READ, William		1	302
READ, William		2	258
READ, William L		2	258
READE, John Henry Loftus		4	166
READER, Albert		2	258
READER, Frederick		5	140
READER, Henry Frank		1	302
READER, James		5	140

Name	Photo	Part No.	Page No.
READING, George		3	226
READING, William Ernest		1	302
READINGS, James		2	258
REAHEAD, Percy Solomy		2	258
REARDON, George Herbert		1	302
REARDON, Samuel Michael		1	302
REARDON, Stephen		5	140
REASON, Patrick Edward		1	302
REAY, William Roland	P	4	166
REBURN, Henry	P	4	166
REDDIN, Henry John		2	258
REDDING, George E		2	258
REDDOCK, Samuel Allan	P	1	302
REDFERN, Henry		2	258
REDFERN, T S		2	258
REDFORD, George		5	140
REDFORD, J R		3	226
REDFORD, Thomas	P	2	258
REDGATE, John William		4	166
REDGLEY, George		2	258
REDHALL, Arthur		4	166
REDHEAD, Robert		4	166
REDHEAD, Thomas		1	302
REDMAN, G H		3	226
REDMAN, Reginald George	P	4	166
REDMAYNE, James	P	1	302
REDMOND, P		3	226
REDMOND, Thomas		2	258
REDMOND, William		1	302
REDMOND, William		4	166
REDNAP,		2	258
REDPATH, James Thomas	P	1	302
REDSHAW, George	P	2	258
REED, Albert		4	166
REED, Albert H		2	258
REED, Arthur Edward		2	258
REED, Charles Enoch		2	258
REED, Ernest William		1	303
REED, Frederick		2	258
REED, George		2	258
REED, George Alfred		2	258
REED, Herbert Lewis		4	166
REED, Horace Alfred		3	226
REED, James Mcgregor		1	303
REED, John Arthur		1	303
REED, John Sleeman		3	226
REED, Joseph John		1	303
REED, Oliver		1	303
REED, Percival John		2	258
REED, Reginald Joseph		1	303
REED, S W		4	166
REED, T		3	227
REED, William		2	258
REED, William		2	258
REED, William Ellis	P	1	303
REEN, Edward	P	4	166
REEP, Alfred Mills	P	2	258
REES, Benjamin		3	227
REES, Benjamin Simon	P	3	227
REES, D		3	227
REES, David John	P	3	227
REES, Edgar George		5	141
REES, Frederick R		2	258
REES, Idris		4	166
REES, William Henry Sebastian	P	3	227

Name	Photo	Part No.	Page No.
REEVE, Herbert Joseph		2	258
REEVES, Arthur Ernest	P	2	258
REEVES, Charles Henry	P	3	227
REEVES, Frank		3	227
REEVES, Geoffrey Browning		3	227
REEVES, Geoffrey Frederick John		1	303
REEVES, Harry Charles	P	2	259
REEVES, Herbert William	P	3	227
REEVES, Leslie Leonhardt		5	141
REEVES, Victor Charles Methuen	P	2	259
REEVES, William		2	259
REEVES, William Wallis		4	167
REFFOLD, Alfred		2	259
REFFOLD, Henry		2	259
REGAN, Edward		1	303
REGAN, J		3	227
REGESTER, Edgar		5	141
REHM, A G		3	227
REID, Alexander Burnett Fraser	P	3	227
REID, Alexander Muir	P	2	259
REID, Alfred		2	259
REID, D H		3	227
REID, Eric B		4	167
REID, Esmond Howard		4	167
REID, Francis Jackson	P	1	303
REID, George		1	303
REID, George	P	3	227
REID, George Christopher		4	167
REID, George Henry Stuart		3	227
REID, George Whiteley		1	303
REID, H		3	227
REID, Hugh Watt	P	4	167
REID, J		3	227
REID, J		3	227
REID, J A F		3	227
REID, James	P	1	303
REID, James	P	2	259
REID, James		2	259
REID, James		2	259
REID, James		2	259
REID, James	P	3	228
REID, James Gray	P	4	167
REID, James Lestock Ironside		4	167
REID, John		2	259
REID, John		3	228
REID, John Clements		2	259
REID, John Elliot	P	3	228
REID, M		3	228
REID, Percy Gargill		3	228
REID, Peter		4	167
REID, Robert Logan		1	303
REID, Samuel	P	3	228
REID, T		2	259
REID, Thomas Henry		4	167
REID, William		3	228
REID, William		3	228
REID, William	P	5	141
REID, William Bramich		1	303
REID, William Heard		3	228
REID, William John	P	3	228
REID, William Leonard	P	1	303
REID, William Mitchell	P	3	228
REILLY, Daniel		2	259
REILLY, Daniel		5	141
REILLY, E		3	228

Name	Photo	Part No.	Page No.
REILLY, J		3	228
REILLY, J		3	228
REILLY, James		2	259
REILLY, P		2	259
REILLY, Ralph Alec		1	303
REILLY, W		2	259
REISS, Stephen Lacy		2	259
RELF, Herbert Alfred		4	167
RELPH, G		3	228
RELTON, Gerald Lyons		4	167
REMFRY, C		3	228
REMNANT, J		3	228
REMNANT, John		2	259
REMNANT, Percy George		2	259
REMON, Walter Thomas	P	3	228
RENDEL, Reginald Dacres		1	304
RENDELL, F		3	228
RENDELL, Leonard Wyndham		4	167
RENDELL, W		2	259
RENDLE, Percival Alfred		4	167
RENNARD, Edward Marmaduke		3	228
RENNICK, H De P		4	167
RENNIE, John		1	304
RENNIE, Robert		2	259
RENNIE, Samuel		4	167
RENNIE, W		2	259
RENNY-TAILYOUR, Henry Frederick Thornton	P	1	345
RENSHAW, Henry		2	259
RENSHAW, Herbert Henry	P	3	229
RENSHAW, J		3	229
RENTON, Charles		4	167
RENTON, Harry Noel Leslie	P	1	304
RENTON, Robert William	P	3	229
RENVOIZE, Albert John		1	304
RENWICK, Adam Dalgleish	P	3	229
REPTON, Arthur		2	259
RESTELL, Percy J D		2	259
RETSALL, A		3	229
RETTIE, Frank		3	229
REVELEY, Edward		1	304
REVELL, David		2	259
REVELL, Leslie Matthew	P	3	229
REVILL, Charles Henry	P	4	167
REVITT, Alfred		1	304
REW, Douglas Jolland		5	141
REX, Reginald George	P	5	141
REYMES-COLE, William Elmer		2	74
REYNELL, Carew	P	1	304
REYNOLDS, Albert John		2	259
REYNOLDS, Alfred Slater	P	3	229
REYNOLDS, C		3	229
REYNOLDS, Charles Edward	P	5	141
REYNOLDS, Charles Hubert	P	2	259
REYNOLDS, Emanuel		1	304
REYNOLDS, Ernest	P	3	229
REYNOLDS, F		2	259
REYNOLDS, Frank		1	304
REYNOLDS, Frederick		2	259
REYNOLDS, Harry		2	259
REYNOLDS, Harry		4	167
REYNOLDS, Henry Clendon Collis	P	1	304
REYNOLDS, Herbert Joseph	P	1	304
REYNOLDS, J		2	260
REYNOLDS, J J		3	229

Name	Photo	Part No.	Page No.	Name	Photo	Part No.	Page No.
REYNOLDS, James		2	260	**RICHARDSON,** Frederick		2	260
REYNOLDS, James	P	5	141	**RICHARDSON,** Frederick		2	260
REYNOLDS, John Ferguson	P	4	167	**RICHARDSON,** Frederick		2	260
REYNOLDS, John Ferguson		5	141	**RICHARDSON,** Frederick Reginald		5	141
REYNOLDS, Joseph		1	304	**RICHARDSON,** G		2	260
REYNOLDS, Louis Victor		1	304	**RICHARDSON,** George	P	1	305
REYNOLDS, R		3	229	**RICHARDSON,** George James		3	230
REYNOLDS, Simon		5	141	**RICHARDSON,** Harold	P	2	260
REYNOLDS, W S		3	229	**RICHARDSON,** Harold		4	168
REYNOLDS, William		2	260	**RICHARDSON,** Harry		2	260
RHODES, Arthur		2	260	**RICHARDSON,** Hector Lawrence		4	168
RHODES, J A		3	229	**RICHARDSON,** Henry Charles		1	305
RHODES, John Harold		3	229	**RICHARDSON,** Herbert James		1	305
RHODES, W		3	229	**RICHARDSON,** Horace Raymond Waterman		4	168
RHODES, W		3	229	**RICHARDSON,** J		3	230
RHODES, William Henry		2	260	**RICHARDSON,** J		3	230
RHODES-MOORHOUSE, William Barnard	P	1	258	**RICHARDSON,** John		2	260
RIBBONS, Henry Thomas		2	260	**RICHARDSON,** John Theodore		1	305
RIBY, Edward		2	260	**RICHARDSON,** John William		1	305
RICARD, Frank	P	1	304	**RICHARDSON,** L		2	260
RICE, Bertie		2	260	**RICHARDSON,** Martin James		4	168
RICE, Eric Vyvyan		2	260	**RICHARDSON,** Maurice Lewis George		3	230
RICE, Henry		2	260	**RICHARDSON,** Mervyn Stronge	P	2	260
RICE, J		3	229	**RICHARDSON,** Reginald Lyman		4	168
RICE, John		2	260	**RICHARDSON,** Richard		4	168
RICE, John Arthur Talbot		4	167	**RICHARDSON,** Robert Harold		3	230
RICE, Owens		5	141	**RICHARDSON,** Rowland		2	260
RICE, Robert	P	4	167	**RICHARDSON,** Russell		1	305
RICH, Alfred Thomas		3	229	**RICHARDSON,** S		2	260
RICHARDS, A		3	229	**RICHARDSON,** S R		3	230
RICHARDS, Alfred Edward		3	229	**RICHARDSON,** Samuel		2	260
RICHARDS, Arthur Hamlet		3	229	**RICHARDSON,** Samuel Alexander		2	260
RICHARDS, Arthur James		2	260	**RICHARDSON,** Stanley George		4	168
RICHARDS, Charles		2	260	**RICHARDSON,** T		3	230
RICHARDS, Charles Morgan		3	229	**RICHARDSON,** Thomas		3	230
RICHARDS, Charlie		4	167	**RICHARDSON,** Thomas Charles		3	230
RICHARDS, Ernest Walter	P	3	230	**RICHARDSON,** Victor		3	230
RICHARDS, Ewart Wilfred	P	4	168	**RICHARDSON,** Walter		2	260
RICHARDS, F L		2	260	**RICHARDSON,** Walter Fairfax	P	1	305
RICHARDS, G C		3	230	**RICHARDSON,** Walter Gardener		4	168
RICHARDS, G W		3	230	**RICHARDSON,** Walter Henry		4	168
RICHARDS, George		5	141	**RICHARDSON,** William		1	305
RICHARDS, George Henry		2	260	**RICHARDSON,** William		2	260
RICHARDS, George Henry		2	260	**RICHARDSON,** William Charles	P	5	142
RICHARDS, George William Willis		3	230	**RICHARDSON,** William John		1	305
RICHARDS, H G		3	230	**RICHARDSON,** William John	P	2	261
RICHARDS, H G		3	230	**RICHENS,** T K		2	261
RICHARDS, Hugh Liddon	P	1	304	**RICHER,** John George Leslie		4	168
RICHARDS, James Ramsey		2	260	**RICHES,** Robert James		1	305
RICHARDS, John		1	304	**RICHES,** Thomas		1	305
RICHARDS, John		5	141	**RICHIE,** Richard Alec		4	168
RICHARDS, Julian David Eaton		2	260	**RICHIE,** William		2	261
RICHARDS, Robert	P	1	304	**RICHMOND,** Henry Sylvester		5	142
RICHARDS, Thomas Ernest		4	168	**RICHMOND,** Leslie		4	168
RICHARDS, W		3	230	**RICKARD,** Henry		1	305
RICHARDS, William Benjamin	P	4	168	**RICKARD,** Henry Cecil		4	168
RICHARDS, William Edward		2	260	**RICKARD,** James		2	261
RICHARDSON, A J		3	230	**RICKARDS,** Hew Wardrop Brooke	P	5	142
RICHARDSON, Arthur		2	260	**RICKMAN,** Stuart Hamilton	P	1	305
RICHARDSON, Charles		2	260	**RICKWOOD,** Walter William	P	3	231
RICHARDSON, E C F		3	230	**RIDDALL,** John George		4	168
RICHARDSON, Ernest	P	3	230	**RIDDEL,** John		4	168
RICHARDSON, F		3	230	**RIDDEL,** John Dean		3	231
RICHARDSON, F		3	230	**RIDDEL,** Robert Mackie		4	168
RICHARDSON, Francis Aymer		4	168	**RIDDELL,** Alexander Grant		4	169

Name	Photo	Part No.	Page No.
ROBERTS, E T		3	232
ROBERTS, Edward		2	262
ROBERTS, Edward		5	143
ROBERTS, Edward J		2	262
ROBERTS, Edwin Alfred		5	143
ROBERTS, Frank		1	307
ROBERTS, Frank William		5	143
ROBERTS, Frederick		4	170
ROBERTS, Frederick Charles		4	170
ROBERTS, Frederick William	P	1	307
ROBERTS, G E		3	232
ROBERTS, George		3	232
ROBERTS, George		5	143
ROBERTS, George Bradley		1	307
ROBERTS, George Hood		4	170
ROBERTS, George William		1	307
ROBERTS, H		3	232
ROBERTS, H		3	232
ROBERTS, H		3	232
ROBERTS, Harold	P	3	232
ROBERTS, Henry		2	262
ROBERTS, Henry George Lloyd	P	1	307
ROBERTS, Herbert Edwin		1	307
ROBERTS, Hugh Stanley	P	2	262
ROBERTS, J		3	232
ROBERTS, J		3	232
ROBERTS, J W		3	232
ROBERTS, James		5	143
ROBERTS, James Rhoderic Trethowan	P	1	307
ROBERTS, Job Harold		5	143
ROBERTS, John		4	170
ROBERTS, John Alfred		1	307
ROBERTS, John George Hill		4	170
ROBERTS, John Lester		5	143
ROBERTS, John Lloyd		3	232
ROBERTS, John Thomas		5	143
ROBERTS, Joseph Baldwin		1	307
ROBERTS, Oscar Howard Salter Roberts		3	232
ROBERTS, Oswald Henry		1	307
ROBERTS, Owen Hughes		2	262
ROBERTS, Philip Hugh Gore	P	2	262
ROBERTS, Richard Bowen	P	3	232
ROBERTS, Richard Henry		5	143
ROBERTS, Robert	P	2	262
ROBERTS, Sidney Herbert		4	170
ROBERTS, Stanley Victor		3	233
ROBERTS, Thomas		1	307
ROBERTS, Thomas		1	307
ROBERTS, Thomas		1	307
ROBERTS, Thomas	P	4	170
ROBERTS, Thomas H		2	262
ROBERTS, Walter Stanley	P	5	143
ROBERTS, Wilfred	P	3	233
ROBERTS, William		2	262
ROBERTS, William		4	170
ROBERTS, William Charles		4	170
ROBERTS, William Clifford		1	307
ROBERTS, William James	P	1	307
ROBERTS, William John		4	170
ROBERTS, William Rowland		4	171
ROBERTS, William Samuel		3	233
ROBERTS OF KANDAHAR, Frederick Sleigh (Roberts)	P	3	232
ROBERTSHAW, James Hartley		5	143
ROBERTSON, Alec Pasley	P	2	262

Name	Photo	Part No.	Page No.
ROBERTSON, Alexander		2	263
ROBERTSON, Alexander		4	171
ROBERTSON, Alexander		4	171
ROBERTSON, Angus		4	171
ROBERTSON, Archibald		2	263
ROBERTSON, Clement		3	233
ROBERTSON, Duncan		2	263
ROBERTSON, Edmund John Macrory	P	1	308
ROBERTSON, Ernest Cecil Lennox	P	2	263
ROBERTSON, Frank	P	1	308
ROBERTSON, Frederick Neal	P	5	144
ROBERTSON, George		2	263
ROBERTSON, George Hawthorne Minot		5	144
ROBERTSON, Gordon		4	171
ROBERTSON, Harvey Young		2	263
ROBERTSON, Hugh	P	3	233
ROBERTSON, Ian Gordon	P	2	263
ROBERTSON, J		2	263
ROBERTSON, James	P	1	308
ROBERTSON, James		1	308
ROBERTSON, James		1	308
ROBERTSON, James		4	171
ROBERTSON, James		4	171
ROBERTSON, James Alexander		3	233
ROBERTSON, James William		4	171
ROBERTSON, John		1	308
ROBERTSON, John		2	263
ROBERTSON, John		2	263
ROBERTSON, John	P	3	233
ROBERTSON, John	P	3	233
ROBERTSON, John		4	171
ROBERTSON, John Adam		5	144
ROBERTSON, John Alexander Tower		3	233
ROBERTSON, John Edmond	P	1	308
ROBERTSON, John Meiklejohn		5	144
ROBERTSON, John Thomas		2	263
ROBERTSON, Lennox Fraser	P	2	263
ROBERTSON, Lewis		4	171
ROBERTSON, Michael		4	171
ROBERTSON, Peter		4	171
ROBERTSON, Robert	P	1	308
ROBERTSON, Robert Currie		3	233
ROBERTSON, Robert Horsburgh	P	1	308
ROBERTSON, Robert John Charles		1	308
ROBERTSON, T		2	263
ROBERTSON, Thomas		1	308
ROBERTSON, Thomas		5	144
ROBERTSON, William		1	308
ROBERTSON, William		4	171
ROBERTSON, William Fleming		2	263
ROBERTSON, William Ford	P	3	233
ROBERTSON, William James	P	1	309
ROBERTSON, William John		1	309
ROBERTSON, William John		4	171
ROBERTSON, William Keith	P	1	309
ROBERTSON, William Sinclair		3	234
ROBERTSON-GLASGOW, Archibald William	P	1	153
ROBERT-TISSOT, Emile Lucien	P	5	163
ROBERT-TISSOT, Jean Ulysse	P	5	163
ROBESON, Herbert		2	263
ROBIN, Charles Harold	P	3	234
ROBINS, Frederick George		4	171
ROBINS, Frederick John		1	309
ROBINS, Henry George		1	309
ROBINS, Joseph Thomas	P	3	234

Name	Photo	Part No.	Page No.	Name	Photo	Part No.	Page No.
ROBINS, W		3	234	**ROBINSON,** William John	P	5	144
ROBINSON, A		3	234	**ROBINSON,** William John		5	144
ROBINSON, A E		3	234	**ROBINSON,** William John		5	145
ROBINSON, Abraham Burchell		1	309	**ROBOTHAM,** Percy William		3	235
ROBINSON, Albert Edward		1	309	**ROBSHAW,** Thomas Arthur		1	310
ROBINSON, Albert Venis		1	309	**ROBSON,** Arnold	P	2	264
ROBINSON, Alfred		1	309	**ROBSON,** Frederick William		4	172
ROBINSON, Alfred		2	263	**ROBSON,** James Herbert		1	310
ROBINSON, Alfred Elliot Somers	P	1	309	**ROBSON,** Jasper Leeming		1	310
ROBINSON, Arthur Gordon		3	234	**ROBSON,** Oliver Augustus	P	1	310
ROBINSON, Austin		5	144	**ROBSON,** Richard Ernest	P	1	310
ROBINSON, Charles Arthur		3	234	**ROBSON,** Thomas		1	310
ROBINSON, Cooper Allen		4	171	**ROBSON,** Thomas William		1	310
ROBINSON, Cyril (Rozee)		2	263	**ROCHE,** Francis		3	235
ROBINSON, Edmond		3	234	**ROCHE,** Gerald Walter	P	5	145
ROBINSON, Edward		2	264	**ROCHESTER,** J		3	235
ROBINSON, Edward	P	3	234	**ROCHFORT-BOYD,** Henry Charles		3	32
ROBINSON, Edwin Hall		3	234	**ROCKLEY,** Ernest		1	310
ROBINSON, Eric Arthur		2	264	**RODDA,** Raymond	P	3	235
ROBINSON, Ernest		2	264	**RODDAM,** Robert Collingwood	P	1	310
ROBINSON, Ernest	P	5	144	**RODDIS,** C A		3	235
ROBINSON, Frank	P	1	309	**RODDIS,** Charles Henry	P	1	310
ROBINSON, Frank		1	309	**RODELL,** Ernest		5	145
ROBINSON, Frank Stanley		1	309	**RODELL,** Robert F		2	264
ROBINSON, Frederick	P	1	309	**RODGER,** James		3	235
ROBINSON, Frederick Bernard		2	264	**RODGER,** Matthew		2	264
ROBINSON, George		2	264	**RODGER,** Walter Washington Buchanan	P	1	310
ROBINSON, George		2	264	**RODGERS,** George		1	310
ROBINSON, George Walter Alfred		4	171	**RODGERS,** John Miniter	P	5	145
ROBINSON, George Whalley	P	3	234	**RODGERS,** William		5	145
ROBINSON, Gordon Edward		2	264	**RODGERSON,** James Stuart	P	3	235
ROBINSON, H		3	234	**RODGERSON,** John		5	145
ROBINSON, Harold Charles		2	264	**RODMAN,** Arthur		5	145
ROBINSON, Harry		3	234	**RODWAY,** Harry		2	264
ROBINSON, Harry Percival		4	171	**ROE,** Edward James		2	264
ROBINSON, Henry Joseph	P	5	144	**ROE,** Frank Edward Mervyn	P	2	264
ROBINSON, I		3	234	**ROE,** Henry Graeme	P	1	310
ROBINSON, James		2	264	**ROE,** Sydney George	P	4	172
ROBINSON, James		2	264	**ROE,** William John		2	265
ROBINSON, James		2	264	**ROGER,** John Millar		2	265
ROBINSON, James Caunce	P	5	144	**ROGERS,** A		3	235
ROBINSON, James George	P	3	234	**ROGERS,** A		3	235
ROBINSON, John		2	264	**ROGERS,** Albert		2	265
ROBINSON, John William		4	171	**ROGERS,** Albert Samuel		1	310
ROBINSON, Joseph Cooper	P	1	309	**ROGERS,** Alfred		2	265
ROBINSON, Joseph Robert		1	309	**ROGERS,** Alfred		4	172
ROBINSON, Kenneth Bardshaw		2	264	**ROGERS,** Alfred Sidney		1	310
ROBINSON, Launcelot Alec (Lannie)	P	1	309	**ROGERS,** Arthur		1	311
ROBINSON, Lawrence Leonard		1	309	**ROGERS,** Arthur Forbes		4	172
ROBINSON, Leonard		4	171	**ROGERS,** Bert		2	265
ROBINSON, Leslie John	P	1	309	**ROGERS,** Cyril Warrilow Pimm		3	235
ROBINSON, M		3	234	**ROGERS,** E		3	235
ROBINSON, Percy Lazenby	P	2	264	**ROGERS,** Edward Eccles		5	145
ROBINSON, Peter		4	171	**ROGERS,** Ernest		4	172
ROBINSON, Ralph Duncan	P	3	234	**ROGERS,** Ernest John		1	311
ROBINSON, Reginald William		1	310	**ROGERS,** F		3	235
ROBINSON, Richard Arthur Wynne	P	3	235	**ROGERS,** Francis Lyttelton Lloyd		3	235
ROBINSON, Robert James		4	171	**ROGERS,** Frank Horace	P	3	235
ROBINSON, Thomas		2	264	**ROGERS,** George Storie		2	265
ROBINSON, Thomas		3	235	**ROGERS,** H G F		3	236
ROBINSON, Thomas Henry		5	144	**ROGERS,** Harold Hildred	P	1	311
ROBINSON, Thomas William		1	310	**ROGERS,** Henry Milward	P	1	311
ROBINSON, William Alexander	P	2	264	**ROGERS,** Hermione Angela	P	3	236
ROBINSON, William Henry		1	310	**ROGERS,** J		2	265
ROBINSON, William J		2	264	**ROGERS,** James		4	172

Name	Photo	Part No.	Page No.
ROGERS, Joseph		1	311
ROGERS, Maurice Croston	P	1	311
ROGERS, Maurice Croston		4	172
ROGERS, P		3	236
ROGERS, P F		3	236
ROGERS, Richard Henry Lyster		3	236
ROGERS, Ronald Joseph	P	1	311
ROGERS, Sidney		3	236
ROGERS, T		2	265
ROGERS, Valentine William		1	311
ROGERS, Wilfrid Frank		4	172
ROGERS, William Alfred		1	311
ROGERSON, Vernon	P	2	265
ROGERSON, William Ernest	P	1	311
ROGIE, Charles		5	145
ROHDE, Harold Turner		3	236
ROKER, Clive Leslie		4	172
ROLFE, S		2	265
ROLLASON, Arthur Gilbert	P	2	265
ROLLESTON, Francis Lancelot	P	1	311
ROLLINGS, Thomas Baker		4	172
ROLSTON, Leslie Hicks	P	4	172
ROLSTONE, James Henry		1	311
ROLT, John		1	311
ROMANS, Alfred		1	311
RONALD, James Mcbain		1	311
RONALD, Kenneth Mcgeorge	P	1	312
RONAN, William		2	265
ROOFF, Eustace Pelham		4	172
ROOK, Percy		5	145
ROOME, Philip William	P	1	312
ROONEY, Thomas James		2	265
ROOPER, William Victor Trevor		4	172
ROOTH, J H		3	236
ROOTH, Richard Alexander	P	1	312
ROOTH, S P		3	236
ROPE, John Arthur	P	2	265
ROPER, Albert John		2	265
ROPER, Albert Victor		2	265
ROPER, Frank	P	5	145
ROPER, William Albert		1	312
ROPER, William Edward	P	3	236
ROPER, William Horace Stanley	P	3	236
RORIE, Thomas Handyside Baxter		3	236
ROSCHER, Max Leopold		4	173
ROSCOE, P		3	236
ROSCOE, Peter		2	265
ROSCOE, Richard		2	265
ROSE, Andrew Mackenzie		4	173
ROSE, Basil Edmund		5	145
ROSE, Benjamin Joseph		1	312
ROSE, Charles Edward		1	312
ROSE, Charles Edward		3	236
ROSE, Clement		1	312
ROSE, D		2	265
ROSE, D		3	236
ROSE, Edward Legh Mildmay		3	236
ROSE, Geoffrey Craig	P	1	312
ROSE, George J		2	265
ROSE, H H		3	236
ROSE, Herbert John	P	1	312
ROSE, Ian		5	145
ROSE, J		3	236
ROSE, J A		3	236
ROSE, J E		3	236

Name	Photo	Part No.	Page No.
ROSE, John		1	312
ROSE, John Alexander		4	173
ROSE, Launcelot St. Vincent	P	1	312
ROSE, Owen William	P	1	313
ROSE, R J		3	236
ROSE, Roland John		2	265
ROSE, Ronald Hugh Walrond	P	1	313
ROSE, Thomas	P	1	313
ROSE, Tom Alfred		1	313
ROSE, W		2	265
ROSE, W		3	236
ROSE, William		2	265
ROSE, William Edward		5	145
ROSEVEARE, Francis Bernard		3	236
ROSEVEARE, Harold William		1	313
ROSEVEARE, Harold William		3	236
ROSEVEARE, R		3	236
ROSEVEARE, Ronald Chard		4	173
ROSEWARNE, Ernest William	P	4	173
ROSEWELL, Frank		2	265
ROSIER, Frederick	P	1	313
ROSIER, George		2	265
ROSKILLY, William A		2	265
ROSLING, Alan Percy		3	237
ROSS, Agnes		4	173
ROSS, Alastair		3	237
ROSS, Alexander		2	265
ROSS, Alexander	P	3	237
ROSS, Alexander		4	173
ROSS, Archibald Seymour	P	1	313
ROSS, Arthur John		4	173
ROSS, Cecil John		1	313
ROSS, Charles Cameron		4	173
ROSS, Colin John		1	313
ROSS, David		4	173
ROSS, George Alexander Sinclair	P	1	313
ROSS, George Inglesby		3	237
ROSS, Henry G		2	265
ROSS, J		2	265
ROSS, J		3	237
ROSS, J		3	237
ROSS, J		3	237
ROSS, James		2	265
ROSS, James John (Eric)		1	313
ROSS, James Oswald		1	313
ROSS, John		2	265
ROSS, John		4	173
ROSS, John Edward		2	265
ROSS, John Shearer		4	173
ROSS, John Thomas		4	173
ROSS, John William		4	173
ROSS, Joseph Morgan	P	3	237
ROSS, Thomas Hesketh	P	5	145
ROSS, W		2	265
ROSS, Walter		2	265
ROSS, Walter A		4	173
ROSS, William		4	173
ROSS, William Alexander		4	173
ROSS, William James		1	314
ROSS, William Lindsay	P	3	237
ROSS, William Munro	P	1	314
ROSSER, John		1	314
ROSSITER, A		3	237
ROSSITER, Philip	P	1	314
ROSSITER, Robert Tully		3	237

Name	Photo	Part No.	Page No.
ROSSON, William Harold	P	1	314
ROSS-TAYLOR, Ian Henry Munro		3	264
ROSTRON, John		1	314
ROTCHELL, Richard		5	145
ROULSTON, James	P	5	146
ROUND, A		3	237
ROURKE, Thomas		1	314
ROUS, Thomas	P	3	237
ROUSE, Frank		4	173
ROUST, Josiah Robert		1	314
ROUTH, Harold		1	314
ROUTHAM, Alfred		2	265
ROUTLEDGE, Calvert	P	3	237
ROUTLEDGE, Frank		2	265
ROUTLEDGE, Herbert Douglas		4	174
ROUTLEDGE, Thomas Kirkbride		4	174
ROUTLEDGE, William		2	265
ROUTLEY, F J		3	237
ROW, Harry Akers	P	1	314
ROW, James Edward		1	314
ROW, William Burnett	P	4	174
ROWAN, Andrew Percival	P	1	314
ROWAN, John Leck	P	1	314
ROWBERRY, Alfred Archibald		2	265
ROWBERRY, Alfred Charles		1	315
ROWBERRY, George Edwin		3	237
ROWBOTHAM, Howard Leeson		4	174
ROWDON, Reuben Frederick		2	266
ROWE, Albert Edward		2	266
ROWE, Arthur		1	315
ROWE, Charles Eli		2	266
ROWE, Frank Charles		1	315
ROWE, Frederick George		4	174
ROWE, George Stephenson Washington		4	174
ROWE, J C		3	237
ROWE, John		1	315
ROWE, Joseph Frank		1	315
ROWE, Joseph James		1	315
ROWE, Philip Henry	P	3	237
ROWE, Thomas		4	174
ROWE, W		3	238
ROWE, William John	P	2	266
ROWELL, H		2	266
ROWELL, H		3	238
ROWEN, Frederick Joseph		2	266
ROWLAND, Augustus Charles	P	4	174
ROWLAND, Edward		2	266
ROWLAND, R D		3	238
ROWLANDS, Jack		4	174
ROWLANDS, Percival Hugh		1	315
ROWLES, W T		3	238
ROWLETT, Thomas		2	266
ROWLEY, B		3	238
ROWLEY, Charles Pelham	P	2	266
ROWLEY, Joseph		3	238
ROWSEN, J		3	238
ROXBURGH, John Hewitt		5	146
ROXBURGH, William Fletcher		4	174
ROY, Kenneth James	P	1	315
ROY, Peter Fraser		4	174
ROYAL, Arthur Charles		1	315
ROYAL, T		2	266
ROYALL, Robert J		2	266
ROYALL, William Edward		1	315
ROYCE, Eric Hooper		4	174

Name	Photo	Part No.	Page No.
ROYES, Thomas Percy		1	315
ROYLANCE, J		2	266
ROYLANDS, Frederick		2	266
RUBY, Alfred James		2	266
RUCK, John Egerton	P	1	315
RUCKER, Robin Sinclair		5	146
RUDALL, Bertram Allen		4	174
RUDD, A		3	238
RUDD, Alexander Richard		1	315
RUDD, E		2	266
RUDD, Frederick Thomas		1	315
RUDD, Kenneth Sutherland	P	5	146
RUDD, William		2	266
RUDDERHAM, Edwin Robert		1	315
RUDDERHAM, Sidney W		1	315
RUDDICK, James John (William J J)		1	315
RUDDIFORTH, Charles Mellville		4	174
RUDDOCK, Harold Edwy Colston	P	1	315
RUDDOCK, J		3	238
RUDDOCK, Thomas		4	174
RUDGE, Arthur		2	266
RUDGE, J A		2	266
RUDGE, Tom		2	266
RUDKIN, Wilfred George		1	315
RUDLAND, William		2	266
RUDMAN, Harry Stanley	P	1	315
RUEGG, Kenneth Stanes		1	315
RUEGG, Maurice Chilton		5	146
RUFF, Ernest		2	266
RUFF, H J		3	238
RUFFLES, Ruben Isaac		5	146
RUFUS, Thomas	P	4	174
RUGG, Edward Ernest		1	315
RUGG, Robert Henry		2	266
RULE, Alfred		2	266
RULER, Herbert John		2	266
RUMBLES, Alfred		1	315
RUMBY, Charles		2	266
RUMMERY, G A		3	238
RUMP, Arthur Herbert		2	266
RUMP, Christopher		2	266
RUNAGLE, Charles Frederick		3	238
RUNCORN, Thomas James		1	315
RUNDLE, Raymond Wallis	P	3	238
RUSCOE, Hugh Henry		4	175
RUSE, George Henry		4	175
RUSH, Henry F		2	266
RUSH, Sydney Walter	P	1	315
RUSHING, Thomas W		2	266
RUSHTON, George Frederick	P	5	146
RUSHTON, William George		4	175
RUSHTON, William Henry (Harry)	P	3	238
RUSHWORTH, A		3	238
RUSLING, T W		3	238
RUSSEL, Michael Leigh		3	238
RUSSELL, A		3	238
RUSSELL, A J		3	238
RUSSELL, Alexander	P	4	175
RUSSELL, Alexander Christopher		2	266
RUSSELL, Alfred		2	266
RUSSELL, Archibald Mckerrow	P	3	238
RUSSELL, Arthur		5	146
RUSSELL, Arthur Henry Eric	P	5	146
RUSSELL, Arthur Sidney		4	175
RUSSELL, Charles Frederick		3	238

Name	Photo	Part No.	Page No.
RUSSELL, Charles Nelson		4	175
RUSSELL, Edric George		5	146
RUSSELL, Edward		2	266
RUSSELL, Edward		3	238
RUSSELL, Edward Francis	P	3	238
RUSSELL, Eric		5	146
RUSSELL, Francis		1	315
RUSSELL, Frank		1	315
RUSSELL, Frederick		1	315
RUSSELL, G E		3	238
RUSSELL, Henry		1	315
RUSSELL, Henry F		2	266
RUSSELL, Henry John		1	315
RUSSELL, Henry John		1	315
RUSSELL, J		3	238
RUSSELL, James		2	266
RUSSELL, James Alexander		4	175
RUSSELL, James Forteath	P	1	316
RUSSELL, Patrick Alfred	P	3	238
RUSSELL, Peter		2	266
RUSSELL, R		2	266
RUSSELL, Ralph William		5	146
RUSSELL, Robert Gordon		4	175
RUSSELL, T		2	267
RUSSELL, W		3	238
RUSSELL, W T		3	238
RUSSELL, Walter	P	5	147
RUSSELL, Walter Tresham		4	175
RUSSELL, William Arthur		4	175
RUSSELL, William George		2	267
RUSSELL, William Henry		4	175
RUST, Edward	P	1	316
RUTHERFORD, H		2	267
RUTHERFORD, H		2	267
RUTHERFORD, J		2	267
RUTHERFORD, James Mcgill		2	267
RUTHERFORD, John Allen	P	2	267
RUTHERFORD, John Thomas Henry		1	316
RUTHERFORD, Thomas Wood		2	267
RUTHERFORD, W		2	267
RUTHERFORD, William	P	4	175
RUTHVEN, W		2	267
RUTLAND, William Edward James	P	5	147
RUTLEDGE, H A		3	238
RUTLEDGE, James Edward		1	316
RUTLEY, Henry W		2	267
RUTTER, Claude Arthur Gordon	P	2	267
RUTTER, Emanuel		1	316
RUTTER, John		1	316
RUXTON, William Ralph	P	1	316
RYAN, Alfred Harold		4	175
RYAN, Charles		1	316
RYAN, George Julian	P	1	316
RYAN, Henry		2	267
RYAN, J		3	239
RYAN, J		3	239
RYAN, James Frederick		2	267
RYAN, John James		1	316
RYAN, John Michael		2	267
RYAN, John P		2	267
RYAN, W		3	239
RYAN, W		3	239
RYDER, C E		3	239
RYDER, Horace	P	3	239
RYDER, J		3	239

Name	Photo	Part No.	Page No.
RYE, Frederick Clement		1	316
RYLANCE, Cyril		2	267
RYLANCE, William Henry		1	316
RYLANDS, Reginald Victor	P	1	316
RYLEY, Charles		4	175
RYMAN, Ernest		2	267
RYOTT, Leonard Gordon		2	267
SABIN, John	P	3	239
SABLES, William		2	267
SACH, Raymond		5	147
SACKER, Henry Edward		5	147
SADD, Robert Douglas	P	3	239
SADDINGTON, J W		3	239
SADDINGTON, William Henry		5	147
SADGROVE, James Thomas	P	5	147
SADGROVE, Leonard Stephen	P	5	147
SADLER, A		3	239
SADLER, E R		3	239
SADLER, Edwin G		2	267
SADLER, G		2	267
SADLER, Henry		2	267
SADLER, R C		2	267
SADLER, Robert Henry		1	317
SADLER, William		1	317
SADLER, William Edward	P	1	317
SADLER, William Reed	P	3	239
SAGE, Albert		2	267
SAGE, John Samuel	P	3	239
SAGGERS, C		3	239
SAIGEMAN, Jack		1	317
SAINSBURY, Charles		4	175
SAINSBURY, Charles W		3	239
SAINT, William Bell	P	2	267
SAIT, John	P	1	317
SAKER, Claude Astley		4	176
SALAMAN, Lewis Henry		2	268
SALAME, John Leonard	P	3	239
SALE, Alexander Gordon	P	1	317
SALE, Frederick Harold		1	317
SALE, Richard Crawford		4	176
SALES, Henry		1	317
SALES, Norman	P	4	176
SALES, William Albert		2	268
SALISBURY, Ernest		3	239
SALKELD, Albert Edward	P	2	268
SALLIS, William		2	268
SALMON, Albert		1	317
SALMON, George		5	147
SALMON, Stanley		4	176
SALMON, T		3	239
SALMON, Walter		2	268
SALMONI, Fred Stanley		1	317
SALT, Thomas Frederick Cyril	P	1	317
SALTER, John		1	318
SALTERN, George Francis		4	176
SALTERSBY, John William		2	268
SALTMARSH, C E		3	239
SALTMARSH, William	P	1	318
SALVAGE, George		4	176
SALVAGE, Harry		4	176
SALVAGE, John Albert		4	176
SALVESEN, Edward Maxwell	P	1	318
SAMPSON, Bertram		4	176
SAMPSON, Frank		4	176
SAMPSON, Frederick John		1	318

Name	Photo	Part No.	Page No.
SAMPSON, Percival Edgar		4	176
SAMPSON, Samuel Edward	P	3	239
SAMS, Harry		1	318
SAMSON, Arthur James		2	268
SAMSON, Arthur Legge		2	268
SAMSON, Hugh		4	176
SAMSON, William Horace		1	318
SAMUDA, Cecil Markham Annesley		4	176
SAMUEL, Felix Leopold		4	176
SAMUEL, Kenneth Clifford		2	268
SAMUELS, J		3	239
SAMWAYS, William Alfred Edwin	P	4	176
SANDALL, James Hosking		3	240
SANDBACH, Gilbert Robertson	P	3	240
SANDBACH, William	P	1	318
SANDBROOK, Henry		2	268
SANDERS, A E		3	240
SANDERS, Alfred Edwin		2	268
SANDERS, Archibald Morton		4	176
SANDERS, Arthur Henry		4	176
SANDERS, Fred	P	5	147
SANDERS, James Donald Gerhardt	P	2	268
SANDERS, Joseph Henry	P	3	240
SANDERS, Lewis	P	4	177
SANDERS, Richard Ingersoll (Jack)	P	1	318
SANDERSON, A		3	240
SANDERSON, Arthur Watson	P	1	318
SANDERSON, Charles Heaney		5	147
SANDERSON, Frederick Borthwick	P	2	268
SANDERSON, Frederick Wilson		5	147
SANDERSON, Harold Scott	P	2	268
SANDERSON, Harry		4	177
SANDERSON, James		2	269
SANDERSON, James Arthur Martin		4	177
SANDERSON, John		1	318
SANDERSON, Philip Noel	P	1	318
SANDERSON, S		3	240
SANDERSON, Wilfred	P	3	240
SANDHAM, James Frederick	P	1	318
SANDHAM, John Benjamin	P	4	177
SANDISON, Alexander Mundell	P	3	240
SANDISON, John Burnett		1	318
SANDRY, James Ralph		4	177
SANDS, Hugh		1	319
SANDY, W J		3	240
SANDYS, Henry John		4	177
SANDYS, Mervyn Keats		4	177
SANFORD, Howard Russell		2	269
SANGAR, Walter Augustine		4	177
SANGSTER, Edward G		2	269
SANGSTER, William John Campbell	P	2	269
SANKEY, Walter		2	269
SANSOM, Alfred John	P	3	240
SANSOM, Robert Andrew		1	319
SANSOME, Arthur		1	319
SANSOME, William		2	269
SANSON, Frederick		2	269
SAPSTEAD, George Frederick		1	319
SARBACH, J		3	240
SARFAS, Albert Edward		1	319
SARGANT, William Edwin		4	177
SARGEANT, William		1	319
SARGEAUNT, Arthur Frederick	P	1	319
SARGEAUNT, Herbert Gaussen		4	177
SARGENT, Alfred		1	319

Name	Photo	Part No.	Page No.
SARGENT, Frederick		1	319
SARGENT, H F		3	240
SARGENT, Henry Benjamin		1	319
SARGENT, Thomas		5	147
SARGENT, Thomas Percival		2	269
SARGOOD, Harry David Mcgregor		2	269
SARGOOD, Hugh Frank		3	240
SASSOON, Hamo Watts	P	2	269
SATTERTHWAITE, George Edward	P	4	177
SAUL, Charles Thomas		1	319
SAUL, George Henry		5	147
SAUNBY, H		3	240
SAUNDERS, Adam Melrose	P	3	240
SAUNDERS, Andrew		2	269
SAUNDERS, Arthur Courtenay	P	1	319
SAUNDERS, C T		3	241
SAUNDERS, Charles Seager	P	3	241
SAUNDERS, Clement	P	3	241
SAUNDERS, E W		3	241
SAUNDERS, Ernest Bertram	P	5	147
SAUNDERS, F		3	241
SAUNDERS, Frederick		1	319
SAUNDERS, Frederick Arthur		4	177
SAUNDERS, George C		2	269
SAUNDERS, Harold		5	147
SAUNDERS, Harry Francis		3	241
SAUNDERS, James		2	269
SAUNDERS, John		5	147
SAUNDERS, Ralph Leonard	P	3	241
SAUNDERS, Richard		1	319
SAUNDERS, Robert Edward		1	319
SAUNDERS, S		3	241
SAUNDERS, S G		3	241
SAUNDERS, Stanley Roland		1	319
SAUNDERS, T		2	269
SAUNDERS, Walter Layton	P	1	319
SAUNDERS, Wilfred		4	177
SAUNDERS, William		1	319
SAUNDERS, William		2	269
SAUNDERS, William Henry		5	148
SAUNDERS-JONES, Henry St. John		3	161
SAUNDERSON, J		3	241
SAUNDERSON, Robert De Bedick		4	177
SAVAGE, Arthur Henry	P	1	319
SAVAGE, Cuthbert Farrar		4	177
SAVAGE, Edwin		1	319
SAVAGE, F		3	241
SAVAGE, Frederick		2	269
SAVAGE, Harry		1	319
SAVAGE, J H		3	241
SAVAGE, John Ardkeen		1	319
SAVAGE, John Ardkeen		4	177
SAVERY, Roger De La Garde		2	269
SAVIGAR, George		4	177
SAVILLE, Edward		4	178
SAVIN, Thomas		1	319
SAVORY, Francis Richard Egerton		2	269
SAVORY, H		3	241
SAW, Noel Humphrey Wykeham	P	5	148
SAWARD, W H		3	241
SAWKINS, Claude Thomas		1	319
SAWYER, Charles		2	269
SAWYER, Ernest Edgar	P	4	178
SAWYER, Herbert Walter	P	3	241
SAWYER, Thomas Henry		1	319

Name	Photo	Part No.	Page No.
SAXON, H		3	241
SAXTON, Harold Henry	P	1	319
SAYER, Edwin		4	178
SAYER, Harold James		5	148
SAYER, Herbert George		2	269
SAYER, Robert William	P	1	320
SAYER, Stanley Kilbourne		1	320
SAYERS, Charles John		2	269
SAYERS, Horace George David		4	178
SAYERS, Joseph		4	178
SAYERS, Percy Langley		5	148
SAYLE, William E		2	269
SAYMAN, William Edward		5	148
SAYNOR, Frank Cyril		5	148
SAYRES, Hugh Wingfield	P	2	269
SAYWELL, Edgar		4	178
SCALBY, John		4	178
SCAMATON, Patrick		1	320
SCAMP, Alfred		2	270
SCANLON, John Joseph Michael		2	270
SCARBROUGH, Reginald John		4	178
SCARFE, Bertie Edward		2	270
SCARFE, Herbert William	P	4	178
SCARFE, John William (Alias Eric Grey)		1	320
SCARFF, Thomas		2	270
SCARLATT, George		2	270
SCARLOCK, E G		3	241
SCARTH, John William	P	1	320
SCARTH, Lawrence Victor	P	3	241
SCATCHARD, T		4	178
SCATCHARD, Thomas	P	1	320
SCHAFER, John Sharpey		5	148
SCHAFER, Thomas Sydney		2	270
SCHILL, Edward Melland	P	2	270
SCHLEIDER, George James William		1	320
SCHLOTEL, Charles Henry Cooper		5	148
SCHMIDT, Henry		1	320
SCHMIDT, Henry John	P	1	320
SCHNEIDER, H H		4	178
SCHNEIDER, Herbert Hugo	P	1	320
SCHOFIELD, Harry	P	3	241
SCHOFIELD, J		3	241
SCHOFIELD, James Alfred		4	178
SCHOFIELD, James Humphrey Clare		3	241
SCHOFIELD, Leonard		4	178
SCHOFIELD, Robert W		2	270
SCHOFIELD, Thomas		4	178
SCHOFIELD, Thos.		1	320
SCHOFIELD, W		3	241
SCHOLES, Fred		4	178
SCHOLES, Percy G		2	270
SCHOLEY, Thomas Edward	P	4	178
SCHOOLEY, Charles Harry		5	148
SCHOOLING, Geoffrey Holt	P	2	270
SCHOOLING, Paul Sydney Bedford	P	4	178
SCHREIBER, Vivian George Edward Spencer	P	1	320
SCHUNCK, Roger Henry		4	179
SCHURER, Louis Henry		1	320
SCHUSTER, Alfred F		4	179
SCHUTZ, J		2	270
SCHWABEN, Henry Robert	P	1	320
SCINDEN, Alfred		1	320
SCOBIE, John (Ian) Allan Mackay	P	2	270
SCOFIELD, W F E J		3	241
SCOONES, Archibald John	P	4	179

Name	Photo	Part No.	Page No.
SCOT, Skirving Archibald	P	1	328
SCOTLAND, David Lothian	P	5	148
SCOTLAND, Thomas	P	4	179
SCOTNEY, G		3	242
SCOTNEY, Harry		3	242
SCOTT, Alexander		1	320
SCOTT, Alexander		2	270
SCOTT, Alexander		5	148
SCOTT, Alexander Stewart		4	179
SCOTT, Andrew Holmes		4	179
SCOTT, Basil John Harrison		2	270
SCOTT, Basil John Harrison		4	179
SCOTT, Campbell Lowe		5	148
SCOTT, Charles		1	320
SCOTT, Charles		2	270
SCOTT, Chrles Edward Arthur		1	320
SCOTT, D		3	242
SCOTT, David Cameron		1	320
SCOTT, Edgar		3	242
SCOTT, Edward Claud	P	1	320
SCOTT, Edward Grigor		4	179
SCOTT, Ernest Robert		2	270
SCOTT, Francis William	P	1	321
SCOTT, Frederick		2	270
SCOTT, Frederick G		2	270
SCOTT, G		3	242
SCOTT, George		1	321
SCOTT, George		4	179
SCOTT, George Frederick		2	270
SCOTT, George Henry Hall	P	3	242
SCOTT, George Kenn		3	242
SCOTT, George William		4	179
SCOTT, H		3	242
SCOTT, H		3	242
SCOTT, Henry Frank	P	1	321
SCOTT, Herbert Lawson		4	179
SCOTT, J		2	270
SCOTT, J		2	270
SCOTT, J		3	242
SCOTT, J		3	242
SCOTT, J		3	242
SCOTT, J D		3	242
SCOTT, John		2	270
SCOTT, John		4	179
SCOTT, John Ford		2	270
SCOTT, Lancelot		2	270
SCOTT, Leslie		5	148
SCOTT, Matthew		4	179
SCOTT, Norman Campbell		4	179
SCOTT, Oliver		4	179
SCOTT, P		2	271
SCOTT, P		2	271
SCOTT, R		3	242
SCOTT, R		3	242
SCOTT, R C		3	242
SCOTT, Ralph Rookby	P	5	149
SCOTT, Richard Thomas Folliott		1	321
SCOTT, Robert		2	271
SCOTT, Robert		3	242
SCOTT, Robert Edward Leslie		5	149
SCOTT, Robert Fraser		1	321
SCOTT, Robert Spence		4	179
SCOTT, Robert Walter Theodore Gordon		3	242
SCOTT, Sidney Maurice		2	271
SCOTT, T		3	242

Name	Photo	Part No.	Page No.
SCOTT, Thomas Hardy		4	179
SCOTT, Victor	P	1	321
SCOTT, W		2	271
SCOTT, W		3	242
SCOTT, W		3	242
SCOTT, W W		3	242
SCOTT, W W		3	242
SCOTT, Wallace		1	321
SCOTT, Walter		2	271
SCOTT, Walter Falconer		4	180
SCOTT, William		1	321
SCOTT, William		1	321
SCOTT, William		2	271
SCOTT, William		4	180
SCOTT, William		4	180
SCOTT, William Ewart		5	149
SCOTT, William G		2	271
SCOTT, William James		2	271
SCOTT, William Leslie		1	321
SCOTT, William Peach	P	3	242
SCOTT, William Peach	P	4	180
SCOUGALL, Alexander	P	1	321
SCOULAR, William		4	180
SCOURFIELD, David Benjamin		4	180
SCOVELL, Reginald Herbert	P	2	271
SCRATTON, Geoffrey Howel		4	180
SCREENEY, Michael		2	271
SCRIMGEOUR, John Alexander	P	3	242
SCRIMGEOUR, Robert Campbell		3	242
SCRIVEN, Frederick		2	271
SCRIVENER, Cyril Alfred		1	321
SCRIVENER, John Sydney	P	3	242
SCRIVENER, W		3	242
SCRIVENER, William		5	149
SCRUTON, Henry		4	180
SCRUTTON, Frank Richards		1	322
SCRYMGEOUR, Paul Mcconnachie	P	3	242
SCULL, Harry Walter		4	180
SCULLY, Charles Richard		1	322
SCULLY, John		2	271
SCUTT, Frank		4	180
SEABROOK, James Herbert	P	1	322
SEABURY, Edgar Raymond		4	180
SEACOMBE, Alfred		2	271
SEAGER, H J		3	242
SEAGER, Thomas		1	322
SEAGER, William Thomas	P	2	271
SEAGO, F W		3	242
SEAL, William	P	3	242
SEALE, E		3	242
SEALE, Rodney Gordon	P	3	242
SEALE, Sidney		2	271
SEALY, Peter Mcintyre		5	149
SEAMAN, G		3	243
SEAMAN, Henry		1	322
SEAR, Albert Alfred		5	149
SEAR, Joseph Sackville	P	1	322
SEARLE, George Charles		1	322
SEARLE, George William Augustus		1	322
SEARLE, H E		2	271
SEARLE, John		1	322
SEARLE, Percy		4	180
SEARLE, William		2	271
SEARLES, Edward Gregory		1	322
SEARS, Horace		2	271

Name	Photo	Part No.	Page No.
SEARS, Percy		4	180
SEARS, Thomas J		2	271
SEATON, George		5	149
SEAVER, Charles		4	180
SEAVERNS, Joel Harrison		2	271
SEBAG-MONTEFIORE, Robert Montefiore		2	228
SEBASTIAN, Skinner Raymond		4	180
SECKER, George Vane		1	322
SECKER, James B		2	271
SECKHAM, Gerald Adair (Robin)		4	180
SECRETT, Albert George		4	180
SECRETT, Walter Frederick		2	271
SEDDON, Daniel Urch		4	180
SEDGELEY, Frank		1	322
SEDGWICK, Arthur Edward		2	271
SEDGWICK, George		1	322
SEDGWICK, Harold		2	271
SEDGWICK, John		4	181
SEDGWICK, John Henry	P	3	243
SEDGWICK, Rupert Charles Bradley	P	2	271
SEDGWICK, Thomas Edward	P	3	243
SEEGER, Frederick Henry	P	3	243
SEELEY, William Alfred		1	322
SEENEY, Hugh		1	322
SEFTON, Thomas Henry		1	322
SEKLES, Henry		2	271
SELBY, Beauchamp Henry		1	322
SELBY, Prideaux Joseph	P	2	272
SELBY-SMYTH, Miles Bury	P	1	333
SELF, Frank Clarence		4	181
SELL, Clarence James		3	243
SELLAR, P L		3	243
SELLEN, Albert Frederick		1	322
SELLENS, George		1	322
SELLEY, Cecil Howard	P	5	149
SELLICK, Walter		1	322
SELLON, Bruce Heckford		4	181
SELLS, William Joseph		2	272
SELMAN, Charles F		2	272
SEMARK, William Richard	P	1	322
SEMMENS, Alfred Frederick William	P	5	149
SEMPLE, Thomas Hubert Galbraith	P	2	272
SENIOR, George Henry		2	272
SENISCAL, William Butler	P	4	181
SENNAR, R		3	243
SERGANT, Ernest		2	272
SERJEANT, W		3	243
SETCHELL, George Thomas		4	181
SETON-BROWNE, Montague William		2	44
SETTER, Auguste Arthur Leopold		1	322
SETTERFIELD, Charles Alfred		1	322
SETTERFIELD, Emmanuel William		1	322
SETTERFIELD, Frank		1	322
SEVERNE, Henry Francis	P	1	322
SEWARD, Frederick		1	322
SEWARD, Robert Francis	P	2	272
SEWART, Harold Yorke	P	3	243
SEWELL, Dougal Clifford Campbell		4	181
SEWELL, Edward William	P	4	181
SEWELL, Henry		1	322
SEWELL, Reuben John		1	322
SEWELL, Robert William	P	5	149
SEWELL, Sidney Davies		1	322
SEWELL, Thomas		1	323
SEWELL, William Fane Dalzell Dalrymple	P	1	323

Name	Photo	Part No.	Page No.
SEXTON, Edwin James	P	3	243
SEXTON, Joseph	P	3	243
SEXTON, Leonard Alfred		4	181
SEXTON, Thomas William	P	3	243
SEYMOUR, C		3	243
SEYMOUR, Lewis Thierry		3	243
SEYMOUR, Thomas William		2	272
SEYMOUR, William		4	181
SEYMOUR, William George		1	323
SEYMOUR, William Percy		4	181
SHACKLADY, W		3	243
SHADBOLT, William	P	3	243
SHADRAKE, Charles		1	323
SHADWELL, Mark B		2	272
SHAFE, Edward James Thomas	P	5	149
SHAFFOND, Charles		1	323
SHAKERLEY, Eric Piers	P	1	323
SHAKESPEARE, William		4	181
SHAKESPEARE, William Henry		2	272
SHALLBERG, John Reginald		2	272
SHAND, James		4	181
SHAND, Peter Lewis Alexander	P	2	272
SHAND, William Whitson		2	272
SHANKIE, James		4	181
SHANKS, Arthur Cain		2	272
SHANKSTER, George	P	2	272
SHANKSTER, Stanley	P	2	272
SHANLEY, James		2	272
SHANN, Reginald Arthur		5	149
SHANN, W		3	244
SHANNON, Ian Herbert Croal	P	1	323
SHANNON, William Henry	P	1	323
SHAPLEY, Archibald Henry		2	272
SHAPTER, Lewis Henry	P	1	323
SHARKEY, John	P	2	273
SHARLAND, Charles Frederic		5	149
SHARMON, Frederick		1	323
SHARP, A		3	244
SHARP, Arthur		1	323
SHARP, Arthur Granville	P	4	181
SHARP, Charles Gordon		4	181
SHARP, E		2	273
SHARP, Frederick Henry	P	2	273
SHARP, Jack Richard		5	149
SHARP, James		2	273
SHARP, John	P	1	323
SHARP, Robert		4	181
SHARP, Vivian King		1	323
SHARP, William		3	244
SHARP, William Charles John		1	323
SHARPE, A		3	244
SHARPE, Albert		2	273
SHARPE, Albert E		2	273
SHARPE, Arthur Noel		4	181
SHARPE, F		3	244
SHARPE, F J		3	244
SHARPE, Harry		2	273
SHARPE, Reginald Albert		3	244
SHARPE, Richard		4	181
SHARPE, Sydney Herbert		2	273
SHARPIN, Frank Lloyd	P	2	273
SHARPLES, F		3	244
SHARRATT, J		2	273
SHARRATT, Simeon	P	1	323
SHATTOCK, Montagu De Mancha	P	1	323

Name	Photo	Part No.	Page No.
SHATTOCK, Thomas Henry		1	324
SHAVE, William James		1	324
SHAW, A		3	244
SHAW, Albert		5	150
SHAW, Alfred		1	324
SHAW, Alfred		2	273
SHAW, Bernard Henry Gilbert	P	1	324
SHAW, Charles		3	244
SHAW, Edward Alfred		4	182
SHAW, Francis Edward		5	150
SHAW, Harry		2	273
SHAW, Hartley		2	273
SHAW, Hugh James	P	1	324
SHAW, James		2	273
SHAW, James	P	5	150
SHAW, John	P	3	244
SHAW, John		5	150
SHAW, John Herbert		4	182
SHAW, Manfred Samuel		1	324
SHAW, Maurice		2	273
SHAW, Peter Boyd		5	150
SHAW, R		3	244
SHAW, Ralph	P	4	182
SHAW, Raymond Pugh	P	1	324
SHAW, Richard	P	2	273
SHAW, Robert Henderson	P	5	150
SHAW, Thomas Walter		4	182
SHAW, Walter Douglas	P	4	182
SHAW, Walter Hunter	P	2	273
SHAW, William		2	273
SHAW, William		2	273
SHAWLEY, P		3	244
SHAYLER, Henry W		2	273
SHEA, Batt		1	324
SHEA, F		3	244
SHEA, James Henry		1	324
SHEAD, H		3	244
SHEARER, Archibald Weir		2	273
SHEARER, Gordon Ross		4	182
SHEARER, William	P	3	244
SHEARIN, Edward		1	324
SHEARING, Harold Southwell		4	182
SHEARMAN, John George		4	182
SHEARMAN, Samuel		1	324
SHEASBY, N		3	244
SHEEHAN, Patrick		2	273
SHEEN, James Edward		4	182
SHEFFIELD, Surtees		2	273
SHEGOG, Richard Wellington		4	182
SHEIL, A		3	244
SHELBOURNE, George		1	324
SHELBOURNE, Percy Edward	P	3	244
SHELDON, John Henry		5	150
SHELDON, Thomas		4	182
SHELDON, William George		1	324
SHELDRAKE, A		3	244
SHELDRAKE, David A		2	273
SHELDRAKE, William		2	273
SHELLEY, Cecil William Charles		2	273
SHENSTONE, W		3	244
SHENTON, Francis Joseph	P	4	182
SHEPHEARD, Richard John		1	324
SHEPHERD, A		3	244
SHEPHERD, Charles Alfred		1	324
SHEPHERD, Frederick		1	324

Name	Photo	Part No.	Page No.
SHEPHERD, George		2	273
SHEPHERD, Gerald A G		4	182
SHEPHERD, Gerald Alexander Gaselee	P	1	324
SHEPHERD, James		1	324
SHEPHERD, James		2	274
SHEPHERD, John	P	3	244
SHEPHERD, John		4	182
SHEPHERD, Lawrence		2	274
SHEPHERD, Norman		4	182
SHEPHERD, Samuel		2	274
SHEPHERD, Thomas	P	4	183
SHEPHERD, W R		3	244
SHEPHERD-CROSS, Cecil Herbert Shepherd	P	3	68
SHEPHERDSON, Robert		5	150
SHEPPARD, Albert		2	274
SHEPPARD, Arthur Vincent		4	183
SHEPPARD, B		4	183
SHEPPARD, Charles Edward		1	324
SHEPPARD, Edgar E		2	274
SHEPPARD, Evelyn Gordon		2	274
SHEPPARD, Frederick		5	150
SHEPPARD, Isaac	P	1	324
SHEPPARD, Lewis Charles Burford		4	183
SHEPPARD, Reginald	P	1	324
SHEPPEE, Frederick John	P	1	324
SHEPPEY, Frederick W		2	274
SHERAN, J		4	183
SHERGOLD, George Henry		1	324
SHERIDAN, Alexander Lindsay		5	150
SHERIDAN, P J		4	183
SHERIFF, George Ross		3	244
SHERIFF, R		3	244
SHERLOCK, Gerard L E		4	183
SHERLOCK, William Reginald		4	183
SHERMAN, Reginald		4	183
SHERRET, Albert		2	274
SHERRING, Frederick William		1	324
SHERWOOD, A B		3	244
SHERWOOD, Sidney William	P	1	325
SHEWRING, F A V		3	244
SHIEL, A		3	244
SHIELD, Frederick Dowson		2	274
SHIELDS, Hugh John Sladen	P	2	274
SHIELDS, Hugh John Sladen		4	183
SHIELDS, Thomas		1	325
SHIELDS, William		5	150
SHIELL, John Dodds	P	4	183
SHIER, Christopher	P	4	183
SHIER, Wilfrid Fowler		4	183
SHIFFNER, Sir John Bridger	P	5	150
SHILCOCK, John		4	183
SHILCOCK, John Wynton		2	274
SHILCOCK, R T		3	244
SHILLINGFORD, Joseph W J		2	274
SHIMMIN, William		1	325
SHINE, J		3	244
SHINER, W J		3	244
SHINGLETON, Arthur Robert		1	325
SHINNIE, Herbert Forsyth Craig	P	1	325
SHIP, Francis Alfred		1	325
SHIP, Joseph J		2	274
SHIPLEY, William		1	325
SHIPP, Gregory		1	325
SHIPTON, Launcelot Bridges		4	183
SHIPWAY, Guy Maxwell		4	183

Name	Photo	Part No.	Page No.
SHIRLAND, Robert		5	150
SHIRLAW, Ninian Frederick	P	3	244
SHIRLEY, Archibald Vincent	P	3	245
SHIRLEY, Daniel		2	274
SHIRLEY, S		3	245
SHIRRA, J		3	245
SHOESMITH, William Copley		4	183
SHOLLIKER, Fred	P	2	274
SHONK, William Charles		1	325
SHOOSMITH, William H		2	274
SHOPLAND, Fred		3	245
SHORE, William		5	150
SHORROCK, Ernest		4	183
SHORT, Albert Frederick	P	1	325
SHORT, Cuthbert William	P	3	245
SHORT, Gladston		2	274
SHORT, James	P	5	150
SHORT, Pursey Frederick		4	183
SHORTER, Bertie Gordon	P	2	274
SHORTER, P		2	274
SHORTER, Percival Arthur	P	2	274
SHORTER, Robert George	P	2	274
SHORTHOUSE, J		2	275
SHOTTON, Rowlandson Hardy		1	325
SHOVE, James		3	245
SHOVE, Victor Albert		1	325
SHRAPNEL, Victor George Fleetwood	P	3	245
SHRIMPTON, John		2	275
SHROSBIE, George Alfred		2	275
SHROSBREE, G A		3	245
SHRUBB, Albert Edward		2	275
SHRUBB, Frank James	P	1	325
SHRUBSALL, W J		3	245
SHURMUR, Harold Thomas		4	183
SHUTE, Albert Edward		3	245
SHUTE, Frederick		2	275
SHUTE, Thomas John	P	1	325
SHUTTLE, H H		3	245
SHUTTLER, Walter Henry		2	275
SHUTTLEWORTH, John		2	275
SHYER, Harry		1	325
SIBBALD, John	P	1	325
SIBBALD, William		4	184
SIBLEY, Edward		4	184
SIBLEY, George James		2	275
SICHEL, Geoffrey Michael John	P	1	325
SIDDALL, Herbert Baker		5	151
SIDEBOTTOM, Arthur	P	3	245
SIDEBOTTOM, George		2	275
SIDNELL, Walter		2	275
SIDWELL, E		3	245
SIDWELL, John		2	275
SIEBERT, Albert Alfred		2	275
SIEVEWRIGHT, Allan Bell		4	184
SIGMUR, William H		2	275
SILBY, William G		2	275
SILCOCKS, Francis Herbert		2	275
SILCOX, William Henry		1	325
SILK, George Dollar		1	326
SILK, Joseph		1	326
SILK, Norman Galbraith	P	1	326
SILKSTONE, Bert		1	326
SILLARS, David Hamilton		2	275
SILLENCE, R H		3	245
SILLER, Alfred		4	184

Name	Photo	Part No.	Page No.
SILLER, Henry		4	184
SILLER, James		4	184
SILLETT, Ernest Henry		1	326
SILLICK, Harold Bertram	P	3	245
SILLS, Charles Caldwell		2	275
SILLS, Charles Caldwell		4	184
SILVER, Charles		1	326
SILVERTON, William Henry	P	1	326
SILVERWOOD, A		3	245
SILVERWOOD, George Henry	P	3	245
SILVESTER, Alfred Ferdinand	P	1	326
SILVESTER, Anson Lloyd	P	1	326
SILVESTER, Arthur John	P	2	275
SILVESTER, George Thomas		2	275
SILVESTER, John		1	326
SILVESTER, Percy Wafford		2	275
SILVESTER, Reginald		2	275
SIM, Andrew		2	275
SIM, George Hedderwick		2	275
SIM, James		2	275
SIM, James	P	4	184
SIM, John Dingwall	P	4	184
SIM, John Gray	P	4	184
SIM, Peter Johnstone	P	4	184
SIMCOCK, Gilbert Alexander		4	184
SIMES, Henry Charles Nathaniel		3	246
SIMKINS, Daniel Frederick	P	3	246
SIMKINS, Henry Ernest		4	184
SIMKINS, Samuel	P	4	184
SIMMONDS, Arthur		2	275
SIMMONDS, Charles Alfred		2	275
SIMMONDS, Edward J		2	275
SIMMONDS, Frederick		2	275
SIMMONDS, George Henry		1	326
SIMMONDS, Guy Bloxham		5	151
SIMMONDS, H		3	246
SIMMONDS, O		3	246
SIMMONDS, Richard Stanley		1	326
SIMMONDS, Robert Thomas		2	275
SIMMONDS, W		2	275
SIMMONDS, William		2	275
SIMMONDS, William		2	275
SIMMONDS, William Edward		2	275
SIMMONDS, William G		2	275
SIMMONITE, George		5	151
SIMMONS, A		3	246
SIMMONS, Albert		1	326
SIMMONS, Albert		1	326
SIMMONS, Alfred L		2	275
SIMMONS, Frederick George		2	275
SIMMONS, J T		3	246
SIMMONS, R		3	246
SIMMONS, Seymour Francis		5	151
SIMMONS, Sidney Charles Stanley		3	246
SIMMONS, Stephen Washington Augustin	P	5	151
SIMMONS, W		2	275
SIMMONS, W H		3	246
SIMMS, Alfred		1	326
SIMMS, George	P	1	326
SIMMS, George Norman	P	1	326
SIMMS, George Norman		4	184
SIMMS, John Basil Palling		4	184
SIMMS, John Edward	P	3	246
SIMMS, John Henry		3	246
SIMMS, Walter George		5	151
SIMON, Eric Conrad		2	275
SIMON, William John		2	275
SIMONDS, Charles Francis	P	3	246
SIMONDS, Charles Henville		4	184
SIMONS, William Vazie Langdale		4	184
SIMPELL, William Mathias		5	151
SIMPER, Albert William		3	246
SIMPKIN, George Henry		2	275
SIMPKINS, Frederick Thomas		1	326
SIMPKINS, James		2	276
SIMPSON, A		2	276
SIMPSON, A		3	246
SIMPSON, Abram	P	1	327
SIMPSON, Albert Victor		1	327
SIMPSON, Alexander		4	185
SIMPSON, Alexander Mathieson	P	1	327
SIMPSON, Alick		4	185
SIMPSON, Anthony Henry	P	1	327
SIMPSON, Archibald		1	327
SIMPSON, Archibald Cranby		1	327
SIMPSON, Arthur John		4	185
SIMPSON, Arthur More		4	185
SIMPSON, Bertram Elsworth		3	246
SIMPSON, Charles		2	276
SIMPSON, Charles Maclaren		2	276
SIMPSON, Christopher Byron	P	2	276
SIMPSON, Claude Middleton	P	5	151
SIMPSON, Clifford Sandford	P	3	246
SIMPSON, David Leonard		4	185
SIMPSON, Edward		1	327
SIMPSON, Frank	P	2	276
SIMPSON, G		2	276
SIMPSON, George		1	327
SIMPSON, George		2	276
SIMPSON, George Kenneth	P	3	246
SIMPSON, H		4	185
SIMPSON, Harry		2	276
SIMPSON, Hector		2	276
SIMPSON, Hubert Zeph	P	1	327
SIMPSON, Hubert Zeph		4	185
SIMPSON, J		4	185
SIMPSON, James		1	327
SIMPSON, James Cowie	P	5	151
SIMPSON, John		1	327
SIMPSON, John		1	327
SIMPSON, John Edmund	P	1	327
SIMPSON, Odo Louis David Mackay	P	4	185
SIMPSON, Richard Dyer		2	276
SIMPSON, Robert Mackie		4	185
SIMPSON, Stephen		5	152
SIMPSON, Thomas C	P	2	276
SIMPSON, W H M		4	185
SIMPSON, William	P	1	327
SIMPSON, William Norman		4	185
SIMPSON, William Russell		1	327
SIMS, Charles	P	5	152
SIMS, Herbert		1	327
SIMS, James Theodore		4	185
SIMS, John		1	327
SIMS, John		1	327
SIMS, William Francis		2	276
SIMS, William John		1	327
SIMSON, Herbert		1	327
SIMSON, Ronald Francis		4	185
SINCLAIR, David		2	276

Name	Photo	Part No.	Page No.
SMITH, Percy Lowe		1	331
SMITH, Peter James		5	154
SMITH, R		2	279
SMITH, R		3	251
SMITH, R		3	251
SMITH, R		3	251
SMITH, R		3	251
SMITH, Richard		2	279
SMITH, Robert		1	331
SMITH, Robert		1	331
SMITH, Robert	P	3	251
SMITH, Robert		4	190
SMITH, Robert		5	154
SMITH, Robert		5	154
SMITH, Robert Charnley		4	190
SMITH, Robert Dunlop	P	3	251
SMITH, Robert Edward		4	190
SMITH, Robert Ernest		1	331
SMITH, Robert James	P	5	154
SMITH, Robert Joshua		1	331
SMITH, Roland		3	252
SMITH, Rowallan William Gordon		5	155
SMITH, S		3	252
SMITH, S		3	252
SMITH, S		3	252
SMITH, S J		3	252
SMITH, Samuel		2	279
SMITH, Sidney		1	331
SMITH, Sidney Charles		1	331
SMITH, Sidney Joseph	P	1	331
SMITH, Stanley		3	252
SMITH, Stanley Fenton		4	190
SMITH, Stanley G		2	279
SMITH, Stanley Ivan		1	331
SMITH, Sydney		1	331
SMITH, Sydney Charles		3	252
SMITH, Sydney Henry		1	331
SMITH, T		2	279
SMITH, T		3	252
SMITH, Thomas		1	331
SMITH, Thomas		2	279
SMITH, Thomas Griffin		1	332
SMITH, Thomas J		2	279
SMITH, Thomas Sidney		2	279
SMITH, Thomas Sydney		1	332
SMITH, Thomas William Edward		4	191
SMITH, Thurston Boyd		4	191
SMITH, Tom		1	332
SMITH, Victor		2	279
SMITH, Victor George		4	191
SMITH, Victor Wheeler	P	3	252
SMITH, W		3	252
SMITH, W		3	252
SMITH, W		3	252
SMITH, W		3	252
SMITH, W		3	252
SMITH, W		3	252
SMITH, W C		3	252
SMITH, W J		3	252
SMITH, W J		3	252
SMITH, Walter	P	3	252
SMITH, Walter Alexander	P	2	279
SMITH, Walter George		2	279
SMITH, Walter Henry		2	279
SMITH, Walter Palmer		1	332
SMITH, Walter S		2	279
SMITH, Walter Sidney		1	332
SMITH, Walter Wyville	P	1	332
SMITH, Wilfred Gaisford	P	2	279
SMITH, William		1	332
SMITH, William		2	279
SMITH, William		2	279
SMITH, William		2	279
SMITH, William		2	279
SMITH, William		2	279
SMITH, William		2	279
SMITH, William		3	252
SMITH, William		4	191
SMITH, William		4	191
SMITH, William		5	155
SMITH, William Charles		4	191
SMITH, William Edmund		1	332
SMITH, William Edward		4	191
SMITH, William Edward George		5	155
SMITH, William Ernest Owen		2	279
SMITH, William Gerald Furness	P	1	332
SMITH, William Harold Vyvyan		4	191
SMITH, William Henry		1	332
SMITH, William Joseph		1	332
SMITH, William Joseph		4	191
SMITH, William Mason		5	155
SMITH, William Oliver		1	332
SMITH, William Wilton		1	332
SMITH GRANT, John Gordon Smith Cheetham		4	68
SMITHERINGDALE, J		3	252
SMITHERS, Harold	P	2	280
SMITHERS, Reginald Cuthbert Welsford	P	3	252
SMITH-MASTERS, George Arthur	P	1	248
SMITHSON, Albert		2	280
SMITTEN, John W		2	280
SMY, Arthur		2	280
SMY, F		2	280
SMYTH, Charles Alfred		5	155
SMYTH, Edmund Fitzgerald	P	3	252
SMYTH, John		2	280
SMYTH, John	P	3	253
SMYTH, Richard Alexander Noel	P	1	333
SMYTH, Robert Richard	P	5	155
SMYTHE, Frederick Fleming		4	191
SMYTHE, Ralph Conran		2	280
SNAITH, George	P	4	191
SNAITH, Thomas	P	4	192
SNARE, Albert		1	333
SNARE, William George		4	192
SNARTT, R		3	253
SNEAD-COX, Geoffrey Philip Joseph		2	82
SNEAD-COX, Richard Mary		2	82
SNEATH, Claude Davis	P	1	333
SNEDDON, J H		2	280
SNEDDON, James	P	1	333
SNEDDON, John Alexander		3	253
SNELGROVE, Sidney Henry	P	1	333
SNELL, Edwin A W		2	280
SNELL, George Nowell		1	334
SNELL, Norris	P	2	280
SNELL, W J		2	280
SNELL, William John		1	334
SNELLING, Frederick John	P	3	253
SNELLING, Jack		2	280
SNEYD, Thomas Humphrey	P	1	334

Name	Photo	Part No.	Page No.
SNOOK, Ralph Edgar	P	3	253
SNOOKS, Frederick E		2	280
SNOSWELL, Thomas Emden		1	334
SNOW, George Wilkie		3	253
SNOW, William Charles		1	334
SNOWDEN, Frederick	P	3	253
SNOWDEN, Harcourt John	P	1	334
SNOWIE, John		3	253
SNOWLEY, Absolom		2	280
SNUDDEN, William John	P	2	281
SOAL, Ernest William		4	192
SOAMES, Harold Martin		4	192
SODIN, Birt		2	281
SOLLEY, Alfred John George		1	334
SOLLITT, George William		1	334
SOLOMAN, Maxwell		2	281
SOLSBURY, William		2	281
SOMERS, W		2	281
SOMERSET, Norman Arthur Henry		4	192
SOMERS-SMITH, John Robert	P	2	280
SOMERS-SMITH, Richard Willingdon		1	333
SOMERTON, Charles Enos		1	334
SOMERTON, Frederick Charles	P	1	334
SOMERVAIL, William Fulton		5	155
SOMERVILLE, Walter Scott		2	281
SOMMERVILLE, George Little	P	2	281
SOMMERVILLE, William		2	281
SONES, Herbert James		1	334
SOOLE, Seymour Waldegrave	P	3	253
SOPER, John Gilbert		4	192
SORE, Alfred George		4	192
SORE, Percy		4	192
SORLEY, Charles Hamilton		2	281
SORSBY, William		1	334
SOTHEBY, Lionel Frederick Southwell		2	281
SOTHERN, John		4	192
SOTHERN, John		5	155
SOUGHTON, Thomas Edward		1	334
SOURBUTTS, Richard		1	334
SOUTAR, A		2	281
SOUTAR, Frederick		2	281
SOUTAR, William		2	281
SOUTER, C		2	281
SOUTER, Charles Jesse		1	334
SOUTER, Henry Fraser		4	192
SOUTER, James George		5	155
SOUTER, R M		2	281
SOUTH, Frederick		1	334
SOUTH, Thomas J		2	281
SOUTHALL, Nathan		5	155
SOUTHERINGTON, Alfred Ernest		4	192
SOUTHERINGTON, George Brown		4	192
SOUTHERN, Edward	P	2	281
SOUTHERN, Henry Walter		1	334
SOUTHERN, John George	P	1	334
SOUTHERN, Joseph		5	155
SOUTHERN, Thomas William		5	155
SOUTHERTON, Harry Percy		1	334
SOUTHERTON, Laurence Cyril		4	192
SOUTHON, John Edward	P	3	253
SOUTHWELL, George A		2	281
SOUTHWICK, Charles Thomas	P	1	334
SOUTHWOOD, Horace George		1	334
SOWDEN, F		3	254
SOWDEN, Francis Henry		2	281
SOWINSKI, Joseph Ladislas	P	4	192
SOWTER, Geoffrey Smart	P	5	155
SOWTER, Unwin Henry Etches		5	156
SPACKESMAN, George Thomas	P	5	156
SPACKMAN, Harold John		1	334
SPAFFORD, Arthur Langworthy	P	2	281
SPAIN, Arthur Charles		4	192
SPAIN, Edward Sydney Stephen		1	334
SPAIN, P F		3	254
SPAIN, Walter		4	192
SPALDING, Frank		1	334
SPALDING, Robert Gordon		2	281
SPALDING, Thomas		2	281
SPARK, Archibald Charles	P	3	254
SPARKES, Charles		1	334
SPARKS, Harry Robert		1	334
SPARKS, John George		5	156
SPARROW, Charles Newman		4	192
SPARROW, Frank Edward		4	193
SPARROW, George Lewis		4	193
SPARROW, Henry Ambrose	P	2	281
SPEAR, Albert Henri		4	193
SPEAR, Norman Victor	P	3	254
SPEAREN, Thomas Alfred		4	193
SPEAREY, Frederick William		1	334
SPEARING, Edward		3	254
SPEARING, Stanley W		2	282
SPEARMAN, E A		2	282
SPEARS, John		4	193
SPEARS, Richard Henry		4	193
SPECK, William Howard		2	282
SPEDDING, Arthur Vivian	P	2	282
SPEECHLY, Tom Martindale		4	193
SPEED, David Nelson	P	4	193
SPEER, Fred		4	193
SPEIGHT, Horace		4	193
SPEIGHT, James Christopher	P	3	254
SPEIGHT, Leonard		4	193
SPEIRS, Andrew Arthur David	P	4	193
SPEIRS, David	P	4	193
SPEIRS-ALEXANDER, Allister Ralph		3	3
SPEKE, The Rev. Hugh	P	1	334
SPELLER, Horace E		2	282
SPELLER, William		2	282
SPELMAN, Peter		2	282
SPENCE, Alexander		4	193
SPENCE, James Mckenzie	P	1	335
SPENCE, Stuart Norman	P	4	193
SPENCE, Thomas J		2	282
SPENCE, William Samuel	P	3	254
SPENCER, A		2	282
SPENCER, Arthur	P	2	282
SPENCER, Arthur	P	3	254
SPENCER, Arthur	P	4	193
SPENCER, B		3	254
SPENCER, Charles James	P	1	335
SPENCER, Edmund		4	193
SPENCER, Francis George		3	254
SPENCER, Frederick W		2	282
SPENCER, Harry Varnals		4	194
SPENCER, Henry	P	5	156
SPENCER, Henry Edmund Kingsley		4	194
SPENCER, John		1	335
SPENCER, John		4	194
SPENCER, John Henry		3	254

Name	Photo	Part No.	Page No.
SPENCER, Joseph Thomas		2	282
SPENCER, Oliver Nevill	P	5	156
SPENCER, Philip Gell	P	3	254
SPENCER, Sam		2	282
SPENCER, Sidney		2	282
SPENCER, William	P	3	254
SPENCER, William John	P	5	156
SPENDLOVE, Gervase Thorpe		4	194
SPENDLOW, John James		1	335
SPENS, Walter Thomas Patrick		5	156
SPICE, Albert		1	335
SPICE, Robert William		1	335
SPICER, Arthur John		1	335
SPICER, Edmund Daniell	P	4	194
SPICER, G		3	254
SPICER, George Henry	P	1	335
SPICER, Maurice Arnott		1	335
SPIDEN, James		2	282
SPIELMANN, Harold Lionel Isidore	P	1	335
SPIERS, Harold Alfred		1	335
SPIERS, William John		1	335
SPILLANE, Cornelius William		1	335
SPILLER, J		4	194
SPILLETTS, Walter		4	194
SPINDLEE, W A		3	255
SPINDLER, David		1	335
SPINKS, Frederick Herman Victor	P	1	335
SPINNER, Percy James		3	255
SPINNER, Sydney John		3	255
SPINNEY, K E		4	194
SPIRES, George		2	282
SPIRES, Henry		2	282
SPITTLE, Frank Thomas		1	336
SPITTLES, Thomas Robert	P	1	336
SPONG, Harry George		4	194
SPOONER, Alexander		1	336
SPOONER, Arthur C		2	282
SPOONER, Charles Albert Victor		1	336
SPOONER, Charles Robert		4	194
SPOONER, Frank		2	282
SPOONER, Frederick Osborn		2	282
SPOONER, George Piercy	P	4	194
SPOONER, Leonard		2	282
SPOONER, Raymond Wilberforce	P	4	194
SPOONER, Seth William George		2	282
SPOONER, William Charles		1	336
SPOORS, George		2	282
SPORTON, George Herbert		1	336
SPRAGGON, George		4	194
SPRAGUE, Reginald		2	282
SPRATT, Harry Osbert William		4	194
SPRECKLEY, Guy Lesingham	P	3	255
SPRIGGS, Frederick Harry	P	4	194
SPRIGGS, Frederick William		3	255
SPRIGGS, Frederick William		4	194
SPRIGGS, William Harris		3	255
SPRINGALL, William Egleton		1	336
SPRINGATE, Arthur Stephen	P	5	156
SPROT, Ivan B		4	195
SPROTT, Maurice William Campbell	P	3	255
SPROUL, John		4	195
SPROUL, William Jardine		4	195
SPRUNT, Alexander Daizell	P	1	336
SPRUNT, Edward Lawrence	P	1	336
SPRY, Ernest John		1	336

Name	Photo	Part No.	Page No.
SPURDEN, William		1	336
SQUIBB, Fred		1	336
SQUIRE, Alan Richard	P	1	336
SQUIRE, Alfred Oliver		2	282
SQUIRE, Arthur		4	195
SQUIRE, Stanley Charles	P	1	336
SQUIRES, A		2	282
SQUIRES, Francis Chavasse	P	1	336
SQUIRES, James Edward		2	282
SQUIRRELL, John William		1	336
ST. AUBYN, The Hon. Piers Stewart		2	268
ST. CALIR, Hon. Charles Henry Murray	P	1	317
ST. CLAIR, Charles Matthew Duncan	P	4	175
ST. CLAIR, William		2	268
ST. GEORGE, Guy Stanforth Wemyss	P	1	317
ST. GEORGE, Howard Avenel Bligh		4	175
ST. HILL, Collis George Herbert		4	176
ST. JOHN-MILDMAY, Bouverie Walter		5	123
STAAL, E		2	282
STABLE, Loscombe Law	P	1	337
STABLE, Loscombe Law		4	195
STABLES, Harold Rolleston		4	195
STABLES, James Howard		5	156
STACE, Oliver George		2	282
STACEY, Douglas William		4	195
STACEY, George		5	156
STACEY, James		1	337
STACEY, Richard John		1	337
STACK, Edward Hugh Bagot		4	195
STACKHOUSE, William Thomas	P	1	337
STACPOOLE, George Eric Guy	P	1	337
STAFF, Samuel Royal		1	337
STAFFORD, Alfred		1	337
STAFFORD, Charles Alfred		2	282
STAFFORD, John Robert		3	255
STAFFORD, Rowland Herbert		1	337
STAFFORD, William G		2	282
STAFFORD-KING-HARMAN, Edward Charles	P	1	173
STAGG, Joseph		2	282
STAGG, Joseph Albert Edward		1	337
STAHL, Ernest Frank	P	1	337
STAINES, J		2	282
STAINFORTH, Richard Terrick		4	195
STAINTHORPE, George		2	282
STALLARD, Francis George		2	282
STALLARD, Herbert		5	156
STALLARD, William Harold		1	337
STAMPER, Geoffrey Sidebottom Parker	P	5	156
STAMPER, J		2	282
STANDING, Alfred Henry		5	156
STANDING, George William		1	337
STANDLEY, Ernest George		1	337
STANDRING, Benjamin Arthur		4	195
STANFORD, Walter	P	5	157
STANIFORTH, Herbert		2	283
STANIFORTH, John	P	5	157
STANLEY, Edwin George	P	3	255
STANLEY, Frederick Harry		1	337
STANLEY, George Thomas		1	337
STANLEY, Harry		2	283
STANLEY, John William		4	195
STANLEY, L G		2	283
STANLEY, Robert George		1	337
STANLEY, W J		3	255

Name	Photo	Part No.	Page No.	Name	Photo	Part No.	Page No.
STANLEY, Walter	P	5	157	STEELE-PERKINS, Cyril Steele	P	1	288
STANLEY, William Joseph John	P	5	157	STEELEY, George William		4	196
STANNARD, Alexander Jewell	P	3	255	STEER, Charles H		2	283
STANNARD, Alfred John		2	283	STEER, George		1	338
STANNARD, Charles Edward	P	5	157	STEER, George Durrell		2	283
STANNARD, Gordon		1	337	STEERS, Alfred Thomas		2	283
STANNETT, Robert		1	337	STEMP, Arthur		2	283
STANSBY, George Buxton		5	157	STENNING, Bernard Clement		4	196
STANTON, George		5	157	STENNING, Leslie Gerald		1	338
STAPLE, William John		2	283	STENNING, William		2	283
STAPLES, John		1	337	STENSON, Peter		2	283
STAPLES, Joseph		2	283	STENT, James John		1	338
STAPLETON, Joseph		4	195	STEPHEN, Albert Alexander Leslie		4	196
STAPLETON, William John		4	195	STEPHEN, David James Shirres	P	4	196
STAPLEY, Henry		2	283	STEPHEN, David Simpson		4	196
STARK, Frederick George	P	3	255	STEPHEN, Edwin Robertson		2	283
STARK, T		2	283	STEPHEN, G		2	283
STARK, William Cant	P	3	255	STEPHEN, G G		2	283
STARK, William Webster	P	2	283	STEPHEN, John		3	257
STARKE, Harry	P	1	337	STEPHEN, William Andrew	P	3	257
STARKIE, Joseph		4	195	STEPHENS, Alfred Sydney		4	196
STARLING, Sydney Ewart		4	195	STEPHENS, Charles		2	283
STARLING, Winifred		5	157	STEPHENS, Edwin Percival	P	3	257
STARMER, George		4	195	STEPHENS, Francis Thomas		4	196
STARMER, John		4	195	STEPHENS, Francklyn F		3	257
STARMER, Lewis Francis	P	4	195	STEPHENS, Frederick William		4	196
STARR, A G		2	283	STEPHENS, George Ernest		1	338
STARR, Francis James		1	337	STEPHENS, George Harry		2	283
STARR, Rupert Kelson	P	4	195	STEPHENS, H A		3	257
STARR, Thomas Adin		1	337	STEPHENS, John		1	338
START, Alfred		3	256	STEPHENS, Richard		5	157
START, Edward		4	195	STEPHENS, Robert Miller		4	196
STATHAM, Arthur Yates	P	3	256	STEPHENSON, Harold	P	1	338
STATHAM, Louis Forsyth		1	337	STEPHENSON, O		2	283
STATHAM, Noel Horner	P	3	256	STEPHENSON, Thomas		2	283
STAVELEY, George Hendley		4	196	STEPNEY, Charles E		2	283
STEAD, Jesse		2	283	STEPTO, Charles P		5	157
STEAD, John Kenneth		3	256	STERLING, John Lockhart		2	283
STEAD, Joseph		5	157	STERLING, Robert William		1	338
STEADMAN, Albert	P	1	338	STERLING, Robert William		1	338
STEADMAN, Alfred	P	2	283	STERLING, William		1	338
STEADMAN, F		3	256	STERLING, William		1	338
STEADMAN, Reginald Walter		5	157	STERN, Leonard Herman	P	1	338
STEANE, Percy Howard	P	1	338	STERN, Sydney Lionel		4	196
STEARN, John Holder	P	3	256	STERN, William		1	338
STEARNS, Eric Gordon	P	1	338	STEUART, Alan John	P	1	338
STEDEFORD, Horace Kingsley		4	196	STEUART, Walter Willox		3	257
STEDMAN, Thomas		2	283	STEVELY, Thomas		2	283
STEDMAN, Thomas W F		2	283	STEVEN, George Hay		2	283
STEEDMAN, William		2	283	STEVEN, James		2	283
STEEDMAN, William		4	196	STEVEN, James	P	3	257
STEEL, Arthur		5	157	STEVEN, Robert	P	3	257
STEEL, Charles Gilbert		4	196	STEVENS, Arthur		1	339
STEEL, Herbert		5	157	STEVENS, Daniel		2	283
STEEL, John		1	338	STEVENS, Ernest Henry	P	2	283
STEEL, John Gordon		3	256	STEVENS, Fred		1	339
STEEL, Joseph		2	283	STEVENS, Frederick Augustus		1	339
STEEL, Robert Kingsley		3	256	STEVENS, G R		2	283
STEEL, Stanley		5	157	STEVENS, Harry		2	283
STEEL, Walter Frank Banfield	P	3	256	STEVENS, Henry Francis Bingham	P	2	284
STEELE, Alfred Harmer		3	256	STEVENS, Herbert		2	284
STEELE, Andrew		4	196	STEVENS, Horace		2	284
STEELE, Matthew James	P	1	338	STEVENS, John		1	339
STEELE, Wilson		1	338	STEVENS, Lothian Basil	P	1	339
STEELE-NICHOLSON, William Herbert Hamilton		4	144	STEVENS, Reginald Walter Morton	P	1	339

Name	Photo	Part No.	Page No.
STEVENS, Richard Henry		4	196
STEVENS, Robert Gray		5	157
STEVENS, Sidney Eric Mackenzie		4	196
STEVENS, Thomas		4	197
STEVENS, Thomas Henry		2	284
STEVENS, William	P	4	197
STEVENS, William Frederick		1	339
STEVENS, William Henry		1	339
STEVENS, William James		4	197
STEVENSON, Alan Macdonald		4	197
STEVENSON, Alexander Campbell		2	284
STEVENSON, Alfred		2	284
STEVENSON, Bertha Gavin (Betty)	P	4	197
STEVENSON, Charles	P	1	339
STEVENSON, Edward Arthur		2	284
STEVENSON, Frederick Arthur		4	197
STEVENSON, Frederick Fotheringham Anderson	P	5	158
STEVENSON, George		1	339
STEVENSON, James		2	284
STEVENSON, James Robert	P	2	284
STEVENSON, John Huntley Wickham	P	3	257
STEVENSON, Talbert	P	3	257
STEVENSON, Thomas		4	197
STEVENSON, Thomas Kerr	P	3	258
STEWARD, Albert Edward		4	197
STEWARD, Arthur Amyot		4	197
STEWARD, Edmund		1	339
STEWARD, John		2	284
STEWART, Adrian Harry		4	197
STEWART, Alexander Murray		4	197
STEWART, Alexander Vivian		4	197
STEWART, Andrew Phillip		4	197
STEWART, Arthur		2	284
STEWART, Bertrand		4	197
STEWART, Charles		1	339
STEWART, Charles Edward	P	4	197
STEWART, Charles Frederic Somes		4	198
STEWART, Donald		1	339
STEWART, Douglas Everard Macbean	P	1	339
STEWART, Frederic Arnold	P	3	258
STEWART, Frederick Arnold	P	4	198
STEWART, Geoffrey	P	1	340
STEWART, Geoffrey		4	198
STEWART, Gerald	P	3	258
STEWART, Gerald Charles	P	2	284
STEWART, Herbert James	P	4	198
STEWART, Hon. Keith Anthony	P	2	284
STEWART, Hubert Francis Liddell		2	284
STEWART, James Alexander Logan	P	1	340
STEWART, James Augustus	P	1	340
STEWART, James Ferguson		2	284
STEWART, James Harvey		4	198
STEWART, John		2	284
STEWART, John		4	198
STEWART, John		4	198
STEWART, John Cecil Grahame		2	284
STEWART, John James Erskine Brown	P	3	258
STEWART, John Maurice	P	2	284
STEWART, John Robertson		4	198
STEWART, John Stewart	P	1	340
STEWART, Nathaniel William (Nathel)		3	258
STEWART, Niel Shaw	P	2	285
STEWART, Robert		4	198
STEWART, Robert Alexander Dean		4	198

Name	Photo	Part No.	Page No.
STEWART, Robert James		4	198
STEWART, Samuel		4	198
STEWART, T		3	258
STEWART, Vernon Forster		4	198
STEWART, W		2	285
STEWART, W		2	285
STEWART, William		5	158
STEWART, William Gibson		4	198
STEWART, William Henry		1	340
STEWART, William Hodson	P	2	285
STEWART, William Marshall	P	4	198
STEWART, William Victor	P	1	340
STICKLAND, Charles Stuart		5	158
STIDSTON, William Popkiss		4	199
STIFF, Edward Thomas	P	5	158
STIFF, Harry		1	340
STIFF, Leonard		2	285
STILES, Frederick		4	199
STILES, George		1	340
STILING, William Charles Henry	P	1	340
STILL, Charles Haselden		5	158
STILL, Thomas		2	285
STILLMAN, John Humphrey		5	158
STINCHCOMBE, W G		3	258
STINTON, Kennedy		4	199
STIRK, Harry Binner		4	199
STIRLING, Gordon Sheffield	P	2	285
STIRLING, Henry Francis Dundas	P	3	258
STIRLING, James	P	1	341
STIRLING, John		5	158
STIRLING, Richard Kellock		2	285
STIRLING, T		2	286
STIRLING, Wilfred Dixon	P	1	341
STIRLING STUART, James		4	202
STITT, J R		3	259
STOBIE, Thomas		4	199
STOCK, Charles Herbert		2	286
STOCK, Frederick Ernest	P	1	341
STOCK, Joseph		4	199
STOCK, Reginald Alfred		5	158
STOCK, Thomas		2	286
STOCKDALE, Cecil		1	341
STOCKDALE, Richard William		4	199
STOCKER, Robert A		2	286
STOCKS, B		3	259
STOCKS, David De Beauvoir		4	199
STOCKS, Frederick		2	286
STOCKS, Harris Lawrence		3	259
STOCKS, Michael George		4	199
STOCKS, Walter Albert		5	158
STOCKWELL, Horace		2	286
STODDART, David		2	286
STODDART, Farquhar		5	158
STODDART, Frederick William		4	199
STODDART, George		5	158
STODDART, Sydney	P	1	341
STOFER, Eric		5	158
STOFFELL, Charles E		2	286
STOKELL, Robert		1	341
STOKER, Frederick William		1	341
STOKES, Alfred Edgar		1	341
STOKES, Arthur Edward		1	341
STOKES, Ernest Alfred		2	286
STOKES, Guy Lennard	P	5	158
STOKES, Haldane Day		1	341

Name	Photo	Part No.	Page No.
STUART, Edward		4	202
STUART, Fremantle Kenneth	P	3	260
STUART, George Douglas Gordon		4	202
STUART, James		4	202
STUART, James Alfred	P	4	202
STUART, James Ogilvie Grant		4	202
STUART, John		1	342
STUART, John Alan		4	202
STUART, John Charles		3	260
STUART, Percy Charles		1	342
STUBBINGTON, William Charles		1	342
STUBBINS, John		2	288
STUBBS, Albert Charles William		1	342
STUBBS, Bernard Castle	P	1	342
STUBBS, Harry		2	288
STUBBS, Herbert Claude		1	342
STUBBS, John	P	4	202
STUBBS, John Duncan	P	1	342
STUBBS, John Duncan		4	202
STUBBS, R		3	260
STUBBS, Wade	P	3	260
STUBBS, Walter		3	260
STUBBS, Walter Bryan		2	288
STUBLEY, Frederick		1	342
STUCHFIELD, Ralph		4	202
STUCKEY, Frederick	P	1	342
STUCLEY, Humphrey St. Leger		4	202
STUDD, Lionel Fairfax	P	1	343
STUDHOLME, Paul Francis William	P	3	260
STUFFIN, Robert		2	288
STUMBLES, Horace George		1	343
STUMP, Leonard Edward		4	202
STURELL, George		2	288
STURGESS, Alfred		2	288
STURGESS, John Robert		4	203
STURGESS, William		5	159
STURGESS, William R		2	288
STURM, A H		2	288
STURMER, Alfred		2	288
STURROCK, Albert George		1	343
STURROCK, David Duff	P	1	343
STURT, John		2	288
STYANCE, Arthur		1	343
STYLES, F		3	260
STYLES, Frederick Ernest	P	1	343
STYLES, Frederick George		1	343
STYLES, Harry		1	343
STYLES, Henry Alfred		4	203
STYLES, James Blair		2	288
STYLES, John	P	1	343
STYLES, Sydney		4	203
STYLES, William Daniel		4	203
SUFFERN, Robert		5	159
SUFFLING, James		2	288
SUGDEN, Ben Roy	P	5	159
SUGDEN, Harry		3	261
SUGDEN, Stanley William	P	5	159
SULIVAN, Eugene Gilbert	P	3	261
SULIVAN, Henry Ernest	P	3	261
SULIVAN, Philip Hamilton	P	1	343
SULLEY, Alan Hereford	P	2	288
SULLIVAN, Bartholomew		1	343
SULLIVAN, Daniel		2	288
SULLIVAN, Douglas D'arcy	P	4	203
SULLIVAN, Eugene	P	5	159

Name	Photo	Part No.	Page No.
SULLIVAN, John		2	288
SULLIVAN, John F		2	288
SULLIVAN, John James	P	1	343
SULLIVAN, John L		2	288
SULLIVAN, M		3	261
SULLIVAN, Michael		2	288
SULLIVAN, Michael		2	288
SULLIVAN, Patrick		2	288
SULLIVAN, Patrick		2	288
SULLIVAN, Patrick		2	288
SULLIVAN, Thomas		4	203
SULLIVAN, William		2	288
SULLY, William		2	288
SUMMERFIELD, Louis Henry		4	203
SUMMERS, Albert Percy		4	203
SUMMERS, Allan Young	P	4	203
SUMMERS, Arthur Charles		4	203
SUMMERS, Frank George		4	203
SUMMERS, Harry Low		4	203
SUMMERS, Jeffrey		4	203
SUMMERS, John William		4	203
SUMMERS, Joseph		2	288
SUMMERS, Samuel William	P	4	203
SUMMERS, Sydney		1	343
SUMMERS, William Wigan		1	343
SUMMERSCALES, Percy		1	344
SUMMERVILLE, W		3	261
SUMNER, Albert George		2	288
SUMNER, R		3	261
SUNDERLAND, Geoffrey	P	5	159
SUNTER, G		3	261
SURCH, Richard		4	203
SURMAN, Arthur Henry		3	261
SURRIDGE, Charles John Logan	P	2	288
SURRIDGE, Kester Thomas		4	203
SURROCK, Christopher William		4	203
SURTEES, William		2	288
SUTCH, Frederick William		1	344
SUTER, Rupert Stanley John		2	288
SUTHERLAND, Adolphus Charles		3	261
SUTHERLAND, Albert Ronald	P	3	261
SUTHERLAND, Alexander		2	288
SUTHERLAND, D		3	261
SUTHERLAND, David Alexander Ingram		4	203
SUTHERLAND, George		4	203
SUTHERLAND, George Alexander	P	1	344
SUTHERLAND, George King		5	160
SUTHERLAND, George Lacey		1	344
SUTHERLAND, J		2	288
SUTHERLAND, James Mckay	P	1	344
SUTHERLAND, John		1	344
SUTHERLAND, John	P	1	344
SUTHERLAND, John		4	204
SUTHERLAND, John Mckay		2	288
SUTHERLAND, John Shand		2	289
SUTHERLAND, Roderick John		4	204
SUTHERLAND, Walter Riddell		5	160
SUTHERLAND, William	P	3	261
SUTHERLAND, William		4	204
SUTTIE, Henry		1	344
SUTTON, Alexander Gordon	P	3	261
SUTTON, Alfred		4	204
SUTTON, Charles Edgar		4	204
SUTTON, Eric Guy	P	3	261
SUTTON, Eustace Martin	P	3	262

Name	Photo	Part No.	Page No.
SUTTON, Evan Richards	P	5	160
SUTTON, Fergus Algernon	P	1	344
SUTTON, Harry		2	289
SUTTON, Henry W		2	289
SUTTON, Hubert	P	1	344
SUTTON, James Thomas		1	344
SUTTON, Stanley George		4	204
SUTTON, Thomas		1	344
SUTTON, Vivian Charles Wolfe		5	160
SUTTON, Wilfred Robert	P	5	160
SUTTON, William		5	160
SUTTON, William Victor Ross	P	3	262
SWAIN, Herbert Richard	P	5	160
SWAIN, Reginald		2	289
SWAIN, Thomas		2	289
SWAINE, Henry Poyntz		4	204
SWAINE, R		3	262
SWAINLAND, William		1	344
SWALES, Edward Arthur	P	3	262
SWALLOW, Hervey Lancelot St. George	P	2	289
SWALLOW, Knight		2	289
SWAN, Andrew Campbell	P	1	344
SWAN, George	P	1	344
SWAN, James Blair	P	1	344
SWAN, Thomas George		1	344
SWAN, William Henry		2	289
SWANBOROUGH, Herbert John		2	289
SWANN, Herbert Edward		2	289
SWANN, J		2	289
SWANN, John David Livermore		1	345
SWANN, Thomas	P	3	262
SWANN, Thomas Henry		1	345
SWANN, William		1	345
SWANSON, Hugh		2	289
SWANSON, J T		3	262
SWANSON, W		2	289
SWANSON, W		2	289
SWANSON, William		4	204
SWANWICK, R Kenneth		4	204
SWASH, Harold		4	204
SWASH, Harold Henry	P	5	160
SWAYNE, Arthur Dudley Cleveland		5	160
SWEATMAN, John Henry		4	204
SWEENEY, Charles		4	204
SWEENEY, J		2	289
SWEENEY, Michael		5	160
SWEET, Frederick Charles		2	289
SWEET, John Hales		4	204
SWEET, Leonard Herbert		4	204
SWEET-ESCOTT, Leslie Wingfield	P	2	113
SWEET-ESCOTT, Murray Robertson	P	1	126
SWEETING, William		1	345
SWEETMAN, E		3	262
SWEETMAN, John Stanley	P	1	345
SWEETNAM, Stanley Joseph	P	3	262
SWEETSUR, James Henry		1	345
SWETENHAM, Edmund	P	1	345
SWETENHAM, Edmund		4	204
SWETENHAM, Foster		4	204
SWIFT, Joseph		1	345
SWIFT, Peter		1	345
SWINDELL, Alfred William		3	262
SWINGLER, William James		4	204
SWINTON, George Lothian		4	204
SWOFFER, Alfred E		2	289

Name	Photo	Part No.	Page No.
SWORDER, Charles Frederick	P	3	262
SWORDER, Hubert Pelham		4	204
SWORDER, John Leslie	P	3	262
SWORDER, John Perkins		4	205
SWYMER, W S		3	262
SYDDALL, George Baxby	P	5	160
SYDENHAM, Humphrey St. Barbe		3	262
SYER, Hubert Lionel		3	262
SYER, Hubert Lionel		4	205
SYGROVE, Charles W		2	289
SYKES, George	P	3	263
SYKES, George Frederick		5	161
SYKES, John William		2	289
SYKES, Joseph		4	205
SYKES, Oliver John	P	2	289
SYKES, Reginald	P	2	289
SYMES, Clarence J		2	289
SYMES, Harold		1	345
SYMES, John Borkwood		1	345
SYMES-THOMPSON, Cholmeley		4	211
SYMINTON, George Charles		4	205
SYMMANS, John		1	345
SYMMS, Charles Fullerton		1	345
SYMONDS, Albert Henry		1	345
SYMONDS, Edgar		1	345
SYMONDS, Edward Charles		4	205
SYMONDS, John E		2	289
SYMONDS, William Harry	P	1	345
SYMONDS, William Percy		1	345
SYMONS, Alfred Albert		1	345
SYMONS, Cecil Henry		4	205
SYMONS, Herbert William		1	345
SYMONS, Herbert William		4	205
SYMONS, William		1	345
SYNNES, Thomas		1	345
SYNNOTT, Fitzherbert Paget	P	2	290
SYPH, Joseph		4	205
SYRED, Frederick Arthur		1	345
SYRETT, Harold Charles	P	2	290
SYRETT, John		1	345
TABBERNER, Thomas Kemp		4	205
TABERNER, Peter	P	3	263
TADD, S		3	263
TAFFS, Charles Reginald	P	4	205
TAILFORD, John Wilson	P	5	161
TAIT, Cecil Leonard	P	4	205
TAIT, Charles		4	205
TAIT, George		4	205
TAIT, George H		2	290
TAIT, Horace William	P	3	263
TAIT, Richard		4	205
TALBOT, Edward Charles	P	1	345
TALBOT, Humfrey Richard		1	345
TALBOT, John Lionel Pemberton	P	5	161
TALBOT, Matthew		4	205
TALBOT, Stanley Alfred		3	263
TALBOT, Thomas		2	290
TALLACK, William Francis Neck	P	1	345
TALLON, Harry		4	205
TALMARSH, V		3	263
TAME, William Edward		2	290
TAMPIN, Charles Thomas		1	345
TANDY, Charles		2	290
TANN, Henry		2	290
TANNER, Charles William		4	206

Name	Photo	Part No.	Page No.	Name	Photo	Part No.	Page No.
TANNER, Ernest Edwin	P	1	345	TAYLOR, Donald	P	2	291
TANNER, Frederick Arthur Albert		2	290	TAYLOR, Douglas Clifton		5	161
TANNER, George Henry		3	263	TAYLOR, Edward		2	291
TANNER, Henry		3	263	TAYLOR, Edward	P	3	264
TANNER, Percival John		3	263	TAYLOR, Edward George		2	291
TANNER, Ralph Eyre	P	1	346	TAYLOR, Ernest		1	347
TANNER, William		2	290	TAYLOR, Ernest	P	3	264
TANSLEY, S E		2	290	TAYLOR, Ernest Albert Isaac		5	161
TANSWELL, R C		3	263	TAYLOR, Ernest Edwin		1	347
TANTON, Ebenezer Frank		5	161	TAYLOR, F		2	291
TAPLEY, Samuel		4	206	TAYLOR, Francis Robert		1	347
TAPLIN, Alfred Charles		1	346	TAYLOR, Frank		1	347
TAPLIN, Percy Charles		1	346	TAYLOR, Frederick Charles		4	207
TAPPENDEN, Alfred Bernard		4	206	TAYLOR, Frederick Thomas		4	207
TAPPER, James Edwin		3	263	TAYLOR, G		3	264
TAPSFIELD, Claude Reginald	P	1	346	TAYLOR, Geoffrey England		5	161
TARGET, Noel Alexander	P	4	206	TAYLOR, George		2	291
TARN, Mark Aitchison	P	1	346	TAYLOR, George		4	207
TARR, William		4	206	TAYLOR, George Joseph	P	4	207
TARRANT, Alfred		4	206	TAYLOR, George Laird		2	291
TARRANT, Ernest William	P	2	290	TAYLOR, George Robert Marmaduke Stanbury		4	207
TARRANT, Frederick Norman	P	2	290	TAYLOR, George Watson		4	207
TARRANT, Frederick W		2	290	TAYLOR, George William		1	347
TARRANT, Oswald Edward	P	2	290	TAYLOR, George William		3	264
TARRANT, William Thomas		1	346	TAYLOR, George William Edward		4	207
TARVIT, William		5	161	TAYLOR, H		3	264
TASKER, Edward		2	290	TAYLOR, Harold	P	2	291
TASKER, James		5	161	TAYLOR, Henry	P	1	347
TATE, Alan Charles Richmond		4	206	TAYLOR, Henry		2	291
TATE, J		3	263	TAYLOR, Henry	P	5	161
TATE, James Henry Charles		2	290	TAYLOR, Henry Edgar Clark		4	207
TATE-SMITH, Robert Ronald	P	5	155	TAYLOR, Henry Noel		2	291
TATHAM, Allan	P	3	263	TAYLOR, Herbert	P	2	291
TATHAM, Trevor Hodgson Stanley	P	1	346	TAYLOR, Hugh		4	207
TATLER, Robert	P	1	346	TAYLOR, J		3	264
TATTERSALL, Eric	P	4	206	TAYLOR, J		3	264
TATTON, Harold	P	5	161	TAYLOR, James	P	4	207
TAUNTON, Cuthbert Andre Patmon	P	2	290	TAYLOR, James		4	207
TAVERNOR, John	P	1	346	TAYLOR, James Albert		2	291
TAVLIN, H		3	263	TAYLOR, James George		2	291
TAWSE, James Gordon	P	3	263	TAYLOR, James Paul		4	207
TAYLER, Eric Hardwick	P	1	346	TAYLOR, James William		4	207
TAYLOR, A		3	263	TAYLOR, John		1	347
TAYLOR, A		3	263	TAYLOR, John	P	5	161
TAYLOR, Albert		2	291	TAYLOR, John Alfred		1	347
TAYLOR, Alex	P	4	206	TAYLOR, John Ellis	P	2	291
TAYLOR, Alexander		4	206	TAYLOR, John Ogilvie		4	207
TAYLOR, Alfred		2	291	TAYLOR, Leo Lambert		1	347
TAYLOR, Alfred	P	3	263	TAYLOR, Maxwell		5	162
TAYLOR, Alfred Daniel		4	206	TAYLOR, Miles Brunskill	P	1	347
TAYLOR, Archibald		1	346	TAYLOR, Nathan		4	207
TAYLOR, Arthur		4	206	TAYLOR, Percy James		2	291
TAYLOR, Arthur Cuthbert Brooke	P	1	346	TAYLOR, Percy Lionel	P	3	264
TAYLOR, Arthur Edwin		4	206	TAYLOR, Robert		4	208
TAYLOR, Arthur Martin		4	207	TAYLOR, Robert Alexander		5	162
TAYLOR, B J		3	263	TAYLOR, Robert Gervais		2	291
TAYLOR, Benjamin		4	207	TAYLOR, Ronald Francis	P	1	347
TAYLOR, Cedric Charles Okey	P	2	291	TAYLOR, Samuel		4	208
TAYLOR, Charles		2	291	TAYLOR, Sidney	P	3	264
TAYLOR, Charles Gordon		2	291	TAYLOR, Sidney		4	208
TAYLOR, Charles Matheson	P	3	263	TAYLOR, Sidney Harold	P	3	264
TAYLOR, Clement Harold	P	1	347	TAYLOR, T		2	291
TAYLOR, Daniel		4	207	TAYLOR, T E		3	264
TAYLOR, Daniel James		1	347	TAYLOR, Thomas		1	347
TAYLOR, David	P	2	291	TAYLOR, Thomas John		1	347

Name	Photo	Part No.	Page No.	Name	Photo	Part No.	Page No.
TAYLOR, Thomas Ralph		4	208	TERRY, Samuel James		2	292
TAYLOR, Thomas William Henry		5	162	TERRY, William		2	292
TAYLOR, Tom Henry Winter		2	291	TERRY, William John		1	348
TAYLOR, W		3	264	TESTARD, Alex		2	293
TAYLOR, W J		3	264	TESTER, F P		3	265
TAYLOR, Walter		1	347	TESTER, Thomas		1	348
TAYLOR, Walter	P	3	264	TETBUTT, Wilfred		4	209
TAYLOR, Walter William	P	1	347	TETLEY, Arthur Norman	P	1	348
TAYLOR, William		1	347	TEUMA, Giovanni		1	348
TAYLOR, William		2	291	TEW, Percy	P	4	209
TAYLOR, William		4	208	TEW, W G		2	293
TAYLOR, William		4	208	THACKER, Frank		3	265
TAYLOR, William		4	208	THACKER, Wilfrid	P	4	209
TAYLOR, William Edgar		4	208	THACKER, William Alfred	P	4	209
TAYLOR, William Ernest Ewart	P	3	264	THACKERAY, Alfred William		1	348
TAYLOR, William Hodgson		3	264	THACKERAY, R W		3	265
TAYLOR, William James		1	347	THAIN, William		4	209
TAYLOR, William Thomas		4	208	THAKE, G A		3	265
TAYLOR-WHITEHEAD, George Edward		4	233	THAKE, William		1	348
TEACHER, William George	P	2	292	THAL, Morris Marcus Van	P	1	348
TEAL, William		4	208	THALLON, Frederick George		4	209
TEALE, A		3	264	THARLE, Robert	P	3	265
TEAPE, Charles Lewarne	P	2	292	THATCHER, John William		2	293
TEASDALE, D		2	292	THELWELL, Ernest James		4	209
TEASDALE, Henry C L		2	292	THEOBALD, Charles E		2	293
TEASDALE, S		3	265	THEOBALD, Harry		2	293
TEAY, Richard		4	208	THEOBALD, William George Morley	P	1	348
TEE, Charles		2	292	THICK, John Charles		1	348
TEE, Henry		2	292	THICKETT, F		3	265
TEELING, Ambrose Mary Anthony		4	208	THISTLE, Robert James	P	3	265
TEESDALE, Albert		2	292	THOM, Alexander John Smith	P	5	162
TEHAN, Edmund Frederick		1	347	THOM, Archibald		2	293
TELFER, William Houston		5	162	THOM, G		2	293
TELFORD, R		2	292	THOMAS, Alexander		2	293
TEMPEST, Wilfrid Norman		3	265	THOMAS, Alma Cyril		4	209
TEMPLE, Claude Castlemain		4	208	THOMAS, Andrew Read		1	348
TEMPLE, John		1	347	THOMAS, Arthur Henry		2	293
TEMPLE, R		3	265	THOMAS, Arthur James	P	3	265
TEMPLE, William Arthur Mould		4	208	THOMAS, Aubrey Jocelyn Nugent		1	348
TEMPLETON, Hugh Miller		4	208	THOMAS, C J		3	265
TEMPLETON, John		2	292	THOMAS, Charles		4	210
TEMPLETON, Robert	P	4	208	THOMAS, Charles Herbert	P	1	348
TEMPLETON, Robert		4	208	THOMAS, Cyril Vaughan	P	4	210
TEMS, Walter Edgar		1	347	THOMAS, D		3	265
TENAILLE, Daniel Jean	P	2	292	THOMAS, Edward Ewart	P	3	265
TENNANT, Charles Grant	P	1	347	THOMAS, Edward George		3	265
TENNANT, D		2	292	THOMAS, Edward Thomas		1	348
TENNANT, Edmund Hubert		4	209	THOMAS, Edward Williams		5	162
TENNANT, George Christopher Serocold		4	209	THOMAS, Ernest		3	265
TENNANT, Harry		2	292	THOMAS, Ernest Edward		2	293
TENNANT, Isaac Robert	P	4	209	THOMAS, Frederick		2	293
TENNANT, John Amherst	P	2	292	THOMAS, Frederick	P	3	265
TENNANT, Philip Lawrence		4	209	THOMAS, Frederick George	P	2	293
TENNANT, William Galbraith	P	2	292	THOMAS, G		3	265
TERRAS, John		4	209	THOMAS, George Henry		4	210
TERRELL, Claud Romako-A-Beckett		4	209	THOMAS, Griffith	P	4	210
TERRELL, Frank William		3	265	THOMAS, Harry C		2	293
TERRY, Alfred H F		2	292	THOMAS, Heber		4	210
TERRY, Charles Henry		1	347	THOMAS, James Samuel		5	162
TERRY, Clifford Hodgson		4	209	THOMAS, John Arloe Edward		1	348
TERRY, Frank Albert		1	347	THOMAS, John Baker		1	348
TERRY, Frederick John Cortorpassi		1	347	THOMAS, John Richard		4	210
TERRY, G		3	265	THOMAS, John Wynford		4	210
TERRY, Harry		1	348	THOMAS, Mathew		5	162
TERRY, Henry George		2	292	THOMAS, Maurice	P	1	348

Name	Photo	Part No.	Page No.	Name	Photo	Part No.	Page No.
TODRICK, Thomas	P	1	351	TOPPING, Herbert	P	3	269
TODRICK, Thomas		4	213	TORR, John		2	297
TOFT, Harry		4	213	TORRANCE, Archibald Henry		2	298
TOLAN, A		2	296	TORRENCE, David		4	214
TOLHURST, Alfred Buckland		4	213	TORRENS, Attwood Alfred	P	3	269
TOLHURST, Charles Alfred		2	296	TOSDEVIN, William Cecil		5	164
TOLHURST, John W		2	296	TOSH, William		1	352
TOLHURST, Walter		1	351	TOTMAN, W W		4	214
TOLLEMACHE, Bevil Douglas	P	1	351	TOTTENHAM, Arthur Henry		3	269
TOLLEMACHE, John Eadred	P	3	268	TOTTENHAM, Desmond Frank Charles Loftus		3	269
TOLLEY, Frank		2	296	TOTTENHAM, Edward L		3	269
TOMBAZIS, James Lyell	P	5	163	TOTTERDALE, G		2	298
TOMBLESON, Cecil		4	213	TOTTIE, Eric Harald		4	214
TOMBS, H		4	213	TOTTMAN, H K		3	269
TOMBS, John Bernard Evelyn	P	1	351	TOUGH, Victor John Arthur		3	269
TOMES, Geoffrey	P	2	296	TOVEY, Frederick John		1	352
TOMLIN, F		2	297	TOVEY, Thomas Hollingsworth		4	214
TOMLIN, George		2	297	TOWLE, John		1	352
TOMLIN, Henry		1	351	TOWLSON, William Holland		4	214
TOMLIN, John		1	351	TOWN, Young Thomas Edward		2	298
TOMLINS, Walter		2	297	TOWNEND, Albert		4	214
TOMLINSON, Frederick Wallace		1	351	TOWNEND, Cecil Pelham		3	269
TOMLINSON, Hugh		4	213	TOWNEND, Francis Whitchurch	P	1	352
TOMLINSON, J		3	268	TOWNER, Frederick Arthur Albert		1	352
TOMLINSON, J		4	213	TOWNLEY, Charles Henry Edmond Lawrence	P	4	214
TOMLINSON, William		1	351	TOWNROW, R		3	269
TOMLINSON, William Benham	P	3	268	TOWNSEND, Arthur Eric		3	269
TOMPKINS, Alexander Samuel	P	5	163	TOWNSEND, Charles		1	352
TOMPKINS, Arthur Vernon		2	297	TOWNSEND, Edwin George		4	214
TOMPKINS, E J		3	268	TOWNSEND, Eric Travis		4	214
TOMPKINS, Edmund Edward		4	213	TOWNSEND, Francis Edward Steavenson		3	269
TOMPKINS, Edwin	P	1	351	TOWNSEND, Fred Selby		4	214
TOMPKINS, George Charles		1	351	TOWNSEND, Frederick Charles	P	4	214
TOMPKINS, Harry		4	213	TOWNSEND, Henry Charles William		1	352
TOMPKINS, William John	P	1	351	TOWNSEND, J		3	269
TOMPKINSON, J S		3	268	TOWNSEND, John	P	4	214
TOMPSETT, William		2	297	TOWNSEND, Leonard	P	4	214
TOMS, Arthur Woodland	P	1	352	TOWNSEND, P		3	269
TOMS, Edgar Harold		2	297	TOWNSEND, Percy		2	298
TOMS, John		1	352	TOWNSEND, Thomas		2	298
TOMSETT, Alfred		2	297	TOWNSEND, William		2	298
TONER, John		2	297	TOWNSEND-GREEN, Henry Russell		1	161
TONGE, J		3	268	TOWNSHEND, Alfred		1	352
TONGE, John Richard		4	213	TOWNSHEND, Charles Henry		1	352
TONKIN, Edwin Cecil		2	297	TOWNSLEY, Thomas		4	215
TONKIN, Jack		4	214	TOWSE, Frederick Peter		4	215
TONKINSON, George		1	352	TOWSON, T		2	298
TOOGOOD, Alfred		1	352	TOY, Percy William		4	215
TOOGOOD, Francis Edward		4	214	TOYNBEE, Geoffrey Percy Robert		4	215
TOOK, Wilfred	P	3	269	TOYNE, William Charles		2	298
TOOKE, Bernard		3	269	TRACEY, Albert James Frederick	P	1	352
TOOLE, Edward Thomas		3	269	TRACEY, F		3	269
TOOLEY, John James		1	352	TRACEY, James Turnbull		2	298
TOOMBS, James Charles		4	214	TRACHTENBERG, Mendel Isadore	P	5	164
TOOMER, Cecil Walter		1	352	TRAFFORD, W		3	270
TOOMEY, Archibald Roche		1	352	TRAFFORD-RAWSON, John Henry Edmund	P	3	225
TOOP, Edward Charles		1	352	TRAHERNE, Llewellyn Edmund	P	1	353
TOOSEN, Endoxil		1	352	TRAIL, David Alexander	P	4	215
TOOTELL, Bernard	P	3	269	TRAILL, J		2	298
TOPHAM, George Samuel	P	1	352	TRAILL, John Murray		4	215
TOPHAM, Henry Angrave Cecil	P	1	352	TRAPP, Thomas Henry	P	3	270
TOPLIS, Roy Herrick	P	2	297	TRATMAN, Leslie William Thomas Draycott		5	164
TOPPER, Ernest William	P	4	214	TRAVERS, Albert John		1	353
TOPPIN, Harry Stanley		4	214	TRAVERS, Alfred		2	298
TOPPING, George		5	163	TRAVERS, F H R		3	270

Name	Photo	Part No.	Page No.	Name	Photo	Part No.	Page No.
TUKE, Hugh Latimer	P	2	299	TURNER, Frank		2	299
TULETT, Thomas		1	355	TURNER, Frederick Harding	P	1	356
TULIP, John James		1	355	TURNER, G		3	272
TULL, Robert George		4	216	TURNER, G A		2	299
TULLETT, F		3	271	TURNER, George		2	300
TULLOCH, Hugh	P	3	271	TURNER, George Corrall		3	272
TULLOCH, James Campbell	P	3	271	TURNER, George Corrall		5	164
TULLOCH, William		4	216	TURNER, George E W		2	300
TULLY, David		1	355	TURNER, George Edward		1	356
TULLY, James Kivas		4	216	TURNER, Harold Frank Barclay		4	217
TUMEY, William George		2	299	TURNER, Harry		1	356
TUNE, Charles Walter		4	217	TURNER, Henry T		2	300
TUNE, Harry Douglas		4	217	TURNER, Henry Thomas		4	218
TUNE, John Skerrow	P	1	355	TURNER, Herbert		4	218
TUNSTALL, James Charles Francis		3	271	TURNER, Herbert Ellery	P	4	218
TUPPEN, Frederick		4	217	TURNER, Herbert John		3	272
TUPPER, Ernest		1	355	TURNER, Horace George		4	218
TUPPER, Victor Gordon	P	3	271	TURNER, J W		3	272
TURBURFIELD, James		4	217	TURNER, James		1	356
TURNBULL, Charles John		4	217	TURNER, James Edward George		5	164
TURNBULL, Derwent Christopher	P	1	355	TURNER, John		3	272
TURNBULL, Henry James	P	2	299	TURNER, John Herbert		2	300
TURNBULL, Hugh Vincent Corbett		4	217	TURNER, John Reginald	P	1	356
TURNBULL, R		3	271	TURNER, Joseph William		1	356
TURNBULL, Stewart B		2	299	TURNER, Montague Alweyne Fisher	P	1	356
TURNBULL, Thomas Russell	P	4	217	TURNER, Noel Price James	P	1	357
TURNBULL, Walter	P	1	356	TURNER, Richard Chase		1	357
TURNBULL, William		2	299	TURNER, Robert		4	218
TURNBULL, William	P	3	271	TURNER, Robert Henry		4	218
TURNELL, A		2	299	TURNER, Robert Nathaniel		1	357
TURNER, A		2	299	TURNER, Robert Wallace	P	5	165
TURNER, A		3	271	TURNER, Roger Bingham	P	3	272
TURNER, Albert		2	299	TURNER, Rowland		2	300
TURNER, Arthur		1	356	TURNER, Thomas		2	300
TURNER, Arthur		1	356	TURNER, Thomas		4	218
TURNER, Arthur		1	356	TURNER, W		3	272
TURNER, Arthur		5	164	TURNER, W		3	272
TURNER, Arthur Harold	P	4	217	TURNER, Walter	P	1	357
TURNER, Arthur Morris	P	1	356	TURNER, Walter		5	165
TURNER, Arthur William		5	164	TURNER, William		1	357
TURNER, Basil		2	299	TURNER, William		1	357
TURNER, Bernard	P	3	272	TURNER, William Charles		4	218
TURNER, Bernard Francis		3	272	TURNER, William Holman		2	300
TURNER, Bernard George	P	1	356	TURNER, William James Oxford		5	165
TURNER, C H		3	272	TURNER, William Stewart	P	1	357
TURNER, C J H		3	272	TURNER, William Thomas		1	357
TURNER, Charles		1	356	TURNEY, Joseph		2	300
TURNER, Charles		2	299	TURNEY, Michael		2	300
TURNER, Charles Alfred		1	356	TURNOR, Christopher Randolph	P	1	357
TURNER, Charles Henry Edward		4	217	TURNOUR, Arthur William Winterton	P	2	300
TURNER, Charles James	P	3	272	TURNS, Sidney Lowe		2	300
TURNER, Charles Robert		2	299	TURPIN, Thomas Cobb		1	357
TURNER, Charles Robert Cornelius	P	3	272	TURRELL, Alfred		1	357
TURNER, Clement Douglas	P	4	217	TURRELL, Arthur Sidney		1	357
TURNER, Clifford		4	217	TURTLE, Clifford Louis	P	2	300
TURNER, Daniel John		4	217	TURTON, C		3	272
TURNER, Donald	P	3	272	TURTON, Richard Dacre	P	3	272
TURNER, Douglas Alfred		4	217	TURTON, Zouch Austin		2	300
TURNER, Edmund Sanctuary	P	2	299	TURVEY, F		3	272
TURNER, Edward		1	356	TUTHILL, John	P	2	300
TURNER, Edward W		2	299	TWEDALE, John James		1	357
TURNER, Ernest Herbert	P	1	356	TWEDDELL, A J		3	272
TURNER, Ernest Thomas		5	164	TWEEDIE, John		2	300
TURNER, F W		3	272	TWEEN, Ernest		2	300
TURNER, Francis Oliver	P	1	356	TWENTYMAN, Arthur		4	218

Name	Photo	Part No.	Page No.		Name	Photo	Part No.	Page No.
VERCO, Walter John		1	360		VIOLIN, Francis		2	302
VERCOE, Henry Steven		1	360		VIPOND, Albert		3	276
VEREKER, Robert Humphrey Medlicott		1	360		VIRGO, James		2	302
VERESMITH, Daniel James Christopher	P	2	301		VIRTUE, William Edward		2	302
VERESMITH, Evelyn Henry	P	2	301		VISCOUNT, John Thomas		1	361
VERGE, Arthur	P	1	360		VIVASH, Harry A		2	302
VERNON, Charles Edward Granville	P	2	301		VIVIAN, Charles Augustus	P	1	361
VERNON, H W		3	275		VOIGTS, Henry James		2	302
VERNON, Herbert Douglas	P	2	302		VOKES, Harold William		4	220
VERNON, Leonard Patrick	P	5	165		VOLLANS, Harry		3	276
VERNON, Roger	P	3	275		VOLLER, Sydney George		3	276
VERNON-INKPEN, Robert Cecil		3	150		VON, Peter		2	302
VERRALL, Charles		3	275		VOSE, James Edward		4	220
VERSO, Cyril Linton		4	220		VOYCE, Harold Edward		2	302
VERTH, William Combe		4	220		VURDETT, Frederick Daniel		5	165
VERYARD, Augustus Ward		2	302		VURLEY, Walter	P	3	276
VESSEY, Charles	P	4	220		VYVYAN, Walter Drummond	P	1	361
VESSEY, Frank	P	4	220		WACHER, Geoffrey Gibbings	P	1	361
VICAT, Horatio John	P	1	360		WACKETT, Frederick James		1	361
VICK, Arnold Oughtred		5	165		WADDELL, David Adams	P	3	276
VICKERS, William H		2	302		WADDELL, James		4	220
VICKERY, Albert E		2	302		WADDELL, James Hamilton	P	4	221
VIGUS, Robert Edward		1	360		WADDELL, William Thomson		4	221
VILE, Solomon Jesse		4	220		WADDIE, Frederick	P	4	221
VILES, William		1	360		WADDIE, John Norman	P	4	221
VILLIERS, H L		4	220		WADDILOVE, Charles John Darley		4	221
VILLIS, Leyshon		1	360		WADDINGTON, Ben Cowper		2	302
VINALL, Charles Cobden		1	360		WADDINGTON, William		3	276
VINALL, Edward Arthur		1	360		WADDY, John Raymond		1	361
VINCE, A J		3	275		WADE, Albert Edwin		4	221
VINCE, Alfred James		2	302		WADE, Frederick Walter		1	361
VINCE, Dan		1	360		WADE, Herbert John Clark		4	221
VINCE, Edmund William		4	220		WADE, Jonathan	P	4	221
VINCE, J		3	275		WADE, Stamper Plaskett		1	361
VINCE, William Lang	P	3	275		WADE, Thomas		1	361
VINCENT, C		3	275		WADHAMS, Joseph		3	276
VINCENT, F W		3	275		WADKINS, William Ferdinand		1	361
VINCENT, George Ernest		3	275		WADLAND, Henry Lawrence		4	221
VINCENT, H		3	275		WADSWORTH, Alfred Charles	P	1	361
VINCENT, H V J		3	275		WADSWORTH, George Frederick		2	302
VINCENT, Howard		4	220		WADSWORTH, H		4	221
VINCENT, Mark Hamilton	P	2	302		WADSWORTH, Thomas Edwin	P	1	361
VINCENT, Oswald		2	302		WADSWORTH, W		4	221
VINCENT, Thomas Ernest		1	360		WAGG, John		4	221
VINCENT, Thomas James		3	275		WAGHORN, L P		4	221
VINCENT, William	P	1	360		WAGHORN, William		2	302
VINCENT, William Morris		3	275		WAGLAND, Isaac William		1	362
VINCENT-JACKSON, Montagu John		3	152		WAGSTAFF, Alfred	P	1	362
VINE, Richard		1	360		WAGSTAFF, Sidney Walter	P	4	221
VINE, Walter	P	4	220		WAGSTAFFE, William Joseph		3	276
VINER-JOHNSON, Percy Joseph Viner	P	1	207		WAIN, Richard William Leslie	P	4	221
VINES, H		3	275		WAINE, Edward		2	302
VINES, Wilfred Edward		3	275		WAINWRIGHT, A		3	276
VINES, Wilfrid		4	220		WAINWRIGHT, Charles	P	3	276
VINEY, Cecil Henry		1	361		WAINWRIGHT, Clifford Ernest		5	166
VINEY, Edward Henry		2	302		WAINWRIGHT, Geoffrey Chauner		4	222
VINEY, Lewis		4	220		WAIT, Herbert Alfred Vincent		5	166
VINEY, Philip Ernest		1	361		WAITE, Arthur Edwin	P	2	302
VINNALL, Edward Arthur		1	361		WAITE, Charles William		1	362
VINSON, Alexander		2	302		WAITE, F A		3	276
VINSON, John R		2	302		WAITE, William		2	302
VINT, G A		3	275		WAITT, George Greenhill		1	362
VINT, Wilfrid George	P	3	276		WAKE, Hugh St. Aubyn		4	222
VINTER, Robert Bagster Wilson		4	220		WAKE, Samuel		2	302
VINTON, William Walter	P	5	165		WAKEFIELD, Arthur James	P	1	362

Name	Photo	Part No.	Page No.	Name	Photo	Part No.	Page No.
WAKEFIELD, Charles Gresley	P	2	302	WALKER, James Langlands		3	277
WAKEFORD, Harold	P	2	303	WALKER, James Thomas		1	363
WAKELIN, J		2	303	WALKER, John		2	303
WAKELIN, John Binham	P	1	362	WALKER, John		3	277
WAKEMAN, Edward Offley Rouse	P	1	362	WALKER, John		3	277
WAKEMAN, Harry		2	303	WALKER, John Binning		4	222
WAKER, Thomas George		5	166	WALKER, John Edward		4	223
WAKINSHAW, James William	P	1	362	WALKER, John George		4	223
WALBEOFFE-WILSON, William		2	319	WALKER, John Haslam		4	223
WALBURN, William Arthur	P	1	362	WALKER, John Haslam	P	5	166
WALCOTT, John Henry Lyons		4	222	WALKER, John James		1	363
WALDECK, Frederick		1	362	WALKER, John James		2	303
WALDEGRAVE, Edmund John		4	222	WALKER, Joseph		2	303
WALDEN, Rand Edwin John	P	3	276	WALKER, Joseph	P	3	277
WALDER, Alfred Sidney Cornelius		4	222	WALKER, Joseph Wilson		3	277
WALDIE, George Strange		4	222	WALKER, Laurence Hall	P	2	303
WALDIE, Robert Broomfield		2	303	WALKER, Leonard Frederick		4	223
WALDOCK, George		2	303	WALKER, Michael Coward		2	303
WALDOCK, George Leonard	P	5	166	WALKER, Peter Croll		4	223
WALDUCK, Luke		1	362	WALKER, Robert		1	363
WALE, Charles William		4	222	WALKER, Robert		5	166
WALE, Charles William		5	166	WALKER, Roland J		2	303
WALE, Edwin		4	222	WALKER, Samuel		2	303
WALFORD, Henry		1	362	WALKER, Samuel Reid	P	1	363
WALFORD, Herbert Ashford		1	362	WALKER, Thomas	P	1	363
WALFORD, Leslie Francis		1	362	WALKER, Thomas Hynaston		3	277
WALFORD, Oliver Robson	P	1	362	WALKER, W		3	277
WALKER, Alexander		4	222	WALKER, William		2	303
WALKER, Alfred Levi		1	362	WALKER, William		3	277
WALKER, Andrew		2	303	WALKER, William Archibald Small	P	1	363
WALKER, Anthony Thornton	P	1	362	WALKER, William Arthur		4	223
WALKER, Archie Norman	P	1	363	WALKER, William James		5	166
WALKER, Arthur John		2	303	WALKLEY, F G		3	277
WALKER, Benjamin		2	303	WALL, Andrew		3	277
WALKER, Charles		1	363	WALL, Charles		2	304
WALKER, Charles		2	303	WALL, Frederick James		3	277
WALKER, Charles Riach		4	222	WALL, George Benjamin		3	277
WALKER, D		3	276	WALL, John Thomas		1	363
WALKER, David Mitchell	P	3	276	WALL, Timothy Henry	P	2	304
WALKER, Edgar W		4	222	WALLACE, Andrew	P	1	364
WALKER, Edmund Basil	P	1	363	WALLACE, Harold Sydney	P	1	364
WALKER, Edward		5	166	WALLACE, Henry Atholl Charles	P	1	364
WALKER, Edward Henry		1	363	WALLACE, James		1	364
WALKER, Ernest		2	303	WALLACE, John		1	364
WALKER, Francis James		4	222	WALLACE, John		2	304
WALKER, Fred	P	4	222	WALLACE, John Roger (Ion)	P	1	364
WALKER, George		4	222	WALLACE, Joseph		1	364
WALKER, George Kay		5	166	WALLACE, T G		3	277
WALKER, George Mccall		4	222	WALLACE, Thomas		1	364
WALKER, Gerald William	P	3	277	WALLACE, W		2	304
WALKER, Godfrey Alan		3	277	WALLACE, W J		3	277
WALKER, H		2	303	WALLACE, William Ernest		3	277
WALKER, Harold Bickerdyke		2	303	WALLACE, William Joseph		1	364
WALKER, Henry Clement		1	363	WALLACE-CRABBE, Keith George	P	1	98
WALKER, Herbert Joseph Griffin	P	2	303	WALLARD, Walter		1	364
WALKER, Hugh B		2	303	WALLBANK, Harry	P	4	223
WALKER, Hugh Percy Wonham		4	222	WALLE, Enrico James	P	3	278
WALKER, J		2	303	WALLEN, George H P		3	278
WALKER, J		3	277	WALLER, Bertram	P	2	304
WALKER, J		3	277	WALLER, Ernest		4	223
WALKER, J		3	277	WALLER, George	P	1	364
WALKER, Jack Gordon		3	277	WALLER, Horace Edmund	P	1	364
WALKER, James		1	363	WALLER, James		1	364
WALKER, James		2	303	WALLER, Reginald John		2	304
WALKER, James Frederick		4	222	WALLER, Richard Hope		4	223

Name	Photo	Part No.	Page No.		Name	Photo	Part No.	Page No.
WALLER, Thomas	P	5	166		WALTHO, Thomas James		1	365
WALLER, Walter	P	5	166		WALTON, Alfred Thomas		2	304
WALLER, William Cecil	P	5	166		WALTON, Frederick	P	4	224
WALLER, William James	P	1	364		WALTON, George Henry		1	365
WALLEY, Geoffrey Stephen	P	2	304		WALTON, George William		1	365
WALLEY, George John		4	223		WALTON, Harold William	P	3	278
WALLEY, John Clifford	P	4	223		WALTON, Henry Marsden		2	304
WALLIKER, Arthur H		2	304		WALTON, Herbert		2	304
WALLINGTON, Nigel Hugh	P	4	223		WALTON, John Leigh		4	224
WALLIS, Alfred George		3	278		WALTON, Joseph Cyril		4	224
WALLIS, Arthur Vincent		4	223		WALTON, Richard Crawhall	P	1	366
WALLIS, Clifford Edward		4	223		WALTON, Thomas		2	304
WALLIS, Cyril	P	5	166		WALTON, Thomas		2	304
WALLIS, Ernest Henry		4	223		WALTON, Thomas	P	4	224
WALLIS, Frederick		1	365		WAND, Thomas Edward		1	366
WALLIS, Henry Digby		4	223		WANDBY, Walter		1	366
WALLIS, Herbert Francis		1	365		WANDS, Andrew Easton		1	366
WALLIS-STOLZLE, Otto	P	3	259		WANN, John		4	224
WALLS, T F		3	278		WANNELL, William		2	304
WALMESLEY, Richard	P	1	365		WANSBURY, Aleck Augustus		2	304
WALMSLEY, Stephen		4	223		WANSTALL, F		2	304
WALN, Edward Ashton	P	5	166		WANSTALL, Percy		2	304
WALPOLE, E		3	278		WAPLINGTON, George		2	305
WALPOLE, Horatio Spencer	P	3	278		WARBIS, Henry John Francis		4	224
WALROND, Francis Hillier	P	3	278		WARBURTON, Frederick		4	224
WALSH, Archibald		1	365		WARBURTON, John Alfred		1	366
WALSH, C		3	278		WARD, A E		3	278
WALSH, Edgar Frank		2	304		WARD, Allan Dudley Walter		4	224
WALSH, Geoffrey Pennell		1	365		WARD, Archibald		2	305
WALSH, James		1	365		WARD, Arthur		1	366
WALSH, James		1	365		WARD, Arthur Claud		4	224
WALSH, James Joseph		1	365		WARD, Arthur Percy		1	366
WALSH, John		3	278		WARD, Arthur Renold		1	366
WALSH, Joseph	P	1	365		WARD, B		2	305
WALSH, Patrick		1	365		WARD, Basil Mignot	P	1	366
WALSH, W		3	278		WARD, G		3	278
WALSH, William		2	304		WARD, G		3	278
WALSHA, Albert Arthur		5	167		WARD, H		3	278
WALSTER, Thomas		2	304		WARD, Harold		4	224
WALTER, Argyle Francis Bradford	P	1	365		WARD, Henry		1	366
WALTER, Aubrey William Thomas		3	278		WARD, Henry		3	278
WALTER, Charles Richard		1	365		WARD, Henry De Courcy	P	1	366
WALTER, Edward James		2	304		WARD, Herbert Alfred		1	366
WALTER, Frank		2	304		WARD, J		3	278
WALTER, George William		1	365		WARD, James		1	366
WALTER, Sydney		4	224		WARD, James Alfred		5	167
WALTERS, Arthur		2	304		WARD, James George Arthur		2	305
WALTERS, Frederick		2	304		WARD, John Edward		1	366
WALTERS, George		1	365		WARD, John Henry		5	167
WALTERS, Harold Victor		3	278		WARD, John William		2	305
WALTERS, Henry James		1	365		WARD, Joseph Thomas		2	305
WALTERS, Robert		2	304		WARD, Joseph Thomas		4	225
WALTERS, Thomas		2	304		WARD, Thomas Leonard	P	1	367
WALTERS, Thomas George	P	2	304		WARD, W		3	278
WALTERS, Thomas J		2	304		WARD, William		2	305
WALTERS, Vivian Arthur Walker		1	365		WARD, William George		1	367
WALTERS, W G		3	278		WARDALE, Clarence		1	367
WALTERS, W J		3	278		WARDE, Brian Edmund Douglas	P	1	367
WALTERS, Walter Andrew		4	224		WARDELL, Harry		3	278
WALTERS, William George		2	304		WARDELL, William Alfred		2	305
WALTERS, William John		4	224		WARDEN, Ernest		1	367
WALTERS, William John	P	5	167		WARDEN, Ernest Alfred		5	167
WALTERS, William Mark		2	304		WARDEN, F		2	305
WALTHAM, William Ernest	P	1	365		WARDEN, Leslie Evers	P	3	278
WALTHEW, Ernest John	P	5	167		WARDEN, Thomas John Blackie	P	2	305

Name	Photo	Part No.	Page No.
WARDEN, William Herbert		4	225
WARDLAW, H		2	305
WARDLE, Arthur		2	305
WARDLE, Charles	P	3	278
WARDLE, James Kenneth	P	2	305
WARDLE, John		2	305
WARDROPPER, Robert William		4	225
WARE, F W		3	279
WARE, G		3	279
WARE, James		2	305
WARE, Robert Cecil		2	305
WAREING, Harry		1	367
WARING, Edward Robert (Teddy)		4	225
WARING, Herbert		2	305
WARING, John		5	167
WARLOW, Theodore William	P	1	367
WARMAN, Charles Thomas		4	225
WARMAN, Edward John		3	279
WARMAN, John Levi	P	5	167
WARMAN, William John		2	305
WARNE, James Felix	P	1	367
WARNER, Albert Charles		4	225
WARNER, Alfred Frederick		2	305
WARNER, Arthur		4	225
WARNER, B W		3	279
WARNER, Cornwallis John	P	1	367
WARNER, Frederick	P	1	367
WARNER, Frederick Leonard		5	167
WARNER, George		2	305
WARNER, Herbert Moline	P	2	305
WARNER, Herbert Moline		4	225
WARNER, John		2	305
WARNER, William Charles		1	367
WARNER, William Henry		1	367
WARNETT, Walter E S		2	305
WARNOCK, Elizabeth Macmath	P	4	225
WARNOCK, Gavin	P	4	225
WARNOCK, George Muir	P	4	225
WARNOCK, Hector Hugh Adolphus		2	305
WARRELL, Alfred		4	225
WARREN, Arthur Ernest		1	367
WARREN, Arthur Ernest	P	2	305
WARREN, Ernest William		1	367
WARREN, F		3	279
WARREN, Frederick James		2	305
WARREN, George William		1	367
WARREN, Henry		2	305
WARREN, James Percy Soltau	P	1	367
WARREN, John Alexander		1	367
WARREN, Mark		1	367
WARREN, Patrick		1	367
WARREN, Reginald Douglas	P	1	368
WARREN, Richard Dunn	P	3	279
WARREN, Robert		1	368
WARREN, Robert		4	225
WARREN, Sydney Chas.		1	368
WARREN, Walter	P	1	368
WARREN, William Stanley	P	3	279
WARRENDER, Andrew Robertson		1	368
WARRY, John Lucas	P	3	279
WARTH, Bernard	P	3	279
WARTH, Edwin Frederick	P	1	368
WARTNABY, George Cecil		4	226
WARTON, Robert Innys Baker	P	1	368
WARWICK, Francis Hugh	P	4	226
WARWICK, John Douglas Barford	P	3	279
WARWICK, L		3	279
WARWICK, R		3	279
WARWICK, Richard		2	305
WASH, Walter		2	305
WASPE, Herbert		2	305
WASSON, Henry		1	368
WATCHORN, Abraham		3	279
WATERFIELD, Frederick Charles	P	1	368
WATERHOUSE, Rennie	P	4	226
WATERING, W		2	305
WATERING, William Ernest	P	1	368
WATERMAN, Charles		2	305
WATERMAN, Frederick	P	3	279
WATERMAN, John Edward		2	306
WATERMAN, Leonard Gordon		1	368
WATERMAN, Robert Albert		1	368
WATERMAN, Walter		2	306
WATERS, Arthur David	P	2	306
WATERS, Arthur Davis		1	368
WATERS, Geoffrey Ernest	P	1	368
WATERS, George Alexander	P	1	368
WATERS, Harry		3	279
WATERS, Jack Fitzroy	P	2	306
WATERS, Kenneth Selby	P	3	279
WATERS, Reginald William	P	5	167
WATERS, Thomas Robert		1	369
WATERS, William Denne	P	1	369
WATERS, William Leslie	P	1	369
WATKIN, Frank Ernest		2	306
WATKIN, Frank Ernest		4	226
WATKIN, Frederick Amos		4	226
WATKINS, Benjamin		2	306
WATKINS, Charles Henry	P	1	369
WATKINS, Charles Robert	P	1	369
WATKINS, Iltyd Edwin Maitland	P	1	369
WATKINS, W		2	306
WATKINS, William John		1	369
WATNEY, Daniel Edward	P	2	306
WATSHAM, Harold Claud		5	167
WATSON, Alexander		1	369
WATSON, Alexander John		4	226
WATSON, Alfred		2	306
WATSON, Alfred James		1	369
WATSON, Arthur Edward	P	2	306
WATSON, C		3	280
WATSON, Cedrick Gordon		1	369
WATSON, Charles Horace Samuel		4	226
WATSON, Charles Victor Macgregor		4	226
WATSON, Daniel		4	226
WATSON, David	P	2	306
WATSON, David Galloway	P	1	369
WATSON, David Henry	P	4	226
WATSON, Dominic Macaulay		4	226
WATSON, Edward Arthur		2	306
WATSON, Enos John		2	306
WATSON, Ernest William John	P	2	306
WATSON, F		3	280
WATSON, Francis Joseph		2	306
WATSON, Frederick		2	306
WATSON, Frederick James		2	306
WATSON, George		2	306
WATSON, George Joseph		1	369
WATSON, George William		1	369
WATSON, Henry Ayton	P	3	280

Name	Photo	Part No.	Page No.
WEBB, Ernest John		4	228
WEBB, Francis W		2	308
WEBB, Frederick		2	308
WEBB, George		4	228
WEBB, Herbert C		2	308
WEBB, James		1	371
WEBB, John Boyer	P	1	371
WEBB, John Herbert	P	2	308
WEBB, Joseph		1	371
WEBB, Matthew Henderson		4	228
WEBB, Noel William Ward		4	228
WEBB, Oswald Brooke	P	2	308
WEBB, Peter Crichton		3	281
WEBB, Samuel Cecil		3	281
WEBB, Stanley Horace	P	4	229
WEBB, Tom Ernest		3	281
WEBB, Trevor	P	3	281
WEBB, Walter		2	308
WEBB, William John		4	229
WEBBER, Charles Henry		1	371
WEBBER, Edward Charles		1	371
WEBBER, Frederick William		2	308
WEBBER, Gustavus Lambert		4	229
WEBBER, Harold Percival	P	1	372
WEBBER, Harold Victor	P	1	372
WEBBER, Hugo		1	372
WEBBER, J		2	309
WEBBER, John	P	1	372
WEBLEY, Herbert John	P	3	281
WEBSTER, Charles Alexander	P	4	229
WEBSTER, Colin Ailesbury	P	1	372
WEBSTER, David Alexander	P	3	281
WEBSTER, Francis Thomas	P	4	229
WEBSTER, George		2	309
WEBSTER, George		4	229
WEBSTER, Godfrey Vassall George Augustus	P	3	281
WEBSTER, Gordon		5	168
WEBSTER, Harry		1	372
WEBSTER, Herbert		4	229
WEBSTER, J		3	282
WEBSTER, James Henry	P	5	168
WEBSTER, Jesse		1	372
WEBSTER, John Frederick		5	168
WEBSTER, John William		4	229
WEBSTER, Lawrence Sydney		4	229
WEBSTER, Robert William Gordon		4	229
WEBSTER, Thomas Robertson		4	229
WEBSTER, Thomas William		3	282
WEBSTER, William		2	309
WEBZELL, Frederick John Benjamin	P	4	229
WEDD, Archibald Nelson	P	4	229
WEDD, Archibald Nelson	P	5	168
WEDD, Herman		4	230
WEDDERBURN, Robert Hamilton Maclagan		1	372
WEDDERBURN-MAXWELL, James	P	5	121
WEDDERSPOON, Jack Henry Butcher		4	230
WEDEKIND, Lawrence	P	2	309
WEDGBURY, C H		3	282
WEEDON, Ernest Hugh	P	4	230
WEEDON, Sydney Charles	P	1	372
WEEDON, Thomas		2	309
WEEDS, James		1	372
WEEKES, John		1	372
WEEKES, Reginald Penkivil Olive		4	230
WEEKS, D H J		3	282
WEGG, Hugh Neville		4	230
WEIGHT, George Harry		4	230
WEIGHT, John Joseph		2	309
WEILL, Abe		5	168
WEIR, Frederick James		2	309
WEIR, Robert W		2	309
WEIR, Walter		4	230
WEIR, William Harold		5	168
WEISBERG, James		2	309
WEISS, G		3	282
WELBURN, Arthur	P	1	372
WELBY, Richard William Gregory	P	1	372
WELCH, Benjamin William		5	168
WELCH, George Richard		1	372
WELCH, John		2	309
WELCH, John W		2	309
WELCH, Samuel Edward		4	230
WELCH, Samuel George		5	168
WELCH, Sydney James	P	5	168
WELCH, Walter George Frederick	P	1	372
WELCH, Walter Leonard		1	373
WELCH, Wilfred		2	309
WELCH, William George		1	373
WELCHMAN, Edward Theodore		1	373
WELDRICK, George Joseph		2	309
WELFARE, Harold Cuthbert		1	373
WELHAM, James		1	373
WELLARD, Herbert William		4	230
WELLBURN, George William	P	2	309
WELLBURN, Henry	P	4	230
WELLBY, John		2	309
WELLER, Charles George		1	373
WELLER, Edward John	P	1	373
WELLER, Harry		4	230
WELLER, Jack		1	373
WELLER, S		3	282
WELLER, Sydney George Walford		3	282
WELLESLEY, Edward Victor Colley William		3	282
WELLESLEY, Lord Richard		4	230
WELLING, Sydney Thomas George		3	282
WELLINGTON, Thomas Haehae		2	309
WELLMAN, James Edward	P	5	168
WELLMAN, John Robert	P	5	168
WELLS, Alfred		2	309
WELLS, Arthur		1	373
WELLS, Edwin William	P	3	282
WELLS, Ernest Arthur		2	309
WELLS, Ernest Maurice	P	1	373
WELLS, Evan Owen		5	168
WELLS, Francis		1	373
WELLS, Frederick Pennson		1	373
WELLS, G		3	282
WELLS, Harry		1	373
WELLS, Harry Stephen		1	373
WELLS, John Douglas	P	1	373
WELLS, John Thomas		1	373
WELLS, Robert		2	309
WELLS, Sladden Joseph		2	309
WELLS, William		2	309
WELLS, William Appleyard	P	1	373
WELLS, William Henry		4	230
WELLS, William John		1	373
WELLWOOD, Frederick Paton	P	3	282
WELLWOOD, Robert		4	230
WELSFORD, Arthur Hadden	P	1	373

Name	Photo	Part No.	Page No.
WHICHELLS, J		3	283
WHICHER, Frederick		1	375
WHICKER, Frederick Paul	P	5	169
WHIDBORNE, George Ferris	P	2	311
WHIDDETT, Frank		2	312
WHIDDETT, Percival J		2	312
WHIFFEN, J		3	283
WHIGHAM, Robert Scott	P	5	169
WHILEMS, George		2	312
WHILES, Sidney Herbert	P	1	375
WHILEY, A		2	312
WHIPP, Frederick		2	312
WHIPPLE, Herbert Connell		4	232
WHIPPY, James Henry		4	232
WHISKIN, Ernest Charles	P	1	375
WHISTLER, Charles E		2	312
WHISTLER, Ralfe Allen Fuller		4	232
WHITAKER, Charles		1	375
WHITAKER, Edward Stanley	P	3	283
WHITAKER, Harold	P	1	375
WHITAKER, Wilfred		4	232
WHITAKER, William E		2	312
WHITALL, Frank		2	312
WHITBY, Charles Barry Douglas	P	1	375
WHITCHURCH, Leslie Sedgwick	P	1	376
WHITCOMBE, Beresford		3	283
WHITCOMBE, Douglas James Aubrey		1	376
WHITCOMBE, Gerald Aubrey		1	376
WHITCOMBE, John	P	1	376
WHITE, A W		3	283
WHITE, Albert Edward John		4	232
WHITE, Alexander Blair		4	232
WHITE, Alexander Clement		5	169
WHITE, Alfred		1	376
WHITE, Alfred John	P	5	169
WHITE, Alfred William		1	376
WHITE, Arthur		2	312
WHITE, Arthur		4	232
WHITE, Arthur		4	232
WHITE, Arthur Ingram	P	4	232
WHITE, Benjamin William		1	376
WHITE, Cecil Wilson Morton	P	2	312
WHITE, Charles		2	312
WHITE, Charles Ernest		3	283
WHITE, Cyril Arthur		4	232
WHITE, Douglas Ughtred Archibald Harold Sherley	P	5	169
WHITE, Edmund Jesse		4	232
WHITE, Edward		1	376
WHITE, Edward		2	312
WHITE, Edward		5	169
WHITE, Edwin Charles		4	232
WHITE, Ernest		1	376
WHITE, Frederick		1	376
WHITE, Frederick Cornelius		3	283
WHITE, Geoffrey Wilfred		3	283
WHITE, George Henry		2	312
WHITE, Geroge Edward		1	376
WHITE, Gilbert Victor	P	1	376
WHITE, Harry Arthur Albert		1	376
WHITE, Henry Francis		2	312
WHITE, Herbert Robert	P	3	284
WHITE, Jack Winter		3	284
WHITE, James		2	312
WHITE, James		2	312

Name	Photo	Part No.	Page No.
WHITE, James		2	312
WHITE, James		2	312
WHITE, James Ernest	P	1	376
WHITE, James Heslop		2	312
WHITE, James Wallis		4	233
WHITE, John		2	312
WHITE, John Cuthbert		5	169
WHITE, Joseph George		2	312
WHITE, Leonard Hale		2	312
WHITE, Leslie Spenser	P	1	376
WHITE, Lloyd Robert		1	376
WHITE, Lynton Woolmer		1	376
WHITE, Melville Arthur	P	3	284
WHITE, Reginald John		2	312
WHITE, Robert		2	312
WHITE, Robert H		2	312
WHITE, Robert Henry	P	1	376
WHITE, Robert R		2	312
WHITE, S		2	312
WHITE, Stafford Charles		4	233
WHITE, Stanley John	P	2	312
WHITE, Thomas		2	312
WHITE, Thomas		2	312
WHITE, Thomas		4	233
WHITE, Thomas David Mcgregor		3	284
WHITE, Thomas Henry		5	169
WHITE, W		2	312
WHITE, W		2	312
WHITE, Walter Edwin		1	376
WHITE, William		2	312
WHITE, William Charles		1	376
WHITE, William Charles		2	312
WHITE, William Charles	P	4	233
WHITE, William Clement		1	376
WHITE, William Darcy		1	376
WHITE, William Hector		2	312
WHITE, William Samuel		5	169
WHITEFORD, Peter	P	1	376
WHITEHEAD, Alfred George		1	376
WHITEHEAD, Charles		1	377
WHITEHEAD, Charles	P	2	312
WHITEHEAD, Charles Hugh Tempest	P	2	313
WHITEHEAD, George		2	313
WHITEHEAD, George William Edendale		5	170
WHITEHEAD, Harry Harding	P	1	377
WHITEHEAD, Henry Montague		1	377
WHITEHEAD, Herbert Howard		3	284
WHITEHEAD, James Hugh Edendale		5	170
WHITEHEAD, James Scullard		1	377
WHITEHEAD, John		2	313
WHITEHEAD, Joseph		4	233
WHITEHEAD, Reuben Alfred		2	313
WHITEHEAD, Samuel		4	233
WHITEHEAD, Thomas R		2	313
WHITEHOUSE, John Walter Glendinning	P	5	174
WHITEHOUSE, T		2	313
WHITEHOUSE, William	P	2	313
WHITEHOUSE, William		4	233
WHITEHURST, Charley	P	1	377
WHITEHURST, Harold	P	1	377
WHITELAW, Alexander	P	1	377
WHITELAW, George Hope		4	233
WHITELOCK, Charles Railton		4	233
WHITEMAN, George Moodie Cassells	P	4	233
WHITEMAN, Harold Shirley		4	233

Name	Photo	Part No.	Page No.	Name	Photo	Part No.	Page No.
WILLIAMS, Noel Griffith		4	236	WILLIS, Frank		2	316
WILLIAMS, Oswald Michael	P	3	286	WILLIS, George		1	381
WILLIAMS, Owen		1	380	WILLIS, H		3	287
WILLIAMS, Owen Wynne		4	237	WILLIS, Hugh Duberly		4	238
WILLIAMS, Percy	P	2	316	WILLIS, John Frederick		2	316
WILLIAMS, Percy		5	171	WILLIS, Russell George		3	287
WILLIAMS, Reginald	P	2	316	WILLIS, Sherlock Amyas	P	3	287
WILLIAMS, Reginald		4	237	WILLIS, Thomas		1	381
WILLIAMS, Reuben		2	316	WILLIS, Thomas		4	238
WILLIAMS, Richard Lloyd		4	237	WILLIS, William Brian De Laval	P	1	381
WILLIAMS, Robert		2	316	WILLIS-HARRIS, Ralph Claudian	P	1	174
WILLIAMS, Robert		2	316	WILLISON, A		3	287
WILLIAMS, Samuel		2	316	WILLMER, Arthur Franklin	P	2	317
WILLIAMS, Samuel Erbery		4	237	WILLMOTT, John Herbert Victor		4	238
WILLIAMS, Shirley Wynn Vaughan		4	237	WILLOCKS, Guy Charles Boileau		3	287
WILLIAMS, Sydney Ernest		1	380	WILLOUGHBY, Nesbit Edward	P	3	288
WILLIAMS, Thomas		2	316	WILLOUGHBY, Thomas		2	317
WILLIAMS, Thomas		4	237	WILLOUGHBY, William		2	317
WILLIAMS, Thomas Charles		1	380	WILLOUGHBY, William		2	317
WILLIAMS, Thomas Henry		4	237	WILLOWS, Bert Hugh		4	238
WILLIAMS, Timothy Davies	P	5	171	WILLOWS, Joseph		2	317
WILLIAMS, Tom James	P	1	380	WILLOWS, Thomas		2	317
WILLIAMS, Vivian Prees		4	237	WILLS, George Edward Leonard		1	381
WILLIAMS, W		3	287	WILLS, J		3	288
WILLIAMS, W E		2	316	WILLS, Sydney Alfred		2	317
WILLIAMS, W H		2	316	WILLS, W		3	288
WILLIAMS, Walter		4	237	WILLS, William George	P	2	317
WILLIAMS, Walter		5	171	WILLSHIRE, Albert William		4	238
WILLIAMS, Walter Kent		1	380	WILLSMORE, A J		3	288
WILLIAMS, Walter Roland		1	380	WILLSON, Francis George Dudley		4	238
WILLIAMS, William		1	380	WILLSON, Frederick James	P	3	288
WILLIAMS, William		2	316	WILLSON, Frederick James	P	4	238
WILLIAMS, William		4	237	WILLSON, Stanley Francis		4	238
WILLIAMS, William Alfred	P	4	237	WILLSON, William Alick Parkinson	P	4	239
WILLIAMS, William Henry		1	380	WILMOT, Henry Cecil		4	239
WILLIAMS, William Henry		4	237	WILMOT, Robert Coningsby		4	239
WILLIAMS, William J		2	316	WILMOT, Thomas Norbury		4	239
WILLIAMS, William James	P	4	237	WILMOT-SITWELL, Stanton Degge	P	1	328
WILLIAMS, William Morris		3	287	WILMOTT, F		3	288
WILLIAMSON, Albert		2	316	WILMSHURST, William Jesse	P	1	381
WILLIAMSON, Albert John		1	381	WILSDON, Alick		2	317
WILLIAMSON, Alexander		2	316	WILSHAW, Dudley George	P	2	317
WILLIAMSON, Alexander John Neeve		4	237	WILSHER, Charles		2	317
WILLIAMSON, Alfred		2	316	WILSHER, Charles		4	239
WILLIAMSON, Ambrose		2	316	WILSHERE, Ernest Edward	P	5	171
WILLIAMSON, Arthur Thomas		4	237	WILSHIRE, Laurence Stanley		4	239
WILLIAMSON, David Millar		1	381	WILSON, A		3	288
WILLIAMSON, F		3	287	WILSON, A		3	288
WILLIAMSON, Frederick		1	381	WILSON, Albert		2	317
WILLIAMSON, George		4	238	WILSON, Albert		2	317
WILLIAMSON, George Hamilton	P	3	287	WILSON, Albert		3	288
WILLIAMSON, Gerald Douglas		4	238	WILSON, Albert Patterson		1	381
WILLIAMSON, Hendrick		2	316	WILSON, Allan		1	381
WILLIAMSON, John George		4	238	WILSON, Ambrose Norris		5	171
WILLIAMSON, John Henry		2	316	WILSON, Arthur		2	317
WILLIAMSON, John Mcleod		4	238	WILSON, Arthur Henry		4	239
WILLIAMSON, Kenneth Harper	P	3	287	WILSON, Arthur Henry Maitland	P	5	171
WILLIAMSON, Peter		1	381	WILSON, Arthur Stafford		3	288
WILLIAMSON, Robert		1	381	WILSON, Arthur Wellesley Alister		4	239
WILLIAMSON, Robert Hamilton	P	1	381	WILSON, C		2	317
WILLIAMSON, William		2	316	WILSON, Cecil Fred		4	239
WILLINGALE, Sidney George		1	381	WILSON, Charles Edgar Andrew	P	3	288
WILLINS, Arthur T		2	316	WILSON, Charles Herbert		4	239
WILLIS, Arthur	P	5	171	WILSON, David		2	317
WILLIS, David		2	316	WILSON, David S		2	317

Name	Photo	Part No.	Page No.
WILSON, Denis Erskine	P	3	288
WILSON, Douglas Henry Vernon	P	1	381
WILSON, Edward		2	317
WILSON, Edward Henry	P	1	381
WILSON, Edwin John		2	317
WILSON, Ennis Norman		1	381
WILSON, Ephraim		2	317
WILSON, Ernest		1	381
WILSON, Evan Welldon		4	239
WILSON, Ewen Holmes Humphrey James	P	1	382
WILSON, F		2	317
WILSON, F		2	317
WILSON, F		3	288
WILSON, F C		3	288
WILSON, Fred Brookfield	P	4	240
WILSON, Frederick Lawrence		3	288
WILSON, G		3	289
WILSON, George		1	382
WILSON, George	P	2	317
WILSON, George Henry		2	317
WILSON, George William		4	240
WILSON, H		2	317
WILSON, Harold Roy	P	3	289
WILSON, Harry		1	382
WILSON, Harry		1	382
WILSON, Harry		2	317
WILSON, Henry George		4	240
WILSON, Henry James		5	171
WILSON, Hugh		5	171
WILSON, Hugh Stanley		1	382
WILSON, Hugh Stanley	P	2	318
WILSON, Humphrey Hamilton		4	240
WILSON, Ian Maclean		2	318
WILSON, J		2	318
WILSON, J		2	318
WILSON, J		3	289
WILSON, J R K		3	289
WILSON, J T		3	289
WILSON, James		1	382
WILSON, James		2	318
WILSON, James		2	318
WILSON, James		2	318
WILSON, James	P	4	240
WILSON, James Adam		3	289
WILSON, James Ernest Studholme	P	3	289
WILSON, James Rose		2	318
WILSON, John		1	382
WILSON, John		2	318
WILSON, John		2	318
WILSON, John		4	240
WILSON, John Andrew Hackett		4	240
WILSON, John Buchanan		4	240
WILSON, John Charles		4	240
WILSON, John Gilmore		4	240
WILSON, John Joseph Dexter		1	382
WILSON, John Norman	P	3	289
WILSON, John William		2	318
WILSON, Lawrence Thomson		5	171
WILSON, M		3	289
WILSON, Oliver		4	240
WILSON, Philip John Conning	P	2	318
WILSON, R		3	289
WILSON, Robert		1	382
WILSON, Robert		5	171
WILSON, Robert Charles		4	240

Name	Photo	Part No.	Page No.
WILSON, Robert Meredith	P	2	318
WILSON, Robert Sym		1	382
WILSON, Rodney	P	5	171
WILSON, Samuel		2	318
WILSON, Samuel Olson		1	382
WILSON, Samuel Thomas		2	318
WILSON, Sidney		2	318
WILSON, T		2	318
WILSON, T		3	289
WILSON, T		3	289
WILSON, Thomas		2	318
WILSON, Thomas A		2	318
WILSON, Thomas Douglas	P	3	289
WILSON, Walton Ronald	P	4	240
WILSON, Wilfred		1	382
WILSON, William		2	318
WILSON, William		4	240
WILSON, William		4	241
WILSON, William Charles Stanley		4	241
WILSON, William Duncan	P	2	318
WILSON, William Edward		4	241
WILSON, William H		2	318
WILSON, William James		4	241
WILSON, William St. John		4	241
WILSON-RAE, Reginald		1	299
WILTON, George		3	289
WILTSHIRE, C E		3	289
WILTSHIRE, E		2	319
WILTSHIRE, E H		3	289
WILTSHIRE, Horace William		2	319
WILTSHIRE, John William		2	319
WILTSHIRE, Joseph Alfred		2	319
WILTSHIRE, Samuel		2	319
WILTSHIRE, Thomas Chalres		2	319
WILTSHIRE, William		2	319
WIMBLE, George Douglas		2	319
WIMBLE, Herbert Ashley		2	319
WIMHURST, Arthur Daniel		1	382
WIMSETT, Frederick Thomas	P	1	382
WINBORN, George A		2	319
WINCH, Albert James		2	319
WINCH, Gordon Bluett	P	4	241
WINCH, Harold Forbes Clarke		2	319
WINCH, William Haffenden	P	2	319
WINCHESTER, John Henry	P	3	289
WINCKLEY, Charles Reginald		3	289
WINDEBANK, Robert Percy		1	382
WINDER, Holloway Elliot	P	4	241
WINDER, J		2	319
WINDER-HOLLOWAY, Elliott		2	170
WINDLE, John		1	382
WINDLE, T		3	289
WINDSOR, Edward Arten George		2	319
WINDSOR, Harold Victor		2	319
WINDSOR, John Henry	P	4	241
WINDSOR, Leslie St. Lawrence		4	241
WINDSOR-CLIVE, The Hon. Archer		2	72
WINFIELD, Stuart James		1	382
WING, L C		3	289
WING, Matthew		1	382
WING, Thomas David		2	319
WINGATE, Alfred Douglas	P	2	319
WINGATE, Thomas Paterson	P	1	382
WINGFIELD, Arthur		3	289
WINGFIELD, Joseph		1	382

Name	Photo	Part No.	Page No.	Name	Photo	Part No.	Page No.
WORSSAM, Leslie Henry	P	3	292	WRIGHT, George Henry		3	293
WORT, L J		3	293	WRIGHT, Harold	P	2	323
WORTABET, John Cecil	P	1	386	WRIGHT, Harold Reginald		4	245
WORTH, Ernest		3	293	WRIGHT, Harry		2	323
WORTH, John Alfred		1	386	WRIGHT, Harry Thomas		1	386
WORTH, William Harry Thorne		3	293	WRIGHT, Henry Gordon	P	3	293
WORTHINGTON, Arthur Guy	P	2	322	WRIGHT, Herbert		4	245
WORTHINGTON, Arthur Tom		1	386	WRIGHT, Herbert		5	173
WORTHINGTON, Claude Arthur	P	2	322	WRIGHT, Howard Caldwell		4	245
WORTHINGTON, Frederick		3	293	WRIGHT, Hugh Stafford Northcote	P	1	386
WORTHINGTON, Ralph	P	3	293	WRIGHT, J		3	294
WORTHINGTON, Reginald George		4	244	WRIGHT, James		5	173
WORTHINGTON, Walter Gustavus		4	244	WRIGHT, James W H		2	323
WORTHINGTON-EYRE, Lionel George	P	3	94	WRIGHT, John		1	387
WORTLEY, Fred		2	323	WRIGHT, John Bremner		4	245
WORTS, Alfred W		2	323	WRIGHT, John Hutton		1	387
WOULIDGE, Leonard Benjamin		5	173	WRIGHT, John Stanley		4	245
WRAGG, Frederick William	P	3	293	WRIGHT, John Thomas William		2	323
WRAGG, George William		4	244	WRIGHT, Jonathan		3	294
WRAIGHT, W G		2	323	WRIGHT, Joseph		2	323
WRAITH, Alfred Osborn	P	5	173	WRIGHT, Lawrence William	P	1	387
WRATTEN, William Henry		1	386	WRIGHT, Leonard Frederick Hall		1	387
WRAY, Herbert John		1	386	WRIGHT, Melville Eugene		4	246
WRAY, James		2	323	WRIGHT, P		2	323
WREFORD-BROWN, Claude	P	1	57	WRIGHT, R		3	294
WREFORD-BROWN, Oswald Eric		3	39	WRIGHT, R		3	294
WREN, Charles Edward		2	323	WRIGHT, Sydney		1	387
WREN, Samuel William	P	4	245	WRIGHT, T		3	294
WREN, T G		3	293	WRIGHT, Theodore		4	246
WREN, Thomas		2	323	WRIGHT, Theodore Archer		3	294
WREN, W J		3	293	WRIGHT, Thomas		1	387
WRENCH, William Seaward		3	293	WRIGHT, Thomas	P	1	387
WREND, John	P	4	245	WRIGHT, Thomas	P	2	323
WRENFORD, Arthur Leonard	P	4	245	WRIGHT, Thomas		4	246
WREST, G A		3	293	WRIGHT, W		2	323
WRIGHT, Albert		2	323	WRIGHT, W		3	294
WRIGHT, Albert George		1	386	WRIGHT, William		1	387
WRIGHT, Albert George (Alias Albert George Smith)	P	2	323	WRIGHT, William		1	387
				WRIGHT, William		1	387
WRIGHT, Allan O'halloran	P	1	386	WRIGHT, William		2	323
WRIGHT, Arthur		4	245	WRIGHT, William		4	246
WRIGHT, Arthur Francis		4	245	WRIGHT, William		5	173
WRIGHT, Bert		2	323	WRIGHT, William D		3	294
WRIGHT, Bruce		2	323	WRIGHT, William Henry		1	387
WRIGHT, C		3	293	WRIGHT, William Richardson		3	294
WRIGHT, Charles		1	386	WRONG, Harold Verschoyle		3	294
WRIGHT, Charles	P	3	293	WROUGHTON, Musgrave Cazenove	P	1	387
WRIGHT, Charles		4	245	WYATT, Arthur Charles		2	323
WRIGHT, Charles	P	5	173	WYATT, Arthur Thomas Elford		4	246
WRIGHT, Charles Benjamin		2	323	WYATT, Charles D G		2	323
WRIGHT, Charles Frank		3	293	WYATT, Ernest John		1	387
WRIGHT, Cyril Vivian		3	293	WYATT, Frederick		2	323
WRIGHT, David		2	323	WYATT, George Alexander	P	2	323
WRIGHT, Douglas Harry		3	293	WYATT, Henry Edward	P	3	294
WRIGHT, E J		2	323	WYATT, Herbert Sydney		4	246
WRIGHT, Edward		1	386	WYATT, John Wynn		4	246
WRIGHT, Edward Leslie	P	3	293	WYER, Herbert		2	323
WRIGHT, Edwin	P	1	386	WYETH, Henry		2	324
WRIGHT, F		3	293	WYKES, William	P	1	387
WRIGHT, Francis		2	323	WYLD, George Richard	P	1	387
WRIGHT, Frederick		2	323	WYLLIE, David	P	4	246
WRIGHT, Frederick		2	323	WYLLIE, George Crichton		3	294
WRIGHT, Frederick Adam		4	245	WYLLIE, Henry		1	388
WRIGHT, Frederick Wilford	P	4	245	WYLLIE, James		1	388
WRIGHT, George		2	323	WYLLIE, James Bulloch		1	388